# A CHRONOLOGY OF EUROPEAN SECURITY & DEFENCE 1945 - 2005

## Acknowledgments

As a Course Director at the Geneva Centre for Security Policy, my time is limited. It would not have been possible to complete the Chronology without the support and commitment of a number of people, including, in the first instance, Emily Munro, who contributed research for a number of the later years, and, in particular, my assistant and co-author Katja Flückiger. I would also like to thank Ambassador Gerard Stoudmann for agreeing to publish the work, Hrair Balian and his team for their efforts on my behalf to prepare it for publication and distribute it thereafter, Damla Süar for the design and invaluable advice on all matters surrounding the publishing process and Curtis Budden for editing. Finally, I am most grateful for the support of the Bertelsmann Foundation, who kindly hosted the Brussels launch of this book. My thanks are sincere and heartfelt.

**Julian Lindley-French**
**Geneva, May 2005**

Photo credits: Page 13, signing of the North Atlantic Treaty: courtesy of NATO,
all other photos (including cover photo): KEYSTONE.

Published by the Geneva Centre for Security Policy
Avenue de la Paix 7bis, P.O. Box 1295
1211 Geneva 1, Switzerland



Designed by Damla Süar, Geneva, Switzerland

Printed in Geneva by Imprimerie Coprint, Switzerland

Die Deutsche Bibliothek lists this publication in the Deutsche Nationalbibliografie; detailed bibliographic data are available in the Internet at http://dnb.ddb.de.

ISBN 2-8399-0080-7

# A CHRONOLOGY OF EUROPEAN SECURITY & DEFENCE 1945-2005

**Julian Lindley-French**
**Katja Flückiger**

# Table of Contents

# A CHRONOLOGY OF EUROPEAN SECURITY & DEFENCE 1945-2005

**Julian Lindley-French**
**Katja Flückiger**

## Introduction

The concept for "A Chronology of European Security & Defence 1945-2005" emerged from my time at the EU Institute for Security Studies in Paris and the Geneva Centre for Security Policy. Countless conversations with policy-makers, practitioners, academics, commentators and students led to the conclusion that such was the complexity of Europe's post-war security and defence story that only a detailed chronology would suffice to close the very evident gap in the literature. Indeed, as a historian, it is impossible to believe that one can adequately explain the present without at least a grasp of the past.

I had developed an initial chronology while studying at the European University Institute in Florence in the 1990s, but it was apparent even then that a mere list of dates would not capture the richness of the story. A thorough extension and update of this initial chronology followed during the last year, and the result is a very personal interpretation of European security and defence and the many events that have formed and shaped it. There are, no doubt, some omissions, for which I apologise. Developing such a chronology is inevitably like cleaning large windows – one always misses something. If the reader can forgive the occasional lapse, however, I am convinced that the Chronology will help plot a way through the jungle of European security and defence that is both informative and enjoyable.

This is but the first edition of what is intended to be a living document. Updates will be made regularly so that the story will continue to be told in a systematic and effective manner.

Finally, the publication of this first edition of the Chronology coincides with that of "The Discourse of European Defence: Europe's Developing Position on Security and Defence in Quotes" by Rem Korteweg/Clingendael Centre for Strategic Studies. Taken together, the two works serve as a comprehensive reference guide for studying the development of European defence throughout the years.

**Julian Lindley-French**

# ABOUT THE AUTHORS

Julian Lindley-French is currently Director of the International Training Course in Security Policy at the Geneva Centre for Security Policy (GCSP). He was born in Sheffield, UK, in 1958. After graduating from Oxford University in 1980, he spent several years working for the British Government and undertaking project management for the United Nations in Geneva and New York, as well as for the International Olympic Committee in Lausanne. He received a Masters Degree in International Relations (with distinction) from the University of East Anglia in 1992 and a Doctorate in Political Science from the European University Institute in Florence in 1996. He was formerly Deputy Director of the International Centre for Security Analysis at the Department of War Studies, King's College London, and Senior Research Fellow at the EU Institute for Security Studies in Paris. He has also acted as a consultant to NATO in Brussels. His main areas of interest are US foreign and security policy and strategic developments in European security and defence structures. He is a regular contributor to "The Wall Street Journal" and the "International Herald Tribune". In June 2004, he published the second Venusberg Report, "A European Defence Strategy".

Katja Flückiger, a Swiss and Dutch national, obtained a Licence in International Relations from the University of Geneva and the Graduate Institute of International Studies (GIIS) in 2003. She is currently studying for a *Diplôme d'Etudes Approfondies* in Political Science at the GIIS and is a Faculty Assistant at the GCSP. Her research interests lie in the field of security and conflict studies, and especially in democratisation, intercommunal relations and consociational politics.

# HOW THE CHRONOLOGY WORKS

**A Chronology of European Security & Defence 1945-2005**
is divided into seven sections:

| | | |
|---|---|---|
| Part 1 | 1945-1949 | The Formative Years |
| Part 2 | 1950-1959 | The Long Haul |
| Part 3 | 1960-1969 | The Dawn of Reason |
| Part 4 | 1970-1979 | The Lukewarm Peace |
| Part 5 | 1980-1989 | Countdown to Freedom |
| Part 6 | [illegible] | New World Order |
| Part 7 | [illegible] | The End of Strategic Vacation |

Each year is treated as a distinct chronological entity. There is an overview of major events and themes that enables the reader to get a flavour of any particular year. Individual events are then organised chronologically, with specific dates given where possible together with an explanatory passage or statement.

The Chronology considers institutional and policy developments and actions taken within and between international bodies such as the European Economic Community/European Community/European Union (EEC/EC/EU), the Conference on Security and Co-operation in Europe/Organization for Security and Co-operation in Europe (CSCE/OSCE), the North Atlantic Treaty Organisation (NATO) and the Western European Union (WEU). Equally, the Chronology also covers developments in specific countries and major world events in order to place European security and defence in context. In addition, those social and economic events that have had a considerable impact upon, and are influenced by, security and defence, are included.

However, a chronology is not, and can never be, an historical analysis. Although, through the commentaries and explanations it provides, the work aims to give the reader more than just a list of events. Rather, it offers perspectives and insights that place European security and defence in their historical context.

Abbreviations in italics at the beginning of the respective entries highlight events that are specific to the development or implementation of the European Defence Community project (EDC), NATO's European Security and Defence Identity (ESDI) and the EU's European Security and Defence Policy (ESDP). Similarly, consequences of the 11 September attacks on the United States (9/11) and the 11 March attacks on Madrid (3/11) are also highlighted, as are the events leading up to, and dealing with the development and consequences of, the 2003 Iraq War (The Iraq War).

On the other hand, there is less focus on aspects of the EU's Common Foreign and Security Policy (CFSP) outside of the ESDP.

# Abbreviations and Acronyms

**A**

| | |
|---|---|
| ABM | Anti-Ballistic Missile |
| ACE | Allied Command Europe |
| ACT | Allied Command Transformation |
| AFSOUTH | Allied Forces Southern Europe (⏩ NATO) |
| JFC Naples | Joint Force Command Naples, Italy (⏩ NATO) |
| ARRC | Allied Command Europe Rapid Reaction Corps |
| AWACS | Airborne Warning and Control System (aircraft) |
| AKP | *Adalet ve Kalkinma Partisi* (Justice and Development Party, Turkey) |

**B**

| | |
|---|---|
| BAOR | British Army of the Rhine |
| Benelux | Belgium, the Netherlands and Luxembourg |
| BiH | *Bosna i Hercegovina* (Bosnia and Herzegovina) |
| BWC | Biological Weapons Convention |

**C**

| | |
|---|---|
| CEDP | Common European Defence Policy |
| CESDP | Common European Security and Defence Policy |
| CFE | Conventional Armed Forces in Europe Treaty |
| CFSP | Common Foreign and Security Policy |
| CJTF | Combined Joint Task Force |
| CoE | Council of Europe |
| Comecon | Council for Mutual Economic Assistance |
| CPA | Coalition Provisional Authority (Iraq) |
| CPSU | Communist Party of the Soviet Union |
| CRRM | Civilian Rapid Reaction Mechanism (⏩ EU) |
| CSCE | Conference on Security and Co-operation in Europe |
| CSU | *Christlich-Soziale Union* |
| CTBT | Comprehensive Test Ban Treaty |
| CWC | Chemical Weapons Convention |

**D**

| | |
|---|---|
| DCI | Defence Capabilities Initiative |
| DPC | Defence Planning Committee (⏩ NATO) |
| DRC | Democratic Republic of the Congo |

**E**

| | |
|---|---|
| EADS | European Aeronautics, Defence and Space Company |
| EAEC | European Atomic Energy Community |
| EAG | European Air Group |
| EAPC | Euro-Atlantic Partnership Council |
| EC | European Communities (⏩ EEC, ⏩ ECSC and ⏩ Euratom), or: European Community, the new name for the ⏩ EEC in the ⏩ TEU |
| ECAP | European Capabilities Action Plan |
| ECSC | European Coal and Steel Community |
| ECU | European Currency Unit, an accounting unit based on a basket of national currencies |
| EDA | European Defence Agency |
| EDC | European Defence Community |
| EDIS | European Defence Industry Study |
| EEA | European Economic Area |
| EEC | European Economic Community |
| EFA | European Fighter Aircraft |
| EFTA | European Free Trade Area |
| ELSO | European Space Vehicle Launcher Development Organisation |

| | |
|---|---|
| EP | European Parliament |
| EPC | European Political Community (1952-1954) |
| EPC | European Political Co-operation (1970-1993) |
| ERM | European Exchange Rate Mechanism |
| ERP | European Recovery Program |
| ERRF | European Rapid Reaction Force |
| ERRM | European Rapid Reaction Mechanism |
| ESA | European Space Agency |
| ESDI | European Security and Defence Identity (⏩ NATO) |
| ESDP | European Security and Defence Policy (⏩ EU) |
| ESDU | European Security and Defence Union (⏩ EU) |
| ESRO | European Space Research Organisation |
| ETA | *Euskadi Ta Askatasuna* (Basque Homeland and Freedom) |
| EU | European Union |
| EUCLID | European Co-operation for the Long Term in Defence |
| EUFOR | ⏩ EU Force in ⏩ BiH |
| EUPM | ⏩ EU Police Mission (⏩ BiH) |
| EUPOL PROXIMA | EU Police Mission in the former Yugoslav Republic of Macedonia |
| Euratom | European Atomic Energy Community |
| EUROFOR | European Operational Rapid Force |
| EUROMARFOR | European Maritime Force |

## F

| | |
|---|---|
| FAWEU | Forces Answerable to ⏩ WEU |
| FBS | Forward Base System |
| FRG | Federal Republic of Germany |
| FRY | Federal Republic of Yugoslavia |
| FYROM | Former Yugoslav Republic of Macedonia |

## G

| | |
|---|---|
| GAC | General Affairs Council (⏩ EU Council of Ministers/Council of the European Union meeting in foreign and defence minister composition) |
| G7/G8 | Group of Seven / Group of Eight |
| GDP | Gross Domestic Product |
| GDR | German Democratic Republic |
| GLCM | Ground-Launched Cruise Missile |
| GPALS | Global Protection Against Limited Strikes |
| GRU | *Glavnoe razvedyvatelnoe upravlenie* (Main Intelligence Directorate, or Soviet military intelligence) |

## H

| | |
|---|---|
| HLG | High-Level Group |
| HR | High Representative |
| HQ | Headquarters |

## I

| | |
|---|---|
| IAEA | International Atomic Energy Agency |
| ICBM | Intercontinental Ballistic Missile |
| ICC | International Criminal Court |
| ICTY | International Criminal Tribunal for the former Yugoslavia |
| IEPG | Independent European Programme Group |
| IFOR | Implementation Force (⏩ BiH) |
| IGC | Intergovernmental Conference |
| INF | Intermediate Nuclear Forces |
| IPTF | International Police Task Force (⏩ BiH) |

| | |
|---|---|
| IRBM | Intermediate-Range Ballistic Missile |
| ISAF | International Security Assistance Force (Afghanistan) |

**J**

| | |
|---|---|
| JFC | Joint Force Command |
| JNA | Yugoslav National Army |

**K**

| | |
|---|---|
| KFOR | Kosovo Force (⏩ NATO) |

**L**

| | |
|---|---|
| LANDJUT | NATO's HQ Allied Land Forces, Schleswig-Holstein and Jutland |
| LTDP | Long-Term Defence Programme |
| LRTNF | Long-Range Theatre Nuclear Forces |

**M**

| | |
|---|---|
| MAD | Mutually Assured Destruction |
| MARAIRMED | Allied Maritime Air Forces Mediterranean |
| MBFR | Mutually Balanced Force Reductions |
| MEP | Member of the ⏩ EP |
| MIRV | Multiple Independent Re-Entry Vehicle |
| MLF | Multilateral Force |
| MLRS | Multi-Launch Rocket System |
| MONUC | *Mission des Nations Unies en République démocratique du Congo* / United Nations Organization Mission in the Democratic Republic of the Congo |
| MRCA | Multi-Role Combat Aircraft |
| MTA | Military Technical Agreement |

**N**

| | |
|---|---|
| NAC | North Atlantic Council |
| NACC | North Atlantic Cooperation Council |
| NATO | North Atlantic Treaty Organisation |
| NAVOCFORMED | Naval Officer Commanding Forces in the Mediterranean |
| NLA | National Liberation Army |
| NPG | Nuclear Planning Group |
| NPT | Treaty on the Non-Proliferation of Nuclear Weapons / Nuclear Non-Proliferation Treaty |
| NRF | NATO Response Force |
| NSC | National Security Council (⏩ US) |
| NSDD | National Security Decision Directive |
| NSDM | National Security Decision Memorandum |
| NST | Nuclear and Space Talks |

**O**

| | |
|---|---|
| OAS | *Organisation de l'Armée Secrète* |
| OCCAR | *Organisation Conjointe de Coopération en Matière d'Armement* |
| OEEC | Organisation for European Economic Co-operation |
| OPEC | Organization of the Petroleum Exporting Countries |
| OSCE | Organization for Security and Co-operation in Europe |

**P**

| | |
|---|---|
| PCC | Prague Capabilities Commitment |
| PD | Presidential Directive |
| PfP | Partnership for Peace |
| PIC | Peace Implementation Conference (⏩ BiH) |
| PLO | Palestinian Liberation Organisation |
| PM | Prime Minister |
| POCO | Political Committee (⏩ EU) |

| | |
|---|---|
| PR | People's Republic |
| PROXIMA | EU Police Mission in ⏩ FYROM (EUPOL PROXIMA) |
| PSC | Political and Security Committee (⏩ EU) |
| QMV | Qualified Majority Voting |
| RAF | Royal Air Force (⏩ UK) |
| RPF | Rwandan Patriotic Front |
| RSFSR | Russian Soviet Federal Socialist Republic |
| SACEUR | Supreme Allied Commander Europe |
| SACLANT | Supreme Allied Commander Atlantic |
| SALT | Strategic Arms Limitation Talks |
| SAMs | Surface-to-Air Missiles |
| SDI | Strategic Defence Initiative |
| SEATO | South East Asia Treaty Organisation |
| SED | *Sozialistische Einheitspartei* (Socialist Unionist Party; the ⏩ GDR's communist party) |
| SFOR | Stabilisation Force (⏩ BiH) |
| SFRY | Socialist Federal Republic of Yugoslavia |
| SHAPE | Supreme Headquarters Allied Powers Europe |
| SIOP | Single Integrated Operation Plan |
| SPD | Social Democratic Party of Germany |
| SSBN | Nuclear Ballistic Missile Submarine |
| SSM | Surface-to-Surface Missile |
| STANAVFORMED | Standing Naval Force Mediterranean |
| STANAVFORLANT | Standing Naval Forces Atlantic |
| START | Strategic Arms Reduction Talks |
| TEC | Treaty Establishing the European Communities |
| TEU | Treaty on European Union |
| TNF | Theatre Nuclear Forces |
| TNW | Theatre Nuclear Weapon |
| UK | United Kingdom of Great Britain and Northern Ireland |
| UN | United Nations |
| UNHCR | (Office of the) United Nations High Commissioner for Refugees |
| UNMIBH | United Nations Mission in ⏩ BiH |
| UNMIK | United Nations Interim Administration Mission in Kosovo |
| UNO | United Nations Organisation |
| UNPA | United Nations Protected Area |
| UNPROFOR | United Nations Protection Force |
| UNSC | United Nations Security Council |
| US | United States |
| USSR | Union of Soviet Socialist Republics |
| WEAG | Western European Armaments Group |
| WEU | Western European Union |
| WEUDAM | De-mining Assistance Mission to Croatia (⏩ WEU) |
| Weucom | WEU Telecommunications Network |

Part 1

# THE FORMATIVE YEARS

# 1945-1949

1945 1947 1949

| At a Glance – Major Events and Themes | |
|---|---|
| | **Big-Three Conferences at Yalta and Potsdam** |
| | **Germany and Japan surrender; World War II ends** |
| | **United Nations is created** |
| | **Atomic bombs dropped on Hiroshima and Nagasaki** |
| | **Growing perception of a Soviet threat** |

# 1945

| Day | Month | Event |
|---|---|---|
| 4-11 | February | Conference of the Crimea (Yalta). Post-war Europe is divided among the victors. US and Soviet hegemony is effectively established in their respective spheres of influence. Zones of occupation are established to avoid any incidents when the forces of the Western Allies meet those of the Soviet Union. This is the last summit for President Franklin D. Roosevelt. |
| 12 | April | US President Roosevelt dies. Vice President Harry S. Truman succeeds him. |
| 8 | May | War in Europe ends as Germany surrenders unconditionally. |
| 12 | May | UK Prime Minister Winston Churchill warns new US President Truman for the first time of a possible Soviet threat. He suggests that Soviet leader Josef Stalin is not interested in partnership, merely domination. |
| 26 | June | Signing of the UN Charter in San Francisco. |
| 17-2 | July-August | UK Prime Minister Clement Attlee, Soviet leader Stalin, and US President Truman meet at the Conference of Berlin (Potsdam) to confirm the Yalta Agreement. President Truman, however, is less well disposed towards Stalin and the Soviet Union than his predecessor. The conference takes place in the shadow of the first atomic-bomb missions over Japan. |
| 26 | July | Attlee defeats Churchill to become the new UK prime minister. |
| 6 + 9 | August | The nuclear age begins as Hiroshima and Nagasaki are destroyed by atomic bombs. East-West relations are to be dominated by the shadow of these weapons hereafter, as the United States strives to maintain its atomic monopoly, and Britain, France, and, above all, the Soviet Union seek to end it. |
| 15 | August | War in the Pacific ends, bringing World War II to a close. |
| | August | Soviet President Mikhail Kalinin verbally attacks the West, signalling to the West that Churchill's analysis at the Yalta Conference – that the world would be divided into spheres of influence in the wake of World War II – is essentially correct and that the US policy of *quid pro quo* is not viable. |

| | | |
|---|---|---|
| 2 | September | Japan surrenders. |
| 11-2 | September-October | First post-war Four-Power Foreign Ministers Conference in London. Soviet Foreign Minister Vyacheslav Molotov takes an uncompromising posture over issues such as the repatriation of prisoners of war, which further suggests to the West that future relations will be anything but cordial. |
| 24 | October | The United Nations Organisation (UNO) is born as its Charter enters into force. |
| 15 | November | In what becomes a one-time-only offer, the US, the UK, and Canada offer the United Nations information on atomic weaponry if an adequate mechanism for control can be developed and headway made towards general and comprehensive disarmament. Little progress is made. |

| At a Glance – Major Events and Themes |
|---|
| **Settlement of the peace** |
| **Kennan's Long Telegram** |
| **Churchill warns of an Iron Curtain** |
| **Atomic-energy discussions** |
| **Churchill calls for a United States of Europe** |

# 1946

| Day | Month | Event |
|---|---|---|
| 14 | January | The US, the UK, and France agree at the Paris Conference on the administration of zones of occupation in Germany. |
| 9 | February | Stalin states in a speech that, "war is inevitable as long as capitalism exists". The already frosty relations between the East and West begin to turn frigid. Western Europe begins to feel particularly exposed, as the Red Army, with more than 3 million men under arms, stands just across the River Elbe from the western half of the now-divided Germany. |
| 22 | February | George Kennan sends the so-called Long Telegram from the US Embassy in Moscow. In the document, Kennan warns of the Soviet Union's expansionist intentions and the implausibility of any US policy for managing the international system in the post-war world that is based on partnership and co-operation with the Soviet Union (such as Roosevelt's old policy of *quid pro quo*). Furthermore, Kennan warns that the Soviets will use both overt and covert means to pursue their ideologically driven goal of a communist world. Secretary of State James F. Byrnes replaces *quid pro quo* with a policy that becomes known as "patient but firm". |
| 5 | March | Churchill makes a speech in Fulton, Missouri, entitled "Sinews of Peace", in which he warns of a descent across Europe of an Iron Curtain. |
| 25-12 | April-July | A conference of foreign ministers is held in Paris concerning Germany and zones of occupation. |
| 14 | June | The United States proposes the Baruch Plan for atomic disarmament at the first UN Atomic Energy Commission. The plan calls for the transfer of all nuclear weapons to a new international authority and for the subsequent supervision of all nuclear-energy projects by this authority. The Soviets reject the proposal, seeing it as an effort by the Americans to uphold their A-bomb monopoly. |
| 1 | July | The first peacetime test of an atomic weapon takes place at Bikini Atoll, using captured German and Japanese ships. The heavy cruiser "Prince Eugen", a veteran of the Bismarck campaign of 1941, meets its demise during this test. |

| | | |
|---|---|---|
| 10 | July | At the conference of foreign ministers in Paris, Molotov pledges Soviet support for a unified Germany with a strong industrial base, but only after reparations are paid. As this is pending, a peace treaty would have to be delayed by "a number of years". |
| 11 | July | US Secretary of State Byrnes proposes merging all zones of occupation economically with the US zone. Only the British agree. |
| 29-15 | July-October | At the Paris Peace Conference, the Allies negotiate peace treaties with Bulgaria, Finland, Hungary, Italy, and Romania. |
| 1 | August | The US Congress passes the McMahon Act, which prevents the transfer of US atomic technology. This leads to tensions between the US and the UK because much of the research that led to the first atomic bombs had been British. |
| 19 | September | Churchill makes a speech at the University of Zurich calling for a United States of Europe, which is seen as a signal by the leaders of an emerging European movement organised around Jean Monnet that the UK is prepared to join an integrated Euopean organisation. Britain's ambivalent relationship with the European project begins. |
| | November-December | At the Four-Power Foreign Ministers Conference in New York, remaining difficulties concerning the Free Territory of Trieste are resolved. |
| 2 | December | US Secretary of State Byrnes and UK Foreign Secretary Ernest Bevin sign an agrement to merge their respective zones of occupation in Germany into the so-called Bizone. |

| At a Glance – Major Events and Themes |
| --- |
| **Division between East and West grows** |
| **Truman Doctrine** |
| **Cominform created** |
| **Treaty of Dunkirk** |
| **The Europe Report and European Recovery Program** |

## 1947

| Day | Month | Event |
| --- | --- | --- |
| 1 | January | French Prime Minister Leon Blum travels to London to discuss an Anglo-French treaty of alliance with the Attlee Government. |
| 1 | January | In Germany, the agreement between the UK and US to create one single economic entity from their two respective zones of occupation comes into effect. The creation of the Bizone is the first step on the road to the creation of the Federal Republic of Germany (FRG). |
| 8 | January | George Marshall becomes US secretary of state. |
| 10 | February | The Paris peace treaties are signed, settling the peace with Germany's allies and co-belligerents in Europe. |
| 21 | February | The UK informs the US that it can no longer afford to provide Greece and Turkey with financial aid. Fearing further Soviet expansion into the region, the Truman administration decides to take over British responsibilities. This decision leads to the policy of containment, which comes to dominate US strategy during the Cold War. |
| 4 | March | The British and French sign the Treaty of Dunkirk, which is designed to confront a resurgent Germany should such an event occur. Importantly, the treaty contains a clause on automatic armed assistance. |
| 10-25 | March-April | US Secretary of State Marshall visits Moscow and comes away convinced of the essential accuracy of Kennan's warnings that the Soviet Union is set upon a course of expansion. |
| 12 | March | US President Truman outlines the Truman Doctrine to the US Congress, committing his administration to the containment of Soviet expansionism. |
| | March- April | At the Four-Power Foreign Ministers Conference in Moscow, peace treaties with Germany and Austria are discussed, but the ministers agree only on the formal dissolution of Prussia. |
| 5 | June | George Marshall announces the European Recovery Program, or Marshall Plan, as it comes to be known. |

| | | |
|---|---|---|
| 27-2 | June-July | UK Foreign Secretary Bevin and French Foreign Minister Georges Bidault meet with Soviet Foreign Minister Molotov to press the Soviet Union to accept aid under the Marshall Plan. Molotov declines on the grounds that such an acceptance would politically compromise the Soviet Union and its satellites. |
| 12 | July | Western European foreign ministers agree to draw up a Europe Report for the Americans, identifying and specifying their needs with respect to aid under the Marshall Plan. |
| 22 | September | The Europe Report is sent to Washington. |
| 22 | September | Cominform is created to disseminate Soviet communist ideas throughout Europe and beyond and to facilitate Moscow's political control. |
| | September | The Treaty of Dunkirk is approved by the British and French parliaments. |
| | November | In London, the Four Powers again discuss peace treaties with Germany and Austria but reach no agreement. |

| | |
|---|---|
| **At a Glance – Major Events and Themes** | **Prague coup** |
| | **Western attempts to organise regionally in response to the Soviets** |
| | **Marshall Plan** |
| | **The Brussels Treaty and the creation of a Western union** |
| | **The Vandenberg Resolution** |
| | **Berlin Blockade and Airlift** |
| | **A European coal and steel community is first proposed** |

## 1948

| Day | Month | Event |
|---|---|---|
| 22 | January | UK Foreign Secretary Bevin informs the House of Commons that a form of union for the Western Allies was required that went significantly further than the Treaty of Dunkirk in its scope and membership. Bevin wants to tie the US to a longer commitment to the defence of Western Europe both as a counter to Soviet power and as a guarantor against a resurgent Germany. |
| 25 | February | With the support of Moscow, Czech Communists seize power in Prague. Kennan's warning is being realised. Tension in Europe and between the US and the USSR increases. |
| | March | The occupation powers agree to allow Belgium, the Netherlands and Luxembourg (the Benelux countries) to have a say over Allied policy on the future of Germany. |
| 13 | March | The European Recovery Program is approved by the US Senate. The Marshall Plan is close to completion. |
| 4-12 | March | Belgium, France, the Netherlands, Luxembourg and the UK meet in Brussels to discuss a Western union: a defensive political, economic and military organisation designed to guard against German revanchism. |
| 17 | March | As a result of discussions on a Western union, the Brussels Treaty of Economic, Social and Cultural Collaboration and Collective Self-Defence is signed. The Western Union, which the Brussels Treaty establishes, is the first truly integrative Western European organisation and establishes a model for future initiatives of this type. |
| 3 | April | President Truman signs the European Recovery Program, and the Marshall Plan becomes US law. |
| 16 | April | A convention creating the Organisation for European Economic Co-operation (OEEC) is signed in Paris by all the Western Powers. |

| | | |
|---|---|---|
| 17 | April | The foreign ministers of the Brussels Treaty powers meet in Paris for the first time to discuss the machinery of the newly formed Western Union. |
| 30 | April | The Western Union Defence Committee, made up of the defence ministers of the Brussels Treaty powers, meets for the first time. They in turn create the Permanent Military Committee. |
| 7-10 | May | The International Committee of Movements for European Unity meets in The Hague, ostensibly to build on Churchill's Zurich speech calling for a United States of Europe. At this meeting, Alcide de Gasperi, Konrad Adenauer, Paul-Henri Spaak, Robert Schuman, Jean Monnet and Paul van Zeeland emerge as the driving forces behind a small but growing body of elite opinion that believes that the avoidance of war in Western Europe can be achieved only through the political and economic integration of states in Europe. |
| 12 | May | Senator Vandenberg proposes a resolution in the US Senate that calls for placing the United States at the core of a series of regional security pacts. |
| 14 | May | The establishment of the State of Israel is proclaimed. |
| 11 | June | The Vandenberg Resolution is passed by the US Congress. |
| 18 | June | The three Western occupying powers announce the introduction of a new German currency in the Bizone and the French occupation zone but say it will not extend to Berlin. |
| 19 | June | Canadian Prime Minister Louis Saint-Laurent proposes a regional defence pact incorporating the US, Canada and the Western European states (excl. Germany). This is the first time that a leading Western statesman makes an overt public proposal for a transatlantic security alliance in the face of the perceived Soviet threat. |
| 20 | June | Currency reform is implemented in the US-UK Bizone and the French occupation zone in Germany. |
| 24 | June | The Berlin Blockade begins as the Soviet Union attempts to force the Western Allies out of the former German capital by closing road and rail access. The reason is Soviet displeasure with discussions in the West aimed at creating the Federal Republic of Germany. The blockade, also known as the First Berlin Crisis or the Berlin Airlift, lasts 323 days. |
| 26 | June | The airlift starts to help the residents of Berlin. |
| 2 | July | President Truman orders the Vandenberg Resolution enacted as soon as possible in order to operationalise the strategy of containment through the establishment of security pacts with friendly states. |
| 17 | July | The first nuclear-capable US B-29 bombers arrive in the UK. |

| | | |
|---|---|---|
| 25 | August | The Treaty of Brussels is ratified. |
| | August | The French ambassador to Washington tells US Secretary of State Marshall that France demands "unity of command at once and immediate movement of US military personnel to France" if France is to join any proposed Atlantic security pact. The Americans view such high-handed behaviour with distaste, and this event establishes the tone of Franco-American relations for much of the Cold War. |
| 10 | September | The National Security Council's (NSC) policy document NSC-30 asserts that the military "must be ready to utilise promptly and effectively all appropriate means available, including atomic weapons" to counter any Soviet conventional attack. The strategy of *massive retaliation* is effectively born. |
| | September | The foreign ministers of the Four Powers meet in Paris and discuss the future fate of the former Italian colonies. The meeting ends inconclusively. |
| 5 | October | UK Field Marshall Bernard Montgomery is appointed chairman of the Western Union's Permanent Military Committee. |
| 25-26 | October | The Brussels Treaty Permanent Commission meets in Paris and announces that it is committed to securing a North Atlantic agreement. |
| | November | André Philip, a colleague of French Foreign Minister Robert Schuman, proposes in the French *Assemblée Nationale* the creation of a European Coal and Steel Community (ECSC) to resolve an old Franco-German problem: namely, that German steel production in the Ruhr relies on French coal in the Saar. |
| 2 | November | Harry S. Truman is elected US president. |
| 10 | December | Talks on a proposed North Atlantic treaty resume in Washington. Norway, Denmark, Iceland, Ireland, Portugal and Italy are invited to join (all except Ireland accept). |

| At a Glance – Major Events and Themes |
| --- |
| Comecon established |
| The Treaty of Washington and the creation of NATO |
| Council of Europe created |
| Berlin Blockade lifted |
| Federal Republic of Germany created |

## 1949

| Day | Month | Event |
| --- | --- | --- |
| 20 | January | Harry S. Truman is inaugurated for his second term as US president. George Marshall resigns as secretary of state. |
| 21 | January | Dean Acheson replaces Marshall as secretary of state. |
| 25 | January | Comecon is established to tie the economies of the Soviet satellite states firmly to that of the USSR. Bulgaria, Czechoslovakia, Hungary, Poland, Romania and the Soviet Union participate. |
| 18 | March | The text of the proposed North Atlantic treaty is published. |
| 28 | March | James Forrestal resigns as US secretary of defense and is replaced by Louis Johnson. |
| 31 | March | The Soviet Union condemns the North Atlantic treaty as contrary to the UN Charter and the Four-Power Foreign Ministers Conferences. |
| 2 | April | The 12 soon-to-be signatories of the North Atlantic treaty reject the Soviet complaint. |
| 4 | April | The North Atlantic Treaty is signed in Washington by Belgium, Canada, Denmark, France, Iceland, Italy, Luxembourg, the Netherlands, Norway, Portugal, the UK and the US. |
| 8 | April | France merges its zone of occupation in Germany with the British-American Bizone. The Trizone is created. |
| | April | At the time, the Western Allies have only 12 active divisions in Western Europe and estimate Soviet strength to be in the region of 175 divisions. Whilst an overestimate, it does indicate the nature of the concern that existed amongst the Western Allies at the time. |
| | April | The French newspaper "Le Monde" suggests that the signing of the North Atlantic Treaty represents a strong step on the road to German rearmament as part of the Western Allies' desire to balance Soviet conventional strength. The paper states that, "The rearmament of Germany is present in the Atlantic Pact as the seed in the egg." |
| | April | André Philip develops the idea of the ECSC at a European Movement Conference in London. |

| | | |
|---|---|---|
| 5 | May | The London Ten-Power Conference creates the Council of Europe (CoE). The CoE has three main organs: the Consultative Assembly, the Committee of Ministers and the Secretariat General. |
| 12 | May | At a meeting of foreign ministers in Paris, it is agreed to lift the Berlin Blockade. |
| 19 | May | The US Joint Chiefs of Staff produce a Short-Range Emergency Plan (1844/13), code-named Half Moon, that is designed to counter, through massive air power, the Soviet Union's ability to fight a war in Europe. It is a "panic" response to the Berlin Blockade and foreshadows the official adoption of the strategic doctrine of *massive retaliation*. |
| 23 | May | The Soviet Union, accepting that its policy of coercion just short of war has failed to force the West to retreat, adopts a more conciliatory line on the questions of the division of Berlin, Germany in general and the proposed Austrian peace treaty. |
| 23 | May | The Basic Law is promulgated the same day, paving the way for the creation of the FRG. |
| 25 | July | President Truman sends the Mutual Defense Assistance Act to Congress. This Act ties the US to entangling foreign alliances even in peacetime and represents an historic shift in US foreign policy. |
| | July | Germany's first chancellor-in-waiting, Konrad Adenauer, writes to French Foreign Minister Schuman to complain about French enthusiasm for the policy of dismantling, whereby the four victors are empowered to remove German equipment by way of war reparations. |
| 14 | August | The first free elections since the war are held in West Germany. |
| 24 | August | The North Atlantic Treaty, also called the Washington treaty, enters into force. The North Atlantic Treaty Organisation (NATO) is born. |
| 29 | August | The Soviet Union explodes its first atomic device, much to the shock of Western leaders, who thought that the USSR was several years further behind in the requisite technology. The USSR had been helped by such celebrated spies as the Rosenbergs, Guy Burgess, Kim Philby and Donald Maclean. |
| 20/21 | September | The FRG formally comes into being. However, it is only partially sovereign. At the same time, the Occupation Status enters into force. |

| | | |
|---|---|---|
| | September | US Secretary of State Acheson, UK Foreign Secretary Bevin and French Foreign Minister Schuman meet to discuss dismantling. The French come under strong pressure to desist from such practices. As a *quid pro quo* for French agreement, Schuman is charged by Acheson and Bevin with finding a solution to the perennial problem of Germany and the threat it has historically represented to its neighbours. |
| 6 | October | President Truman signs the Mutual Defense Assistance Act into US law. |
| 12 | October | US Chief of Staff General Omar Bradley says that the Soviet Union has some 2.5 million military personnel. |
| 16 | October | Bradley increases his estimate to 5 million during hearings before the Senate Armed Services Committee. |
| 31 | October | The FRG becomes a full member of the OEEC. |
| 23 | November | The Western Union Defence Committee decides at a meeting in London to place the Western Union structure within the North Atlantic framework. |
| | November | France, the UK and the US agree to stop the practice of dismantling German industry. |
| 11 | December | The North Atlantic Defence Committee accepts the Western Union Defence Committee's recommendation to place itself under the aegis of NATO. |

Part 2

# THE LONG HAUL

# 1950 - 1959

1950

1957

1959

| At a Glance – Major Events and Themes | |
|---|---|
| | **Nuclear stand-off begins** |
| | **The Schuman Plan and the European Coal and Steel Community** |
| | **The Korean War starts** |
| | **The movement towards creating a North Atlantic community intensifies** |
| | **US proposes German rearmament** |
| | **Adenauer proposes economic union between France and Germany** |
| | **The Long Haul begins** |
| | **Churchill calls for a European army** |
| | **The Pleven Plan for a European Defence Community** |
| | **The Spofford Proposals** |

## 1950

| Day | Month | Event |
|---|---|---|
| 27 | January | President Truman approves the plan for an integrated defence of the North Atlantic area. |
| 31 | January | The US decides to proceed with the construction of a hydrogen bomb that is many times more potent than the atomic weapons used on Japan. The dawn of the nuclear age (as opposed to the atomic age) begins. |
| 21 | March | German Chancellor Adenauer suggests an economic union between France and Germany. |
| 28 | March | UK Prime Minister Attlee affirms that, "We have set our face - the United States, France and ourselves - against the re-arming of Germany." |
| 1 | April | The NATO Defence Committee approves the first draft of a four-year (medium-term) defence plan. |
| 16 | April | Monnet, Paul Reuter and Etienne Hirsch draft the first version of the so-called Schuman Plan. The document proposes a solution to the German Problem by focusing on the Saar/Ruhr divide first through the creation of the European Coal and Steel Community (ECSC) and then on to eventual federation of Western European states covered by the Western Union. |
| | April | US policy document NSC-68 is presented to President Truman. The document proposes a strategy of comprehensive Western rearmament focused upon, and led by, the United States. It represents a final acceptance of the enduring nature of the now-established Cold War. The so-called Long Haul begins. |

| | | |
|---|---|---|
| 5 | May | The UK complains to the Soviet Union about the creation and rearming of the so-called *Volkspolizei* in the Eastern *Länder* of Germany under Soviet occupation. The British claim that this is in breach of the Four-Power agreement not to rearm the Germans. |
| 9 | May | In the so-called Declaration of 9 May, the French Cabinet accepts the Schuman Plan for an ECSC. This declaration is regarded as the start of the process of European integration. It states: "World peace cannot be safeguarded without the making of constructive effort proportionate to the dangers which threaten it. The contribution which an organised and living Europe can bring to civilisation is indispensable to the maintenance of peaceful relations. In taking upon herself for more than 20 years the role of champion of a united Europe, France has always had as her essential aim the service of peace. A united Europe was not achieved and we had war. Europe will not be made all at once, or according to a single, general plan. It will be built through concrete achievements, which first create a de facto solidarity. The gathering of the nations of Europe requires the elimination of the age-old opposition of France and the Federal Republic of Germany. The first concern in any action undertaken must be these two countries." |
| 11 | May | A Four-Power Foreign Ministers Conference takes place. There is no substantive progress made between the adversaries. |
| 11 | May | In a debate in the UK House of Commons, Britain comes out against joining the Schuman Plan and the ECSC. |
| 2 | June | The UK formally rejects membership of the ECSC. The French say that they will press ahead anyway. |
| 3 | June | The French Government sends a memorandum outlining the conditions for UK membership of the ECSC. The "difficult" terms contained therein have been taken as evidence by some authorities that Schuman had no real desire to see the UK join, for that would have disrupted French leadership of the fledgling integrationist institution. |
| 5 | June | The so-called Six (Belgium, France, Germany, Italy, Luxembourg and the Netherlands) agree to pool their steel and coal industries under a High Authority. |
| 12 | June | The National Executive Council of the UK Labour Party publishes a pamphlet entitled "European Unity", which strongly attacks the concept of supranationality that they believe is envisaged in the ECSC. |
| 20 | June | Work starts in Paris on an ECSC treaty under the chairmanship of Jean Monnet. |
| 25 | June | North Korea invades the South. The Korean War starts. |

| | | |
|---|---|---|
| 24 | July | General Graf von Schwerin is appointed advisor to German Chancellor Adenauer on technical security issues. Following this, he commences work on an intelligence appreciation of the Soviet threat. |
| 22 | July | The US high commissioner in Germany states "that it is very difficult to deny the Germans the right and the means to defend their own soil". |
| 26 | July | The UK Government reaffirms its opposition to German rearmament. |
| | July | UK War Minister Emanuel Shinwell "confirms" Western intelligence estimates that the Soviet Union has some 175 active military divisions. |
| 3 | August | The UK Government announces that it is increasing defence expenditure to an historic high of £3.4 billion per annum. |
| 9 + 10 | August | *European Defence Community (EDC).* In a debate in the Assembly of the CoE, French representative Paul Reynaud calls for a European minister of war. However, the German Social Democrat Carlo Schmid says that German rearmament would destroy European defence. |
| 11 | August | *EDC.* Churchill calls for the creation of a European army. Once again, this is taken to imply that the British would be part of such an integrated force. |
| 11 | August | *EDC.* In the Strasbourg Resolution, the CoE calls for "the creation, for a common defence of Europe, of a European Army under political institutions of a United Europe". |
| 11 | August | Summing up much of the popular feeling in Western Europe, a headline in the Italian newspaper "Quotidiane" reads: "A 38th Parallel Runs through Berlin". |
| 29 | August | In a security memorandum, Chancellor Adenauer offers German participation in the defence of Western Europe. |
| | August | The French Government announces that it is increasing its forces significantly to 20 divisions with a 28-group air force. This increase is to be realised by 1953. |
| 9 | September | President Truman decides to increase the level of US forces in Western Europe. |
| 12-14 | September | *EDC.* French Foreign Minister Schuman, British Foreign Secretary Bevin, and US Secretary of State Acheson meet at the Waldorf Astoria in New York. Acheson proposes an integrated military command and a German contribution of 10 divisions. Schuman leaves the meeting shocked by the prospect and knowing that such a development would be utterly unacceptable to the French Government and people. |
| 15 | September | The US lands forces at Inchon in Korea. The Americans exert pressure on the Europeans to increase available military manpower. The German rearmament crisis beckons. |

| | | |
|---|---|---|
| 16 | September | At the North Atlantic Council meeting in New York, it is agreed to place the Western defensive line as far east as possible. The so-called forward strategy is born. |
| 18 | September | The North Atlantic Council meeting ends inconclusively. The other Western Allies believe that the US is forcing the German issue upon them. However, the foreign ministers of France, the UK and the US agree to continue discussing the problem. |
| 26 | September | *EDC.* The North Atlantic Council reconvenes and accepts the US plan for an integrated command. However, France refuses to shift its position over any possible German contribution to Western defence. How Germany will contribute is therefore put off to a meeting of the NATO Defence Council that is planned for 28 October. Importantly, France recognises that it needs to produce an alternative strategy if it is to avoid isolation at that meeting. The concept of what eventually becomes the European Defence Community (EDC) is the result. Schuman charges the same team that drew up the ECSC plan to devise an integrated solution to this latest version of the German Problem. |
| 14 | October | *EDC.* The ECSC team, under the direction of Monnet and including such notable figures as Etienne Hirsch, Pierre Uri, Bernard Clappier, Paul Reuter, Hervé Alphand and Jacques van Helmont, complete the basic plan for an integrated European army that becomes known as the Pleven Plan, after the French prime minister of the time, René Pleven. |
| 23 | October | *EDC.* The French Cabinet accepts the Pleven Plan at an emotional meeting. The plan includes the following key elements:<br>a) France is implacably opposed to the creation of a German Army with a separate general staff;<br>b) Germany is to be allowed to rearm only under the auspices of a supranational high command and organisation that will provide for common equipment and common financing under a single high authority (*à la* ECSC); and<br>c) No agreement is to be signed before the ECSC Treaty. |
| 24 | October | *EDC.* The French *Assemblée Nationale* grudgingly agrees to the Pleven Plan, but the prime minister concludes that this position is as far as he can go. |
| 28 | October | *EDC.* France introduces the Pleven Plan to its Allies at the NATO Defence Committee. |
| 2 | November | *EDC.* "The Washington Post" reports that France and the other Allies remain split over the question of German rearmament. |

| | | |
|---|---|---|
| 3 | November | The Soviet Union proposes a meeting of the Big Four (France, UK, US, USSR) to discuss what it calls "the fulfilment of Potsdam". The USSR is concerned by the prospect of German rearmament. |
| 13 | November | *EDC.* As a response to the Pleven Plan, the US makes the so-called Spofford Proposals, after Charles Spofford, the American lawyer charged with finding a solution to the impasse of the German Problem within NATO. The proposals, based upon an American analysis that the immediate military crisis is more important than any fear over a resurgent Germany in the longer term, involve a German element within NATO that would not exceed 20% of the overall force levels. However, such an element would require Germany to be a NATO member, which would also entail equality, independence and the right to secede, something that is unacceptable not only to the French but to all European Allies. The proposals also include the following key elements:<br>a) A distinction between short-term and long-term political requirements;<br>b) They dissociate the creation of German units from the creation of a European army, saying that longer-term developments would depend upon the development of an appropriate institutional framework;<br>c) The proposals accept the concept of a European army as a means of strengthening the Atlantic Alliance but only if it is militarily viable and operates within the framework of NATO;<br>d) The creation of a European army, however, raises profound problems vis-à-vis attendant political institutions, and these would have to be considered at length;<br>e) The forward strategy requires German units as soon as possible;<br>f) Any German military contribution would have to be subject to several safeguards:<br>i) The stationing of Allied forces in Germany;<br>ii) The express prohibition of any German general staff or national army;<br>iii) No heavy armoured formations;<br>iv) No chemical, biological or atomic weapons; and<br>v) A limited German navy and air force;<br>g) The NATO Council to invite the three Allied Occupation Powers to discuss German participation with the Government of the Federal Republic;<br>h) The Powers concerned to keep the other Powers fully informed;<br>i) The proposals in no way intended to grant Germany equality of rights or treatment in the military field; and<br>j) The proposals draw the attention of the NATO Council to the French intention to call a conference of countries that wish to participate in a European army. |

| | | |
|---|---|---|
| 15 | November | In a debate in the UK House of Commons, War Minister Emanuel Shinwell asks "whether British public opinion, French public opinion or American public opinion would tolerate a situation in which British, American and French soldiers and airmen were engaged in the defence of German territory without some contribution from the German people". |
| 24 | November | *EDC.* The Consultative Assembly of the CoE makes a formal recommendation to the Council of Ministers urging governments to create a European army. |
| | November | China attacks UN forces in Korea across the Yalu River. |
| 18 | December | The NATO Defence Committee approves the Spofford Proposals. |
| 19 | December | General Dwight D. Eisenhower, the Allied commander on D-Day, is appointed the first supreme Allied commander Europe (SACEUR) of NATO. |
| 21 | December | It is agreed that the FRG shall have "equality of rights and treatment". |

| At a Glance – Major Events and Themes | |
|---|---|
| | **The Paris Conference on a European army** |
| | **The Petersberg Conference and West German contribution to European defence** |
| | **US augments production of material for nuclear weapons** |
| | **Supreme Headquarters Allied Powers Europe (SHAPE) established** |
| | **Paris Four-Power Conference** |
| | **The Paris Treaty establishing the European Coal and Steel Community (ECSC)** |
| | **Resolution 99** |
| | **Eisenhower calls for a European federation** |

# 1951

| Day | Month | Event |
|---|---|---|
| 9 | January | The Petersberg Conference convenes outside Bonn in West Germany to discuss a possible German contribution to the defence of Western Europe. From the outset, the Germans make it clear to their American, British and French negotiating partners (the three respective high commissioners) that they demand "equality of rights and equality of treatment" before they will consider making a contribution. |
| 12 | January | The main points of the Spofford Proposals are leaked to "The Times" of London. |
| 1 | February | *EDC.* General Eisenhower calls for Germany to be given equality of status with the other Western Allies. |
| 12 | February | *EDC.* In an address to the UK House of Commons, Attlee raises several conditions for German rearmament:<br>a) The rearmament of NATO should precede that of Germany;<br>b) The build-up of NATO forces should precede that of Germany;<br>c) The German contribution should be wholly integrated into a European army so as to avoid the possibility of a German army;<br>d) Rearmament should be carried out only with the agreement of the German people. |
| 15 | February | *EDC.* The Paris Conference on the creation of a European army commences. Known officially as *La Conférence pour l'Organisation de l'Armée Européenne*, it has five participants – France, Germany, Italy, Belgium and Luxembourg – and six observers – Canada, Denmark, the Netherlands, Norway, the UK and the US. France dominates proceedings from the start, including naming Hervé Alphand as chairman. |

| | | |
|---|---|---|
| 20 | February | *EDC.* "Izvestiya" accuses the Pleven Plan of being a Washington tool. |
| | March | The UK War Office estimates Soviet armed strength at 4 million military personnel. |
| 4 | April | The US Senate approves Resolution 99, which commits the US to sending six divisions to Western Europe. |
| 18 | April | *ESDP.* Belgium, France, Germany, Luxembourg, the Netherlands and Italy sign the treaty establishing the ECSC in Paris. The Six are born. |
| 4 | June | *EDC.* The Petersberg Conference ends in failure due to German insistence upon equality of treatment and French determination to prevent it. As a consequence, the US switches its support to the EDC negotiations as a means of engaging German manpower in the defence of Western Europe. |
| 10 | June | *EDC.* As part of what becomes known as the US change of heart, the US high commissioner to Germany is recalled to Washington to discuss future US policy towards Germany. |
| 30 | June | *EDC.* The Paris Conference Military Committee succeeds in producing an interim draft report. |
| 3 | July | *EDC.* Eisenhower calls for a European federation and starts to put his weight behind a European army. |
| 24 | July | *EDC.* The Paris Conference approves the report of the Military Committee and recommends the creation of a European army. The military formation of division, so painful to the French, is replaced by groupement. |
| 30 | July | *EDC.* Truman formally authorises US backing for the EDC approach. |
| 15-20 | September | The NATO Council meeting in Ottawa examines the vexed issue of contractual agreements, which proved the stumbling block during the ill-fated Petersberg Conference. The contractual agreements are aimed at transforming the status of Germany from that of an occupied power to that of an Ally. However, France demands that any such agreement be linked to an EDC treaty, which simultaneously constitutes a European army, thus preventing German freedom of action. |
| 15-20 | September | At the same meeting, NATO establishes the Temporary Council Committee to enable the Alliance to match military requirements with economic and financial capabilities. |
| 22 | October | The protocol inviting Greece and Turkey to join NATO is concluded. |
| 26 | October | Labour loses UK elections to the Conservatives. Winston Churchill is elected to a second term as prime minister. |
| | October | *EDC.* As a result of a change in attitude by Dutch Foreign Minister Dirk Stikker, the Netherlands changes its position from observer to participant at the Paris Conference. |

| | | |
|---|---|---|
| | October | The US carries out a test on the first sub-kiloton bomb. The so-called baby bombs are the first generation of tactical nuclear weapons. |
| | October | *EDC.* The UK sends a military officer to Paris. However, it is unclear whether the UK is to enter into a formal relationship with any European army. The concession is a result of US pressure. |
| | October | *EDC.* The conference on a European army becomes the Conference on a European Defence Community, mainly to ease British fears. |
| 24-28 | November | No substantive progress is made at the Rome meeting of the North Atlantic Council. |
| 28 | November | *EDC.* UK Foreign Secretary Anthony Eden says at a press conference that UK units will not participate in an EDC. The UK-French rift becomes ever more apparent, as the UK senses that it can back away from EDC talks as US support appears to wane. The British home secretary, Sir David Maxwell Fyfe, echoes the words of the foreign secretary. |
| 28 | November | *EDC.* Responding to the comment of the British home secretary, the French representative to the CoE states that: "Britain must not now repudiate Churchill's resolution ... If Britain ... refuses to join ... what a powerful argument for the European Army's opponents in parliaments." |
| | November | The US Army Command and General Staff College complete a report entitled "The Tactical Use of Atomic Weapons - FM 100-31". |
| 1 | December | *EDC.* Dean Acheson, the US secretary of state, tells Truman that the EDC talks are not going well. |
| 10 | December | *EDC.* Robert Schuman suggests a college of ministers similar to the political control of the British Commonwealth in order to overcome British concerns over loss of sovereignty implied by the EDC. This proposal becomes known as the new Schuman Plan. |
| 15 | December | *EDC.* While concluding a visit to Paris, British Prime Minister Churchill issues a *communiqué* saying that the UK will not join the EDC but will co-operate as closely as possible with it. |
| 20 | December | *EDC.* Dean Acheson hopes that the new Schuman Plan for the EDC is enough to persuade the UK to participate. |
| 27-30 | December | *EDC.* The foreign and defence ministers of the Six EDC states agree that the community is a step along the path to eventual European unification. The ministers also agree to develop a plan for European confederation or federation. |
| | December | NATO Allies announce that they have 35 divisions in Western Europe. They also state that they possess 3,000 operational aircraft compared with a 1949 level of 1,000. However, former UK Defence Secretary Shinwell has suggested that the Soviets have 19,000. |

| | |
|---|---|
| **At a Glance – Major Events and Themes** | **London Foreign Ministers Conference in support of the EDC** |
| | **Greece and Turkey join NATO** |
| | **Stalin proposes German unity** |
| | **The Eden Plan on political control of the EDC** |
| | **The contractual agreements signed, giving the Federal Republic of Germany equal treatment** |
| | **The treaty establishing the European Coal and Steel Community (ECSC) enters into force** |
| | **First UK atomic-bomb test** |
| | **First US hydrogen-bomb test** |
| | **Adenauer calls for a common foreign policy** |
| | **NATO force levels reach 7 million** |
| | **The US Joint Chiefs of Staff authorise NATO's Supreme Allied Commander Europe Eisenhower to start planning for the use of tactical nuclear weapons** |
| | **The UK Chiefs of Staff produce the Global Strategy Paper, which advocates *massive retaliation*** |
| | **A small group of French officers under Colonel Charles Ailleret advocate a French nuclear deterrent** |

## 1952

| Day | Month | Event |
|---|---|---|
| 5-9 | January | *EDC.* Churchill goes to Washington to discuss the situation with Truman and to ensure the "special relationship" remains intact in spite of the UK refusal to join the EDC. |
| 26-27 | January | *EDC.* The foreign ministers of the Six meet in Paris and agree that the Board of Commissioners that will oversee the work of the EDC should consist of nine members, each serving for six years. |
| | January | *EDC.* The refusal of the UK to join the EDC threatens its failure, as France fears having to counterbalance potential German power without the active and assured support of the British. |
| 3 | February | *EDC.* Adenauer suggests that German membership of the EDC and an accord for the contractual agreements might take place only if Germany is given NATO membership and if there is a bilateral settlement of the Saar/Ruhr dispute with France. Adenauer is testing the political climate, and, following the hostile reaction his suggestion receives, he quickly backs away. |

| | | |
|---|---|---|
| 8 | February | The *Bundestag* votes for a resolution demanding equal status for Germany and an end to the occupation if it is to accept the EDC. |
| 17-19 | February | *EDC.* During the London Foreign Ministers Conference, the US and the UK offer to support the EDC fully (although short of British membership) and to play their full role in the defence of Western Europe. They also agree a position on future NATO/EDC relations. This agreement averts the failure of the EDC. |
| 18 | February | Greece and Turkey accede to NATO. |
| 19 | February | *EDC.* In an historic and heated debate, the French *Assemblée Nationale* votes narrowly in favour of the EDC. However, French representatives are worried that the EDC will enable Germany to enter NATO by the back door. As a result, they want the US and the UK to guarantee the EDC. |
| 20-25 | February | The North Atlantic Council meets in Lisbon and sets a force target of 96 divisions, which is to be achieved by 1954 (at mobilisation plus 30 days). |
| 10 | March | In a note to France, the UK and the US, Stalin proposes a peace treaty for Germany, offering German unity and sovereignty with rearmament sufficient for self-defence within one year and strict neutrality of all troops. |
| 13 | March | Lord Ismay is appointed secretary general of NATO. He is famous for stating that the purpose of NATO is "to keep the Russians out, the Americans in and the Germans down". |
| 14 | March | *EDC.* Paris Conference asks the UK "to enter into a formal treaty relationship with the EDC, including accepting a provision for an automatic armed assistance" clause similar to that contained in Article IV of the Treaty of Brussels (Article V in the modified treaty of 1954). |
| | March | *EDC.* The UK responds by invoking Article 51 of the UN Charter and Article 5 of the North Atlantic Treaty in order to claim that a *de facto* guarantee of the EDC already exists. |
| | March | *EDC.* In a further move to avoid the EDC structure, UK Foreign Secretary Anthony Eden proposes that the CoE should become the political-control body for the EDC because it is run through an intergovernmental Council of Ministers. The so-called Eden Plan is designed to ensure French support for the EDC and to involve the UK partially, but not fully, in the integration process, and, as such, it foreshadows British support for the process of European Political Co-operation, which starts in the 1970s. |
| 25 | March | In response to Stalin's proposal for German unity, the West makes free elections under UN control a precondition for negotiating a peace treaty. |

| | | |
|---|---|---|
| 4 | April | Lord Ismay takes up his positions as secretary general of NATO and vice-chairman of the North Atlantic Council (NAC). |
| 9 | April | In a note to the Western Powers, the Soviet Union insists that Germany remain free from alliances but agrees to allow free elections in Germany if they are supervised by the Four Powers instead of the UN. |
| 30 | April | *EDC.* The UK Labour Party demands a fresh general election before any decision is made that will commit the UK to the EDC. |
| 1 | May | General Matthew Ridgway becomes SACEUR, succeeding Eisenhower. |
| 9 | May | *EDC.* The text of the *Traité Instituant la Communauté Européenne de Défense* is initialled in Paris. |
| 12 | May | *EDC.* UK Field Marshal Earl Alexander visits Paris and offers the French strong UK support in the form of close British military association with the EDC in exchange for French commitment to the EDC. This eases French concerns. |
| 26 | May | *EDC.* The contractual agreements, which end the status of Germany as an occupied power, are signed in Bonn. |
| 27 | May | *EDC.* The EDC treaty is signed in Paris. |
| 2 | June | *EDC.* In a letter to the US Senate, President Truman expresses his satisfaction with the EDC treaty. |
| | June | *EDC. Le Comité Intérimaire de la Conférence pour l'Organisation de la Communauté Européenne de Défense* is established in Paris. |
| 23 | July | The Treaty Establishing the European Coal and Steel Community (ECSC) enters into force. |
| 31 | July | *EDC.* After a tense debate in the UK House of Commons, Parliament approves the EDC. However, the final motion is worded in such a way as to remind members of the 1951 Attlee conditions. |
| 23 | August | French Premier Antoine Pinay, a strong supporter of the EDC, steps down from office. |
| 25 | August | *EDC.* The USSR attacks the EDC as being in breach of the Potsdam Agreement not to rearm Germany. |
| 5 | September | *EDC.* The East German *Volkskammer* attacks the EDC. |
| 10 | September | *EDC.* The Eden Plan is killed off as Italian Foreign Minister Alcide de Gasperi suggests that a new ECSC assembly should be the focus of EDC political control. |

| | | |
|---|---|---|
| 10 | September | *EDC.* At an ECSC meeting in Luxembourg, the Six agree to appoint a special assembly to interpret Article 38 of the EDC treaty, which spells out its institutional structure, and to draw up a draft treaty for a European Political Community (EPC). This political community would take over the powers and institutions of the ECSC and the EDC along de Gasperi's ideas, but the success of the initiative depends on the ratification of the EDC treaty. |
| 3 | October | The UK carries out its first test explosion of an atomic device. |
| 3 | October | Stalin proposes to Adenauer a "pan-German solution", offering military autonomy to prevent the conclusion of treaties between the Western Powers and Germany. Adenauer rejects the proposal. |
| 17 | October | *EDC.* French Socialists attack the EDC as "unconstitutional". Worryingly, Edouard Herriot, the president of the *Assemblée Nationale*, leads the attack. |
| 1 | November | The first US hydrogen bomb is exploded. |
| 4 | November | Dwight D. Eisenhower is elected president of the United States. |
| 15 | November | The French Government puts the EDC treaty before the *Assemblée Nationale* for detailed examination in committee. |
| | November | *EDC.* René Pleven talks of alternatives to the EDC but says that he himself remains committed. |
| 3 | December | The UK Foreign and Commonwealth Office says West German troops number 100,000. This estimate is accurate. |
| 5 | December | *EDC.* The *Bundestag* approves the EDC in its second reading but puts off voting on it in a third reading for fear of its being rejected. |
| 15 | December | *EDC.* Adenauer suggests the need for a common foreign policy, saying that it is not possible to have a common defence policy without one. |
| 15-18 | December | *EDC.* The NATO Council affirms that there remains a need for the EDC, but none of the Six wants to be the first to ratify. |
| 23 | December | *EDC.* The French Government formally resigns, dealing an important blow to the EDC. |

| At a Glance – Major Events and Themes | |
|---|---|
| | **The EDC falters** |
| | **Dwight D. Eisenhower sworn into office as US president** |
| | **John Foster Dulles becomes US secretary of state** |
| | **Charles de Gaulle attacks the EDC** |
| | **Josef Stalin dies** |
| | **Call for a new European assembly** |
| | **The Dulles Deadline** |
| | **Korean final armistice signed at Panmunjan** |
| | **First Soviet thermonuclear device tested** |
| | **NATO adopts doctrine of *massive retaliation*** |
| | **Dulles warns of an "agonising reappraisal" of US policy towards Western Europe** |
| | **UK, US and France each establish defence expenditure at around 10% of GDP** |
| | **European economies have increased defence expenditure by some 250% on average since 1949** |

## 1953

| Day | Month | Event |
|---|---|---|
| 7 | January | *EDC.* Adenauer says that he is prepared to meet the French to discuss their concerns over the EDC. |
| 8 | January | *EDC.* René Mayer becomes prime minister of France. He demands more guarantees from the US and UK before France will ratify the EDC treaty. Schuman is replaced by Georges Bidault as French foreign minister. |
| 20 | January | Eisenhower is sworn into office. |
| 21 | January | John Foster Dulles and Charles E. Wilson begin their terms as US secretary of state and US secretary of defense, respectively. |
| 29 | January | *EDC.* "Frankfurter Allgemeine Zeitung" military expert Adalbert Weinstein says that France is only interested in maintaining the "fiction" of the EDC whilst at the same time keeping its own national army. |
| 31 | January | *EDC.* Dulles starts a tour of Western European capitals in order to push for the ratification of the EDC treaty. |
| 12 | February | *EDC.* Dulles tells the American people that the failure to ratify the EDC treaty is "worrying", and that NATO suffers from a "fatal weakness" without Germany and the EDC. |

| | | |
|---|---|---|
| 12-13 | February | *EDC.* At the Anglo-French summit, the two sides discuss French national sentiment over their army, enhanced guarantees from the UK prior to ratification and protocols to the treaty concerning French engagement in Indo-China. |
| 23-25 | February | *EDC.* Foreign ministers of the Six meet in Rome. Although concern at what is regarded as French tampering with the EDC treaty is delayed, it cannot now be avoided. |
| 25 | February | Charles de Gaulle bitterly attacks the EDC. |
| | February | *EDC.* Dulles says that the EDC treaty must be ratified by all the participants or else the US will cut its military aid. |
| 1 | March | *EDC.* René Mayer says the EDC represents the last guarantee against the rebirth of German militarism. |
| 5 | March | Josef Stalin dies. A power struggle commences over his succession between Georgi Malenkov and Nikita Khrushchev. |
| 5/6 | March | Malenkov is named chairman of the Council of Ministers of the USSR and first secretary of the Communist Party of the Soviet Union (CPSU). |
| 10 | March | *EDC.* Italy's Prime Minister de Gasperi formally puts forward a new plan for the political control of the ECSC and the EDC through an elected assembly. This plan, known as Article 38 (referring to the EDC treaty), kills off the Eden Plan and any realistic chance of the UK's being in any way involved with either the ECSC or the EDC. |
| 10 | March | The *ad hoc* assembly instituted by the ECSC agrees on the text of the treaty establishing an EPC. |
| 13 | March | Malenkov has to resign from his post as first secretary of the CPSU. |
| 19 | March | The German Constitutional Court rules that a two-thirds majority from both German chambers is necessary to ratify the EDC treaty. |
| 19 | March | *EDC.* The German *Bundestag* finally votes for the ratification of the EDC treaty after a bitter debate. However, approval by the upper house, the *Bundesrat*, is still needed for ratification. |
| 23 | March | US President Eisenhower establishes the post of assistant to the president for national security affairs, to become known as national security advisor. Robert Cutler, who wrote the report on the organisation of the NSC that triggered Eisenhower's decision, becomes the first national security advisor. |
| 1 | April | *EDC.* The so-called Dulles Deadline is reached for the EDC treaty. However, no country has ratified the treaty yet. |
| 6-19 | April | *EDC.* During a visit to the US and Canada, Adenauer goes to Washington and is given pledges of US aid for having ratified the EDC treaty. |

| | | |
|---|---|---|
| 23-25 | April | At the North Atlantic Council meeting in Paris, the US pushes hard for the ratification of the EDC treaty but faces stiff opposition from the French in particular. |
| 11 | May | *EDC.* In a famous speech in the UK House of Commons, Prime Minister Churchill attacks France and its "anti-British" position on the EDC. He says that the UK has done more than anyone to support the treaty and was getting absolutely no thanks for its efforts. He states that, "we are with them but not of them". |
| 15 | May | *EDC*. The German upper house, the *Bundesrat*, also approves the EDC treaty. |
| 17 | June | Anti-Soviet demonstrations commence in East Berlin. They are ruthlessly suppressed. |
| 26 | June | Lavrenti Beria, the head of the Soviet secret police, is arrested. |
| 30 | June | *EDC.* In France, the Mayer Government falls and is replaced by the anti-EDC Joseph Laniel. The EDC is failing. |
| | June | *EDC.* French Foreign Minister Bidault says that France will not ratify the EDC treaty until there is a further Western attempt at an overall East-West settlement to the German Problem and other related disputes. |
| | June | The US commences the transfer of control of nuclear weapons from the civilian-controlled Atomic Energy Commission to the military. |
| 11 | July | General Alfred Gruenther replaces General Matthew Ridgway as NATO's SACEUR. |
| 27 | July | A final armistice is signed at Panmunjon to end hostilities on the Korean Peninsula. The original dynamic behind the need for the EDC is removed, although the Red Army remains ominously strong across the Central Plain of Europe. |
| 28 | July | *EDC.* De Gasperi is toppled as prime minister of Italy. This represents another blow to the EDC treaty ratification process. |
| 4 | August | The Soviet Union rejects a Western request for a meeting to discuss free and open elections in all of Germany. The West uses this rejection to reinforce its image of a wholly intransigent and undemocratic USSR. |
| 12 | August | The Soviet Union explodes its first thermonuclear device. |
| 20 | August | The Soviet Union announces that it possesses a hydrogen bomb. |
| 6 | September | *EDC.* Adenauer wins decisively in elections in the FRG, and hopes for a successful EDC are renewed. |
| 7 | September | Khrushchev is named first secretary of the CPSU. |

| | | |
|---|---|---|
| 15 | September | The US secretary of the army reveals that six 280-millimetre cannons are on their way to Germany. These cannons are nuclear-capable. |
| 8 | October | The first of the 280-millimetre cannons arrives in West Germany. |
| 27-29 | October | *EDC.* In yet another blow to the EDC ratification process, the French *Assemblée Nationale* calls on its government to protect French interests. Specifically, it calls upon the UK to formally commit itself to balancing German power within the EDC. |
| 30 | October | Eisenhower approves NSC-162/2, which advocates extensive reliance on nuclear weapons and strategic air power to deter Communist expansion and agression. Eisenhower authorises an expansion of the US nuclear arsenal. The document lays the administrative foundation of the *new strategic look* concept and advocates containment and the doctrine of *massive retaliation*. While it does not advocate a roll-back, i.e., actively pushing back the Soviet Union from its zones of influence in Europe, the doctrine does endorse military initiatives against lesser adversaries. |
| | October | Under the title of *massive retaliation*, NATO formally adopts the US National Security Doctrine enshrined in NSC-162/1 and commits itself to the use of theatre nuclear weapons in the event of a conflict in Europe. |
| 12 | November | *EDC.* Charles de Gaulle once again attacks the EDC. |
| 18-27 | November | *EDC.* In a key debate in the French Assembly, the anti-treaty forces carry the day, and the prospect of the successful ratification of the EDC treaty becomes even more remote. |
| 30 | November | The Soviet Union finally agrees to a Four-Power meeting to discuss Germany. |
| 4-8 | December | Bermuda Conference between the US, the UK, and France. Among other international issues, discussions also focus on the EDC. Churchill and Eden once again try to persuade the French to support the treaty. If the EDC fails, they want to prepare ground for German integration into NATO, fearing that without a German contribution the US would withdraw from Europe. For Eisenhower, however, "it's [only] the EDC and we must get it done". Bidault requests US and UK guarantees for a troop presence in continental Europe for 20 years; otherwise, he says, *Assemblée Nationale* support for the EDC would be difficult to obtain. |
| 14 | December | *EDC.* At the North Atlantic Council meeting, US Secretary of State Dulles warns of an "agonising reappraisal" of US policy towards Western Europe if the EDC treaty is not ratified. |

| | | |
|---|---|---|
| 14-16 | December | The North Atlantic Council (NAC) reports that defence expenditure among members is 3.5 times higher in real terms than in 1949 and 13% up on 1952. However, the NAC gives up on the achievement of the force goals set at the Lisbon Conference. |
| 17 | December | *EDC.* Churchill again raises the prospect of Germany's being given membership of NATO if France does not ratify the EDC treaty. |
| 23 | December | *EDC.* René Coty is elected president of France. |
| 23 | December | After being found guilty of high treason and collaboration with foreign intelligence services, Lavrenti Beria, the former chief of the Soviet secret police, is executed. |
| | December | President Eisenhower says that nuclear weapons have "virtually achieved conventional status" within the US armed forces. |

| At a Glance – Major Events and Themes | |
|---|---|
| | **Four-Power Conference in Berlin; Soviet Union calls for general European treaty on collective security** |
| | **French garrison at Dien Bien Phu attacked and falls** |
| | **France deploys more than 100,000 troops to Algeria** |
| | **EDC fails** |
| | **South East Asia Treaty Organisation formed** |
| | **London conference held to expand the 1948 Brussels Treaty to include a rearmed Germany and Italy; Western Union becomes Western European Union** |
| | **West German contribution to the NATO defence structure agreed** |
| | **German membership of NATO agreed** |
| | **General Gruenther suggests that the introduction of theatre nuclear weapons could reduce the need for manpower by as much as two-thirds** |
| | **The first Soviet nuclear-capable TU-16 Badger bomber is deployed in Eastern Europe** |
| | **Soviet forces receive their first operational atomic weapons** |

# 1954

| Day | Month | Event |
|---|---|---|
| 6 | January | *EDC*. Eisenhower raises the prospect of US withdrawal from Europe: "It is the EDC or nothing." |
| 12 | January | The US formally announces that its strategic doctrine is based upon the concept of *massive retaliation* and the early use of nuclear weapons in the event of a Soviet conventional attack in Europe. |
| 25 | January | The Four-Power Conference opens in Berlin. The Soviet Union proposes a general European treaty on collective security. The West rejects it on the grounds that it would formalise the division of Europe. |
| 18 | January | The Four-Power Conference fails due to the Soviet refusal to allow free and open elections in East Germany. The Four Powers do agree, however, to convene a Geneva conference on Indo-China and Korea in the same year. |
| | January | General Gruenther (SACEUR) formally announces that NATO has a theatre nuclear capability. |
| 9 | February | A Western tripartite statement tries to explain the reasons for the failure of the Four-Power Conference. France is finally convinced that there is no solution to the EDC dilemma. |

| | | |
|---|---|---|
| 26 | February | The German *Bundestag* discusses Germany's military contribution to the EDC, as the Basic Law of 1949 left the question open. The Federal Republic of Germany's exclusive legislative jurisdiction is extended to defence, including compulsory military service, and EDC treaties are declared compatible with the Basic Law. |
| 13 | March | The French garrison at Dien Bien Phu in Indo-China is attacked by Communist irregulars. |
| | March | Chairman of the Council of Ministers of the USSR Malenkov states in a speech that nuclear war might bring about the end of civilisation. He is subsequently criticised by Molotov and Khrushchev for this statement. |
| 7 | April | The German *Bundestag* refuses to recognise the German Democratic Republic (GDR) as a sovereign state and instead insists that the Federal Republic of Germany (FRG) is the only legal successor of the German Reich and thus the only legitimate representative of German interests. |
| 13 | April | *EDC.* The EDC ratification process is given a boost when the UK signs an Agreement Regarding Co-operation Between the UK and the EDC in Paris. |
| 26 | April | The first Geneva Conference on a possible solution to the Indo-China conflict opens on the question of Korea. |
| 2 | May | The Soviet Union recognises the GDR as a sovereign state. |
| 7 | May | Dien Bien Phu falls to Communist irregulars in Indo-China. |
| 8 | May | The Geneva Conference turns to the issue of Indo-China. |
| | May | *EDC.* De Gasperi's hope of a supranational assembly to control the EDC is finally dashed. De Gasperi dies shortly thereafter. |
| 18 | June | *EDC.* In what proves to be a fatal blow for the EDC process, Pierre Mendès France is appointed prime minister of France. |
| | June | General Gruenther states that NATO has achieved a level of 100 divisions. |
| | June | However, the US announces plans to cut its military personnel from 3.3 million to 2.8 million by June 1957. |
| | June | Gruenther confirms that he fully intends to deploy nuclear weapons in support of NATO ground forces. |
| | June | France deploys 117,000 troops in Algeria, as pressure for independence mounts. |
| 18 | July | The Geneva Conference resumes. |
| 20 | July | Geneva Conference reaches an accord on the future of Indo-China. France is to withdraw, and the US is to guarantee security through a new regional security organisation, the South East Asia Treaty Organisation (SEATO). |
| 24 | July | The Soviet Union repeats its proposal made at the Berlin Conference and calls for an all-European security treaty. |

| | | |
|---|---|---|
| 30 | August | *EDC.* In an historic debate, the French *Assemblée Nationale* adjourns the discussion of the EDC treaty *sine die*. France effectively refuses to join, and the EDC is dead. |
| 8 | September | SEATO is founded in Manila, the Philippines, by Australia, France, New Zealand, Pakistan, the Philippines, Siam, the UK and the US. |
| 10 | September | UK Foreign Secretary Eden replies to the Soviet Union's proposal for a European security treaty, recalling the Berlin discussions in January and asserting that for any progress to be made Germany should be united in freedom and be allowed to hold free elections under international supervision and that the USSR should sign the Austrian Peace Treaty. |
| 28-3 | September-October | *EDC.* The UK foreign secretary "rescues" Western European defence from the debacle of French rejection of the EDC by hosting a Nine-Power Conference in London. The conference decides to terminate the occupation regime in the FRG, to invite West Germany and Italy to accede to the Brussels Treaty, to allow Germany to undertake some rearmament, and to invite Germany to join NATO. A conference paper sets out "A German Defence Contribution and Arrangements to Apply to SACEUR's Forces on the Continent". Historically, Britain commits itself to a permanent presence on the Continent and agrees to station four divisions and a tactical air force in Germany. It allows itself the escape clause, however, that if its economic or political circumstances change, it can withdraw from the commitment. European defence is therefore maintained; France has a UK presence to counterbalance Germany; the US has access to German manpower; and Germany has equality of status. The EDC era is brought to an end. |
| 22-23 | October | The North Atlantic Council approves the decision taken at the Nine-Power Conference on permitting Germany to join NATO. |
| 23 | October | *European Security and Defence Identity (ESDI)/European Security and Defence Policy (ESDP).* The four treaties implementing the "EDC alternative" designed during the London Nine-Power Conference are signed in Paris: The Western Union becomes the Western European Union (WEU) and is expanded to include West Germany and Italy; the occupation of the FRG is ended and its full sovereignty restored; the FRG is invited to join NATO; and a French-German treaty foresees a European status for the Saar/Sarre region, subject to a referendum by the region's inhabitants. |
| | October | French troops leave what is now Vietnam. |
| | November | Conflict breaks out in Algeria. |
| 17-18 | December | NATO formally adopts the New Look Strategic Concept, which enshrines *massive retaliation* and the forward strategy. This is very much a result of US pressure. The Allies are not given much choice in the matter. |

| **At a Glance – Major Events and Themes** | |
|---|---|
| | **President Eisenhower reconfirms that nuclear weapons are to be regarded like any other weapon within the NATO arsenal** |
| | **The UK commits itself to develop a hydrogen bomb** |
| | **Warsaw Treaty Organisation formed** |
| | **Dual-key control over nuclear delivery system** |
| | **West Germany joins NATO** |
| | **The first Honest John theatre nuclear missiles arrive in West Germany** |
| | **France ratifies revised Brussels Treaty** |
| | **Austrian Peace Treaty** |
| | **The Geneva Conference on European security, disarmament and German unification** |
| | **US President Eisenhower proposes Open Skies to the USSR** |
| | **Jean Monnet creates the Action Committee for the United States of Europe** |
| | **US forward-based system exceeds 500 nuclear-capable force units** |

## 1955

| Day | Month | Event |
|---|---|---|
| 8 | February | Malenkov is forced to resign as chairman of the Council of Ministers of the USSR. Nikolai Bulganin succeeds him following a recommendation by Khrushchev. |
| 16 | March | US President Eisenhower states that, "A-bombs can be used ... as you would use a bullet". |
| 2 | April | Belgian Foreign Minister Paul-Henri Spaak proposes to German Chancellor Konrad Adenauer the relaunch of European co-operation by extending the responsibility of the European Coal and Steel Community's High Authority to include other sources of energy and transport. |
| 4 | April | Jean Monnet also proposes to Adenauer, Antoine Pinay and Italian Foreign Minister Gaetano Martino an extension of European economic integration and calls for a meeting of the Six to that end. |
| 5 | April | Winston Churchill resigns as UK prime minister. |
| 7 | April | Anthony Eden becomes UK prime minister. |
| | April | The US agrees to "share" nuclear weapons with other NATO members. The so-called dual-key system is introduced, by which NATO members will control nuclear delivery systems but the US will maintain control over the warheads. |

| | | |
|---|---|---|
| 5 | May | *ESDP*. France ratifies the revised Brussels Treaty. Although there is much opposition to German rearmament within the *Assemblée Nationale*, the French know that to procrastinate any longer will result in France's isolation. However, the level of US pressure that they are subjected to further sours an already tense and complex intra-Alliance relationship. |
| 5 | May | The Warsaw Treaty Organisation (Warsaw Pact) is formed as a Soviet-inspired counterbalance to NATO and the rearming of West Germany. |
| 5 | May | The emerging power of Khrushchev, as he consolidates his victory over Malenkov in the Kremlin power struggle, leads to an increasingly sophisticated Soviet policy shift in its dealings with the West. |
| 5 | May | *ESDI.* The High Commission in Germany is dissolved; the Federal Republic of Germany declares its sovereignty and undertakes to contribute to NATO defence efforts by setting up the *Bundeswehr*. |
| 6 | May | *ESDP.* The amended Brussels Treaty enters into force. |
| 6 | May | *ESDI.* The FRG joins NATO. |
| 9-11 | May | *ESDI.* The North Atlantic Council in Paris welcomes Germany's accession to NATO and stresses the Alliance's purely defensive character. |
| 15 | May | At the Vienna Four-Power Conference, the Treaty on a Democratic and Independent Austria is signed. The peace treaty ends the Four-Power occupation of that country and prohibits a future *Anschluss*. It represents the first really positive sign of the Soviet policy shift. |
| | May | The first Honest John theatre nuclear missiles arrive in West Germany. |
| 1-3 | June | The foreign ministers of the Six meet in Messina, Italy, to discuss the future of European integration. They propose economic integration through a common market as an instrument to create a political union. They also welcome the idea of a European Atomic Energy Community. The ministers decide to set up the Intergovernmental Committee on European Integration, chaired by Belgian Foreign Minister Spaak, to have it write a report on the necessary treaties and to prepare the conference to draft them. |
| 16 | June | Churchill decides that the UK should go ahead with the development of a hydrogen bomb. |
| 23-28 | June | The first Western exercise simulating the use of tactical nuclear weapons takes place in West Germany. Known as Operation Carte Blanche, the result suggests a staggering degree of damage in the event such a conflict occurred on the territory of the FRG. |

| | | |
|---|---|---|
| | June | The B-52 long-range US bomber becomes operational, and the first truly intercontinental atomic delivery system comes into service. |
| 18-23 | July | A conference of four heads of government and foreign ministers takes place in Geneva regarding European security and German reunification, disarmament and East-West contacts. West and East German delegations participate as observers. This constitutes a considerable valorisation for the German Democratic Republic (GDR). |
| 21 | July | At the Four-Power Conference in Geneva, US President Eisenhower proposes Open Skies (unarmed reconnaissance flights for mutual verification of capabilities and deployment by the US and the USSR over each other's territory to reduce the risk of a surprise attack). The USSR rejects the proposal. |
| 23 | July | The West Germans authorise the raising of the first volunteer troops for the newly created *Bundeswehr*. |
| 26 | July | Khrushchev declares in East Berlin that: (a) reunification concerns only the Germans and presupposes rapprochement; and (b) that the social acquisitions of the GDR need to be retained. This kills all Western hopes of rapid reunification. |
| | September | The first tangible signs of Soviet expansion into the Middle East occur when Czechoslovakia signs an arms deal with President Gamal Abdel Nasser's Egypt. |
| 13 | October | *ESDP.* Jean Monnet announces the establishment of the Action Committee for the United States of Europe. This committee will prove an extraordinary instrument for influencing and lobbying political parties, trade unions and European governments over the following twenty years. |
| 22 | October | The inhabitants of the Saar/Sarre vote by 67.7% in favour of reintegration into Germany, thereby rejecting the European status foreseen in the French-German Paris Treaty of 1954. |
| 26-16 | October-November | A Four-Power Foreign Ministers Conference is held in Geneva on Germany, disarmament and East-West contacts. Just as at the July conference involving heads of government, no agreement is reached. |
| | December | French deployment in Algeria now reaches a level of 517,000. Most of these troops have been withdrawn from NATO duty in Germany or France. France justifies this by saying that the deployment in Algeria is part of the West's global policy of containment of Soviet expansionism. |

| At a Glance – Major Events and Themes | |
|---|---|
| | **De-Stalinisation begins** |
| | **Spaak Report** |
| | **Polish workers revolt** |
| | **West Germany passes the so-called Service Bill, and conscription begins** |
| | **Hungarian crisis** |
| | **Suez crisis** |
| | **At the NATO Council, European members demand access to control of nuclear weapons on their soil** |
| | **Eisenhower states: "Nuclear production is now so vast that it may be possible to have everything that is needed"** |

# 1956

| Day | Month | Event |
|---|---|---|
| 25 | February | At the 20th Congress of the CPSU, General Secretary Nikita Khrushchev attacks Stalin. The process of de-Stalinisation gets under way. |
| 6 | March | West Germany agrees to raise an army of 500,000. |
| 21 | April | The Intergovernmental Committee on European Integration presents the Spaak Report to the foreign ministers of the Six. The report proposes a common market on the basis of a customs union and urges the establishment of an atomic-energy organisation to ensure European independence in this field. |
| 29-30 | May | In Venice, the foreign ministers of the Six approve the Spaak Report as a basis for negotiations and decide to hold an Intergovernmental Conference (IGC) to draw up the two treaties proposed by the report, one establishing a European Economic Community (EEC), and one for a European Atomic Energy Community (Euratom). |
| 26 | June | The IGC to set up the two treaties establishing the EEC and Euratom opens in Brussels. |
| 28-29 | June | A Polish workers revolt is ruthlessly crushed by Soviet troops. |
| 7 | July | West Germany passes a law on general conscription. |
| 26 | July | President Nasser "renationalises" the Suez Canal, thus technically depriving the British and the French of what they continue to regard as a vital strategic artery that has hitherto been under their control. |
| | July | News leaks that the US Joint Chiefs of Staff are planning a cut of 800,000 in the US Army. This greatly concerns the West German leadership. |

| | | |
|---|---|---|
| | September | Adenauer proposes to cut the length of conscription from 18 months to 12, which, with leave, barely allows time for basic training of conscripts. |
| 16 | October | Franz Josef Strauss of the CSU, a conservative party based in Bavaria, becomes the West German defence minister. |
| 23 | October | Hungary revolts, and the Soviets move to suppress it. The operation is effective, but it is another blow to Soviet attempts to present themselves as the purveyors of socialist democracy. |
| 29 | October | With Anglo-French collusion, the Israelis invade the Sinai Desert of Egypt. The Suez Crisis begins. |
| 31 | October | Using the pretext of separating Israeli and Egyptian forces as a *casus belli*, the two old imperial powers – the UK and France – attack Egypt. It is a set-up to regain control of the nationalised Suez Canal, and the Americans are appalled. |
| 6 | November | Dwight D. Eisenhower is elected US president for the second time. |
| 20 | November | General Lauris Norstad replaces Gruenther as SACEUR. |
| 13-14 | December | North Atlantic Council in Paris. European NATO members demand access to the control of nuclear weapons that are stationed on their soil. |
| 19 | December | Partly as a result of humiliation and anger at the overt American opposition to the Suez fiasco, France makes public its determination to develop an independent nuclear deterrent. |
| 22 | December | Under intense US pressure, the UK and France are forced to withdraw from Egypt, and a UN Emergency Force takes over control of the region. The humiliation they suffer leads to the fall of Anthony Eden as UK prime minister and abruptly marks the end of the Imperial Age in Europe. |

| At a Glance – Major Events and Themes | |
|---|---|
| | **General Norstad proposes the stationing of a 300-700-missile medium-range ballistic-missile force in Western Europe** |
| | **The Saar region returns to Germany** |
| | **UK/US Bermuda Conference to discuss UK nuclear deterrent** |
| | **The Treaties of Rome establishing the European Economic Community and the European Atomic Energy Commission** |
| | **The Göttingen Appeal** |
| | **UK announces end to conscription** |
| | **UK tests first thermonuclear device** |
| | **The USSR launches Sputnik into orbit. The Space Race begins** |
| | **Euro-deterrent created** |

## 1957

| Day | Month | Event |
|---|---|---|
| 1 | January | The Saar Treaty enters into force, and the Saar thus becomes part of the Federal Republic of Germany. |
| 9 | January | Anthony Eden resigns as UK prime minister. |
| 10 | January | Harold Macmillan becomes the new UK prime minister and sets about repairing the "special relationship" so badly strained by the Suez Crisis. |
| 12 | March | An agreement is signed between the Soviet Union and the German Democratic Republic on the temporary stationing of Soviet troops in East Germany. |
| 15 | March | The US announces that its troops stationed in West Germany have nuclear weapons. |
| 20-24 | March | Macmillan and Eisenhower meet at the Bermuda Conference and discuss the UK nuclear deterrent. |
| 25 | March | *ESDP.* The Treaty Establishing the European Economic Community (EEC) (the Treaty of Rome) is signed by the six ECSC members (Belgium, France, Germany, Italy, Luxembourg and the Netherlands). The treaty solemnly declares that it aims to "lay the foundations of an ever closer union among the peoples of Europe". |
| 25 | March | The Treaty Establishing the European Atomic Energy Community (Euratom) is signed. |
| | March | Israel withdraws from Sinai to the 1949 borders, and the Suez Canal is reopened for shipping. |

| | | |
|---|---|---|
| 4 | April | At a press conference, West German Chancellor Adenauer advocates nuclear armament of the *Bundeswehr*. |
| 12 | April | Reflecting the growing tide of public concern about the possession and use of nuclear weapons in Western Europe, a group of eminent German scientists issue the so-called Göttingen Appeal, calling for the Federal Republic to abrogate the possession of such munitions. |
| 15 | May | The UK tests its first thermonuclear device. |
| | May | The United Kingdom declares an end to conscription and is immediately attacked by the Western European Union states, which openly question whether the British will be able to fulfil their treaty obligations. |
| 29 | July | The US, the UK, France and West Germany sign a Berlin Declaration on German unity that calls for Four-Power negotiations and the conclusion of a peace treaty providing for a freely elected all-German government. The Western Powers also undertake not to negotiate disarmament with the Soviet Union without the Germans. |
| 27 | August | Khrushchev states that the Soviet Union has acquired ICBM capability. |
| 4 | October | The Soviet Union proves its grasp of the essential technology for an ICBM by successfully launching the Sputnik satellite, the first venture of humanity into space. The effect on the West is to create a belief that there is a "missile gap" with the Soviets. |
| | October | In the shadow of the Sputnik launch, Eisenhower and Macmillan meet again to discuss the UK deterrent. As a result, the US president promises to request that Congress relax the Atomic Energy Act, which prohibits the sharing of such technology with other countries, in order for the British to get US nuclear technology. The US/UK talks reflect an emerging European concern that in the event of nuclear parity between the US and the Soviet Union, the American extended deterrent would no longer be credible. |
| 16-19 | December | Further reflecting the growing European concerns about a Soviet strategic nuclear force nullifying the effects of the US deterrent, the North Atlantic Council agrees to place theatre nuclear weapons under the command of SACEUR (and not the US president) as part of a Euro-deterrent. |
| | December | France agrees to station US intermediate-range ballistic missiles (IRBMs) on its territory in return for US nuclear technology. This partly reflects problems that France is having with its own development programme and a desire not to be left behind in this vital field. |

| | |
|---|---|
| **At a Glance – Major Events and Themes** | **Charles de Gaulle is elected president of France** |
| | **The McMahon Act becomes US law** |
| | **De Gaulle calls for a Triple Entente between France, the UK and the US** |
| | **The second Berlin Crisis commences** |
| | **The first West German force contingent becomes available to the NATO Command** |
| | **The British Army of the Rhine completes its preparations to fight a nuclear war** |
| | **First British regiment of theatre nuclear weapons stationed in West Germany** |

## 1958

| Day | Month | Event |
|---|---|---|
| 1 | January | The Treaties of Rome (EEC and EAEC) enter into force. |
| | January | The UK announces that it is to reduce the British Army of the Rhine (BAOR) from 77,000 to 55,000. This produces protests from all the NATO Allies. |
| 22 | February | The UK and the US agree to station 60 Thor missiles, each with a range of 2,400 kilometres, in the UK under the dual-key arrangement, also known as the double-veto agreement. |
| 27 | March | Khrushchev becomes chairman of the Council of Ministers of the USSR, replacing Bulganin. Khrushchev now formally gains complete control of state and party. |
| | March | Adenauer says that NATO deployment of theatre nuclear weapons will go ahead in spite of public opinion and that the Federal Republic must either accept these weapons on its soil or leave NATO. |
| | April | French Prime Minister Felix Gaillard authorises French construction of a French nuclear deterrent following progress in the development programme. |
| 1 | June | In the midst of the Algerian crisis, General de Gaulle is returned to power as president of France. This augurs badly for the future political cohesion of the NATO Alliance. |
| 2 | July | The McMahon Act, which permits the transfer of American nuclear technology to favoured third parties, becomes US law. The way in which the law is drafted means that it clearly favours the UK, not France. |
| 3 | July | The US and UK sign an agreement allowing for the "exchange" of nuclear technology for weapons purposes. |

| | | |
|---|---|---|
| 17 | September | *European Security and Defence Identitiy (ESDI).* In an attempt to break what he regards as Anglo-Saxon control of the Western Alliance, de Gaulle proposes a new *Triple Entente* between France, the UK and the US as a method for the collective control of NATO. The Americans and the British reject this proposal almost out of hand, which only serves to consolidate de Gaulle's anti-American and anti-British views. |
| | October | US President Eisenhower and UK Prime Minister Macmillan issue a Joint Declaration of Common Purpose, which confirms a special relationship between the two countries. The two leaders also agree to henceforth work together closely on defence matters. |
| 10 | November | In a speech at a Soviet-Polish friendship meeting in Moscow, Soviet leader Khrushchev asserts that the Western Powers have long since lost all legal rights to remain in West Berlin because they have broken all other Four-Power agreements on Germany, especially concerning the latter's demilitarisation. He declares that the Berlin situation must be "normalised", meaning that the Western Powers leave West Berlin and that any remaining questions regarding Berlin be addressed to the East German Government. The second Berlin Crisis begins. |
| 26 | November | In response to Khrushchev's speech, US Secretary of State Dulles says, "We are most solemnly committed to hold West Berlin, if need be, by military force." He demands that the Soviet Union respect its "explicit obligation" to assure "normal access to and egress from Berlin". |
| 27 | November | The Soviet Union pronounces a double ultimatum: Western Allied troops have to withdraw from Berlin, and an agreement on Berlin as a "free city" has to be reached. If there is not sufficient progress on these issues within six months, Moscow will sign a separate peace treaty with the German Democratic Republic (GDR) and transfer control over access routes between West Germany and West Berlin to the GDR. The West threatens the use of nuclear weapons. |

| | | |
|---|---|---|
| 16-18 | December | The North Atlantic Council issues a Berlin Declaration stating that: "no state has the right to withdraw unilaterally from its international engagements. ... the denunciation by the Soviet Union of the inter allied agreements on Berlin can in no way deprive the other parties of their rights or relieve the Soviet Union of its obligations. ... The member states of NATO could not approve a solution of the Berlin question which jeopardized the right of the three Western Powers to remain in Berlin as long as their responsibilities require it, and did not assure freedom of communication between that city and the free world. ... the Berlin question can only be settled in the framework of an agreement with the USSR on Germany as a whole. [The Council] recalls that the Western Powers have repeatedly declared themselves ready to examine this problem, as well as those of European security and disarmament. They are still ready to dicuss all these problems." |
| 21 | December | General Charles de Gaulle wins the French presidential election and becomes the first president of the Fifth Republic. |
| 31 | December | Cuban President Fulgencio Batista resigns amidst political and social turmoil. |

| At a Glance – Major Events and Themes | |
|---|---|
| | **Castro comes to power in Cuba** |
| | **Second strike and mutually assured destruction** |
| | **Soviets create a Strategic Rocket Force** |
| | **First Polaris nuclear ballistic-missile submarine commissioned by US Navy** |
| | **With the deployment of SS-4 missiles in Eastern Europe, the USSR probably deploys the first operational theatre nuclear capability** |
| | **The British start to receive their first Honest John and Corporal theatre nuclear missiles from the Americans** |

## 1959

| Day | Month | Event |
|---|---|---|
| 1+2 | January | Fidel Castro comes to power in Cuba after the fall of a corrupt US-supported regime. |
| 8 | January | General Charles de Gaulle is inaugurated as president of France. |
| | January | The term *second strike* appears in an article by Albert Wohlstetter entitled "The Delicate Balance of Terror". With it comes the concept of mutually assured destruction (MAD), which is to dominate American strategic nuclear doctrine for the next two decades. |
| 23-3 | February-March | Macmillan visits the USSR and meets with Khrushchev. Discussions focus on Berlin and Gemany and ways to stop nuclear testing and nuclear armament, as well as on cultural exchanges. |
| | March | The US announces that it intends to base 15 Jupiter theatre nuclear missiles in Italy. |
| | March | As a sign of the rising tension within NATO and continuing French problems in Algeria, the French withdraw their Mediterranean Fleet from the control of SACEUR. |
| 15 | April | Dulles resigns as US secretary of state. |
| 11 | May | Geneva Four-Power Conference begins. |
| 20 | June | The Geneva Four-Power Conference is adjourned. |
| 20 | June | As a first sign of a major Sino-Soviet split, the USSR rescinds the Sino-Soviet Nuclear Agreement. |
| | June | *ESDP*. De Gaulle decrees that there can be no stockpiling on French soil of theatre nuclear weapons that are not French. |
| 13 | July | The Geneva Four-Power Conference reopens. |
| 21 | July | Seven members of the OEEC – the UK, Denmark, Norway, Sweden, Austria, Portugal and Switzerland – decide to create the European Free Trade Area (EFTA). |

| | | |
|---|---|---|
| 23-1 | July-August | US Vice President Richard Millhouse Nixon visits the USSR. He is allowed to make a television address, in which he criticises communism and warns against any attempt to spread it beyond the borders of the USSR. Khrushchev demands a removal of "bases on foreign land". |
| 3 | August | The US and the Soviet Union announce that Eisenhower will visit the Soviet Union, and Khrushchev the US, later in the year. |
| 5 | August | The Geneva Four-Power Conference ends without agreement. The US, UK and France insist that Germany must be reunified through free elections before there can be a peace treaty or a European security plan and also that Western troops would stay in Berlin until such time. The USSR, however, proposes the transformation of West Berlin into a demilitarised free city, separate peace treaties with the two Germanys and the establishment of a zone in Central Europe within which arms and troops would be banned or limited. |
| 15-27 | September | Khrushchev visits the US. |
| 25 | September | Eisenhower and Khrushchev begin Camp David talks. |
| | November | *ESDP*. De Gaulle states that, "it is necessary that the defence of France be French", and he presents a plan to develop an all-French nuclear capacity, the so-called *force de frappe*. |
| 30 | December | The first Polaris-class nuclear ballistic-missile submarine (SSBN), the "George Washington", is commissioned by the US Navy. This marks the first move towards invulnerable second-strike systems. |
| | December | The Soviet Union creates a Strategic Rocket Force. The era of American invulnerability appears to be coming to an end. However, the Soviets are having considerable difficulty with their first-generation ICBMs, the SS-6. |

Part 3

# THE DAWN OF REASON

# 1960 - 1969

1960

1967

1969

| At a Glance – Major Events and Themes | |
|---|---|
| | **European Free Trade Association is created** |
| | **France detonates first atomic device** |
| | **U2 incident: US spy plane over USSR shot down by Soviet missile** |
| | **The US Navy establishes the US Polaris submarine base at Holy Loch in Scotland** |
| | **John F. Kennedy elected president of the United States** |
| | **US offers Europeans a multilateral force to control use of nuclear weapons** |
| | **The UK ends conscription** |
| | **The US announces that it has 18,000 warheads in Western Europe** |
| | **Due to the Algerian struggle, French forces in West Germany fall to a level of 50,000 troops and eight air squadrons** |
| | **The West German defence budget exceeds 6% of GDP** |
| | **France refuses to operate completely under the control of SACEUR** |
| | **The US secretary of state, Dean Rusk, implies that European fears of a "de-coupling" of the US strategic deterrent from the defence of Western Europe may well have grounds when he says that any conventional attack upon NATO should be met first by conventional forces** |
| | **US General Maxwell D. Taylor publishes a book entitled "The Uncertain Trumpet", in which he coins the phrase *flexible response*** |

# 1960

| Day | Month | Event |
|---|---|---|
| 4 | January | The treaty establishing the European Free Trade Association (EFTA) is signed by Austria, Denmark, the Netherlands, Norway, Portugal, Sweden and Switzerland. EFTA aims to be a counterbalance to the EC in terms of market access and size, but, in contrast to the latter, EFTA members maintain full political independence. Agriculture and fisheries are not included in the free-trade area due to disagreements among its members. |
| 13 | February | France explodes its first atomic device at Reggane, Algeria. |
| | March | At Camp David, the US and UK reach an agreement in which the US promises the UK Skybolt, a high-altitude bomber for air-launched ballistic missiles. In return, Britain is to make available bases on the Scotland's west coast for US Navy Polaris missile submarines. |

| | | |
|---|---|---|
| 1 | May | The Cold War heats up as US pilot Gary Powers is shot down by a SAM2 missile in his U2 spy plane over the Soviet Union. |
| 3 | May | The EFTA Treaty enters into force. |
| 16 | May | Khrushchev walks out of Paris Four-Power Summit after the US refuses to apologise for spy-plane flights. |
| 18 | July | All Soviet advisors are recalled from China as the tension increases between the two communist giants. The tension centres upon border disputes and a long-running Chinese belief that the Soviets are not promoting the communist struggle with the Americans energetically enough. |
| 20 | July | The first test-firing of a US Polaris submarine-launched ballistic missile takes place. |
| | July | The US Navy decides to establish a US Polaris submarine base at Holy Loch in Scotland. |
| 16 | August | Cyprus gains independence, which is guaranteed by Greece, Turkey and the UK. Some British bases on the island remain under UK sovereignty. |
| | August | A US State Department policy-planning official, Robert Bowie, presents the department with a report about the future of NATO. He suggests that a multinational missile-submarine force under joint command and financing and mixed crews be set up to ease NATO's nuclear dilemma between the natural development of national forces and the need for international co-operation. He hopes such a force will bring about a feeling of nuclear control and, at the same time, prevent any members from withdrawing. A build-up of European conventional forces is implicit in his proposal. |
| 12 | October | At the UN General Assembly in New York, Khrushchev angrily pounds his shoe on the table after the Philippine delegate accuses the USSR of imperialism in Eastern Europe. |
| 8 | November | John F. Kennedy is elected president of the United States. One of his main campaign pledges is to plug the so-called missile gap with the Soviet Union. |
| | November | In a clear move away from the doctrine of *massive retaliation* and with it the assumption of early first use of nuclear weapons by the NATO Alliance, General Norstad tells the NATO Parliament that the threshold over which the use of nuclear weapons is countenanced in a war in Europe must be high. This is prompted partly by US fears for the vulnerability of the United States in the event of war and the hostile reaction of Western European publics to the use of tactical nuclear weapons. |

| | | |
|---|---|---|
| 16-18 | December | *European Security and Defence Identitiy (ESDI)*. In an attempt to soothe general Alliance concerns over lack of accountability of American control of nuclear weapons in Western Europe (particularly French ones), outgoing Secretary of State Christian Herter offers the Europeans a so-called multilateral force (MLF). This would involve all the Allies in a much closer degree of military integration over the use of nuclear forces. The US State Department has altered Bowie's concept since mixed manning seems too complex. |

| At a Glance – Major Events and Themes | |
|---|---|
| | **Eisenhower warns of the "military-industrial complex"** |
| | **Robert McNamara becomes US secretary of defense** |
| | **Dean Rusk becomes US secretary of state** |
| | **Failed US-backed invasion of Cuba** |
| | **First manned space flight** |
| | **The US/USSR Vienna Conference** |
| | **Berlin Wall is built during the second Berlin Crisis** |
| | **As a prelude to the Cuban Missile Crisis of October 1962, leading German SPD politician Helmut Schmidt suggests that the stationing of US missiles in Turkey is insensitive** |
| | **The Soviet SS-5 theatre nuclear missile is deployed** |
| | **The first Soviet ICBMs are deployed** |
| | **Kennedy places five SSBNs at Holy Loch under the control of SACEUR** |

## 1961

| Day | Month | Event |
|---|---|---|
| 17 | January | In his farewell address, President Eisenhower warns against the influence of what he terms the "military-industrial complex". In coining a phrase that will soon become famous, he hints that procurement policy might be pushed as much by special-interest groups in the military and the defence industry as by a hard assessment of the strategic environment. |
| 20 | January | John F. Kennedy is inaugurated as president of the United States. |
| 21 | January | Robert McNamara becomes secretary of defense under Kennedy. Coming from a business background, "Mac", as he is popularly known, immediately starts introducing strategic business practices into the Department of Defense, including models based on game theory. |
| 21 | January | Dean Rusk becomes US secretary of state. |
| 3 | March | Submarine tender "USS Protay AS-19" arrives at Holy Loch, Scotland. |
| 8 | March | The first Polaris submarine, "USS Patrick Henry" (SSBN 559), arrives at Holy Loch, Scotland. |
| | March | At a Warsaw Pact Summit, Khrushchev promises to conclude a separate peace treaty with East Germany if a general settlement with the West cannot be reached. |

| | | |
|---|---|---|
| | March | In preparing a report for Kennedy entitled "A Review of North Atlantic Problems for the Future", Dean Rusk hints at changes in US strategic doctrine that will move away from *massive retaliation* to what becomes known as *flexible response*. This new doctrine is designed from its outset to afford the Alliance a graduated response capability short of all-out nuclear war in the event of a Soviet conventional attack in Europe. |
| 15-20 | April | In a disastrous attempt to overthrow Fidel Castro in Cuba, CIA-trained Cuban irregulars attempt to land at the Bay of Pigs. The mission is a fiasco, and the Americans are made to look aggressive and inept. |
| 12 | April | Yuri Gagarin becomes the first man in space, further enhancing the public perception that the USSR is ahead in missile technology. |
| | April | *ESDI*. Kennedy addresses the NATO Military Committee and suggests that significant improvements need to be made to the capabilities of conventional forces. This is widely accepted both within the Alliance and without as a thinly disguised attempt to end the automatic use of the US strategic nuclear capability in the event of a Soviet conventional attack in Europe. |
| 5 | May | Alan Shepard becomes the first American in space. |
| 17 | May | In a speech to the Canadian Parliament, US president Kennedy confirms the Polaris offer, i.e., five nuclear submarines under US control to NATO, and proposes that a NATO sea-borne force be formed. Kennedy stresses the multilateral character of the force. |
| 3-4 | June | Khrushchev and Kennedy meet at a Vienna conference but reach no solution on the German/Berlin problem. Khrushchev threatens to sign a peace agreement with the German Democratic Republic (GDR) in December that might restrict Western rights in Berlin if the US refuses an interim agreement. |
| Throughout | July | East German authorities try to stop the "haemorrhaging" after more than 33,000 people flee to the West. The second Berlin Crisis comes to a head. |
| 25 | July | Kennedy states that blocking Western access to Berlin by East Germany or the Soviet Union would mean war. |
| 4 | August | Khrushchev makes a secret speech at a Warsaw Pact meeting in reaction to Kennedy's speech of 25 July. He insists on a West Berlin peace treaty and worries about the possibility of war and nuclear destruction. He also speaks about the need to raise living standards in the GDR. |
| 13-16 | August | In a desperate attempt to stop the flow of escapees from East to West, the Berlin Wall is constructed. |
| | October | Nuclear artillery shells become available to the British. |

| | |
|---|---|
| **At a Glance – Major Events and Themes** | **The Evian peace agreement ends the Algerian conflict** |
| | **The MLF talks continue** |
| | **McNamara attacks the doctrine of *massive retaliation*** |
| | **Cuban Missile Crisis** |
| | **The US/UK Nassau summit leads to agreement over UK access to US Polaris nuclear technology** |
| | **The French seek to buy a Polaris nuclear missile system from the US** |
| | **Despite deploying ICBMs by the end of the 1962, the USSR has only 30 operational ICBMs against America's 200 as a result of continuing technical difficulties** |

# 1962

| Day | Month | Event |
|---|---|---|
| 6 | February | Chancellor Adenauer announces that the FRG is willing to participate in a multilateral nuclear force under NATO. |
| 20 | February | John Glenn is the first American to orbit the planet. |
| 23 | February | France's *Conseil de Défense* decides to build a ballistic surface-to-surface missile (SSM) and a sea-to-surface, submarine-launched missile force. |
| | February | The UK announces that it is to station forces in its crown colony Aden in Yemen. |
| 18 | March | De Gaulle finally extracts France from the turmoil of Algeria with a peace agreement signed at Evian. The agreement gives Algeria independence, even though it was technically a *département* of France, rather than a colony. This policy is seen as a humiliating climbdown by the French military and earns de Gaulle many enemies in the armed forces. Extremists start a terrorist network known as the OAS (*Organisation de l'Armée Secrète*), and the Fifth Republic appears to be going the way of its four predecessors. |
| 4-6 | May | *ESDI.* In a meeting of NATO foreign and defence ministers in Athens, US Secretary of State McNamara bluntly tells the Allies that the US is no longer ready to respond automatically in kind to a nuclear attack upon them. He also demands US control of all NATO planning and that conventional forces be improved. The Allies like neither the tone nor the content of the speech, which simply reinforces the determination of the British and French to get their hands on their own nuclear deterrent. |

| | | |
|---|---|---|
| 14-28 | October | In what was probably the most dangerous superpower confrontation of the Cold War, the Cuban Missile Crisis occurs when the USSR attempts to station IRBMs in Cuba and inside the US early-warning capability. Kennedy orders the US Navy to stop any Soviet ships carrying missiles *en route* to Cuba and threatens to bomb existing sites if all missiles are not returned to the Soviet Union. Khrushchev finally recalls the ships after Kennedy promises that the US will not invade Cuba. Six months later, the US secretly begins dismantling its nuclear missiles based in Turkey and Italy, thereby *de facto* conforming with a second request by Khrushchev. Both sides seem genuinely frightened by how close to the brink they come. The end of the crisis marks the start of a more pragmatic period of nuclear management between the two sides: a thaw that eventually leads to arms control and *détente*. |
| 20 | October | The first Sino-Indian War breaks out. India is quickly defeated, but, rather than advancing, the Chinese withdraw. |
| | October | Khrushchev officially acknowledges a Sino-Soviet split. |
| 16 | December | The first fully successful flight of Skybolt takes place, but the US cancels the programme forthwith. This is an attempt by the US to rid Britain, to which Skybolt had been solemnly promised, of its independent nuclear deterrent. |
| 18-21 | December | At the Nassau Summit between UK Prime Minister Macmillan and US President Kennedy, the Americans confirm their decision to terminate US procurement of Skybolt, but they eventually agree to allow the UK to purchase the Polaris SSBN system at a reduced price. Under the agreement, the missiles for the system (the A-4) will be American and will be serviced by the US. This greatly qualifies the "independence" of the UK's deterrent. |
| 31 | December | The US Skybolt programme is officially terminated. |

| | |
|---|---|
| **At a Glance – Major Events and Themes** | **De Gaulle rejects US MLF proposals** |
| | **Elysée Treaty between France and Germany** |
| | **Hot Line established between Washington and Moscow** |
| | **In a speech in Berlin, US President Kennedy declares: "Ich bin ein Berliner"** |
| | **France withdraws its Atlantic Fleet from NATO control** |
| | **First Nuclear Test Ban Treaty initialled by UK, US and USSR** |
| | **US and USSR renounce the use of nuclear weapons in space** |
| | **Communist coup in Vietnam** |
| | **Kennedy assassinated** |
| | **The UK proposes mixed manning of weapons systems instead of a multilateral force** |
| | **US Secretary of State McNamara admits that when the US deployed the Thor and Jupiter missile systems in 1957 they were the only strategic missiles that NATO had; this has created much of the dynamic behind the missile-gap myth** |
| | **McNamara tells the US Senate Armed Services Committee that there is little chance of containing a nuclear war once one has started** |

## 1963

| Day | Month | Event |
|---|---|---|
| 14 | January | Unwilling to have *de facto* American control over the French nuclear deterrent, President de Gaulle rejects the American offer of Polaris, and thus the MLF proposals, and at the same time rejects the British bid for membership of the EEC on the grounds that the UK is in effect an American "fifth column". In reality, de Gaulle is aware that British membership of the Community would weaken France's control over it. |
| 14 | January | Just a few hours after de Gaulle's announcement, Kennedy lays out his vision of the MLF in his State of the Union address: "For the first time, the door is open for the nuclear defense of the Alliance to become a source of confidence, instead of contention." |
| | | *ESDP.* The Franco-German Elysée Treaty of Friendship is signed, which sets the seal on reconciliation between the two countries and creates the institutional framework for close German-French co-operation. The treaty provides for regular meetings between French and German ministers of armed forces/defence, chiefs of staff and relevant authorities |

| | | |
|---|---|---|
| 22 | January | in the field of education and youth. With regard to foreign affairs, "The two Governments will consult each other, prior to any decision, on all important matters of foreign policy, [on defence matters], ... on the level of strategy and tactics, [and they] endeavour to harmonize their doctrines with a view to arriving at mutual concepts, [and] [e]xchanges of personnel between the armed forces will be increased." |
| | January | US Special Ambassador to NATO Livingston Merchant tours Europe to test opinion on the MLF proposal. He receives only a lukewarm response. |
| | February | US President Kennedy proposes a new structure to implement MLF: the force should be based on ships instead of submarines. This would be cheaper and quicker to produce and could be carried out in several European countries. |
| 5 | April | In the first attempt to avoid an accidental nuclear war or war through misunderstanding, the US and USSR establish the so-called Hot Line between Washington and Moscow. From the Soviet point of view, the American position reflects a growing recognition on the part of the United States that they are in a situation of nuclear stalemate with their Communist adversary. |
| 26 | June | In front of 120,000 West Berliners, US President Kennedy gives a speech intended to boost the morale of the Berlin population and to give a strong signal to the USSR about the Allies' determination to stay in West Berlin. Kennedy ends his speech with the words, "Ich bin ein Berliner." |
| | June | France withdraws its Atlantic Fleet from the control of the Supreme Allies Commander, Atlantic (SACLANT). |
| 25 | July | In recognition of the huge environmental damage that atmospheric nuclear tests are causing, the UK, US and USSR initial the Nuclear Test Ban Treaty, which prohibits nuclear testing in the atmosphere, in Outer Space and underwater, but allows tests conducted underground. The treaty is important for several reasons. First, a culture of "nuclear management" is developing between the superpowers. Second, the two burgeoning nuclear powers, France and China, are conspicuous by their absence. |
| | October-November | During the so-called Tailgate Crisis, access between West Germany and West Berlin is blocked for several days. |
| 3 | October | At the UN General Assembly, the US and the USSR renounce the deployment of nuclear weapons in space. The commitment of the two countries' space programmes to ostensibly peaceful purposes is a further confidence-building step on the road to the SALT talks. |

| | | |
|---|---|---|
| 1 | November | A communist-inspired coup takes place in South Vietnam against the corrupt, US-backed Government of Diem. America's Vietnam saga begins. |
| 22 | November | President John F. Kennedy is assassinated in Dallas. Vice President Lyndon B. Johnson is sworn in as new interim president. |
| 30 | November | Greek Cypriot leader Makarios proposes changes to the Cypriot Constitution that would abrogate power-sharing arrangements. The Turkish side subsequently withdraws from power-sharing. |
| | November | Two working groups established to explore several aspects of the MLF proposals begin their work. The Paris working group begins considering issues of control and international legality of the MLF proposal, and the Washington working group starts examining military implications of MLF. |
| 21 | December | Inter-communal violence erupts on Cyprus. |
| 27 | December | British troops assume positions between fighting groups on Cyprus. |
| | December | At a NATO Council meeting, UK Defence Secretary Peter Thorneycroft puts forward the idea of mixed manning of weapons systems as a counterproposal to MLF. |

| At a Glance – Major Events and Themes | |
|---|---|
| | **Gulf of Tonkin Resolution** |
| | **First Mirage IV, France's strategic bombers, deployed** |
| | **Nikita Khrushchev deposed as general secretary of the CPSU** |
| | **China explodes its first atomic device** |
| | **Lyndon B. Johnson elected president of the United States** |
| | **The MLF proposals fail** |

## 1964

| Day | Month | Event |
|---|---|---|
| | January | Washington and Paris MLF working groups produce reports and recommendations. |
| | February | The first Mirage IVs are delivered to the French Air Force. They are to form France's first two nuclear bomber squadrons. The Mirage IV is the only plane in the world able to fly at Mach 2 for more than half an hour. |
| | February | Attacks by Greek Cypriots spark renewed fears of Turkish landing on the island. The UK appeals to the UN. |
| 26-27 | February | UK Minister of Defence Thorneycroft announces that the UK will build a fifth Polaris submarine and stresses the importance of an independent nuclear deterrent. |
| 4 | March | The UN Security Council establishes a peacekeeping force in Cyprus, UNFICYP, to prevent the recurrence of fighting between Greek and Turkish Cypriot communities and to contribute to the restoration of normal conditions. |
| | May | Assembly begins on the "USS Biddle", a US mixed-manned, guided-missile destroyer to be equipped with surface-to-air missiles and anti-submarine rockets. This is supposed to demonstrate the feasibility of mixed manning. |
| 10 | June | Thorneycroft confirms his proposal of December 1963: "[I]t would be sensible to consider the possibility of mixed manning some of the weapons systems that people are going to buy anyway since this might achieve the political objective much cheaper than any other method." |
| 26 | June | The French chief of staff of the armed forces, General Charles Ailleret, criticises *flexible response*, saying that, "immediate strategic nuclear action remains the best guarantee of the elimination of external attack". |
| | June | The "USS Biddle" is ready. It is manned with seamen from the US (50%, captain and executive officer), UK, Federal Republic of Germany, the Netherlands, Italy and Turkey. |

| | | |
|---|---|---|
| 2 | July | At a meeting of the Paris working group, the UK presents proposals for applying the concept of mixed manning to aircraft and land-based missiles. |
| 2+11 | July | The Soviet Union protests against MLF, which it judges to be "primarily a means of camouflaging the fact that West Germany is in fact being given access to nuclear weapons". |
| 23 | July | De Gaulle states at a press conference: "It is apparent that Europe, provided it wishes to do so, is henceforth called to play a role of its own." |
| 27 | July | NATO working groups on military aspects of MLF plans begin considering the UK proposals. |
| 7 | August | After an incident in the Gulf of Tonkin off North Vietnam, when the American frigate "USS Maddox" is supposedly attacked, the US Congress passes the Gulf of Tonkin Resolution, which allows the president almost unrivalled and unquestioned powers in the conduct of defence operations against the North Vietnamese. The Imperial Presidency becomes an increasing reality. Ironically, the pretext for the resolution, which takes Congress 40 minutes to pass, is the belief that the "Maddox" was the victim of an unprovoked attack on the open seas. It later transpires that the ship had been operating in support of South Vietnamese aircraft that were attacking a North Vietnamese port. |
| 1 | October | The Mirage IV, France's strategic bomber, is deployed for the first time. |
| 14 | October | Khrushchev is deposed partly as a result of his increasing reliance upon nuclear weapons as the Soviet Union's only instrument of armed force and because of the discontent that such a policy engenders both within the Red Army and the CPSU. Leonid Brezhnev takes over as general secretary in a move that is meant to signify the return to collective leadership within the Politburo. |
| 15 | October | British Conservatives lose elections. A new Labour Government is formed under Harold Wilson. Wilson is very critical of the Nassau agreement. |
| 16 | October | China explodes its first atomic device. |
| 3 | November | Lyndon B. Johnson is elected US president by promising to maintain the Kennedy legacy of US strength allied to a domestic New Deal-type programme called the Great Society. |
| 16 | December | The *Loi programmation d'équipment militaire* is given final approval by the French *Assemblée Nationale*. It provides for nuclear weapons carried by ballistic missiles and a start in equipping forces with national tactical nuclear weapons. |
| | December | US President Johnson declares MLF dead. |

1960-1969

| At a Glance – Major Events and Themes |
| --- |
| **Vietnam conflict starts** |
| **The Merger Treaty** |
| **Dispute over Kashmir and East Pakistan results in the second Indo-Pakistan War** |
| **The US proposes a NATO nuclear force instead of the MLF, or Third Force, concept** |
| **De Gaulle announces intention to withdraw from integrated military structure of NATO** |

## 1965

| Day | Month | Event |
| --- | --- | --- |
| 7 | February | The US commits troops to Vietnam, and the bombing of the North commences. The European Allies steadfastly refuse to join in the operation; eventually, it is only Australia that sends troops. |
| 4 | March | UK Secretary of State for Defence Denis Healey states: "Britain cannot go it alone in the nuclear age. Until disarmament is achieved, her survival and national security must depend on the strength and solidarity of the alliance with the US and Western Europe." |
| 8 | April | The Merger Treaty is signed in Brussels. It provides for a single Commission and a single Council of the three European Communities. |
| 23 | April | India and Pakistan fight a major battle in the Rann of Kutch, leading to the second Indo-Pakistan War. |
| 25-30 | April | Invited by France, Andrei Gromyko visits Paris and meets with de Gaulle and Prime Minister Georges Pompidou. |
| 31-1 | May-June | At a Paris Foreign Ministers Conference, McNamara mentions a Committee on Nuclear Planning within NATO instead of MLF. This gives MLF the final death blow. |
| 30 | June | Unwilling to let the EEC have a common budget, and rejecting qualified majority voting (QMV) on the issue, French President de Gaulle commences the empty-chair policy: France will not take part in Council or permanent representatives' committee meetings. |
| 5 | August | The second Indo-Pakistan War breaks out in a dispute over Kashmir and the separation movement in East Pakistan. |
| 9 | September | *ESDI/ESDP.* Concern about restoring France's "grandeur" and giving it more strategic independence, as well as fear of faltering US commitment to the nuclear defence of Europe (because of the US change in strategy from *massive retaliation* to *flexible response*), leads de Gaulle to announce his intention to withdraw French forces from the integrated military structure of NATO by 1969. |
|  | November | The incoming Labour Government in the UK make it clear they are not in favour of the MLF proposal and will thus not attempt to revive it. |

| At a Glance – Major Events and Themes | |
|---|---|
| | **The Chinese Cultural Revolution begins** |
| | **France leaves the military structure of NATO** |
| | **A grand coalition comes to power in the Federal Republic of Germany under Willy Brandt** |
| | **Georges Pompidou says that the US would never have allowed France to get its hands on nuclear technology and as such France's decision to leave NATO was entirely justified** |
| | **The Soviet Union deploys the SS-11 ICBM** |

## 1966

| Day | Month | Event |
|---|---|---|
| 28-29 | January | The Luxembourg Compromise ends France's empty-chair policy. Member states agree that if important interests of one or more partners are at stake in cases of decisions that are normally taken by majority vote on the proposal of the Commission, then the Council members should make an effort to find a solution that can be adopted by all Council members in a reasonable time. The French delegation, however, says that if these matters concern very important interests, then discussion should continue until unanimity is reached. Thus, there is disagreement on what to do in the absence of complete conciliation. Despite this, normal working procedures are taken up again; France decides to participate in Council meetings again. |
| | January | The Chinese Cultural Revolution begins. In what amounts to a purge by Mao Tse Tung of the communist old guard, the Great Helmsman uses the young revolutionary guard to eradicate opposition to his control and to shift the blame for the catastrophic failure of the Great Leap Forward, a programme of forced industrialisation started in 1959. |
| 7+10 | March | *ESDI/ESDP.* In a final break with the Americans and the British, de Gaulle officially announces to the US and then to the other Allies that France will withdraw from the integrated command structure of the Alliance. However, de Gaulle leaves the back door open by maintaining French membership of the organisation. French officers who are serving NATO commanders are increasingly regarded by de Gaulle as "traitors". De Gaulle also orders all NATO forces and functionaries to leave France by 1 April. |
| 1 | July | *ESDI/ESDP.* French representatives step down from their positions in the military organisations of NATO. |
| 26 | October | NATO decides to set up headquarters in Brussels. |
| 27 | October | German Government coalition falls over a debate on tax increases or cuts. The ministers of the liberal coalition member, the *Freiheitlich Demokratische Partei* (FDP), step down. |

| | | |
|---|---|---|
| 10 | November | The NATO Defence Planning Committee (DPC) requests that the Military Committee of the Alliance transfer from Washington to Brussels. |
| 14 | November | *ESDP.* The UK announces that it will try to join the EEC again. |
| 30 | November | German Chancellor Ludwig Erhard steps down after coalition negotiations between the FDP, the *Christlich-Demokratische Union* (CDU) and the *Christlich-Soziale Union* (CSU) fail and the Social Democrats reach an agreement with the Christian Union parties (CDU and CSU). |
| 1 | December | Kurt Georg Kiesinger is elected German chancellor and builds a Grand Coalition of Social Democrats and Christian Union parties. Willy Brandt becomes foreign minister. |
| 14 | December | Germany declares that diplomatic recognition of the GDR is possible only after democratic legitimisation. |
| 14 | December | At a NATO DPC meeting, it is agreed to create a high-level Nuclear Planning Group (NPG). |
| 14 | December | German Federal Foreign Minister Willy Brandt states before WEU representatives that the new West German Government does not aspire to any atomic participation within NATO. |
| 15-16 | December | During a ministerial meeting of the NATO DPC, Belgian Foreign Minister Pierre Harmel calls for a fundamental reappraisal of the political, military and economic aims of the Alliance, given what he sees as the fundamental changes that have taken place over the preceding years. |

| At a Glance – Major Events and Themes | |
|---|---|
| | **The US nuclear arsenal reaches a peak of 32,000 warheads** |
| | **The US informs its Allies of the details of the nuclear weapons that it is holding on the territory of its partners** |
| | **The US completes its programme for the construction of 41 SSBNs, carrying 656 missiles in total, each with a range of between 2,400 and 4,000 kilometres** |
| | **At the Glassboro Summit, the US indicates, for the first time, its willingness to begin talks with the Soviet Union on strategic arms control** |
| | **Konrad Adenauer dies** |
| | **Six Day War** |
| | **China explodes its first thermonuclear device** |
| | **The Merger Treaty enters into force, setting up a single Council and a single Commission for the EEC, Euratom and ECSC** |
| | **The first British Polaris SSBN, the "HMS Resolution", enters service** |
| | **Harmel Report completed and *flexible response* formally adoted by NATO** |

## 1967

| Day | Month | Event |
|---|---|---|
| 18 | January | The NATO Defence College is inaugurated in Rome. |
| 29 | March | The first French SSBN, "Le Redoutable", is launched. |
| 31 | March | The inauguration of the SHAPE Headquarters takes place at Mons in Belgium. |
| 1 | April | Deadline for the withdrawal of all NATO forces from France. |
| 6-7 | April | The first meeting of NATO's NPG takes place in Washington. |
| 19 | April | Konrad Adenauer, the first chancellor of post-war Germany, dies. Adenauer did more than any other politician to create confidence in the Western Allies that enabled the Federal Republic to develop a political identity and to rearm on the road to equal treatment. |
| 21 | April | In Greece, a group of colonels seizes power in a *coup d'état* and installs an authoritarian regime that suppresses civil liberties. |

| | | |
|---|---|---|
| 5 | June | Following the massing of Egyptian, Jordanian and Syrian troops near the Israeli border and blockades of waterways, Israel attacks a coalition of Arab forces. In the Six Day War that follows, the Arabs suffer heavy losses, and East Jerusalem, the Golan Heights and the Sinai Desert fall to Israel. |
| 17 | June | China explodes its first thermonuclear device. |
| 23-25 | June | At the Glassboro Summit between President Johnson and Prime Minister Aleksei Kosygin, the US indicates that it is willing for the first time to enter into talks with the Soviet Union on strategic arms control. This greatly concerns the Europeans, who fear that the Americans might negotiate over their heads and, by formally accepting the strategic stalemate, render Europe vulnerable to a Soviet conventional attack – thus making a European war "winnable" for the USSR. This foreshadows the dual-track debate that erupts in the 1970s with the Soviet deployment of the SS-20 IRBM. |
| 1 | July | The Merger Treaty enters into force, merging the executive bodies of the three European Communities: the EEC, Euratom and ECSC. A single Commission and a single Council thus begin to operate for all three Communities. The treaty also provides for a common budget. |
| 8 | August | Indonesia, Malaysia, the Philippines, Singapore and Thailand sign the treaty establishing the Association of Southeast Asian Nations (ASEAN). |
| 2 | October | The first British Polaris SSBN, the "HMS Resolution", joins the British Fleet. |
| 16 | October | The inauguration of the new NATO seat in Brussels takes place. |
| 29 | November | The last British forces leave Aden, Yemen, which became their main base in the region after the loss of the Suez Canal. The territory is left to the National Liberation Front. |
| 12 | December | NATO continues to examine options for the Allies to join in nuclear planning. |
| 13-14 | December | *ESDI.* Following the completion of the Harmel Report on NATO doctrine, the NAC formally adopts the strategy of *flexible response*. This enables the Alliance to envisage some degree of conventional warfare before it is deemed necessary to cross the nuclear threshold. The move to a graduated response to a Soviet attack enshrines nuclear weapons at the heart of NATO strategy. It also precludes any no-first-strike agreement with the Soviet Union. Not surprisingly, Moscow endeavours to exploit this. |

| At a Glance – Major Events and Themes | |
|---|---|
| | **The Prague Spring** |
| | **UK announces withdrawal of all forces east of the Suez Canal** |
| | **First British Polaris missile fired** |
| | **Mass student demonstrations in Paris destabilise the Fifth Republic** |
| | **Treaty on the Non-Proliferation of Nuclear Weapons signed** |
| | **Warsaw Pact countries invade Czechoslovakia** |
| | **Brezhnev Doctrine enunciated** |
| | **Harmel Plan presented to the WEU** |
| | **Richard Millhouse Nixon elected president of the United States** |
| | **NATO's Eurogroup established** |

## 1968

| Day | Month | Event |
|---|---|---|
| 5-20 | January-August | Prague Spring: under new Communist Party leader Alexander Dubcek and, as of March, new President Ludvik Svoboda, liberal reforms are introduced in Czechoslovakia, including the freedoms of speech and assembly. |
| 13 | January | Standing Naval Forces Atlantic (STANAVFORLANT) is inaugurated at the Royal Navy's base at Portland in the United Kingdom. |
| 16 | January | The UK announces that it intends to withdraw from all of its bases east of the Suez Canal by 1971. |
| 31 | January | The Americans receive their first major shock of the Vietnam War when the North Vietnamese launch the Tet offensive and get to within a few kilometres of the South's capital, Saigon. |
| 15 | February | The "HMS Resolution" fires Britain's first Polaris missile. |
| 2-16 | May-June | Mass student demonstrations create the impression that the Fifth Republic in France might fall. After open conflict between the student movement and French riot police on the streets of Paris, however, the government brings the situation under control. |
| 23 | June | De Gaulle's conservative party and its allies triumph in French parliamentary elections. |
| 24-25 | June | The North Atlantic Council publishes a declaration calling for mutually balanced force reductions (MBFR) involving conventional forces. |

| | | |
|---|---|---|
| 1 | July | The Treaty on the Non-Proliferation of Nuclear Weapons is signed in Washington, London and Moscow. Due to enter into force on 5 March 1970, the treaty commits the so-called Nuclear Weapons States to eventual disarmament. All other states are formally obliged not to develop nuclear weapons. There are some notable absentees. |
| 20-21 | August | After a period of experimentation with democratic socialism under Alexander Dubcek known as the Prague Spring, the Soviet Union, East Germany, Poland, Hungary and Bulgaria invade Czechoslovakia to enforce Communist orthodoxy. The invasion marks the end of any crusading appeal of Soviet-style Communism in the West. |
| | August | The USSR surpasses the US in numbers of ICBMs deployed. This is a somewhat semantic point, for both superpowers now possess enough warheads to destroy life on the planet several times over. The term *overkill* enters the lexicon. |
| 25 | September | The Brezhnev Doctrine is unofficially enunciated in the Soviet newspaper "Pravda". The doctrine restricts socialist countries' sovereignty in that it makes a turn towards capitalism in one socialist country the concern of other socialist countries and justifies certain military interventions to overcome such a turn. |
| 3 | October | *ESDI/ESDP.* Pierre Harmel, the foreign minister of Belgium, tells a press conference that at the next ministerial meeting of the WEU Council scheduled for 21 -22 October, the Benelux countries will submit a plan for co-operation between the EEC and the UK in the fields of foreign, defence, technological and monetary policy. This plan becomes known as the Harmel Plan. European integration is essential and must move ahead even if some countries are not ready.<br>At this juncture, it is clear that Harmel is aiming his comments at the increasingly intransigent French Government. He goes on to say that the "hegemony" of any one EEC or WEU member must be avoided. Furthermore, he suggests that political co-operation should move from "occasional" to "compulsory" consultation. With regard to a common defence, he suggests that the seven WEU members should aim to establish a European pillar within NATO through a process of systematic consultation. The basis for Eurogroup is established. |
| 21 | October | *ESDI/ESDP.* The Harmel Plan is presented to the Ministerial Council of the WEU. |
| 5 | November | Richard Millhouse Nixon is elected president of the United States. |

| | | |
|---|---|---|
| 12 | November | In a speech at the fifth Congress of the Polish United Workers' Party, CPSU General Secretary Brezhnev enunciates his doctrine: "When forces that are hostile to socialism and try to turn the development of some socialist country towards capitalism, it becomes not only a problem of the country concerned, but a common problem and concern of all socialist countries." |
| 13-14 | November | *ESDI.* At a NATO meeting, it is agreed to establish Eurogroup in an effort to better co-ordinate all the defence activities of the European pillar of NATO. |
| 21 | November | MARAIRMED (Allied Maritime Air Forces Mediterranean) is activated. |

| | |
|---|---|
| **At a Glance – Major Events and Themes** | **The Soames Affair** |
| | **The US moves to enhance its ICMB capability through multiple independent re-entry vehicles (warheads) on each missile** |
| | **Soviet-Chinese border dispute starts** |
| | **Neil Armstrong and Edwin Aldrin walk on the moon** |
| | **Nixon Doctrine enunciated** |
| | ***Ostpolitik* launched by Willy Brandt** |
| | **Strategic Arms Limitation Talks agreed** |
| | **The Hague Summit of the EEC; Davignon Report on European political union authorised** |

# 1969

| Day | Month | Event |
|---|---|---|
| 4 | February | *ESDI/ESDP.* President de Gaulle has lunch with the British ambassador to Paris, Christopher Soames, to discuss what is termed "the future of European co-operation". At the meeting, the British claim that de Gaulle demands that Europe become totally independent of the US and that Britain could join the EEC if it dismantled NATO. Furthermore, de Gaulle tells Soames that he wants discussions on all the European issues that divide the two countries and favours the creation of a core of countries consisting of Britain, France, Germany and Italy to act as a kind of political directorate. Soames duly passes the information on to London. Unfortunately, the British note of the meeting is made public. |
| 6-7 | February | *ESDP.* France commences a boycott of the Western European Union following the Harmel Plan and a sharp deterioration in its relations with the United Kingdom during what is soon called the Soames Affair. In what also becomes known as the "WEU crisis", France reserves its position on the co-ordination of foreign policy through the Council of Ministers of the WEU. The dispute develops after the UK elaborates its position and attempts to exploit the Harmel Plan on co-operation between itself and the six EEC members on areas not covered by the Treaty of Rome, such as defence, security, technological and monetary policy. |
| 11 | February | The go-ahead is given for the development of an accurate new theatre nuclear missile for Europe. This decision is detected by Soviet military intelligence, the GRU, and ironically becomes one of the Soviet military's rationales for developing the SS-20, which in turn leads to the Euromissile crisis of the 1970s. |

| | | |
|---|---|---|
| 14 | February | *ESDP.* In a strongly worded *communiqué*, France states that it fundamentally objects to the UK's using the machinery of the WEU in an attempt to outflank French objections to British membership of the EEC by establishing other links with members of the Community. Furthermore, France is irritated by what it regards as the unceasing efforts of the other members of the EEC to force it to change its position with regard to its veto over UK membership of the Community. Unquestioned French leadership of the Community is beginning to crack as France boycotts first NATO, then the Community and finally the Western European Union. |
| 21 | February | Through Agence France Presse, the French Government angrily denies the British interpretation of the meeting that took place between President de Gaulle and Christopher Soames, the British ambassador. Furthermore, the press release disavows the suggestion that Britain could join the EEC. |
| 24 | February | France formally protests to the UK, via Christopher Soames, over its handling of the ambassador's note of the meeting with de Gaulle. |
| 24 | February | *ESDI.* In an address to the North Atlantic Council in Brussels, US President Nixon offers what he calls "a two-way street" with the NATO Allies in an attempt to resolve what he acknowledges as discontent on the part of the Europeans, who feel too often talked at rather than talked to. |
| | March | Soviet and Chinese troops start fighting in Manchuria over the disputed border. |
| 10-11 | April | A meeting of the North Atlantic Council in Washington celebrates 20 years of NATO. |
| 28 | April | French President Charles de Gaulle resigns over a lost referendum on regionalisation and reform of the Senate. |
| 28 | May | NATO's DPC decides to create Naval Officer Commanding Forces in the Mediterranean (NAVOCFORMED). |
| 15 | June | Georges Pompidou is elected French president. |
| 1 | July | The Non-Proliferation Treaty (NPT) is signed. Its 59 initial members (189 as of March 2005) agree to renounce the use of nuclear weapons, and the five existing nuclear powers agree to work towards disarmament and to assist the other signatories with help and advice concerning the peaceful use of nuclear energy. |
| 20 | July | Neil Armstrong becomes the first man to walk on the moon. The US therefore wins the Space Race, and President Kennedy's 1962 claim that an American would walk upon the Earth's only terrestrial satellite before the end of the decade is realised. |

| | | |
|---|---|---|
| 25 | July | President Nixon announces the Nixon Doctrine, which amounts to courting China in a bid to force the Soviet Union on the defensive whilst keeping the lines of communication open to Moscow. |
| 21 | October | Willy Brandt of the Social-Democratic Party is elected German federal chancellor. |
| 28 | October | Brandt launches his famous *Ostpolitik* drive aimed at a German-led rapprochement with the East. The US sees this as a dangerous precedent because a leading NATO member has broken ranks and thus the *de facto* American monopoly over the political leadership of the Alliance. |
| 17 | November | At Helsinki, the US and Soviet delegates have their first discussion over the practicalities of entering into arms-control discussions, to be called the Strategic Arms Limitation Talks (SALT). |
| 25 | November | Building upon the goodwill generated by the NPT, the US renounces biological warfare and the first use of chemical weapons. |
| 1-2 | December | *ESDP.* At the Hague summit, the heads of state of the six member states of the European Economic Community reach an agreement to build a European Community that is based on economic and monetary union. They also instruct their foreign ministers to "study the best way of achieving progress in the matter of political unification, within the context of enlargement" of the European Communities. The preparation of the so-called Davignon Report on political union is authorised. The summit also paves the way for the opening of membership negotiations with the UK, Ireland, Denmark and Norway. |
| | December | The US and the USSR reach an agreement to begin SALT in 1970. |
| | December | Soviet/German talks begin in Moscow about recognition of the Federal Republic and its recognition of the German Democratic Republic. |
| | December | By the end of 1969, the Soviet Union has 1,190 strategic nuclear missiles deployed and the Americans 1,054. However, the US seeks to upgrade its weapons by providing its ICBM capability (the Minuteman III system) with multiple independent re-entry vehicles (MIRV) on each missile. |

Part 4

# THE LUKEWARM PEACE

# 1970 -1979

| At a Glance – Major Events and Themes | |
|---|---|
| | **President Nixon states what has become increasingly clear to the Western Europeans: namely, that the US is not prepared to commit suicide through the automatic launching of a full-scale nuclear response in the wake of a Soviet nuclear attack upon Western Europe. The problem of de-coupling becomes a major issue in transatlantic relations** |
| | **Nuclear non-proliferation treaty enters into force** |
| | **SALT I talks commence** |
| | **Invasion of Cambodia by US** |
| | **NATO calls for unilateral balanced force reduction** |
| | **First F-111 nuclear bombers arrive in Europe** |
| | **Werner Report on European economic and political union presented** |
| | **Davignon Report (Luxembourg Report): European Political Co-operation commences** |

## 1970

| Day | Month | Event |
|---|---|---|
| | January | The Soviet Union establishes a military relationship with President Anwar Al-Sadat of Egypt. This raises alarm both in Washington and in Tel Aviv. |
| 1 | March | Iceland joins EFTA. |
| 5 | March | The NPT enters into force. |
| 16 | April | The main round of SALT talks commences in Vienna. The objective is arms control rather than disarmament with the first target being the stabilisation of the strategic arms race through the establishment of nuclear strategic parity between the superpowers. Both the US and Soviet economies are suffering the strain of prolonged confrontation. In particular, the US economy is being badly affected by the Vietnam War, as the budget deficit balloons and the US Federal Reserve prints dollars to fund the debt. |
| 29+30 | April | The invasion of Cambodia by American and South Vietnamese troops begins and is announced the next day by President Nixon under the guise of winding down the Vietnam War. |
| 26-27 | May | The North Atlantic Council issues a declaration calling for MBFR in Europe with the Warsaw Treaty Organisation. Western economies are moving into recession, and the cost of the Cold War is proving prohibitive. |
| 20 | July | *ESDP.* The foreign ministers of the six EEC member states accept in principle the Davignon Report on political union. |

| | | |
|---|---|---|
| 12 | August | In the first overt demonstration of the thaw in Soviet-West German relations since 1945, the two countries sign a non-aggression treaty in Moscow. |
| 19 | August | The US deploys the first MIRVed missile, the Minuteman III. |
| 12 | September | The first lighter delivery aircraft, the F-111, arrive in Europe. Deployed as a way of calming European fears over the stalemate in the strategic nuclear balance, this nuclear-capable aircraft is capable of penetrating Soviet air defences as part of the US forward base system (FBS). As such, it creates an "action-reaction cycle", for the Soviet high command perceives the need for a highly accurate, mobile theatre nuclear missile that can both attack the home bases of the F-111 and threaten Western European governments. The SS-20 is born. |
| 7 | October | *ESDP.* The so-called Werner Report on European economic and monetary union is presented to the Council of Ministers and the Commission for consideration. This document, which advises the six member states to increase co-operation between their central banks, is the first step on the way to the Euro and eventually leads to the Single European Act of 1986. |
| 27 | October | *ESDP.* The foreign ministers of the Six formally endorse the Report on the Problem of Political Unification, known as the Davignon Report or Luxembourg Report, and thus the movement towards political union. As a result, the concept of European Political Co-operation (EPC) is born. A Political Committee is established to bring together foreign policy officials of member states responsible for political affairs. EPC is intergovernmentalist, i.e., based upon the traditional nation-state. However, it requires them to work so closely together that the co-ordination of policy in key areas in principle takes the form of integration for all intents and purposes. |
| 9 | November | Former French President Charles de Gaulle dies. |
| 2-4 | December | *ESDI.* Following the AD-70 report by NATO suggesting Warsaw Pact forces have undergone a major programme of qualitative upgrading, the 10 members of NATO's Eurogroup decide to embark upon a force improvement package. This is in spite of the economic difficulties that many of them are beginning to experience. |
| 7 | December | West Germany and Poland sign a treaty that normalises their relations. |

| At a Glance – Major Events and Themes | |
|---|---|
| | **US-Soviet treaty to de-nuclearise the seabed** |
| | **The Mansfield Resolution tabled in US Congress** |
| | **Pentagon Papers published** |
| | **Nixon accepts invitation to visit China** |
| | **French nuclear SSMs on Plateau d'Albion enter into operation** |
| | **Four-Power agreement on Berlin** |
| | **Joseph Luns becomes secretary general of NATO** |
| | **The first of the French SSBNs, "Le Redoutable", enters service** |

# 1971

| Day | Month | Event |
|---|---|---|
| 11 | February | In a further step along the road to confidence-building between the nuclear superpowers, a treaty to de-nuclearise the seabed is signed. |
| 13 | May | US Senator Mike Mansfield tables a motion calling upon the administration to withdraw 50% of US forces from Western Europe if the NATO Allies are not seen to be doing more for their own defence. |
| 20 | May | The Mansfield Resolution is defeated, but it sets the tone for an increasingly acrimonious debate within the Alliance over the fraught question of burden-sharing. |
| 13 | June | The Pentagon Papers are published by "The New York Times", revealing, in detail, the thinking in the McNamara Pentagon in the build-up to the Vietnam *imbroglio*. |
| 15+16 | July | As part of his policy of forcing the Soviet Union to confront threats on two fronts, Nixon engineers and accepts an invitation to visit Communist China in what is an historic rapprochement between the two former ideological adversaries. |
| 2 | August | France's surface-to-surface nuclear-cabable Pluton IRBM force, stationed at Plateau d'Albion, enters into operation. |
| 3 | September | In a reaffirmation of the *status quo*, the Four Powers (France, the UK, the US and the USSR) reach agreement over the continued partition of Berlin and of the corridor that links West Berlin with the Federal Republic. |
| 30 | September | The US and the Soviet Union reach an agreement on the avoidance of nuclear accidents. It requires from the signatories a pledge to maintain and improve safeguards against accidental or unauthorised use of nuclear weapons. |

| | | |
|---|---|---|
| 1 | October | Dr. Joseph Luns of the Netherlands becomes secretary general of NATO. This post is normally held by a European to offer some balance to the fact that the supreme allied commander Europe (SACEUR) is always an American. |
| 25 | October | The Government of the People's Republic of China (PR China) replaces the Republic of China (Taiwan) as the "only lawful representative of China to the UN". |
| 23 | November | PR China takes up China's permanent seat at the UN Security Council. |
| | November | The first F-111s in Europe become operational. |
| 1 | December | The first French SSBN, "Le Redoutable", enters active service. Together with the deployment of the surface-to-surface IRBM on Plateau d'Albion and the nuclear-capable Mirage IV fighter-bomber, the French *force de frappe* becomes a reality. It is an American strategic Triad in microcosm and, as such, is considerably more extensive than the British "minimum deterrent". |

| At a Glance – Major Events and Themes | |
|---|---|
| | **Paris peace talks on Vietnam** |
| | **Nixon visits China** |
| | **SALT I and ABM treaties signed** |
| | **Four-Power agreement on future of Berlin signed** |
| | **First summit of the enlarged EEC in Paris** |
| | **Nixon re-elected US president** |
| | **SALT II talks begin in Geneva** |
| | **MBFR talks start in Vienna** |
| | **East and West Germany recognise each other's sovereignty** |

## 1972

| Day | Month | Event |
|---|---|---|
| 22 | January | Denmark, Ireland, Norway and the UK sign Accession Treaties with the European Communities. |
| 25 | January | US President Nixon reveals that Henry Kissinger has been secretly negotiating with North Vietnam. |
| 28 | January | The first operational patrol of the French SSBN "Le Redoutable" takes place. |
| 21-28 | February | President Nixon visits China. He pledges to reduce US troops and military installations on Taiwan as tensions in the area diminish and affirms complete withdrawal as its ultimate objective. Nixon also promises not to support either the independence of Taiwan or the military return of Taiwan to mainland China. Nixon's visit and his pledges break the ice and mark the beginning of a normalisation process between the US and PR China. |
| 23 | March | The US begins boycotting Vietnam peace talks, citing North Vietnamese refusal to seriously discuss concrete issues. |
| 26 | March | US President Nixon suspends Vietnam peace talks. |
| 30 | March | North Vietnam launches a major military offensive. |
| 7 | April | PR China invites US table tennis players to visit China. |
| 14 | April | Chinese leader Zhou Enlai receives table tennis teams from Canada, Colombia, Nigeria and the US in the Great Hall of the People in Beijing. A few hours after the reception, US President Nixon announces a relaxation of the US embargo against China. |
| 27 | April | Paris peace talks on Vietnam resume after bombing of North Vietnam intensifies. |
| 4 | May | The US and South Vietnam suspend Paris peace talks indefinitely in response to North Vietnamese offensive. |

| | | |
|---|---|---|
| 22-30 | May | President Nixon visits Moscow to sign the SALT I and ABM treaties. |
| 26 | May | The US and USSR sign the SALT I Interim Agreement together with the Anti-Ballistic Missile (ABM) treaty. These two agreements are designed to stabilise the strategic nuclear balance by fixing offensive parity and by preventing a destabilising advance through a technological breakthrough in the field of anti-ballistic-missile technology. Partially successful as arms-control and diplomatic exercises, the core of the agreements are progressively weakened as confidence is undermined with the advent of increasingly accurate warheads, MIRVs and missile-launcher mobility. |
| 29 | May | US President Nixon and Soviet General Secretary Brezhnev sign Basic Principles of Detente. The agreement asserts the principle of peaceful co-existence and opens economic markets between the two countries. |
| 3 | June | The Four-Power agreement over the future of Berlin is signed by the foreign ministers of France, the Soviet Union, the United Kingdom and the United States. After two years of negotiations, West Berlin's status and the city's relationship with the two German states are regularised. The agreement paves the way for the normalisation of relations between East and West Germany and their entry into the UN. |
| 17 | June | Five men are arrested trying to bug offices of the Democratic Party at the Watergate Hotel in Washington. The Watergate Affair begins. |
| 18 | June | The second round of the SALT I signing process takes place, as the Soviet Union signs. |
| | June | Talks start for a treaty on the prevention of nuclear war. |
| 13 | July | Vietnam peace talks resume in Paris. |
| 18 | July | President Anwar Al-Sadat of Egypt demands the removal of all Soviet advisors from Egypt. |
| 3 | August | The ABM treaty is approved by the US Senate. |
| 5 | September | Munich Olympic Massacre: the radical Palestinian Black September movement kills 11 Israeli participants. A German policeman and five terrorists are also killed. |
| 25 | September | The Norwegian people reject EC membership in a referendum. |
| 29 | September | "The Washington Post" reports that a secret Republican fund used for widespread intelligence-gathering operations against the Democrats existed under the control of John Mitchell in 1971 and 1972, during his mandate as attorney general. |

| | | |
|---|---|---|
| 8 | October | Stalemate ends at the Paris peace talks between Kissinger and Le Duc Tho, the top US and North Vietnamese negotiators, respectively, as both sides agree to major concessions. |
| 10 | October | The US Federal Bureau of Investigation says that the break-in at the Watergate Hotel was part of a massive campaign of political spying and sabotage conducted in an effort to secure the re-election of President Nixon. |
| 19-21 | October | *ESDP.* The first summit of the enlarged EEC is held in Paris. In a key passage of the agreed final text, the *communiqué* states: "In line with its political aims, the construction of Europe will allow the continent to assert its personality in the loyalty of its traditional friendships and in the alliances of its member states and to make its mark in world affairs as a distinct entity determined to promote a better international balance which respects the United Nations Charter. The member states of the Community, the driving wheels of European construction, declare their intention of converting their entire relationship into a European Union before the end of this decade." |
| 22 | October | Henry Kissinger visits South Vietnamese leader Nguyen Van Thieu to discuss the compromise reached between the US and North Vietnam. Thieu refuses to allow North Vietnamese troops to remain in South Vietnam indefinitely. |
| 7 | November | With more than 60% of the vote, Richard Nixon is elected president of the United States for the second time. |
| 9 | November | The Norwegian Government announces that it is not bringing before parliament a bill on the ratification of EC membership. |
| 21 | November | SALT II talks begin in Geneva. The objective of these talks is more ambitious than SALT I in that they aim to actually reduce the number of launchers and warheads. Moreover, the target is to complete an agreement prior to the end of the SALT I Interim Agreement in 1977. |
| 22 | November | In what is regarded as a major breakthrough for Western diplomacy, the preliminary talks of the MBFR negotiations begin in Vienna. |
| 22 | November | Preparatory talks on the Conference on Security and Co-operation in Europe (CSCE) begin in Helsinki. |
| 13 | December | Vietnam peace talks end abruptly as Kissinger presents North Vietnam with a new version of their compromise, which now includes 69 changes demanded by South Vietnamese leader Thieu. |
| 14 | December | Willy Brandt is re-elected German federal chancellor. |

| | | |
|---|---|---|
| 20 | December | Mainly at French instigation, but demonstrative of an increasingly independent European line in technological development, a European Space Conference decides to fuse the two Eurolauncher organisations – the European Space Vehicle Launcher Development Organisation (ELDO) and the European Space Research Organisation (ESRO) – into a new organisation, the European Space Agency (ESA). |
| 21 | December | As the most overt sign of the progress of *Ostpolitik*, East and West Germany recognise each other's sovereignty. |

| At a Glance – Major Events and Themes | |
|---|---|
| | **UK, Ireland and Denmark join the EEC** |
| | **Vietnam ceasefire agreed; US begins to scale down its operations in Vietnam** |
| | **Kissinger's "year of Europe"** |
| | **Brezhnev visits Washington** |
| | **US/USSR Agreement on the Prevention of Nuclear War** |
| | **Conference on Security and Co-operation in Europe opens in Helsinki** |
| | **Yom Kippur War** |
| | **US War Powers Act passed** |
| | **Arab oil embargo starts** |
| | **The EEC Copenhagen Summit adopts the concept of a European Identity; EPC is operationalised** |
| | **The Watergate Affair intensifies** |

## 1973

| Day | Month | Event |
|---|---|---|
| 1 | January | *ESDP.* The United Kingdom, Denmark and Ireland join the European Economic Community (EEC). The Six become the Nine. |
| 8 | January | Henry Kissinger and chief North Vietnamese negotiatior Le Duc Tho start a new round of negotiations. |
| 15 | January | US President Nixon announces the suspension of offensive action in Vietnam because of progress in the peace talks. |
| 23 | January | As a result of talks in Paris, a ceasefire agreement is announced in Vietnam. Nixon now starts to extricate the US from that war. |
| 27 | January | The Vietnam ceasefire agreement offically enters into force. US troops are to withdraw within 60 days. North Vietnam is to release prisoners-of-war within 60 days. |
| 21 | February | A peace agreement is signed in Laos between the royal government and the pro-communist opposition. |
| 23 | April | In an attempt to win back an increasingly hostile Western Europe, US Secretary of State Kissinger declares 1973 the "year of Europe". |
| 18 | May | The Watergate Senate hearings begin. |
| | May | Standing Naval Force Mediterranean (STANAVFORMED) is formed as a NATO response to increased activity by the Soviet Black Sea Fleet in the Mediterranean. |
| 18-25 | June | Just over a year after Nixon's historic visit to Moscow, General Secretary Brezhnev visits Washington. |

| | | |
|---|---|---|
| 22 | June | On the 32nd anniversary of the German invasion of the Soviet Union, the US and the USSR conclude an Agreement on the Prevention of Nuclear War. The core tenet of this treaty, which enters into force the same day, is that both parties commit themselves to consulting one another if a nuclear conflict appears at all likely. The agreement sends shock waves around Western European capitals, for it suggests a degree of symbiosis that indicates to them that "*détente*" might be turning into "*entente*". European members of NATO are becoming increasingly worried about the credibility of the US extended deterrent at the heart of NATO and thus fear de-coupling. |
| 3 | July | The Conference on Security and Co-operation in Europe opens in Helsinki. Divided into three "baskets", the political/security discussions are backed up by discussions on greater freedom of movement and expression, enhanced trade and technical transfers and human rights. |
| 13 | July | Former Presidential Appointment Secretary Alexander Butterfield testifies before the US Congress that Nixon has recorded all conversations and phone calls in his offices since 1971. |
| 27 | July | EEC leaders adopt the Copenhagen Report, the second report on EPC. It endorses the Davignon (Luxembourg) Report and further develops European Political Co-operation by formalising several already well-established features of EPC. It foresees that the member states' permanent representatives to international organisations "will regularly consider matters together and, on the basis of instructions received, will seek common positions in regard to important questions dealt with by those organisations." More generally, it contains a political commitment that foreign ministers consult with each other on foreign-policy issues and undertake joint action "wherever it appears possible and disirable." |
| 31 | July | A European Space Conference confirms the decision taken on 20 December 1972 that a European Space Agency (ESA) will be formed out of the ESRO and the ELDO. |
| 6 | October | Arab forces led by the Egyptians cross the Suez Canal and attack Israeli forces. In the early days of the war, the Arab coalition seems to be winning, and the Americans rush materials and weapons to support Israel. As the Yom Kippur War progresses, however, the Arabs begin to suffer heavy losses, and Syria and Egypt, both client states of the Soviet Union, appeal to Moscow for help. For a brief period, it seems that the two superpowers could be dragged into a third world war as the doomsday scenario begins to play itself out. Confronted with a determined US, however, the Soviet Union, cautious in such situations, seeks compromise. |

| | | |
|---|---|---|
| 17-28 | October | The Organization of the Petroleum Exporting Countries (OPEC) decides to place an embargo on oil exports to the US and the Netherlands. Oil exports will be cut until the territories occupied by Israel in the Yom Kippur War are liberated and the rights of the Palestinian people reinstated. |
| 25 | October | US President Nixon places US forces on DEFCOM 4 (a state of readiness just short of war) as the Yom Kippur War intensifies. However, he fails to warn, tell or in any way involve the European Allies. As a result, the political cohesion of NATO is once again brought seriously into question. |
| 30 | October | The MBFR talks open in Vienna. Aimed at achieving an equitable conventional-force balance in Europe between NATO and Warsaw Pact forces, the talks are to prove extremely difficult due to political problems and the problem of agreeing on comparability in the weapons inventories of the two sides. |
| | October | A group of visiting US senators are shocked at the anger of the European Allies over the recent spate of agreements between the US and the USSR. They warn that the US policy of bargaining without any referral or consultation with Allies is an extremely dangerous practice that could lead to the very problem of de-coupling that the Europeans are so keen to avoid. |
| 5 | November | OPEC announces a general 25% cut in oil-production levels (on the basis of September 1973 levels). The world oil price has doubled since September 1973. |
| 6 | November | The EC foreign ministers "strongly urge that the forces of both sides in the Middle East conflict should return immediately to the positions they occupied on 22 October", stress "the need for Israel to end the territorial occupation which it has maintained since the conflict of 1967" and recognise that, "... in the establishment of a just and lasting peace, account must be taken of the legitimate rights of the Palestinians." |
| 6-7 | November | NATO's NPG establishes two committees – the Military Implications Team and the Political Implications Team – tasked with examining the likely impact of cruise and Pershing 2 missile technology on NATO strategy. The Euromissile debate commences. |
| 7 | November | In a response to the Vietnam debacle, and with the backdrop of Nixon's threat to deploy US forces in the Yom Kippur War, the US Congress passes the War Powers Act. The act demands that a president come to Congress 60 days after the deployment of US troops in a war zone to gain approval. |

| | | |
|---|---|---|
| 7 | December | *ESDI.* With the implied threat of US withdrawal from Europe as context, NATO's DPC starts to look at ways of reducing the US costs associated with the Alliance and the problem of burden-sharing. |
| 14-15 | December | *ESDP.* At the Copenhagen Summit of the leaders of the EEC, the concept of a European Identity is adopted, in which "(t)he nine countries affirm their common will to speak with one voice in important world affairs". Furthermore, the final *communiqué* goes on: "It was agreed that the Foreign Ministers of the Member States should, at their next meeting decide on the means by which a common position should be worked out quickly in times of crisis. The development of political co-operation will also enable them to make joint assessments of crisis situations, with the aim of foreseeing them and of taking measures needed to deal with them." |
| 22-24 | December | Six OPEC countries decide to raise the price of crude oil from $5.18 to $11.65 a barrel effective 1 January 1974. The West stands on the brink of a severe depression. Western Europe feels particularly aggrieved, as it believes it is being pressured into supporting Israel when its oil interests suggest neutrality in the conflict might serve its interests (and economies) more effectively. |

| At a Glance – Major Events and Themes | |
|---|---|
| | **Schlesinger Doctrine** |
| | **Portuguese coup** |
| | **India explodes a nuclear device** |
| | **The first Transatlantic Declaration** |
| | **Turkey invades Cyprus** |
| | **The Watergate Affair results in the resignation of President Nixon** |
| | **Greece withdraws from NATO's integrated military structure** |
| | **The USSR decides to develop the SS-20 IRBM for deployment in Eastern Europe** |
| | **US-USSR Vladivostok summit** |
| | **Tindemans Report on European integration launched at EEC Paris summit** |

# 1974

| Day | Month | Event |
|---|---|---|
| 1 | January | With the increase of the crude oil price announced by OPEC in December 1973 coming into effect, the world oil price has quadrupled since September 1973. |
| 7-9 | January | OPEC decides to freeze oil prices until 1 April. |
| 10 | January | The so-called Schlesinger Doctrine, or NSDM-242, becomes US policy. Named after Secretary of Defense James Schlesinger, the objective of the policy is to reassure nervous West Europeans that in the event of a war some effort would be made to limit "collateral damage" by concentrating on low-yield, deep-strike targets, such as counterforce opportunities, i.e., Soviet command and control facilities and military installations. |
| 18 | March | The OPEC oil embargo ends. However, Libya maintains its oil embargo against the US. |
| | March | US Secretary of Defense Schlesinger is forced to admit that the Single Integrated Operating Plan, by which US nuclear forces (and British) are targeted and deployed, is still "massive" and "pre-planned", in spite of the policy of *flexible response* in NATO and the Schlesinger Doctrine. There is little room for flexibility or a limited nuclear strike given existing US command and control systems. |
| 2 | April | French President Georges Pompidou dies. |

| | | |
|---|---|---|
| 25 | April | In the so-called Carnation Revolution, the right-wing government in Portugal is overthrown by an apparently left-wing coup. Moscow is encouraged, but NATO becomes increasingly concerned over the reliability of Portugal as a member. |
| 6 | May | West German Chancellor Willy Brandt steps down over a spy scandal. |
| 16 | May | Helmut Schmidt is elected German federal chancellor. |
| 18 | May | India explodes a nuclear device. Along with Israel, India joins the five acknowledged nuclear powers. India is not a party to the NPT. |
| 19 | May | Valéry Giscard d'Estaing is elected French president. |
| 24 | May | Valéry Giscard d'Estaing takes office as French president. |
| 26 | June | To mark the 25th anniversary of NATO, and against the back-drop of tensions within the Alliance over the oil embargo by the Arabs, US policy towards the Soviet Union and the emerging disagreement over the credibility of the American extended deterrent, the NATO heads of government sign a declaration on future transatlantic relations. |
| 20 | July | After a Greek-backed coup in Cyprus with the aim of reunification with Greece, Turkey invades the island and occupies the northern portion. |
| 23-24 | July | The colonels are forced out of power in Greece, and the country returns to democracy. |
| 24 | July | Rejecting claims for executive privilege, the US Supreme Court rules that President Nixon must turn over White House tape recordings. |
| 27 | July | Charging obstruction of justice, the US House Judiciary Committee passes the first of three articles of impeachment against President Nixon. |
| 8 | August | US President Nixon announces his resignation to avoid being impeached following the Watergate Affair. |
| 9 | August | Nixon resigns as US president. Vice President Gerald R. Ford takes over as commander-in-chief of US forces and president of the United States. |
| 14 | August | In protest at what it regards as an insufficient response by NATO Allies to the Turkish invasion of Cyprus, Greece withdraws from the integrated command structure of the Alliance. |
| 16 | August | The UN Security Council expands UNFICYP's mandate to include the supervision of the *de facto* ceasefire on the island and the maintenance of a buffer zone. |

| | | |
|---|---|---|
| | November | The Politburo of the Soviet Union decides to proceed with the development and deployment of the SS-20 missile in Eastern Europe. This mobile, triple-warhead, MIRV, mobile nuclear missile system destabilises the theatre nuclear balance in Western Europe through its ability to strike the US FBS in Western Europe with little or no warning. With a range of more than 1,500 kilometres, it is seen by the Americans and the Western Europeans as a significant qualitative upgrading of Soviet theatre capabilities. |
| 23-24 | November | The Vladivostok Summit between President Ford and General Secretary Brezhnev takes place. The Soviets drop, for the first time, their hitherto determined insistence that the US FBS in Western Europe be included in the SALT process. Brezhnev indicates that he has had much trouble with the military to get them to agree to this and that, in return, he has allowed them to develop a new theatre nuclear system, the SS-20. He insists, therefore, that in return for this concession the US agree to an equal, aggregate number of strategic missile launchers and an equal sub-ceiling on the number of MIRVs. The US resists since Soviet weapons systems tend to be larger, with heavier throw-weights, more warheads and greater kilo tonnage in each warhead. The US eventually agrees, but, soon after the summit, the Soviets place the question of the FBS back on the negotiating agenda. The Europeans regard what they see as American weakness as another US retreat from extended deterrence. |
| 9-10 | December | *ESDP*. At an EEC meeting in Paris, it is agreed to give new impetus to the process of European integration. As part of the final *communiqué*, the heads of government agree that, "with a view to progress towards European unity, the Heads of Government reaffirm their determination gradually to adopt common positions and to co-ordinate their diplomatic action in all areas of international affairs which affect the interests of the European Community". Belgian Prime Minister Leo Tindemans is invited to prepare a report on the progress towards European Union. Furthermore, it is also agreed to proceed with plans for an elected European Parliament (EP), although Britain and Denmark reserve their respective positions. |
| 12-13 | December | At a meeting of the North Atlantic Council, increases in Warsaw Pact forces are noted and the determination to improve NATO forces reaffirmed. The impact of inflation upon defence expenditure is also discussed. |

| | |
|---|---|
| **At a Glance – Major Events and Themes** | **Biological Weapons Convention enters into force** |
| | **Economic recession in Western Europe undercuts defence budgets** |
| | **Saigon falls** |
| | **European Space Agency founded** |
| | **Helsinki Final Act signed** |
| | **The Jordan Report: Amos Jordan, the US principal assistant secretary of defense for international security affairs, says that: "...the thing that is troubling our European Allies in particular... is not our military capability but what they perceive to be shaky coherence and national unity which may make it impossible to use those military capabilities. It is the credibility of our commitment, not the existence of our commitments or the strength of our forces that is the doubt in their minds"** |

## 1975

| Day | Month | Event |
|---|---|---|
| 26 | March | The Biological Weapons Convention (BWC) enters into force. |
| 29 | April | In what represents a final humiliation for the Americans, Saigon falls to the North Vietnamese. The remaining Americans are forced to leave the US Embassy compound clinging to the last helicopters that can make the journey. It is a far cry from the far-off days in 1964 when the Americans first arrived in Vietnam in strength. |
| | April | The UK, the Netherlands, Belgium and Denmark announce significant unilateral defence cuts that are at variance with NATO's policy of pursuing force improvement programmes. The cause is deep economic recession in these countries. |
| 9 | May | After almost twenty years of existence, the Action Committee for the United States of Europe set up by Jean Monnet is dissolved by its founder. |
| 23 | May | *ESDI.* At a ministerial session of NATO's DPC, the strategic situation in the Mediterranean is examined and Eurogroup encouraged to improve the overall effectiveness of the European pillar of NATO. |
| 29-30 | May | A North Atlantic Council meeting in Brussels is attended by heads of state and government. Tension is rising within the Alliance over the Soviet deployment of SS-20 theatre nuclear weapons (TNW). |
| 30 | May | The member states of ESRO and ELDO – Belgium, Denmark, France, the FRG, Italy, the Netherlands, Spain, Sweden, Switzerland, and the UK – sign the Convention for the Establishment of a European Space Agency. |

| | | |
|---|---|---|
| 5 | June | After extensive work by British and French mine sweepers and engineers, the block ships and mines that have prevented the use of the Suez Canal since 1967 are removed, and the canal is reopened to traffic. |
| 21 | July | The second phase of the Conference on Security and Co-operation in Europe ends. |
| 1 | August | The so-called Helsinki Final Act of the Conference on Security and Co-operation in Europe is signed. It contains a set of "politically binding" principles for all signatory states, such as sovereign equality; territorial integrity; the right to freely choose and develop one's political, economic and cultural systems; respect for international law; peaceful settlement of disputes; non-intervention in internal affairs; and respect for human rights and fundamental freedoms. Concretely, the document also provides for confidence-building measures on certain aspects of security and disarmament, such as prior notification of major military manoeuvres and exchange of observers. Furthermore, signatories agree on co-operation in the fields of economics, science, technology and the environment, as well as on co-operation and exchanges of culture, education and information. Moreover, facilitated contacts between, and reunification of, familiy members dispersed in Eastern and Western countries are foreseen. The Helsinki Final Act succeeds in making human-rights issues a legitimate subject of dialogue between East and West for the first time. It also offers a permanent channel of communication through follow-up conferences, a normative code of conduct and a long-term programme of co-operation. |
| 30 | October | Prince Juan Carlos, the heir-designate, takes over as provisional head of state in Spain, effectively ending General Franco's reign. |
| 19-20 | November | Donald Rumsfeld replaces James Schlesinger as US secretary of defense. |
| 20 | November | Spain's General Franco dies. |
| 22 | November | Juan Carlos is sworn in as King of Spain. After 36 years of authoritarian rule under General Franco, Spain is becoming a democracy. |
| 9-10 | December | The Defence Planning Committee of NATO, in ministerial session, notes with concern the increase and improvements in Warsaw Pact forces and discusses NATO's own progress in the fields of "standardisation" and "interoperability". |
| 16 | December | At the Vienna talks on MBFR, US Secretary of Defense Rumsfeld indicates that the US is willing to discuss the question of the FBS in Europe with the Soviet Union. Once again, there is no real consultation with the Western Europeans, who regard this latest action as further evidence that the US is becoming an increasingly untrustworthy Ally. |

| At a Glance – Major Events and Themes |
| --- |
| **European Tornado multi-role combat aircraft programme launched** |
| **Mao Tse Tung dies in China** |
| **US forward base system rethought** |
| **Jimmy Carter is elected president of the United States** |

# 1976

| Day | Month | Event |
| --- | --- | --- |
| 8 | January | Zhou Enlai dies in China. |
| 21-22 | January | At a ministerial session of NATO's NPG meeting in Hamburg, the growth in Soviet nuclear capability is discussed, particularly with regard to its theatre nuclear capability, and the possibility of stabilisation through the SALT process is examined. |
| 2 | February | On invitation by Dutch Defence Minister Henk Vredeling, defence ministers from all European NATO members except Iceland establish the IEPG to provide co-operation in the area of research, development, and production of defence equipment. |
|  | February | *ESDI/ESDP.* For the first time since departing from the NATO command structure in 1966, France participates in an Alliance Eurogroup meeting to discuss the co-ordination of arms procurement and production. This lays the foundation of the Independent European Programme Group (IEPG). |
| 7 | April | In China, Deng Xiaoping is ousted from his top government and party positions by left-wing radicals around Mao. |
| 20-21 | May | At the North Atlantic Council in Oslo, ministers note the Helsinki Final Act and restate their determination to press Western demands for progress in the MBFR talks in Vienna. |
| 10-11 | June | *ESDI.* At a NATO DPC meeting (ministerial session), ministers restate their commitment to Eurogroup and their worries over Warsaw Pact force improvements, and they endorse force goals for the period 1977-82. |
| 14-15 | June | A NATO NPG meeting (ministerial session) discusses proposals for improving NATO's theatre nuclear capability. In particular, the Europeans demand a replacement for ageing Honest John and Jupiter missiles in the form of cruise and Pershing 2. |
| 2 | July | The Socialist Republic of Vietnam is proclaimed. |

| | | |
|---|---|---|
| 29 | July | *ESDI/ESDP.* West Germany, Italy and the UK give the go-ahead to full production of the programme to build the multi-role combat aircraft (MRCA). This strike/fighter aircraft becomes known as the Tornado and represents a major step forward in defence collaboration between the Europeans, who are later joined by Spain in the project. However, France remains outside. |
| 8 | September | Chairman Mao Tse Tung dies. China goes into official mourning, and the search for a successor begins. |
| 3 | October | The US Air Force deploys another 84 F-111 nuclear-capable fighter-bombers to the UK as a short-term counter to the Soviet SS-20s in Eastern Europe. However, the reliance of these aircraft upon fixed conventional runways makes them vulnerable to either a first strike or counterforce attack. In a sign of American policy thinking, the USAF therefore initiates a study to enable them to replace the F-111s in the FBS with ground-launched cruise missiles (GLCMs). |
| 7 | October | The "Gang of Four" (the chief members of a radical faction with key roles during the Chinese Cultural Revolution under Mao) are arrested, opening the way for Deng Xiaoping to regain his influential positions. |
| 2 | November | Running on a ticket designed to capitalise on the tide of disenchantment that is felt in the United States against the Washington establishment, James Earl (Jimmy) Carter is elected president. |
| 9-10 | December | At the NAC in Brussels, it is decided to further increase NATO forces by way of response to what is now described as the "incessant" build-up of Warsaw Pact forces. NATO totally rejects Warsaw Pact proposals to renounce the first use of nuclear weapons and to limit the participation of European states in alliances. |

| At a Glance – Major Events and Themes | |
|---|---|
| | **Cruise missiles given the go-ahead** |
| | **NATO Long-Term Defence Programme agreed** |
| | **Vance-Gromyko meeting in Geneva** |
| | **The Gelb Paper** |
| | **SALT I agreement expires** |
| | **NATO High-Level Group meets for first time** |
| | **Helmut Schmidt makes a speech attacking US nuclear policy to the International Institute for Strategic Studies** |
| | **SS-20 deployed in Central and Eastern Europe. The Euromissile crisis begins** |
| | **The Carter administration estimates that a major nuclear exchange would result in 140 million casualties in the US and ca. 113 million casualties in Western Europe** |



## 1977

| Day | Month | Event |
|---|---|---|
| 7 | January | Czech civil-rights movement Charta 77 publishes an eponymous resolution demanding that the Czech Government respect human and civil rights as estabished in the Helsinki Final Act. Many of the petitioners are arrested. |
| 18 | January | The US Defense Department gives the Air Force the go-ahead to develop GLCMs. |
| 20 | January | Jimmy Carter becomes the first Democratic US president since John F. Kennedy. |
| 23 | January | Cyrus Vance becomes US secretary of state; Harold Brown, secretary of defense; and Zbigniew Brzezinski, national security advisor. |
| 21 | March | The "Frankfurter Allgemeine Zeitung", with the alleged backing of the German Foreign Ministry, publishes an article in which it states that, "Bonn is concerned that Jimmy Carter is a man ruling the White House whose moral and religious convictions are incompatible with the demands of world politics." This pejorative piece comes to encapsulate the difficult relationship that develops between Carter and the German SPD chancellor, Helmut Schmidt. |
| 25 | March | NATO's DPC meets in ministerial session to discuss the purchase of a NATO airborne early-warning capability. |
| 10-11 | May | *ESDI.* The NAC meets in London at the level of heads of state and government, together with ministers, and decides to undertake a long-term study of East-West relations and to develop a Long-Term Defence Programme (LTDP). |

| | | |
|---|---|---|
| 10-11 | May | At the same meeting, Carter and Schmidt confront each other over the issue of NATO defence planning. Upon taking office, Carter ordered Presidential Memorandum No. 10, which was a full review of the US force posture and structure in Western Europe. The West Germans have learned that one of the key proposals to emerge from the review was for the Americans to withdraw "temporarily" from the forward areas they hold in the event of conflict. This has infuriated the Germans. |
| 18-21 | May | At a meeting between US Secretary of State Cyrus Vance and Soviet Foreign Minister Andrei Gromyko in Geneva, the Americans make a radical proposal that would involve a delay of three years in the deployment of ground-launched and sea-launched cruise missiles in return for a moratorium on the deployment of the SS-20. Unfortunately, the Americans once again fail to discuss this matter first with their Europeans Allies. |
| | May | As a result of European anger, Carter orders that a report be prepared for the Allies that explains to them in detail the US technical and operational analyses of the issue of theatre nuclear forces (TNF). After much wrangling, it is eventually prepared by Leslie Gelb, the director of the State Department's Bureau of Politico-Military Affairs, and, as such, becomes known as the Gelb Paper. The American view of the TNF issue is found to be at considerable variance to that of the Europeans. Its key finding is that the deployment of cruise missiles would have the effect of de-coupling the US strategic arsenal from the defence of Europe because it would create a Eurostrategic balance and therefore reduce the credibility of the US strategic deterrent and extended deterrence. This is a diametrically opposing view to that held by the European Allies. |
| 6 | June | "The Washington Post" reports that the US is seeking to build an enhanced radiation weapon, or neutron bomb. The weapon is designed to destroy Soviet tanks through minimal blast but enhanced radiation and to reduce the degree of collateral damage in West Germany in particular. Unfortunately for NATO, the Soviet propaganda campaign caught the imagination of the public in the West and the resurgent anti-nuclear movement by presenting it as a weapon that kills people but does not destroy buildings. Consequently, it becomes known as the Capitalist Bomb. |
| 8-9 | June | The NATO NPG meeting in ministerial session in Ottawa notes with concern the development by the Soviet Union of long-range theatre nuclear forces (LRTNF), the SS-20, and examines options open to the Alliance for similar improvements. |
| 30 | June | SEATO is dissolved. |

| | | |
|---|---|---|
| 22 | July | Deng Xiaoping is reinstated in China as vice-chairman of the Central Committee, vice-premier of the State Council, vice-chairman of the Military Commission and chief of the General Staff of the People's Liberation Army, effectively making him the leader of the Chinese Communist Party and Government. |
| 23+25 | September | The US and the USSR agree to continue to abide by the terms of the SALT I interim agreement, which is to officially expire on 3 October 1977, even though a SALT II agreement has not yet been reached. |
| 4 | October | The first CSCE follow-up meeting starts in Belgrade. |
| 11-12 | October | At the first meeting of the NATO High-Level Group, the West Germans demand that the Americans adjust their negotiating position in the SALT II talks in order to allow for the deployment of cruise missiles. The Americans refuse. |
| 28 | October | In a speech to the International Institute for Strategic Studies in London, German Chancellor Helmut Schmidt responds to the American refusal to remove cruise missiles as a bargaining chip. He says that, "Strategic arms limitations confined to the United States and the Soviet Union will inevitably impair the security of the West European members of the Alliance vis-à-vis Soviet military superiority in Europe if we do not succeed in removing the disparities of military power parallel to the SALT negotiations." Crucially, the British agree with him. They, too, want a counter to the SS-20. |
| | December | The Soviet Union deploys the SS-20 in Eastern Europe and the Eastern republics of the USSR. East-West relations take a decidedly chilly turn. West-West relations are not much better. |

| At a Glance – Major Events and Themes | |
|---|---|
| | **Plans to deploy neutron bomb shelved** |
| | **US Secretary of Defense Donald Rumsfeld states in his annual report that attempts to control nuclear war would be little more than an attempt to stave off disaster. The same report also recommends the deployment of cruise missiles as a vital component in the Western arsenal** |
| | **UN General Assembly Special Session on Disarmament takes place** |
| | **The European Monetary System is created** |
| | **NATO Long-Term Defence Programme launched** |
| | **EEC forms Three Wise Men Committee on institutional efficiency** |
| | **Vietnam invades Cambodia** |
| | **US announces normalisation of its relationship with China** |

# 1978

| Day | Month | Event |
|---|---|---|
| | January | In response to the Soviet deployment of the SS-20, the NATO HLG suggests the need for an "evolutionary upward adjustment" in NATO LRTNF. |
| 9 | March | The first CSCE follow-up meeting ends. |
| 14/15 | March | Israel invades Lebanon following an attack on the Tel Aviv-Haifa road that killed 37 people and for which the Palestinian Liberation Organisation (PLO), based in Lebanon, claims responsibility. |
| 19 | March | The UN Security Council calls for an Israeli ceasefire and withdrawal from Lebanon. The UN Interim Force in Lebanon (UNIFIL) is established and mandated to create a buffer zone in southern Lebanon. |
| 7 | April | The Americans are forced to shelve plans for the deployment of an enhanced radiation weapon, or neutron bomb, due to intense public pressure in Western Europe, which started with the article in "The Washington Post" on 6 June 1977. The decision to withdraw it makes the Soviets believe that they can manipulate Western public opinion to their own advantage given the inability of Western governments to lead in the face of popular criticism. |
| 18-19 | April | At a ministerial meeting of NATO's NPG at Frederikshavn in Denmark, the ministers note with deep concern the growth in Soviet LRTNF (SS-20s) with multiple warheads and confirm the importance of NATO modernisation in this field. |
| 18-19 | May | NATO ministers meeting at the DPC in Brussels approve improvements to NATO forces in certain priority areas and give the go-ahead to submitting the LTDP to heads of state and government. |

| | | |
|---|---|---|
| 23-1 | May-July | The UN General Assembly Special Session on Disarmament takes place. It achieves consensus on a Final Document laying down basic objectives on disarmament, arms control and non-proliferation and giving priority in disarmament negotiations to "nuclear weapons; other weapons of mass destruction, including any which may be deemed to be excessively injurious or to have indiscriminate effects; and reduction of armed forces". The session also creates the Committee on Disarmament, later called the Conference on Disarmament. |
| 30-31 | May | At the North Atlantic Council, heads of state and government give the go-ahead to the LTDP. |
| | June | Israel withdraws from Lebanon under intense US pressure. The UN peacekeeping force UNIFIL can now fulfil its mandate. |
| 20 | August | "The Economist" writes: "Some Europeans have always doubted whether the Americans would fight a nuclear war for Europe; and even the trusters are beginning to think that what might have been true when the United States had a commanding lead is not necessarily true now." |
| | August | US President Carter accepts an interagency study group report on LRTNF and opts for an "evolutionary upward adjustment", which requires the deployment of cruise and Pershing 2 missiles. |
| 17 | September | At Camp David in the US, President Anwar Al-Sadat of Egypt and Prime Minister Menachem Begin of Israel sign the Camp David Accords, a framework for the conclusion of a peace treaty between Egypt and Israel within three months. |
| 19 | November | NATO launches its third Alliance military communications satellite. |
| 5 | December | The Brussels meeting of the European Council instructs Barend Biesheuvel (the Netherlands), Edmund Dell (United Kingdom) and Robert Marjolin (France) to prepare a report on the efficient operation of the EEC's institutions. The committee becomes known as the Three Wise Men. |
| 7-8 | December | At the NAC, the go-ahead is given for the purchase of the American AWACS (airborne warning and control system) aircraft. Based upon the airframe of the venerable Boeing 707, the Alliance agrees to purchase 18 of these aircraft, which are to be registered in Luxembourg. |
| 15 | December | The US announces the transfer of diplomatic recognition from Taipei to Beijing (as of 1 January 1979), which is now under the pragmatic leadership of Deng Xiaoping. His brand of communism calls for "modernisation", which requires opening up the Chinese giant to the West. |
| 25 | December | Vietnam invades Cambodia in an attempt to put an end to the regime of Pol Pot and his Khmer Rouge, who are believed to have massacred some 7 million people as part of their attempt to return the country to what they call Year Zero. |

| | |
|---|---|
| **At a Glance – Major Events and Themes** | **Guadeloupe Summit of Western leaders** |
| | **Shah or Iran toppled; Ayatollah Khomeini seizes power** |
| | **China invades Vietnam** |
| | **Margaret Thatcher elected prime minister of the United Kingdom** |
| | **Relations between the superpowers worsen, *détente* falters, and the so-called second Cold War begins** |
| | **First elections to the European Parliament held** |
| | **SALT II Treaty signed** |
| | **Agreement reached within NATO on the deployment of cruise and Pershing 2 missiles in Europe; 1983 set as year of deployment** |
| | **US Embassy seized in Tehran; hostage crisis begins** |
| | **Three Wise Men Report completed** |
| | **NATO's dual-track decision on the deployment of IRBMs** |
| | **USSR invades Afghanistan** |
| | **US and Western Europeans split over their reaction to Soviet invasion of Afghanistan** |
| | **First European Ariane rocket launched** |

## 1979

| Day | Month | Event |
|---|---|---|
| 1 | January | The US and China formally normalise their diplomatic relations. |
| 5-7 | January | At the Guadeloupe Summit of Western leaders, the Americans adopt a "get tough" policy in the wake of the neutron-bomb fiasco. Ironically, it is now West German leaders who are facing an embarrassing climbdown in the face of strong public opinion against the stationing of nuclear weapons on German soil. However, Carter and his national security advisor, Zbigniew Brzezinski, insist that the Germans take Pershing 2 and cruise missiles on their territory, even though they no longer have the political strength to force the Germans to accept such a demand. |
| 16 | January | Shah Mohammed Reza Pahlevi is forced to leave Iran, America's major client state in the Middle East. Ill with cancer, the Shah has led an increasingly oppressive regime through the use of his secret police, SAVAK. Led by the octogenarian Ayatollah Ruhallah Musavi Khomeini, Islamic fundamentalists seize power, and the US becomes the Great Satan. Carter's decision to allow the Shah into the US for medical treatment only serves to exacerbate the difficulties in relations between Washington and Tehran, and thus the very cornerstone of US Middle East policy is removed. |

| | | |
|---|---|---|
| 17 | February | China invades Vietnam to punish the latter for its invasion of Cambodia, which it regards as a client state. |
| | March | Israel and Egypt sign a peace agreement. Israel hands back the Sinai to Egypt. |
| 11 | April | NATO creates a Special Group to examine the implications involved in the escalation of LRTNF. |
| 3 | May | Representing the start of a steady shift to the political right amongst all the major NATO Powers, Margaret Thatcher is elected prime minister of the United Kingdom in what is a landslide victory for the Conservative Party over the ruling Labour Party. |
| 30-31 | May | The North Atlantic Council meets in Washington to celebrate the 30th anniversary of the signing of the North Atlantic Treaty, which brought NATO into being. As it does so, relations between East and West are once again deteriorating, *détente* falters and the stage is set for the second Cold War. |
| 1 | June | US General Bernard Rogers is appointed SACEUR. |
| 7-10 | June | The first elections take place to the recently created EP, based in Strasbourg, France. To supporters of European integration, this event marks the start of a genuine move in that direction. |
| 18 | June | The SALT II Treaty is signed. If it were to have been ratified by the US Congress, the treaty would have meant the first actual cut in strategic nuclear weapons on both sides and stabilisation at a lower level of nuclear balance. However, the signing itself takes place in a declining strategic environment, and ratification is to be overtaken by other events. |
| | September | Former US Secretary of State Henry Kissinger tells Western Europeans to stop being unrealistic about the theoretical use of the American strategic nuclear deterrent in their defence. It would never happen. The utterance by such a senior US statesman at this sensitive time in East-West relations only serves to deepen mistrust in what becomes known as the West-West relationship. |
| | September | Spain indicates a willingness to join NATO. |
| 4 | November | Following President Carter's decision to allow the former Shah of Iran into the US for cancer treatment, anti-American demonstrations orchestrated by the new Islamic regime in Tehran culminate in the seizing of the US Embassy and the taking of hostages. |

| | | |
|---|---|---|
| 13-14 | November | Based on a report by the High-Level Group, a meeting of the NPG agrees to deploy 464 cruise missiles and 108 Pershing 2s in Europe by the end of 1983. All the Pershing 2s are to be deployed in West Germany; of the 464 cruise missiles, 160 are destined for the UK, 96 for Italy, and 48 to each of Belgium and the Netherlands. The NPG also reaffirms "the need for arms control to be pursued in parallel". |
| 29-30 | November | *ESDP.* The Three Wise Men formally present their 100-page "Report on European Institutions" to a European Council meeting in Dublin. The key passages with regard to EPC are as follows: "We have been asked to report on the adjustments to the machinery and procedures of the institutions which are required for the proper operation of the Communities, and for progress towards European Union. ... An analysis of the reasons for concern – the failures, omissions and inadequacies in Community performance – will show that their deeper causes are not mechanical or procedural. ... More important were the political and economic strains that discouraged initiative and limited resources, and the lack of clear guidelines for advance such as existed at an earlier stage. ... In these conditions, the role of the machinery and institutional procedures is a strictly secondary one." The report suggests that the Council must have its workload reduced to be able to concentrate on the truly political (as opposed to technical) issues. If subsidiary bodies are to take over some responsibility for decision-making, however, this will require more use of QMV. The report recommends that: "In all cases where the Treaty does not impose unanimity, and very important interests are not involved for any State, voting should be the normal practice after an appropriate but limited effort for consensus has been made. ... Each State must remain the judge of where its very important interests lie." |
| 11-12 | December | The NATO Defence Planning Committee (ministerial meeting) adopts its Force Plan for the five-year period 1980-1984. |
| 12 | December | A special meeting of NATO foreign and defence ministers agrees that, unless the Soviet Union withdraws its SS-20 IRBMs from Central and Eastern Europe, the Alliance will deploy counterforces in the form of Tomahawk cruise missiles and Pershing 2 IRBMs in December 1983. However, in what becomes known as the dual-track decision, the more cautious members of the Alliance, such as the Netherlands, Belgium and Germany, demand greater effort from the Americans to achieve an arms-control agreement with the Soviet Union over Euromissiles. |
| 15 | December | "The Economist" writes: "In recent months, the growing Soviet nuclear superiority in Europe has posed NATO with one of its greatest challenges yet, both from the Russians and from those West Europeans who are reluctant to face up to the need to restore the balance." |

| | | |
|---|---|---|
| 24 | December | The first Ariane rocket launcher places a satellite into Earth's orbit, and the ESA (which does not yet exist formally, as its founding treaty has not yet entered into force) under French leadership joins the space club. Between 24 December 1979 and 22 February 1986, 11 vehicles in total are launched, nine of which are successful. |
| 27 | December | The Soviet Union invades Afghanistan, claiming to do so at the request of a fellow Communist regime in Kabul. In reality, it is alarmed by the spread of Islamic fundamentalism on the doorstep of its volatile southern republics, and the regime in Kabul is a puppet. As a result, the second Cold War begins as the West attacks the Soviets for blatant adventurism and aggression and commences to assist the resistance forces, known as the Mujahadeen, in Afghanistan. |
| | December | The United States and the Western Europeans react differently to the Soviet invasion of Afghanistan. The Americans see it as the end of *détente*, whereas the Western Europeans see no reason why such a policy should not continue. |

Part 5

# COUNTDOWN TO FREEDOM

# 1980 -1989

| At a Glance – Major Events and Themes | |
|---|---|
| | **US Senate suspends consideration of SALT II** |
| | **The Carter Doctrine is declared** |
| | **Marshall Tito dies in Yugoslavia** |
| | **Presidential Doctrine 59 on the build-up of US forces** |
| | **The Gdansk Agreement and the founding of Solidarnosc** |
| | **Military coup in Turkey** |
| | **Iraq attacks Iran** |
| | **Ronald Reagan elected president of the United States** |
| | **The Madrid Conference on Security and Co-operation in Europe opens** |
| | **The Luxembourg European Council** |

# 1980

| Day | Month | Event |
|---|---|---|
| 3 | January | In the wake of the Soviet invasion of Afghanistan, the US Senate suspends consideration of SALT II as the Carter administration withdraws. With the twin decisions of the West to deploy LRTNF in Europe and the Soviets to invade Afghanistan, the SALT phase of arms control is effectively dead and *détente* along with it. |
| 15 | January | The EEC foreign ministers attack the Soviet Union for invading Afghanistan. In a strongly worded statement, they say that, "the nine Ministers have re-affirmed their grave concern with regard to the crisis created by the military intervention of the Soviet Union in Afghanistan, which represents a serious violation of the principles of international relations enshrined in the Charter of the United Nations". |
| 23 | January | President Carter enunciates the Carter Doctrine, which commits the US to adopting a policy of confrontation and containment with the USSR but reaffirms the aspiration for *détente*. |
| 24 | January | NATO creates a new Special Consultative Group to examine the limitations of all LRTNF and other TNF weapons systems as military tools. |
| | April | As a result of domestic opposition, the Belgian Government again postpones its announcement of the base for the deployment of cruise missiles that it is to accept in 1983. |
| 4 | May | Yugoslav leader Marshal Josip Broz Tito dies in Belgrade, and Yugoslavia begins its long slow drift towards war. |
| | June | The UK announces sites for the deployment of the cruise missiles that it will accept in 1983. |

| | | |
|---|---|---|
| | June | The Soviet Union announces that it is ready for bilateral negotiations with the US over the question of LRTNF. |
| 19-3 | July-August | The Moscow Olympics take place. The Americans boycott the Games, but the Western Europeans participate. |
| 25 | July | President Carter issues Presidential Directive 59 (PD-59), which orders a major build-up in American military capability with a focus on the development of a rapid deployment force and an American capability to intervene successfully in two wars anywhere in the world simultaneously. The Soviet invasion of Afghanistan is used as the pretext for the decision when it becomes public knowledge the following month. |
| | July | At the invitation of Altiero Spinelli, founder of the European Federalist Movement, former commissioner, and member of the European Parliament (MEP), a group of nine MEPs meet in Strasbourg to discuss ways to reform the European institutions. |
| | August | As the superpower relationship freezes, the people in Eastern Europe take action. As part of the so-called Gdansk Agreement, the independent trade union Solidarnosc (Solidarity) is formed under the leadership of a charismatic shipyard worker, Lech Walesa. Strikes are crippling the Polish economy, and the Communist Government in Warsaw decides to attempt to co-habit with this new political force. Moscow and the Red Army look on nervously. |
| 12 | September | A military coup takes place in Turkey. |
| 22 | September | In an old-fashioned piece of opportunistic power politics, President Saddam Hussein Al-Majit Al-Tikriti of Iraq orders his troops to attack Iran. |
| | September | The Netherlands announces that it is unable to comply with the NATO decision of 1977 to increase defence expenditure by a year-on-year average of 3%. |
| 20 | October | Following a break of some six years, Greece is reintegrated into the NATO command structure after Turkey lifts its veto. |
| 30 | October | Having been ratified by all 10 members of ESRO and ELDO, the convention establishing ESA enters into force. ESA now legally replaces ESRO and ELDO. |
| 4 | November | Ronald Reagan is elected president of the United States in a landslide victory. After the victory of Thatcher in Britain, the New Right has its greatest moment with the capture of the White House. Reagan vows to continue the decision of PD-59 to further build up US forces to combat the Soviet Union. |
| 11 | November | The Madrid Conference on Security and Co-operation in Europe (the second CSCE follow-up meeting) opens with the nine EEC countries having adopted a common position through the machinery of EPC. |

| | | |
|---|---|---|
| | November | Belgium is still unable to decide whether or not to accept cruise missiles on its territory. |
| 1-2 | December | *ESDP.* At the European Council in Luxembourg, it is agreed that Europe must make a greater contribution to the efforts to ensure global peace, particularly within the context of East-West relations. To that end, the Council issues a *communiqué* that states: "In the face of the disquiet caused by developments in the international situation, the European Council is conscious of the responsibilities devolving upon Europe. The Council considers that Europe's experience and resources make it one of the essential factors of equilibrium and peace in the world. It is in the context of the solidarity which unites a strong America and a Europe confident of itself and of its role that dialogue and co-ordination between them will best serve the cause of peace and freedom. The European Council will therefore ensure that Europe acquires greater cohesion and that its voice is heard." |

| At a Glance – Major Events and Themes | |
|---|---|
| | **Greece joins the EEC** |
| | **Bonn-Rome initiative** |
| | **François Mitterrand elected French president** |
| | **London Report on EPC** |
| | **Spain applies to join NATO** |
| | **The Draft European Act** |
| | **Talks begin on intermediate nuclear forces** |
| | **Martial law imposed in Poland** |

# 1981

| Day | Month | Event |
|---|---|---|
| 1 | January | Greece joins the EEC. The Nine become the Ten. |
| 20 | January | Ronald Reagan becomes president of the United States. He appoints General Alexander Haig, Jr. (former NATO SACEUR), as secretary of state and Caspar Weinberger as secretary of defense. Weinberger, in turn, appoints Fred Ikle as under-secretary for policy and Richard Perle as assistant secretary for international policy. With backgrounds in the RAND Corporation, these men are well-known for their anti-Soviet fervour. Furthermore, Richard Allen, national security advisor, and Richard Pipes, on the NSC staff, are also regarded as hawks on this matter. |
| | January | *ESDP.* In an effort to revitalise the concept of European Union, Hans-Dietrich Genscher, the German foreign minister, and his Italian counterpart, Emilio Colombo, suggest strengthening the political and security aspects of the Community in what becomes known as the Bonn-Rome initiative. |
| 23-24 | February | Lt-Col Antonio Tejero and 200 Guardia Civil storm the Spanish Parliament, which is about to elect a new prime minister. At the same time, General Miláns del Bosch declares a state of emergency, and army tanks take to the streets of Valencia. After several hours, King Juan Carlos makes a televised speech, demanding that Spain's democratic process continue peacefully. The hostage-takers surrender without bloodshed some hours later. |
| | February | The Soviet Union proposes a moratorium on the deployment of LRTNF in Europe. However, such a moratorium would leave the Soviet Union with a distinct advantage. |
| 28-3 | February – March | The 26th congress of the CPSU reaffirms Soviet commitment to *détente* in the wake of the invasion of Afghanistan and calls upon the US to reciprocate. |
| 9 | May | In an address at Syracuse University, US Secretary of State Haig says that, "the task ahead for this vital decade is the management of global Soviet power". |

| | | |
|---|---|---|
| 4-5 | May | At the North Atlantic Council meeting in Rome, Western Allies reject the Soviet proposal for a moratorium on the deployment of LRTNF in Europe. |
| 10 | May | François Mitterrand is elected president of France. |
| | July | The EP sets up an Institutional Affairs Committee to draw up a plan for amending the existing treaties. Spinelli, who started the parliamentary debate on relaunching the European institutions in July 1980, is the co-ordinating rapporteur. |
| | August | Italy takes a decision to deploy cruise missiles and names its chosen sites. The Netherlands is still unable to make such a decision. |
| 13 | October | *ESDP.* The third report (the London Report) on EPC is issued. It is a reaction to the EC's poor collective response to several crises in the 1970s. Member states recognise the usefulness of the Commission's involvement in EPC at all levels, indicating a step beyond intergovernmentalism. The report also broadens the EPC mechanism to include "political aspects of security" and reinforces the adjustment of policies among member states by a crisis mechanism. |
| 19 | October | US President Reagan approves National Security Decision Directive 13 on Nuclear Weapons Employment Policy. It contains a return to a strong counterforce strategy in vision of an extended nuclear war. |
| | October | Spain makes a formal application to join NATO. |
| 6-12 | November | *ESDP.* The German and Italian Governments write to the other EEC member states to present a draft European Act that includes both a draft declaration on economic integration and proposals in the political and security fields. |
| 19 | November | Genscher and Colombo present their draft European Act to the EP. The document proposes to extend the EC's powers into new areas, including foreign policy, defence and justice, as well as a revival of QMV. |
| 21 | November | In Amsterdam, 400,000 people demonstrate against cruise missiles in Europe. |
| | November | After a break of some two years, the Reagan administration begins negotiations with the Soviet Union over theatre nuclear forces in Europe. The so-called intermediate nuclear forces (INF) talks have been forced upon the Americans by nervous Western European Allies who are facing hostile public opinion in the political vacuum that has been created between the dual-track decision of December 1979 and the aggressive rhetoric and negotiating inaction of the Reagan White House. |
| | November | The Dutch Government again postpones a decision on the deployment of cruise missiles upon its territory. |

| | | |
|---|---|---|
| 10-11 | December | NATO ministers reaffirm their commitment to deploy new LRTNF missiles in Western Europe in 1983 but also reaffirm their commitment to arms control. |
| 13 | December | In Poland, General Wojciech Jaruzelski stages what is in effect a military coup. He imposes martial law and suppresses the independent trade union Solidarnosc. The United States and Western Europe react with differing degrees of condemnation. The Europeans, however, remain keen to continue with a policy of *détente*. |
| | December | In a Soviet-inspired attempt to fuel West German public opposition against the proposed deployments of cruise and Pershing 2 missiles, discussions take place between the two Germanys over the issue of NATO deployment. |

| At a Glance – Major Events and Themes | |
|---|---|
| | **US presents Zero Option at INF talks in Geneva** |
| | **Falkland Islands conflict** |
| | **Reagan administration approves National Security Decision Directive 32 on US National Security Strategy** |
| | **Spain joins NATO** |
| | **George P. Shultz becomes US secretary of state** |
| | **START talks begin** |
| | **Helmut Kohl elected West German chancellor** |
| | **Brezhnev dies, Andropov succeeds** |
| | **US National Security Decision Directive 75** |

## 1982

| Day | Month | Event |
|---|---|---|
| 2 | February | The Americans provide a first draft for discussion at the INF talks in Geneva. In what becomes known as the Zero Option, the director of the State Department Bureau of Political-Military Affairs, Richard Perle, calls this a "simple, straightforward US approach". It proposes that the Soviets withdraw all SS-20s from the European side of the Urals in return for which the US would not deploy cruise and Pershing 2 missiles. |
| 4 | February | The Soviets table counterproposals at Geneva that demand compensation for existing British and French nuclear systems and the withdrawal of the American FBS in Western Europe if the USSR is to withdraw SS-20s from Eastern Europe and the European portion of the USSR. |
| 10 | February | The Soviet plan at the INF talks in Geneva is categorically rejected by the US. The objections cited are essentially three-fold: first, the Americans claim that by including French and British systems the Russians are not accepting the principle of equality between the superpowers; second, the Soviet proposals would allow the USSR to continue to replace the ageing SS-4 and SS-5 missiles with the SS-20; third, the USSR is counting launchers rather than warheads, so the actual threat to Western Europe would hardly diminish. |
| 2 | April | Argentina invades the Falkland Islands / Islas Malvinas and South Georgia, British dependent territories. The UK vows to recapture them. However, Foreign Secretary Lord Carrington resigns over the failure of the Foreign Office to foresee the invasion. The UK rapidly establishes a task force for the capture of the Falklands but has to withdraw some of NATO's best units for the mission. |
| 10 | April | The EEC adopts a series of measures against Argentina for its invasion of the Falkland Islands in solidarity with the United Kingdom. These include the banning of all Argentine imports into the Community. |

| | | |
|---|---|---|
| 5 | May | NATO publishes an official document on force comparison with the Warsaw Treaty Organisation that paints the Western Alliance as being in an alarmingly weak and vulnerable position. |
| 20 | May | The Reagan administration approves a new US National Security Strategy (National Security Decision Directive 32). It reflects American attempts to move away from MAD towards a a strategic posture aimed at fighting and winning a nuclear war. This not only greatly concerns the Western Europeans but finds an ironic echo in the thinking of the Soviet first deputy defence minister and chief of the General Staff, Marshal Nikolai Ogarkov, and his war-waging concept known as *proval blitzkriga*. Even more ironically, the Ogarkov view comes after the Soviet Union has modified its military doctrine and renounced superiority and belief in the winnability of a war in the nuclear age. |
| 30 | May | *ESDI.* At a special meeting of the NATO Eurogroup, Argentina is condemned for its attack on the Falkland Islands. |
| | May | Spain joins NATO. |
| 6 | June | Israel invides southern Lebanon again. The PLO leaves its base in the Lebanese capital Beirut. |
| 14 | June | The British retake Port Stanley after the surrender of all Argentine forces on the Falkland Islands. The longest sea-borne invasion in history is successful, and British military and political standing in the world are undoubtedly enhanced. |
| 25 | June | Alexander Haig is replaced by George P. Shultz as secretary of state. With a background in big business, Shultz is regarded as more pragmatic in his attitude towards relations with the Soviet Union than his predecessor. |
| 29 | June | The Strategic Arms Reduction Talks (START) commence. The objective is to follow up where the abortive SALT II talks left off by going for actual reductions in the nuclear arsenals of the two superpowers. However, there is no great enthusiasm within the US administration for the talks. The US believes it has been forced into discussions by Western European concern over the renewed arms race. |
| | September | Israeli troops march into West Beirut. |
| 1 | October | Helmut Kohl is elected chancellor of the FRG. |

| | | |
|---|---|---|
| 10 | November | Leonid Brezhnev dies. In power in the Soviet Union since the overthrow of Khrushchev in 1964, his regime has become stagnant and corrupt and his foreign policy all but static. He is succeeded as general secretary of the CPSU by a former head of the KGB, Yuri Andropov, who is reputed to have some reform credentials, although he is still a party disciplinarian. |
| | December | President Reagan finally codifies US policy towards the USSR in National Security Decision Directive 75 (NSDD-75). The directive is a compromise between the ideological-confrontational tendency of the NSC staff and civilian leadership in the Pentagon and the pragmatic geopolitical tendency represented by Shultz and the professionals in the Department of State. The directive's main thrust is pragmatic. It establishes three long-term objectives:<br>a) To contain Soviet expansion and to moderate Soviet international behaviour;<br>b) To encourage, by the limited means at the disposal of the United States, change in the Soviet system towards greater liberalism over time; and<br>c) To negotiate agreements that are in the interests of the United States. |

| | |
|---|---|
| **At a Glance – Major Events and Themes** | **Reagan calls the USSR "the evil empire" and "the focus of evil in the modern world"** |
| | **Strategic Defense Initiative (Star Wars) launched** |
| | **The Solemn Declaration on European Union leads to the birth of a Common Foreign and Security Policy** |
| | **South Korean Airlines Boeing 747 (KAL 007) shot down** |
| | **Deployment of cruise and Pershing 2 missiles begins in Europe** |

# 1983

| Day | Month | Event |
|---|---|---|
| 8 | March | At a meeting of Evangelicals in Orlando, Florida, US President Reagan calls the Soviet Union the "evil empire" and states that, "those who live in that totalitarian darkness ... are the focus of evil in the modern world". |
| 23 | March | President Reagan announces in an address to the US on national television that he is backing an initiative that will be designed to render ICBMs obsolete through the deployment of a futuristic space-based defence system. Known officially as the Strategic Defense Initiative (SDI), it becomes known colloquially as Star Wars. The Soviets complain on the grounds that the testing and deployment of such a system would constitute a clear breach of the 1972 Anti-Ballistic Missile Treaty. The original US negotiating team for the ABM agree with the USSR. |
| 16 | June | The sixth successful launch of the ESA's Ariane rocket takes place. |
| 19 | June | *ESDP.* The heads of state or government of the 10 EEC member states, "resolved to continue the work begun on the basis of the Treaties of Paris and Rome and to create a united Europe, which is more than ever necessary in order to meet the dangers of the world situation, capable of assuming the responsibilities incumbent on it by virtue of its political role, its economic potential and its manifold links with other peoples" and "convinced that, by speaking with a single voice in foreign policy, including political aspects of security, Europe can contribute to the preservation of peace", issue a Solemn Declaration on European Union, also called the Stuttgart Declaration. The concept of a Common Foreign and Security Policy (CFSP) is born. More generally, the document, which reflects the 1982 draft European Act, presages the transformation of the EC into the European Union (EU) by beginning to curtail the national right of veto, increasing the powers of the EP, advancing the single market and urging greater co-operation in many fields. |

| | | |
|---|---|---|
| 28 | June | In a speech to a meeting of leaders of the CPSU, General Secretary Andropov characterises the current situation in East-West relations as "marked by confrontation, unprecedented in the entire post-war period by its intensity and sharpness, of two diametrically opposite world outlooks, two political courses: socialism and imperialism". |
| 31-1 | August-September | A South Korean Boeing 747 civilian airliner, flight number KAL 007, is shot down over Sakhalin Island after passing directly over Soviet submarine construction pens at Petropavlovsk. The West immediately accuses the USSR of a barbaric act and states that the plane was simply off course. The Soviets claim that it was challenged many times and failed to respond and was therefore shot down for spying on Soviet naval facilities. Two hundred sixty-nine people are killed, including a member of the US House of Representatives. No satisfactory answer has ever been forthcoming from either side for what happened that night. The second Cold War takes a dangerous turn for the worse. |
| 9 | September | The CSCE Madrid Conference (second follow-up meeting) concludes. |
| 28 | September | In a response to US accusations over the KAL 007 disaster, General Secretary Andropov attacks US policy as a "militarist course that represents a serious threat to peace. Its essence is to try to ensure a dominating position in the world for the United States of America without regard for the interests of other states and peoples." However, he reaffirms the Soviet policy of "peaceful co-existence". |
| 23 | October | Two hundred forty-one US marines and 56 French troops are killed in two bomb attacks on military headquarters in Beirut, Lebanon. The suicide bombers are thought to belong to a group of Lebanese Shi'a Muslims, part of an extremist militia faction based in Syrian-occupied eastern Lebanon. |
| 23 | November | With the failure of the INF talks to make any substantial progress, 572 cruise and 108 Pershing 2 missiles (LRTNF) begin being deployed in Western Europe. The Soviets walk out of the INF talks in Geneva as a result. |
| 8-9 | December | At the North Atlantic Council in Brussels, Denmark and Greece dissociate themselves from the NATO decision to deploy LRTNF. |

| | |
|---|---|
| **At a Glance – Major Events and Themes** | **Reagan administration accuses the Soviet Union of violating the ABM treaty** |
| | **Andropov dies, Chernenko succeeds in Moscow** |
| | **The European Parliament approves draft treaty establishing the European Union** |
| | **Lord Carrington appointed NATO secretary general** |
| | **European Parliament approves draft treaty establishing European Union** |
| | **Rome Declaration reactivates the Western European Union** |
| | **President Reagan calls for "constructive negotiations" with the Soviet Union** |
| | **Reagan re-elected US president. Peace through Strength becomes the rallying call of the second Reagan administration** |
| | **Thatcher and Gorbachev meet** |

# 1984

| Day | Month | Event |
|---|---|---|
| 23 | January | The Reagan administration sends a report to Congress charging the Soviet Union with seven specific violations and probable violations of the ABM treaty. This is part of an attempt to persuade Congress that even if the US is breaking the ABM treaty due to SDI it is justified as a result of Soviet non-compliance. The administration's case is based on the ambiguous wording of Article 2 of the treaty and what or what does not constitute exotic technology, as well as whether, thereafter, it is treaty-specific or treaty-exempt. |
| 17 | January | A CSCE meeting on confidence- and security-building measures (CSBM) opens in Stockholm. |
| 18 | January | After walking out of INF talks in Geneva last month, Soviet Foreign Minister Gromyko meets with US Secretary of State George Shultz to discuss confidence-building measures. There is little progress. |
| 9 | February | Yuri Andropov dies of kidney failure 15 months after succeeding Leonid Brezhnev as general secretary of the CPSU. His successor is Konstantin Chernenko, an elderly contemporary of Brezhnev who is little more than a compromise placeman. He is also in ill health. It is clear that a power struggle between conservatives and reformers is taking place within the Politburo. |
| 14 | February | *ESDP.* The EP approves a draft treaty establishing the European Union, based on proposals elaborated by the Spinelli committee set up in 1981. The draft treaty aims for a balance of power between the EP and the Council of Ministers and provides for a bicameral legislature. |

| | | |
|---|---|---|
| 23 | May | First commercial launch of the ESA's Ariane rocket. |
| 25 | June | *ESDI.* Lord Carrington is appointed secretary general of NATO. His deputy is Dr. Joseph Luns of the Netherlands. |
| 29 | June | Impressed by the resolve being shown by Ronald Reagan and worried about the lack of contact with the United States in the wake of their walk-out from the INF talks in December 1983, the Soviet Union takes the unusual step of proposing negotiations on the prohibition of the militarisation of Outer Space and, once the talks begin, on a moratorium on the testing and deployment of such weapons. |
| | June | The Fountainebleau European Council decides to set up an *ad hoc* committee of the personal representatives of the heads of state and government to make proposals for improving the functioning of the Community system and of EPC. The committee's chairman is James Dooge, representative of Irish Prime Minister Farrett FitzGerald. |
| | June | Belgium announces that it will proceed with preparations for the deployment of cruise missiles on its territory. |
| | June | The Netherlands decides to postpone the deployment of cruise missiles on its territory at least until 1988. |
| 12 | August | In an interview with the "Newsday" magazine, former Secretary of State Alexander Haig admits that the US START proposal was "a non-negotiable package ... a two-faced proposal that was clearly going to fall of its own weight and did". Indeed, for the US is not prepared to accept cuts in its own build-up of counterforce capabilities comparable to the drastic reductions sought in Soviet counterforce capabilities. While the US proposals are nominally equal, they would apply unequally. For example, the proposed limit of 5,000 missile warheads for each side would involve a sizeable and equitable cut of about one-third in the arsenals of both sides. But a sub-ceiling of 2,500 warheads on land-based missiles, and further sub-limits of 210 on MX-sized ICBMs (for example, the Soviet SS-18 and SS-19 and the US MX) and of 100 on very large ICBMs (the Soviet SS-18) would mean a cut of more than one-half of Soviet ICBM warheads and two-thirds of SS-18 and SS-19 warheads, while the US could deploy additional ICBM warheads, including the then-planned 200 MX missiles. Moreover, other US strategic modernisation programmes could continue as well: Trident II sea-launched ballistic missiles, air-launched cruise missiles, submarine-launched cruise missiles, and the Pershing 2 and GLCM European-based systems. One Soviet general states on seeing the proposals: "You want to solve your vulnerability problem by making our forces vulnerable." |
| 24 | September | In a shift in US policy towards a less overtly confrontational stance, President Reagan states in an address to the UN General Assembly that, "America has repaired its strength ... we are ready for constructive negotiations with the Soviet Union." |

| | | |
|---|---|---|
| | September | In a sign of the power struggle taking place within the Soviet Union over negotiations with the United States, the powerful and hawkish chief of staff and deputy minister of defence, Marshal Nikolai Ogarkov, is removed from his posts for "unparty-like behaviour". |
| 26-27 | October | *ESDP.* On the initiative of the Belgian and French Governments, a preliminary joint meeting of the foreign and defence ministers within the WEU framework is held in Rome. The ministers agree to reactivate the organisation and adopt the Rome Declaration to this aim. The objective is to strengthen Western Europe's ability to contribute to its own defence and to enable France to play a fuller and more integrated role. The ministers decide "to hold comprehensive discussions and to seek to harmonise their views on specific conditions of security in Europe, in particular defence questions; arms control and disarmament; the effects of developments in East-West relations on the security in Europe; Europe's contribution to the strengthening of the Atlantic Alliance ...; and the development of European co-operation in the field of armaments ...." The WEU Council is henceforth to hold two meetings a year at ministerial level. The Rome Declaration is seen by some commentators as being a first step towards the WEU's becoming the defence arm of the EC. |
| | October | In a response to the Soviet initiative of 29 June to open talks on the banning of space weaponry, the US offers umbrella talks to cover a flexible combination of arms limitations on various strategic offensive and defensive arms, covering both Outer Space and nuclear weapons. |
| 6 | November | President Reagan is returned to office with another overwhelming majority. The second Reagan administration now promises to concentrate upon Peace through Strength. |
| 17 | November | Surprisingly, the Soviet Union reacts positively to the offer made by the US in October and agrees to nuclear and space talks (NST). |
| | November | *ESDI.* The IEPG meets at the ministerial level for the first time. Ministers agree to undertake a thorough review of the operational requirements of European defence procurement and to work harder to harmonise them. They also agree not to duplicate similar efforts elsewhere. The European Defence Industry Study (EDIS) is also launched at the meeting. |
| 16 | December | Mikhail Gorbachev, secretary responsible for agriculture within the Central Committee of the CPSU, and widely regarded as the next Soviet leader, visits the UK and speaks with Prime Minister Margaret Thatcher. |
| 17 | December | Thatcher tells the press: "I like Mr. Gorbachev. We can do business together." |

| At a Glance – Major Events and Themes | |
|---|---|
| | **Rogers re-appointed SACEUR** |
| | **Chernenko dies** |
| | **Gorbachev comes to power in the USSR** |
| | **Dr Hans van Eekelen appointed secretary-general of the WEU** |
| | **INF talks resume in Geneva** |
| | **The USSR announces unilateral suspension of the deployment of intermediate nuclear weapons in Europe** |
| | **Eduard Shevardnadze appointed Soviet foreign minister** |
| | **The USSR announces a unilateral moratorium on nuclear testing** |
| | **Eurofighter given the go-ahead** |
| | **Gorbachev visits Paris** |
| | **Reagan and Gorbachev meet in Geneva** |

## 1985

| Day | Month | Event |
|---|---|---|
| 7-8 | January | US Secretary of State Shultz and Soviet Foreign Minister Gromyko agree at a meeting to make progress in arms-control talks under the umbrella approach covering both nuclear-capable and space-based weapons. The Soviet Union is, however, determined to link any progress to the scrapping of the US SDI programme. |
| | January | In an address on Soviet television, Foreign Minister Gromyko tells viewers: "If the United States continues to deploy its medium-range weapons in Europe, then I must say bluntly that the situation will be made more complicated, and greatly more complicated. The fact that we proposed a freeze on these weapons is well known. Indeed, in Geneva we warned the United States quite clearly that, if it did so – if it continued with the deployment; and it was at great pains to emphasise that it had plans, and that it intended to carry out those plans – then it would put in question the talks that were due to begin in accordance with the understanding reached in Geneva. I repeat – we warned the United States about this." Gromyko also insists that, in forthcoming talks, "British and French armaments must also be taken into account. ... It would be most unjustified if the North Atlantic Alliance obtained a kind of addition, a bonus if you like, in the form of the British and French armaments. This is the crux of the disagreement in connection with the discussion of the medium-range-weapons problem." |
| | February | *ESDI.* US General Bernard Rogers is reappointed SACEUR by NATO. |

| | | |
|---|---|---|
| 10 | March | General Secretary of the CPSU Konstantin Chernenko dies after pulmonary emphysema. He is to be the last of the Brezhnevites and the sclerosis in the Soviet decision-making process that set in with the decline of Brezhnev's health in the late 1970s. Mikhail Sergeyevich Gorbachev takes power as general secretary of the CPSU. The first post-war Soviet leader not to have actually fought in World War II, Gorbachev is only 54. He is a known as a reformer. |
| 12 | March | Following the agreement between the USSR and the US on NST in November 1984, the INF talks recommence in Geneva after a delay of almost 15 months. This is the first concrete indication that there is new thinking in the Kremlin following the appointment of Gorbachev as general secretary. The Soviet Union maintains its determination to link any agreement to the scrapping of the US SDI programme. |
| 29-30 | March | The Dooge Committee, set up in 1984, presents its report. It proposes enhancing EPC by increasing adjustment of policy concerning security issues and calls for co-operation in the armaments sector. |
| 29 | May | At a reception for Italian President Bettino Craxi, Gorbachev reiterates that if the Soviet Union is to agree to a treaty on LRTNF in Europe, then it will insist on compensation for British and French warheads and the removal of cruise and Pershing 2 missiles. However, the United States has not shifted from its own position of demanding a balance between cruise and Pershing 2 missiles and SS-20s with neither British nor French weapons counted. |
| 14 | June | Belgium, France, Luxembourg and the Netherlands sign the Schengen Agreement to gradually abolish checks at their common borders. |
| 25-26 | June | The Milan European Council decides to convoke an IGC to consider the power of the institutions, the extension of Community activities to new areas and the establishment of a "genuine" internal market. |
| | June | Israel partially withdraws from Lebanon. |
| | June | *ESDI.* A further meeting of NATO's IEPG takes place in order to discuss improvements in co-operation in the area of weapons procurement in Western Europe. |
| | July | As a gesture towards the West and the INF talks, the Soviet Union announces the unilateral suspension of the deployment of nuclear weapons in Europe. |

| | | |
|---|---|---|
| 2 | July | Andrei Gromyko, the Soviet foreign minister and confidant of Molotov as far back as the Nazi-Soviet pact of August 1939, is finally relieved of responsibility for foreign policy, as Gorbachev moves to strengthen his control over its direction. Gromyko is given the decorative position of chairman of the Presidium of the Supreme Soviet. In his place, Gorbachev promotes Eduard Shevardnadze, a Georgian fellow reformer who has little experience of foreign policy. |
| 9 | July | Talks are held in the Kremlin between select members of the two committees of the Supreme Soviet on Foreign Affairs and members of Britain's House of Commons Foreign Affairs Committee. The Soviet chairman states: "To the extent that the countries of the EEC act as a political whole we are ready to seek a common language with it ... on concrete international questions." This is the first time that the Soviet side has treated the EEC as anything other than an object of its policy via the Americans and thus represents a clear shift towards treating the Western Europeans as a separate entity from the United States within the Western Alliance. |
| 16 | July | The first round of the resumed INF talks in Geneva ends with no substantial progress. The determination of the United States to avoid "linkage" between INF and SDI results in a stalemate. It is clear that the US administration is not very bothered about whether or not there is an agreement. The onus shifts to Soviet side. |
| 6 | August | The Soviet Union announces a unilateral moratorium on nuclear testing. |
| | September | *ESDI/ESDP.* Britain, Germany, Italy and Spain agree to build the European Fighter Aircraft (EFA). Work allocation is divided strictly on investment levels, with the UK and Germany leading the way. France is, at this stage, outside, as it remains committed to building a wholly French aircraft, the Rafael. |
| 2 | October | Gorbachev arrives in Paris where he stresses the Soviet Union's wish to resolve "accumulated European and world problems". |
| 3 | October | Gorbachev, in a speech to the deputies of the French *Assemblée Nationale*, makes clear that his wish to resolve foreign-policy disputes has an economic imperative. The first real suggestion that *perestroika* is driving new Soviet thinking in foreign policy is made graphically clear. |
| 3 | October | In the same speech to the French *Assemblée Nationale,* Gorbachev offers direct talks with France and Britain. France, in particular, objects to direct talks between the Soviet Union and the United States over issues that it regards as its special interest. Gorbachev lays the foundation for a later concept of the Common European |

| | | |
|---|---|---|
| | | Home and his subsequent attempts to de-couple the Americans and Western Europeans in a manner far more subtle than those employed in the past. However, he goes on to say that the Soviet Union cannot ignore British and French nuclear forces because: "This capability is growing rapidly and we can no longer close our eyes to it." |
| | October | Gorbachev offers to drop the Soviet linkage between SDI and INF if the British and French start talks with the USSR about their own nuclear systems with the USSR. |
| 19-21 | November | Gorbachev meets President Reagan in Geneva. The summit falters, as Reagan tries to convince Gorbachev of the mutual benefit to be gained from continued US research and development of the SDI system. However, both sides agree to accelerate progress towards a 50% cut in strategic nuclear forces (START) and interim agreement on LRTNF in Europe. |
| | December | *ESDI/ESDP.* In what represents a major change of policy, France agrees to participate in the EFA project if the aircraft can be redesigned to suit the requirements of the French Air Force. |

| At a Glance – Major Events and Themes | |
|---|---|
| | **Spain and Portugal join the EC** |
| | **Reagan and Gorbachev meet in Reykjavik, Iceland** |
| | **Gorbachev makes radical proposal to cut nuclear weapons** |
| | **Single European Act signed; the European Community is born with an overt foreign, security and defence element** |
| | **Switch in Soviet doctrine to defence sufficiency** |
| | **US attacks Tripoli** |
| | **Report Towards a Stronger Europe on improving the competitiveness of European defence-equipment industry presented to IEPG ministers** |

## 1986

| Day | Month | Event |
|---|---|---|
| 1 | January | Spain and Portugal join the European Communities, bringing its membership to 12. |
| 1 | January | Finland, an EFTA associate member since 1961, becomes a full member of the organisation. |
| 14 | January | Gorbachev writes to UK Prime Minister Margaret Thatcher, outlining the proposals for a cut in nuclear forces on both sides that he is to make public the following day. |
| 15 | January | Gorbachev issues a statement, probably without full Politburo backing, that the USSR and the US should "reduce by one half the nuclear weapons that can reach one another's territory". As to the remaining systems, each side would retain no more than 6,000 warheads. This would be dependent upon mutual renunciation of "the development, testing and deployment of space strike weapons". The first stage would include "the adoption and implementation of a decision on the complete elimination of medium-range missiles of the USSR and the USA in the European zone". The Soviets also include the non-transfer provision that they had consistently attempted and failed to get the Americans to accept during the SALT I and SALT II talks. "The United States should undertake not to transfer its strategic and medium-range missiles to other countries." The most innovative element, however, is the disappearance of the insistence upon compensation for existing British and French systems by suggesting that, "Great Britain and France should pledge not to build up their respective nuclear arsenals". |
| 15 | January | Western Europeans react to the Soviet proposal by suggesting that the USSR was once again trying to de-couple the US from its NATO Allies. |

| | | |
|---|---|---|
| 17 | February | *ESDP.* The Single European Act (SEA), elaborated during the IGC convoked in 1985, is signed in Luxembourg. EPC is incorporated into the treaty: "The High Contracting Parties ... shall endeavour jointly to formulate and implement a European foreign policy." They also pledge to develop "a European identity in external policy matters." The SEA contains the legal codification of EPC structures and processes, including Commission involvement in the EPC. It also creates a small EPC Secretariat. Thus, the European Community (as the EEC, ECSC and Euratom became in 1967) contains for the first time an element of security, foreign and defence policy. Although still vague, intergovernmental and, as far as security is concerned, restricted to non-military aspects, it represents an important precedent. |
| 23 | February | The US rejects the Soviet offer of 15 January. |
| | February | The United States expresses an interest in joining the consortium building the EFA. |
| 10 | March | NATO Secretary General Lord Carrington reacts to the Gorbachev proposal of 15 January and echoes British Prime Minister Margaret Thatcher by saying that Britain and France could not be expected to accept "perpetual nuclear obsolescence". |
| 16 | March | Seventy-five per cent of Swiss voters reject UN membership, largely because of fears of losing neutrality and independence. |
| 26 | March | "Izvestiya" reports that, at the 27th Congress of the CPSU, General Secretary Gorbachev made a speech redefining the Soviet concept of security away from preparedness to take the offensive to one of defence sufficiency. This is in order to meet certain preconditions for talks that the British and French have insisted upon with regard to their own nuclear forces. "Security", he declared, "can only be mutual", and Soviet military doctrine was "purely defensive". "Our country", he argued, "is in favour of keeping military capability within the limits of reasonable sufficiency". |
| 5 | April | Three people die in a bomb explosion at a disco in Berlin. A Berlin court later finds Libya co-responsible for the attack. |
| 15 | April | The US attacks the Libyan capital, Tripoli, in retaliation for what it regards as Libyan complicity in the terrorist attack in Berlin in which several Americans were killed. The NATO Allies are split over the American action, with only the UK offering full and unquestioning support. |

| | | |
|---|---|---|
| 25-26 | April | Chornobyl disaster. A testing procedure in reactor number 4 of the nuclear plant in Chernobyl, Ukraine, gets out of control. The ensuing chemical explosions blow off the reactor's heavy steel and concrete lid. Radioactive clouds are released for more than 10 days and spread over parts of Europe. The accident kills around 30 people immediately and more than 15,000 in the emergency clean-up afterwards. As a result of the high radiation levels in the surrounding 30-kilometre radius, 135,000 people have to be evacuated. Estimations of the total short- and long-term death toll of the disaster range from 15,000 to 56,000. It is estimated that a million more people become ill or suffer disability because of the disaster. |
| 4-6 | May | Group of Seven Tokyo Summit: political debate on terrorism. The EC countries' position was previously consolidated within the EPC framework and is transported into the final document: they give preference to strategies founded on diplomacy and political sanctions rather than economic sanctions or military action. |
| 22 | May | NATO's DPC rubber-stamps the US administration's decision to resume the production of chemical weapons. |
| 25 | July | President Reagan extends an invitation to General Secretary Gorbachev to visit the United States. However, Gorbachev is reluctant to go unless a deal on SDI is in the offing. |
| 19 | September | Soviet Foreign Minister Shevardnadze hands US Secretary of State George Shultz a reply to the Reagan invitation for Gorbachev to visit the US. He says that the two leaders should be personally involved in preparations for the summit. |
| 19 | September | The CSCE meeting on CSBM concludes. |
| 20 | September | To help the Americans accept the idea of a pre-summit summit, Soviet Foreign Minister Shevardnadze announces that the Soviet Union has dropped its demand that British and French nuclear forces be frozen at existing levels. |
| 11-12 | October | President Reagan and General Secretary Gorbachev meet in Reykjavik. The Soviet side surprises the US by arriving with a radical arms-control package. The Soviets suggest that, first, the two sides should both cut strategic weapons by 50% in the first five years of any agreement and then the remaining 50% in the following five. Initially, Reagan agrees to apply this proposal to all intercontinental weaponry. The Soviets then suggest the complete liquidation of US and Soviet medium-/intermediate-range missiles in Europe. However, British and French forces are to be totally excluded. The Soviets agree to freeze SS-23 short-range weapons and SS-12 (model 2) IRBMs at existing levels as a prelude to negotiations. However, the talks fail when Gorbachev links cuts to the scrapping of the US SDI programme. |

| | | |
|---|---|---|
| 21-22 | October | *ESDI.* NATO defence ministers meeting at Gleneagles Hotel in Scotland express continuing concern at the US's negotiating over their heads and agree to meet West German concerns by providing for constraints on operational-tactical missiles along with the reduction of LRTNF. However, the British and French continue to express unease over apparent US willingness to negotiate away weaponry that is peripheral to US security (LRTNF) but seem to be unprepared to negotiate on weaponry central to US security (SDI). |
| 25 | October | *ESDI.* In an article in "The Economist", French Foreign Minister André Giraud is reported as saying that the withdrawal of all American missiles from Europe "would weaken the security of Europe, especially in view of other imbalances, such as those in conventional and chemical weapons". |
| 4 | November | The third CSCE follow-up meeting opens in Vienna. |
| | December | The European Defence Industry Study (EDIS), chaired by former Dutch Defence Minister Henk Vredeling, presents its report "Towards a Stronger Europe" to IEPG ministers. The report's proposals for an improvement of the competitiveness of Europe's defence-equipment industry contain the following elements: an opening of procurement markets, promotion of mergers, the strengthening of technical capabilities, the principle of fair return, support for the development of the armaments sector in weaker countries and the establishment of an IEPG secretariat in order to ensure that Western European countries can be technical leaders. |
| | December | *ESDP.* In an address to the WEU Assembly, French Prime Minister Jacques Chirac proposes that the WEU draw up a Western European Charter of security principles. The Assembly strongly endorses this and recommends that the Council draw up such a document. |

| At a Glance - Major Events and Themes | |
|---|---|
| | **France withdraws from plans for an EFA** |
| | **Turkey applies to join the WEU** |
| | **WEU Platform on European Security Interests** |
| | **Intermediate Nuclear Forces Treaty signed** |

# 1987

| Day | Month | Event |
|---|---|---|
| | January | *ESDP.* Greece enquires about joining the WEU. |
| 8 | January | Soviet leader Gorbachev accepts defeat over his attempt at Reykjavik to link cuts in strategic and intermediate nuclear forces with the scrapping by the US of its SDI programme by stating through the TASS news agency that the INF issue could be singled out from the rest for negotiation. |
| | February | *ESDI/ESDP.* France withdraws support for the EFA due to design incompatibility with the requirements of the French Air Force. |
| 3-4 | March | The US delegation to the INF talks tables a draft INF agreement. The Soviets respond by accepting the proposal in principle and agreeing to intrusive on-site inspections, which has been one of the major stumbling blocks to progress. However, Western Europeans remain uneasy about the American proposals. To satisfy the Germans, the Americans agree to insist that Soviet short-range nuclear weapons be included within the treaty framework. The Soviets object on the grounds that the American equivalent (the ageing Pershing 1A) is not included. |
| | March | The US withdraws its interest in participating in the building of the EFA. |
| | April | Turkey makes a formal application to join the WEU. |
| | June | Karoly Grosz becomes Hungarian prime minister and begins to introduce tough economic reforms, to relax censorship legislation, to allow independent political groups and to legalise the right to strike and to demonstrate. |
| 15-17 | September | During a visit to the United States by Soviet Foreign Minister Shevardnadze, the Americans inform him that the West Germans have agreed to withdraw their objections to the inclusion of the Pershing 1A within the INF treaty to offset Soviet conventional superiority. All the "final issues of principle" are resolved. |
| | September | The North Atlantic Assembly produces a report recommending Allied participation in the US Strategic Defense Initiative. However, it is clear that any involvement will be peripheral. |

| | | |
|---|---|---|
| 27 | October | *ESDI/ESDP.* The WEU Ministerial Council adopts a Platform on European Security Interests. The document is the result of consultations following a December 1986 proposal by French Prime Minister Chirac. Recognising that "the constitution of an integrated Europe will remain incomplete as long as it does not include security and defence, [WEU foreign and defence ministers] intend therefore to develop a more cohesive European defence identity" by setting out European security conditions and criteria and the specific responsibilities of Europeans for their defence within the Atlantic Alliance after the negotiations between the United States and the USSR on the withdrawal of intermediate nuclear forces. In the platform, the WEU links its fate to the EC for the first time. |
| 4 | November | *ESDI/ESDP.* US President Reagan welcomes the WEU Platform and emphasises the unshakeable nature of the United States' commitments to the Alliance and to European security. |
| 11 | November | *ESDI/ESDP.* The NAC also welcomes the WEU Platform, which affirms "a positive identity in the field of European security within the framework of the Atlantic Alliance, conducive to the strengthening of the transatlantic partnership and of the alliance as a whole." |
| 13 | November | At the 50th French-German summit in Karlsruhe, German Federal Chancellor Kohl and French President Mitterrand announce that a joint German-French brigade will be set up shortly. |
| 8 | December | The Treaty Between the United States of America and the Union of Soviet Socialist Republics on the Elimination of Their Intermediate-Range and Shorter-Range Missiles (INF Treaty) is signed by Reagan and Gorbachev in Washington. Both parties agree to eliminate all their intermediate- and medium-range missiles and launchers within 18 months of the ratification of the treaty. This covers SS-20s, SS-4s, SS-5s, SS-12s and SS-23s on the Soviet side; Pershing 2s, Pershing 1As and GLCMs on the American side. Replacement missiles are banned. On-site inspection is provided for at all operating bases and support facilities. The treaty is for unlimited duration. |
| | December | An *Intifada* (uprising) begins in the West Bank and the Gaza Strip. The Palestinians protest with civil disobedience and riots against the Israeli occupation. |

| | |
|---|---|
| **At a Glance – Major Events and Themes** | **Withdrawal of Soviet troops from Afghanistan** |
| | **Faced with economic difficulties, the Kádár regime in Hungary, one of the most liberal in Central and Eastern Europe alongside Poland, is replaced by reform communists** |
| | **Iranian airliner shot down by US warship** |
| | **Iran-Iraq War ends** |
| | **Mikhail Gorbachev becomes head of state of the USSR** |
| | **George Bush elected US president** |
| | **Pan Am Flight 103 explodes over Scotland** |
| | **Arafat recognises Israel** |

# 1988

| Day | Month | Event |
|---|---|---|
| 22 | January | A German-French Defence and Security Council is founded. It gives the two countries' security and defence co-operation a broad institutional basis. The council is composed of the heads of state and government and the foreign and defence ministers and meets at least twice a year. The council's work is to be prepared by a council's committee, which bases itself on reports by the German-French Permanent Commission for Security and Defence. |
| 23 | March | Mikhail Gorbachev speaks in favour of more private initiative in agriculture. |
| 14 | April | Afghanistan and Pakistan sign an agreement, with the US and the USSR as guarantors, calling for the withdrawal of Soviet military forces from Afghanistan. |
| 19 | April | *ESDP.* The Council of the WEU issues a political statement voicing its grave concern at the increase in hostilities in the Persian Gulf and the need to respect the principle of free navigation, and it calls urgently for an immediate end to all mine-laying and other hostile activities against shipping in international waters. This is the first application of Article VIII.3 of the modified Brussels Treaty, which foresees that at the request of any of the High Contracting Parties the Council should be "immediately convened in order to permit them to consult with regard to any situation which may constitute a threat to peace, in whatever area this threat should arise, or a danger to economic stability." The Council consultations lead to Operation Cleansweep, which helps to clear the Gulf waters of mines, providing the first example of a joint military operation co-ordinated by the WEU. |
| 15 | May | Soviet troops begin to withdraw from Afghanistan. |

| | | |
|---|---|---|
| 23 | May | An extraordinary party congress of the Hungarian Socialist Workers' Party agrees profound changes in, and reform of, the top leadership and a separation of functions between state and party. Party head János Kádár is replaced by Karoly Grosz, who became prime minister in 1987. |
| 29 | June | At a press conference in Moscow chaired by General Secretary Gorbachev, leading Soviet politicians and economists demand major political and economic reforms in order to allow the democratisation process to proceed. |
| 3 | July | The "USS Vincennes", a US cruiser, shoots down an Iranian airliner in the Persian Gulf, killling 290 people. The US Government says the "USS Vincennes" mistook the airliner for an Iranian F-14 Tomcat in spite of being warned of its presence by a nearby British warship. |
| 3 | July | The All-Union Congress of the CPSU endorses proposals for dramatic reform of political institutions. |
| 20 | August | A ceasefire ends the Iran-Iraq War after Iran, feeling militarily isolated, offers peace negotiations to Iraq. |
| | September | The Hungarian Democratic Forum, an umbrella movement for opposition groups, is formed. |
| 1 | October | Gorbachev is elected chairman of the Supreme Soviet and thus head of state. |
| 8 | November | George Bush is elected US president. |
| 9 | November | *ESDP.* IEPG ministers accept the Action Plan on a Stepwise Development of a European Armaments Market, which they commissioned in 1987. The action plan (which is based on the Vredeling Report of 1986, "Towards a Stronger Europe") proposes an opening of armament markets to competition, the principle of *juste retour*, technical transfers, more research and developement, and special assistance for countries with developing defence industries. Funding for community projects is to come from national budgets. Ministers also agree to set up a small IEPG secretariat in Lisbon. |
| 14 | November | *ESDP.* Spain and Portugal sign the accession protocol to the WEU. |
| 1 | December | The Supreme Soviet of the USSR approves the establishment of a new legislative body, the Congress of People's Deputies. |
| 21 | December | Two hundred seventy people are killed as an on-board bomb causes Pan Am Flight 103 to explode over Lockerbie, Scotland. The US and UK suspect Palestinian or Iranian involvement, the former possibly with Lebanese support. |
| | December | Palestinian leader Arafat recognises the State of Israel and condemns terrorism in all its forms. |

| At a Glance – Major Events and Themes | |
|---|---|
| | **Solidarnosc legalised in Poland** |
| | **Slobodan Milosevic elected president of Serbia** |
| | **Tiananmen Square massacre** |
| | **Reformist governments are elected in Poland and in Czechoslovakia** |
| | **Gorbachev enunciates the Sinatra Doctrine** |
| | **UTA DC-10 explodes over Sahara Desert** |
| | **The Berlin Wall falls** |
| | **Czechoslovakia's Velvet Revolution** |
| | **Execution of Ceausescu in Romania** |
| | **Democratic changes begin in Bulgaria** |

## 1989

| Day | Month | Event |
|---|---|---|
| 19 | January | The CSCE follow-up meeting in Vienna closes. |
| 20 | January | Bush is inaugurated as US president. Brent Snowcroft becomes national security advisor. |
| 25 | January | James Baker III becomes US secretary of state. |
| 15 | February | The last Soviet troops leave Afghanistan. |
| 24 | February | The Hungarian Socialist Workers' Party renounces its constitutionally based claim to leadership. |
| 9 | March | The US Senate rejects President Bush's first nomination for the post of secretary of defense, John Tower. |
| 10 | March | US President Bush nominates Richard B. (Dick) Cheney as secretary of defense. |
| 17 | March | Dick Cheney becomes US secretary of defense. |
| 26 | March | For the first time, Soviet citizens can choose from among several candidates in elections to the first Congress of Soviet People's Deputies. Many reformist candidates are elected. |
| 17 | April | The Polish trade union and opposition movement Solidarnosc is legalised and allowed to run for elections. |
| 19 | April | Tens of thousands of Chinese students start protests for democracy and freedom on Beijing's Tiananmen Square. The protests go on for weeks, and the number of demonstrators swells to over a million, gaining large support also from urban workers. |
| 8 | May | Slobodan Milosevic is elected president of Serbia by the National Assembly. |

| | | |
|---|---|---|
| 12 | May | Picking up on an idea that US President Eisenhower had in 1955, President George Bush makes another Open Skies proposal, which is to involve NATO and Warsaw Pact Allies. Open Skies is meant to serve as a confidence-building tool, lead to increased transparency and be used for the surveillance of arms-control and disarmament agreements, and possibly later on for crisis managment and environmental protection. The proposal is also a test by the US president of how serious the Soviet Union is about political reforms. Unlike in 1955, this time the US proposal receives a positive response from the Soviet Union. |
| 15 | May | *ESDP.* Dr Hans van Eekelen is appointed secretary-general of WEU. His appointment is an interesting one, for he is a former Dutch minister of defence and an expert on European defence, suggesting that the member states of the WEU are serious about upgrading the status of the organisation. |
| 15-18 | May | President of the Supreme Soviet and General Secretary of the Central Committee of the CPSU Gorbachev pays an official visit to China and meets Deng Xiaopeng. The visit brings about formal restoration of party-to-party relations and completes a process of normalisation of the relationship between the two countries that began with Gorbachev's coming to power. |
| 20 | May | Martial law is declared by Chinese leaders. The demonstrations are widely covered by the international media, which is present due to Gorbachev's visit. |
| 25 | May | Gorbachev is elected state president with special powers by the Congress of Soviet People's Deputies. |
| 29-30 | May | *ESDI.* NATO agrees to a Comprehensive Concept of Arms Control and Disarmament. |
| | May | Hungary opens its borders to Austria. |
| 4 | June | Chinese leaders decide to use force to end protests. Thousands are killed. The international image of China is seriously damaged. |
| 5 | June | Elections in Poland bring a resounding victory for the Solidarnosc movement. This inspires a succession of mostly peaceful anti-communist revolutions in Eastern Europe. |
| 27 | June | *ESDI.* At an IEPG meeting in Estoril, Portugal, the European Co-operation for the Long Term in Defence (EUCLID), endowed with 120 million ECU, is accepted. |
| 7 | July | At an Eastern bloc summit in Bucharest, Soviet leader Gorbachev concedes that every socialist state has the right to choose its own way of development. This invalidates the Brezhnev Doctrine of 1968 and creates the so-called Sinatra Doctrine: they can do it their way. |

| | | |
|---|---|---|
| | July | In Hungary, Prime Minister and Socialist Party leader Grosz has to cede power to three more-radical reformers including Imre Pozsgay. A four-person ruling presidency that includes Grosz is formed. |
| throughout | August | East German citizens flood to the West German embassies in Berlin, Budapest and Prague, demanding to leave the GDR. |
| 19 | August | Some 900 people flee over the "green border" from Hungary to Austria, taking advantage of a so-called Pan-European Picnic initiated by the president of the Pan-European Union, Otto von Habsburg. |
| 23 | August | Tens of thousands of people form a human chain between the capitals of Estonia and Lithuania, Tallinn and Vilnius, respectively, to protest against the 50th anniversary of the Hitler-Stalin Pact. |
| 24 | August | The Hungarian Government grants permission to 108 East German citizens camping in the West German Embassy in Budapest to leave for the West in what is called a one-time humanitarian action. |
| 4 | September | The first Monday Demonstration takes place in Leipzig, East Germany. Participants demand more freedom of travel and the closing down of the Ministry for State Security. |
| 10-11 | September | Hungary allows all GDR citizens presently on its territory to leave for the West. It does so without prior discussion with GDR authorities. |
| 18 | September | At talks between the government and the opposition, the introduction of a multiparty system is agreed in Hungary and approved by the parliament the same day. |
| 19 | September | UTA DC-10 Flight 772 explodes over the Sahara Desert in southern Nigeria, killing 171 people. |
| 30-1 | September-October | Chartered trains transport some 7,600 GDR refugees who sought refuge at the Prague and Warsaw West German embassies over GDR territory to West Germany. Stations and tracks are closed and the carriages barred to prevent more people from jumping onto the trains. |
| 3 | October | The East German communist party, the SED, closes the GDR's borders with Czechoslovakia. |
| 7 | October | Gorbachev participates in celebrations of the 40th anniversary of the founding of the GDR. He speaks about the necessity of reforms and says pointedly, "He who arrives late is punished by life." |
| 9 | October | Seventy thousand people demonstrate in Leipzig. Their rallying cry becomes famous: "We are the people." |

| | | |
|---|---|---|
| 18 | October | East German leader Erich Honecker steps down from his posts as general secretary of the SED and chairman of the State Council. He is replaced by Egon Kranz, who cannot, however, stop the rapid crumbling of the country's communist system. |
| 23 | October | After giving Imre Nagy a state funeral, Hungary adopts a series of refoms: restrictions on emigration are eased, the Constitution is revised to allow for multiparty democracy, and the state's name is changed from People's Republic of Hungary into Republic of Hungary. |
| | October | At a Congress of the Hungarian Socialist Workers' Party, a split occurs, and a group of reformers launch the Hungarian Socialist Party. |
| 3 | November | The GDR Government decides that its citizens can leave the country without formalities via the territory of Czechoslovakia. |
| 4 | November | Between 500,000 and 1 million people demonstrate in favour of democratic reforms in East Berlin. GDR television broadcasts the events live. |
| 7 | November | The GDR Government and Politburo step down. |
| 9 | November | After hundreds of people converge on crossing points along the Berlin Wall, East Germany's rulers give permission for gates along the Wall to be opened, and tens of thousands of people break through to the West. |
| 10 | November | The head of the Bulgarian state and Communist Party, Todor Zhivkov, is replaced by Petre Mladenov, hitherto prime minister. The party gives up its political and ideological monopoly, and a multiparty system is introduced in Bulgaria. |
| 17 | November | Communist riot police severely beat participants in a peaceful student demonstration in Prague. The Velvet Revolution that follows ends in the overthrow of the Communist Government. |
| 26 | November | Civic forum leaders and one representative of Charta 77 meet with Czechoslovak Prime Minister Ladislav Adamec in Prague. They discuss the setting up of independent political parties and a transition to democracy. A further release of political prisoners is announced after the discussions. The opposition groups maintain the call for a two-hour general strike to take place the next day. The same evening, a massive rally takes place in Prague and is broadcast live on TV. |

| | | |
|---|---|---|
| 26 | November | Hungary conducts a referendum on four issues: putting off scheduled presidential elections until after parliamentary elections, the withdrawal of party organisations from the work place, that the Hungarian Socialist Workers' Party should give account of its property and the dissolution of workers' militia. |
| 27 | November | A Czechoslovak general strike is observed by millions. |
| 29 | November | The Czechoslovak Parliament abolishes the leading role of the Communist Party. |
| 7 | December | In Bulgaria, 13 opposition organisations form the Union of Demcoratic Forces (UDF). |
| 17 | December | Romanian leader Nicolae Ceausescu orders regular military forces and Securitate secret-service forces to fire on anti-communist demonstrators in the city of Timisoara. The demonstrations quickly spread to Bucharest. |
| 20 | December | The US invades Panama after the Panamanian Government fails to recognise the victory of Guillermo Endarma in presidential elections, citing US interference. |
| 22 | December | The Romanian Army fraternises with the demonstrators. Ceausescu and his wife flee in a helicopter. The pilot lands after faking an engine failure, and the Ceausescus are captured by the Romanian Army at a roadblock. |
| 25 | December | Ceausescu and his wife are executed in Romania after a secret military tribunal finds them guilty of crimes against the state. |
| 27 | December | Having achieved their objective, US troops begin to withdraw from Panama. |
| 29 | December | Vaclav Havel is elected president of a transitional government in Czechoslovakia. |

Part 6

# NEW WORLD ORDER

# 1990 -1999

| At a Glance – Major Events and Themes | |
|---|---|
| | **Lithuania declares independence from the USSR** |
| | **End of Communist rule in Hungary** |
| | **Spain and Portugal join the WEU** |
| | **Germany and France propose a European Union** |
| | **Dublin Convention (on allocation of asylum applications between countries) and Convention Implementing the Schengen Agreement (on free cross-border movement) signed** |
| | **Iraq invades Kuwait** |
| | **Germany reunifies** |
| | **Conventional Forces in Europe Agreement signed** |
| | **NATO and Warsaw Treaty Organisation no longer enemies** |
| | **Transatlantic Declaration signed** |
| | **Two EC Intergovernmental Conferences begin on monetary and political union** |

# 1990

| Day | Month | Event |
|---|---|---|
| | January | The US announces its National Security Strategy. |
| 3 | February | The Bulgarian parliament elects economist Andrei Lukanov as prime minister. He is replacing a hard-line communist. |
| 5 | February | Soviet leader Gorbachev proposes to the Central Committee the introduction of a multiparty system and to abandon Article 6 of the Soviet Constitution, which enshrines the leading role of the CPSU. |
| 12-28 | February | The first round of negotiations between NATO and Warsaw Pact states on an Open Skies treaty take place in Ottawa, Canada. There are disagreements over the resolution of optic sensors on planes and on information-sharing. |
| 11 | March | The Lithuanian parliament declares the re-establishment of independence. |
| 13 | March | Article 6, prescribing the leading role of the Communist Party, is removed from the Constitution of the Soviet Union. |
| 15 | March | Gorbachev is elected president of the USSR. The next election is to be by popular vote. |
| 25+8 | March+April | First free elections in Hungary. A coalition of centre-right parties led by the Hungarian Democractic Forum wins. |
| 27 | March | *ESDP.* Portugal and Spain become full members of the WEU. |

| | | |
|---|---|---|
| 30 | March | The Estonian parliament declares the Soviet annexation to have been illegal and re-establishes the country's independence. |
| 10 | April | The Bulgarian Communist Party changes its name to Bulgarian Socialist Party. |
| 23-2 | April-May | The second round of Open Skies negotiations takes place in Budapest. Progress is again slowed by disagreements on technical issues such as camera resolution, and the US still rejects the Soviet proposal of data-sharing. |
| | April | *ESDP.* Germany and France propose the creation of a European Union. |
| 4 | May | The Latvian parliament declares the union with the USSR illegal and states its intention to restore full Latvian independence after a transition period. |
| 20 | May | Parliamentary and presidential elections take place in Romania. The elections are not fully free, but the outcome reflects the will of the people. The National Salvation Front of Ion Iliescu wins, and Iliescu becomes president. He is a fomer top party and state official who had fallen into disfavour with Ceausescu. |
| 31-3 | May-June | US/USSR Summit: agreement on START follow-up talks to reduce first-strike incentives, i.e., no warheads on MIRVs. |
| 10 | June | The Bulgarian Socialist Party (the former Communist Party) wins the first free parliamentary election in the country. |
| 15 | June | The Dublin Convention is signed by all EU member states except Finland, Sweden and Denmark. The convention sets out criteria to determine which state is responsible for examining an application for asylum lodged in a member state of the EU. This aims to assure that applications cannot be made in several countries but also that every application is dealt with. |
| 17 | June | Multiparty elections take place in Bulgaria. The former communists gain a relative majority of 45%. |
| 19 | June | The Convention Implementing the Schengen Agreement is signed by Belgium, France, the FRG, Luxembourg and the Netherlands. It contains measures to create a common area of security and justice following the abolition of common border checks. |

| | | |
|---|---|---|
| | June | During Conventional Armed Forces in Europe (CFE) negotiations in Vienna, NATO members table the idea of an aerial inspection regime. Since there is not enough time to settle the details of such a regime, a general provision is included that allows for aerial inspections throughout the area of application of the treaty. Russia soon begins to relocate weapons and equipment beyond the Urals, where the CFE does not apply but where the Open Skies treaty will apply. Thus, the CFE negotiations give new impetus to the Open Skies negotiations. |
| | June | The Russian Soviet Federal Socialist Republic (RSFSR) declares independence. |
| 6 | July | President Petar Mladenov resigns in Bulgaria. |
| 5-6 | July | *ESDI.* NATO NAC in London:<br>a) President Mitterrand announces that France will withdraw all troops from Germany by 1994;<br>b) NATO to reduce forward presence;<br>c) Nuclear weapons to be NATO's "last resort".<br>The preparation of a new military strategy is announced. NATO members propose to Warsaw Pact states a joint declaration containing a commitment to non-aggression and a statement that the two organisations are no longer enemies. NATO ministers also invite Eastern and Central European leaders to address NATO and to establish regular diplomatic liaison with NATO. Ministers assert that the "Alliance will do its share to overcome the legacy of decades of suspicion" and that they are "ready to intensify military contacts, including those of NATO Military Commanders, with Moscow and other Central and Eastern European capitals". |
| 25 | July | UK Defence Secretary Tom King announces the Options for Change Programme for the British armed forces. King states that between 1990 and 1994 cuts of roughly 18% in current manpower levels will be made. British forces in Germany will be cut by around 50%. |
| 25 | July | The US ambassador in Baghdad, April Glaspie, meets with Saddam Hussein and tells him that the US has no position with regard to regional border disputes. However, she adds that the US "strongly believe[s] that they should be settled peacefully". She also makes it clear that the US is concerned by the massive Iraqi troops deployment at the Kuwaiti border. |
| 27 | July | Belarus's newly elected Supreme Soviet adopts a Declaration of Independence. |
| | July | The US agrees to halt production of chemical weapons. |
| 2 | August | Iraq invades Kuwait. The UN Security Council demands an immediate Iraqi withdrawal. |

| | | |
|---|---|---|
| 3 | August | Italian Prime Minister Giulio Andreotti confirms before an Italian Senate committee the existence of Gladio, a clandestine military force that is an armed covert subdivision of the military secret service. The senators demand a written report on this force, whose task was to fight a potential Soviet invasion. |
| 6 | August | The UN Security Council imposes economic sanctions against Iraq. |
| 21 | August | *ESDP.* The WEU Ministerial Council meets in Paris to discuss the situation in the Persian Gulf. Ministers reactivate and extend the co-ordination mechanisms approved in 1988. A high-level group of foreign and defence ministers' representatives is made responsible for "the most effective coordination in capitals and in the region". Ministers emphasise that, "coordination within WEU should also facilitate cooperation with other countries deploying forces in the region, including those of the United States." |
| 12 | September | The Treaty on the Final Settlement with Respect to Germany, also called the Two-Plus-Four Treaty, is signed by the FRG, the GDR, France, the Soviet Union, the UK and the US. It accords the unified Germany a *de facto* peace treaty and full sovereignty, as the Allied sovereign rights are discontinued as of 3 October 1990. |
| 3 | October | German reunification: the GDR – and thus the newly created East German *Länder* of Brandenburg, Mecklenburg-Western Pomerania, Saxony, Saxony-Anhalt and Thuringia – accedes to the FRG. |
| 18 | October | Italian Prime Minister Andreotti presents his report on Gladio to the Senate. It confirms that Gladio is still active, that the CIA built up the force after World War II, that similar structures exist all over Western Europe and that NATO co-ordinated these secret armies. |
| | October | The USSR agrees to remove all troops from Germany by the end of 1994. |
| 19 | November | The Conventional Armed Forces in Europe (CFE) treaty is signed by 22 states at a CSCE summit in Paris. The CFE treaty establishes a complex system of military balance between the Eastern and Western alliances from the Atlantic to the Urals. In particular, it provides for equal ceilings for major weapons and equipment systems for both groups of states, which are then translated into national limits for each state party. |
| 19-21 | November | CSCE participating states sign the Charter of Paris for a New Europe. The Charter marks the formal end of the Cold War and begins the institutionalisation of the CSCE by setting up three permanent bodies: the Secretariat, the Conflict Prevention Centre and the Office for Free Elections. |

| | | |
|---|---|---|
| | November | While the CIA, the US Government and NATO all refuse to comment on the Gladio affair, the European Parliament holds a special session on the issue. It is very concerned that such secret armies could exist without any democratic oversight and urges governments to conduct profound and precise investigations into these networks. |
| | November | NATO and the Warsaw Treaty Organisation issue a statement that they are no longer enemies. |
| 23 | November | *ESDI.* A Transatlantic Declaration is signed and a new era of US-European relations hailed. The key components are the maintenance of the transatlantic security pact and a determination to modify NATO so that the Alliance will be able to cope with post-Cold War strategic realities. |
| 29 | November | In its Resolution 678, the UN Security Council issues an ultimatum to Iraq, demanding it withdraw from Kuwait by midnight of 15 January 1991. All member states co-operating with Kuwait are authorised "to use all necessary means to uphold and implement resolution 660 (1990) and all subsequent resolutions and to restore international peace and security in the area" in the event of Iraqi non-compliance with the ultimatum. |
| 29 | November | Confronted with a wave of protests and riots, Bulgarian Prime Minister Andrei Lukanov falls from power. |
| 15 | December | *ESDP.* Two year-long EU IGCs begin, one on political union, the other on monetary union. The results of the IGCs form the basis for the Treaty on European Union (Maastricht treaty). |
| | December | In Bulgaria, the dominant Socialist Party forms a coalition government that includes the reformist UDF. |

| | |
|---|---|
| **At a Glance – Major Events and Themes** | **Comecon and the Warsaw Pact dissolve** |
| | **Gulf War** |
| | **US announces Global Protection Against Limited Strikes** |
| | **First meeting of Visegrad Group** |
| | **Armenia, Azerbaijan, Belarus, Estonia, Georgia, Kazakhstan, Kyrgyzstan, Latvia, Moldova, Tajikistan, Turkmenistan, Ukraine and Uzbekistan declare independence from the USSR** |
| | **UNSCOM created to inspect Iraqi weapons capabilities** |
| | **Allied Rapid Reaction Corps agreed in principle** |
| | **Boris Yeltsin elected president of the Russian Soviet Federal Socialist Republic** |
| | **Yugoslavia dissolves as Slovenia, Croatia and Macedonia declare independence** |
| | **START Treaty signed** |
| | **August coup by hard-line communists in the USSR fails** |
| | **First EC peace conference on ex-Yugoslavia** |
| | **First fully democratic elections in Bulgaria** |
| | **European Economic Area agreed** |
| | **Germany and the US call for establishment of North Atlantic Cooperation Council** |
| | **NATO adopts New Strategic Concept** |
| | **Nunn-Warner Act** |
| | **Treaty on European Union (Maastricht treaty) approved** |
| | **Declaration on the role of the WEU and its relations with the European Union and Atlantic Alliance** |
| | **North Atlantic Cooperation Council founded** |
| | **The USSR is dissolved** |

# 1991

| Day | Month | Event |
|---|---|---|
| 5 | January | The Executive Committee of Comecon agrees to disband the organisation. In its place, the Organisation for International Economic Co-operation will be created. |
| 10 | January | Economist Albertas Simenas is appointed Lithuanian prime minister. Gorbachev sends a telegram to the Lithuanian parliament, demanding it revoke unconstitutional acts, i.e., the declaration of independence. |

| | | |
|---|---|---|
| 13 | January | The Soviet Union cracks down on Lithuania in an attempt to reverse its independence. |
| 15 | January | *ESDP.* In order to establish common rules of engagement for WEU forces, given Iraq's non-compliance with the Security Council ultimatum, the WEU Naval Co-ordination Authority is established. |
| 15-18 | January | The CSCE draws up a procedure for the peaceful settlement of disputes at Valetta, Malta. |
| 17 | January | After the Security Council ultimatum against Iraq elapses without success, US-led coalition forces begin Operation Desert Storm with aerial bombardment of Iraq. |
| 29 | January | US President Bush announces a new, scaled-back missile defence project named Global Protection Against Limited Strikes (GPALS). It is intended to protect the US from unauthorised, accidental attacks from Soviet warheads or limited attacks from so-called rogue states. |
| 9 | February | In Lithuania, a referendum on independence from the Soviet Union takes place. |
| 15 | February | First meeting of the Visegrad Group (Czechoslovakia, Hungary, Poland) in Hungary. |
| 22 | February | Iraq agrees to a Soviet ceasefire proposal. The US rejects it but gives Iraq 24 hours to withdraw without being attacked. |
| 24 | February | The US launches Desert Sabre, the ground operation in Iraq. |
| 26 | February | Iraqi forces begin to withdraw from Kuwait. |
| 27 | February | Kuwait is liberated, and coalition forces cease hostilities. |
| | February | *ESDP.* France and Germany re-emphasise their commitment to a European Union. |
| | February | The Serbian minority in Croatia's Knin region declares independence as the Autonomous Region Krajina. |
| 3 | March | Latvia holds a referendum on its independence. |
| 17 | March | Seventy-eight per cent of voters in the Soviet Union vote for the retention of the USSR in a modified form. Ukraine and Belarus boycott the plebiscite. |
| 31 | March | Communists gain a majority in the first multiparty elections in Albania. |
| 31 | March | The military components and structures of the Warsaw Pact are abolished. |
| 3 | April | In its Resolution 687, the UN Security Council decides that Iraq shall "unconditionally accept the destruction, removal, or rendering harmless, under international supervision, of: a) All chemical and biological weapons and all stocks of agents and all related subsystems and components and all research, |

| | | |
|---|---|---|
| | | development, support and manufacturing facilities; (b) All ballistic missiles with a range greater than 150 kilometres and related major parts, and repair and production facilities". Iraq shall also "unconditionally agree not to acquire or develop nuclear weapons or nuclear-weapons-usable material or any subsystems or components or any research, development, support or manufacturing facilities related to the above." The Security Council creates the United Nations Special Commission (UNSCOM) to carry out immediate on-site inspection of Iraq's biological, chemical and missile capabilities and mandates the International Atomic Energy Agency (IAEA) to verify Iraq's disarmament of its nuclear-weapons programmes. |
| 9 | April | Georgia declares independence. |
| 24 | April | Gorbachev offers his resignation as general secretary of the CPSU to the Central Committee, but it is rejected. |
| | April | The US announces a Basic Force Plan for restructuring US forces and their command functions. |
| | April | High-level parliamentary leaders from CSCE participating states set up the CSCE Parliamentary Assembly. |
| 28-29 | May | *ESDI.* NATO's DPC agrees in principle to establish an Allied Command Europe Rapid Reaction Corps (ARRC). |
| 6-7 | June | *ESDI/ESDP.* At the NAC in Copenhagen, the US threatens to pull out of European security if the EC takes responsibility for security matters. At the same meeting, ministers refuse to give security guarantees to Eastern Europe but state that the security of those countries is indivisible from their own. |
| 12 | June | Boris Yeltsin is elected president of the RSFSR. |
| 23 | June | EC foreign ministers meeting in Luxembourg. Ministers agree not to recognise any of the Yugoslav republics unilaterally and to support the unity of Yugoslavia. |
| 25 | June | Slovenia and Croatia declare independence from Yugoslavia. |
| 27 | June | Yugoslav troops invade Slovenia. Fighting also starts within Croatia between Croats and ethnic Serbs supported by the Yugoslav National Army (JNA). |
| 27 | June | *ESDP.* At the WEU Vianden meeting, ministers agree to set up a Satellite Data Interpretation Centre in Torrejon, Spain. |
| 28-29 | June | Comecon is formally dissolved. |
| 29 | June | An EC Troika composed of Jaques Poos, Hans van den Broek and Gianni de Michelis arrives in Zagreb to try to stop the war in Croatia. |
| 1 | July | The Warsaw Pact is formally dissolved. |

| | | |
|---|---|---|
| 1 | July | The Slovenian leadership and a delegation of the Yugoslav Government headed by Prime Minister Ante Markovic agree on a peace deal in Ljubljana. The JNA has already been defeated. |
| 2 | July | The Slovenian delegation and the European Troika agree on a ceasefire on the basis of the agreement concluded on 1 July. |
| 4 | July | EC foreign ministers meeting in The Hague. German Foreign Minister Genscher insists on warning the JNA, with reference to the right to self-determination. The majority of EC members disagree, however, citing the principle of the unity of Yugoslavia. |
| 5 | July | The European Community (EC) issues an arms embargo on the whole of Yugoslavia. |
| 7-8 | July | Under EC auspices, a meeting of leaders of the Socialist Federal Republic of Yugoslavia (SFRY), Slovenia and Croatia takes place. They adopt the Brioni Declaration, under which all parties accept principles for a peaceful resolution of the crisis in Yugoslavia, such as the urgent beginning of negotiations and abstention from unilateral steps. The Croatian and Slovenian declarations of independence are suspended for three months. International monitoring missions are agreed for Slovenia but only envisaged for Croatia. An agreement between Yugoslavia and Slovenia ends hostilities: Slovenia retains control over its borders, including external borders, and Slovenian forces end a blockade of JNA units, which return to barracks. POWs are released. The war in Croatia continues, however, and JNA troops withdrawing from Slovenia are stationed in Croatia. |
| 9 | July | The European Parliament adopts a resolution on Yugoslavia in which it states that it does not support any unilateral action. |
| 10 | July | Boris Yeltsin takes office as president of the RSFSR. |
| 10 | July | EC foreign ministers meet in The Hague and confirm their support for the Brioni Declaration. |
| 12 | July | The SFRY Presidency endorses the Brioni Declaration and decides to demobilise. |
| 12 | July | The Bulgarian parliament passes a new, democractic constitution. |
| 18 | July | The SFRY Presidency agrees to withdraw the JNA from Slovenia. Meanwhile, fighting between the JNA and Croats intensifies. |
| 19 | July | The EC sets up an *ad hoc* working group on Yugoslavia. |

| | | |
|---|---|---|
| 31 | July | The START Treaty is signed. It reduces the two superpowers' nuclear arsenals to a limit of about 3,500 warheads apiece and, in so doing, raises the relative importance of the Anglo-French nuclear deterrents. |
| | July | Dutchman Henry Wynaendts is sent to Yugoslavia by the EC in the framework of EPC to enquire about a political solution to the conflict. |
| 18-21 | August | August coup in the USSR. Feeling threatened by Gorbachev's *perestroika* policy and his plans for a new union treaty between the Soviet republics, a group of hard-line communists mount a coup. They hold Gorbachev under house arrest at his *dacha* in the Crimea, publicly declaring that he is ill. The putschists issue emergency decrees declaring a return to the pre-*perestroika* period and order tanks and troops to Moscow. Russian President Boris Yeltsin prevents the success of the coup by encouraging the public to take to the streets to resist the coup. After three days, the coup implodes, as its proponents give up in the face of resistance by the population and large parts of the military. The events leave three people dead. Yeltsin has managed to make use of a unique opportunity and emerges as the new leader in the USSR. |
| 20 | August | Estonia declares independence from the USSR. |
| 21 | August | Latvia declares independence from the USSR. |
| 24 | August | Gorbachev resigns as general secretary of the CPSU but remains head of state, i.e., president of the USSR. Yeltsin closes the party newspaper "Pravda" and suspends the CPSU. |
| 24 | August | Russia recognises the independence of Estonia, Latvia and Lithuania. |
| 24 | August | Ukraine declares independence from the USSR. |
| 25 | August | Belarus declares independence from the USSR. |
| 27 | August | Moldova declares independence from the USSR. |
| 27 | August | EC foreign ministers urge Serbia to co-operate at the Yugoslavia conference; otherwise, the EC will search for a solution to the conflict without Serbia. |
| 30 | August | Azerbaijan declares independence from the USSR. |
| 31 | August | Kyrgyzstan declares independence from the USSR. |
| 1 | September | Uzbekistan declares independence from the USSR. |
| 6 | September | The Soviet Union recognises Latvian, Estonian and Lithuanian independence. |
| 7 | September | First EC peace conference on former Yugoslavia opens in The Hague. |

| | | |
|---|---|---|
| 8 | September | Macedonia conducts a referendum on independence from the SFRY. Sixty-eight per cent of voters express that they are in favour of an independent state. |
| 9 | September | Tajikistan declares independence from the USSR. |
| 17 | September | Macedonia declares independence from the SFRY. |
| 20 | September | Yugoslav President Stjepan Mesic declares that he has no more control over the JNA and that the the latter is conducting a dirty war against Croatia. |
| 21 | September | Armenia declares independence from the USSR. |
| 25 | September | The UN Security Council imposes a general and complete arms embargo on the whole of Yugoslavia. |
| 28 | September | EC ministers announce that they will take restrictive measures against "unco-operative participants" in the Yugoslavia conference, by which they mean Serbia. |
| | September | *ESDP.* France and Germany propose placing a WEU interposition force in Croatia, but they are blocked by the British. |
| 3 | October | Four members of the Yugoslav federal presidency oust President Mesic and the federal parliament from power. |
| 4 | October | *ESDP.* A UK-Italian declaration calls for a permanent European command structure for general defence missions. |
| 5 | October | Gorbachev announces that he will reduce the Soviet arsenal by 1,000 more warheads than required by START. |
| 5-6 | October | EC foreign ministers at Haarzuilens in the Netherlands confirm the decision of the Yugoslavia conference of two days earlier to envisage a political solution that comprises the possibility of recognition of Slovenia and Croatia. The EC stops considering the Yugoslav presidency as representing all its constituent republics. |
| 7 | October | The CoE stops co-operation with Yugoslavia on the grounds of human-rights violations. |
| 8 | October | The three-month moratorium imposed by the Brioni Declaration ends. Slovenia and Croatia confirm their declarations of independence. |
| 10 | October | The Dutch EC Presidency, represented by Foreign Minister van den Broek, asserts that the recognition of Slovenia and Croatia is planned if negotiations do not succeed within two months. France and the UK agree under the condition that recognition can only be the result of a consensus reached in negotiations among all parties. Germany, however, sees van den Broek's assertions as representing an ultimatum. |
| 13 | October | The UDF wins 110 out of 240 seats in elections in Bulgaria. The first truly non-communist government since 1946 is formed. |

| | | |
|---|---|---|
| 14 | October | *ESDP.* In a letter to the European Council, Chancellor Kohl and President Mitterrand propose to expand the French-German joint brigade into "the basis for a Eurocorps, to which the armed forces of other WEU member-states could be added." |
| 21-22 | October | The Agreement on the European Economic Area (EEA) is signed between EC and EFTA countries. It is designed to allow EFTA member states to participate in the EU single market by providing for the free movement of goods, services, capital and persons among EEA countries. |
| 25 | October | A declaration by the European Community sees the JNA as the main party responsible for the escalation of the Croation conflict. |
| 27 | October | Turkmenistan declares independence from the USSR. |
| | October | The USSR responds to US President Bush's GPALS initiative by agreeing to discuss limited ABM defence systems. |
| | October | Kazakhstan and Belarus agree to centralised Russian control of all nuclear weapons in the former Soviet Union. |
| | October | *ESDP.* The WEU and the EC accept the primacy of the UN in the crisis in former Yugoslavia. This marks the failure of the EC to find a solution and a reverse for Europe's attempts to be taken seriously as an international actor. |
| | October | Germany and the US propose the establishment of a North Atlantic Cooperation Council. |
| | October | Israelis, Syrians, Jordanians and Palestinians discuss peace in the Middle East. |
| 4-8 | November | Open Skies negotiations resume in Vienna. Major concessions by both the USSR and the US allow a draft treaty to be set up for final review by all states. |
| 7-8 | November | *ESDI.* NATO's Rome Summit adopts the New Strategic Concept and establishes the framework for the development of the ARRC. The New Strategic Concept is based on a broad concept of security and on co-operation with all European states. NATO moves away from frontal defence and towards a strategy of involvement in the security and stability of the so-called new democracies. "To protect peace and to prevent war or any kind of coercion, the Alliance will maintain for the foreseeable future an appropriate mix of nuclear and conventional forces based in Europe and kept up to date where necessary, although at a significantly reduced level. ... the overall size of the Allies' forces, and in many cases their readiness, will be reduced [and] the maintenance of a comprehensive in-place linear defensive posture in the central region will no longer be required. ... [Alliance forces] will require enhanced flexibility and mobility and an as sured capability for augmentation when necessary .... For |

| | | |
|---|---|---|
| | | the Allies concerned, collective defence arrangements will rely increasingly on multinational forces, complementing national commitments to NATO." |
| 7-8 | November | NATO heads of state and government call for a strengthening of the CSCE process. |
| 14 | November | A British investigation concludes that two Libyan nationals were responsible for the Pan Am bombing. They are charged with conspiracy, murder and contravention of the Aviation Security Act. The US issues a similar indictment. Libya refuses to hand the suspects over for trial, which results in UN sanctions against Libya. |
| 18 | November | *ESDI/ESDP.* At a Bonn meeting of the WEU Council, the attending foreign and defence ministers discuss the place and specific role of the WEU in the European security architecture. They welcome NATO's New Strategic Concept and repeat "the objective of developing the WEU as the defence component of the European unification process and as a means of strengthening the European pillar in the Atlantic within the Alliance." |
| 26 | November | Poland joins the CoE. |
| 27 | November | German Chancellor Helmut Kohl announces Germany's intention to recognise Slovenia and Croatia before Christmas 2004 if they fulfill the necessary criteria. |
| | November | The Warner-Nunn Act is passed by the US Congress. It calls for the deployment by 1996 of an ABM-treaty-compliant ground-based anti-ballistic-missile defence system in the US. |
| | November | The CPSU is formally disbanded. |
| 1 | December | The majority of Ukrainians vote for independence. |
| 2 | December | The EC lifts its economic sanctions from Croatia, Slovenia, Bosnia and Herzegovina (BiH) and Macedonia, leaving only Serbia and Montenegro. |
| 4 | December | The Croatian parliament adopts new legislation on minority protection. |
| 6 | December | French Foreign Minister Roland Dumas describes the German attitude on the recognition of Croatia and Slovenia as harmful to the Community. |
| 7 | December | The first assessment of the EC Badinter Commission is presented by the Dutch Presidency of the EC. It speaks of a "process of dissolution" in Yugoslavia. |
| 8 | December | The leaders of Belarus, Ukraine and Russia, Stanislau Shushkevich, Leonid Kravchuk and Boris Yeltsin, respectively, meet in Minsk and set up the Commonwealth of Independent States (CIS). They also annul the 1922 treaty establishing the Soviet Union, and declare that, "the USSR, as a subject of international law and a geopolitical reality, is ceasing its existence." |

| | | |
|---|---|---|
| 9-10 | December | *ESDP.* The Treaty on European Union (TEU) is negotiated and approved at Maastricht, the Netherlands. Title V of the treaty contains "Provisions on a common foreign and security policy" and Article J.4.1 states that, "the implementation of a common foreign and security policy including the eventual framing of a common defence policy, which might in time lead to a common defence" is the goal. However, there are profound disagreements among the member states over how to proceed. |
| 10 | December | In a letter to Dutch Foreign Minister van den Broek, UN Secretary-General Javier Pérez de Cuéllar expresses concern that a premature, selective recognition of Yugoslav republics might exacerbate the conflict and cause an explosive situation, "particularly in Bosnia and Herzegovina and also in Macedonia." |
| 10 | December | *ESDI/ESDP.* The Declaration on the Role of the Western European Union and its Relations with the European Union and with the Atlantic Alliance is signed. The member states of the WEU agree to "develop a genuine European Security and Defence Identity and a greater European responsibility on defence matters." The declaration likewise indicates that, "this identity will be pursued through a gradual process involving successive phases." The declaration also states that the re-examination of the WEU's provisions "will take account of the progress and experience acquired and will extend to relations between WEU and the Atlantic Alliance." This specific reference to NATO is consistent with the definition of the role of the WEU as "the defence component of the European Union and as a means to strengthen the European pillar of the Atlantic Alliance." Under the declaration, member states also undertake to further examine enhanced co-operation in the field of armaments with the aim of creating a European armaments agency. |
| 12 | December | The Maastricht European Council issues a Declaration on Areas which Could be the Subject of a Joint Action. The CSCE process, disarmament and arms-control policy in the EU, nuclear non-proliferation and economic aspects of security are cited as being such areas. |
| 13 | December | The Government of the FRG announces that it will recognise Croatia and Slovenia before Christmas. |
| 15 | December | The UN Security Council agrees to send peacekeeping troops to Yugoslavia. |
| 15 | December | The two year-long IGCs that led to the Maastricht treaty come to an end. |
| 16 | December | Kazakhstan declares independence from the USSR. |

| | | |
|---|---|---|
| 16-17 | December | EC foreign ministers meet in Brussels on the issue of Yugoslavia. They agree that those Yugoslav republics that wish to obtain recognition must apply for it by 23 December and that recognition will then be granted on 15 January 1992. German Foreign Minister Genscher insists that Germany can pronounce recognition already before Christmas. |
| 19 | December | Germany decides to grant recognition to Croatia and Slovenia on 23 December. |
| 20 | December | The North Atlantic Cooperation Council (NACC) is created. It is a consultative forum for NATO member states and nine Central and Eastern European countries, initially including the Soviet Union. However, at the closing session, Moscow sends instructions to delete all references to the USSR in the documents. The Soviet ambassador assumes that all agreements concerning the NACC are valid for the successor states to the Soviet Union. |
| 21 | December | The CIS is expanded to include Armenia, Azerbaijan, Kazakhstan, Kyrgyzstan, Tajikistan, Turkmenistan, and Uzbekistan. Georgia participates as an observer. The participant states agree that, "with the formation of the Commonwealth of Independent States, the Union of Soviet Socialist Republics ceases to exist." They also declare that, "Member states of the Commonwealth support Russia in taking over the USSR membership in the UN, including permanent membership in the Security Council." |
| 23 | December | Slovenia adopts a new constitution. |
| 23 | December | Germany recognises Slovenia and Croatia, to be effective on 15 January. |
| 24 | December | Yeltsin informs the secretary-general of the UN that the Russian Federation will continue the membership of the USSR in the UN, including in the Security Council. He also requests "that the name 'Russian Federation' should be used in the United Nations in place of the name 'the Union of Soviet Socialist Republics'." |
| 25 | December | Gorbachev steps down. |

| | |
|---|---|
| **At a Glance – Major Events and Themes** | **Maastricht treaty signed** |
| | **UNPROFOR created to demilitarise parts of former Yugoslavia** |
| | **Open Skies treaty signed** |
| | **Elections in Albania end 47 years of communist rule** |
| | **Bosnia and Herzegovina declares independence from Yugoslavia** |
| | **War in Bosnia and Herzegovina starts** |
| | **Eurocorps created** |
| | **WEU Petersberg Declaration and Tasks** |
| | **Greece admitted as full member to the WEU** |
| | **US Senate approves START I** |
| | **William Jefferson Clinton elected US president** |
| | **EUROFOR and EUROMARFOR created** |
| | **EU draws up report on future of CFSP** |

# 1992

| Day | Month | Event |
|---|---|---|
| 9 | January | Serbian President Slobodan Milosevic declares the war against Croatia over. |
| 10 | January | *ESDP.* President Mitterrand proposes a common European nuclear strategy. |
| 10 | January | The BAOR's I Corps is disbanded. It becomes the nucleus of the ARRC. The various brigades and divisions of the BAOR in Germany are disbanded or reorganised. |
| 11 | January | The EC Badinter Commission presents its second report on the situation in Yugoslavia. It endorses the recognition of Slovenia and Macedonia but demands improvements in the constitutional protection of minorities in the case of Croatia. |
| 13-20 | January | A further conference on Open Skies is held in Vienna. Russia participates in place of the former Soviet Union. Ukraine and Belarus take part as observers. The US agrees to the so-called Taxi Proposal, by which an observed nation can insist that an observer state use aircraft and equipment of the observed party and not its own. The signing of the treaty is confirmed for March 1992. |
| 15 | January | The EU announces its readiness to recognise Slovenia and Croatia. |
| | January | The French *Loi Programmation de la Défense* 1992-1994 reduces the proportion of the defence budget spent on nuclear forces from 30% to 20%. |
| | January | NATO Status of Forces treaty is revised in order to remove special privileges. |

| | | |
|---|---|---|
| | January | France agrees not to deploy the Hades TNW due to German protests. |
| | January | *ESDP.* The WEU chief of staff asks the WEU Presidency to define the mandate of a proposed Military Planning Cell. |
| | January | The US Congress throws out the Warner-Nunn Act. |
| 3 | February | Turkey establishes a forum of states that border the Black Sea. |
| 7 | February | *ESDP.* The TEU is signed. It establishes the Common Foreign and Security Policy (CFSP), which replaces EPC. It also changes the name of the EEC to simply the European Community (EC) and establishes a structure of three pillars, of which the EC is the central one. Together, they form the European Union (EU). The TEU enables the EU to request the WEU to implement EU decisions with defence implications. |
| 21 | February | The UN Security Council establishes the United Nations Protection Force (UNPROFOR) to "create the conditions of peace and security required for the negotiation of an overall settlement of the Yugoslav crisis." UNPROFOR's mandate is to ensure the demilitarisation of the three United Nations Protected Areas (UNPAs) in Croatia and the protection of all persons residing in them. |
| 29 | February | BiH conducts a plebiscite on independence. Bosnian Croats and Bosnian Muslims are largely in favour, while Bosnian Serbs are largely against, although most of the them boycott the vote. |
| 6 | March | *ESDI/ESDP.* Independent European Programme Group (IEPG) ministers agree to analyse the future of the IEPG in the new European security architecture. |
| 22+29 | March | The second multiparty parliamentary elections in Albania result in the victory of the Democratic Party, ending 47 years of communist rule. |
| 24 | March | Twenty-four states sign the Treaty on Open Skies in Helsinki. |
| 31 | March | The UN imposes a flight and arms embargo and a selective travel ban on Libya. Libyan citizens are suspected of having caused the UDA and Lockerbie flight bombings with the support of the Libyan Government. Diplomatic and consular relations with Libya are to be reduced. |
| | March | The NACC is expanded to include all CIS states. |
| 5 | April | BiH declares independence from the SFRY. |
| 5 | April | Serbian militants open fire on peace demonstrators in Sarajevo. |
| 6 | April | The EU and the CIS recognise BiH. |
| 6-7 | April | Republika Srpska declares independence from BiH. |

| | | |
|---|---|---|
| 8 | April | France declares a moratorium on nuclear testing. |
| 27 | April | The remainder of the SFRY gives itself the new name of Federal Republic of Yugoslavia (FRY). |
| 30 | April | STANAVFORMED is inaugurated by NATO. |
| 30 | April | The UN secretary-general redeploys 40 military observers from the UNPAs in Croatia to the Mostar region in BiH due to the deteriorating situation there. |
| | April | German Defence Minister Volker Rühe rejects plans for a *Führungskommando* to unify command of German forces. It is too much like a general staff. |
| 2 | May | The complete siege of Sarajevo by Serbian forces starts. |
| 7 | May | Bulgaria joins the CoE. |
| 14 | May | Slovakia joins the CoE. |
| 14 | May | As the conflict in BiH intensifies further, UN military observers are withdrawn back to Croatia. |
| 15 | May | Azerbaijan, Armenia, Belarus, Kazakhstan, Moldova, the Russian Federation, Ukraine and Georgia sign the Agreement on the Principles and Procedures for the Implementation of the Treaty on Conventional Armed Forces in Europe (Tashkent Agreement) to establish the maximum levels of conventional armaments of these successor states of the USSR. Russia and Ukraine are to have forces as large as, or larger than, any other European state. |
| 16-17 | May | Around two-thirds of UNPROFOR headquarters personnel in Sarajevo are withdrawn. |
| 21-22 | May | *ESDP.* Franco-German Summit: the Joint Report Concerning the Creation of the European Corps (La Rochelle Report) of the French and German defence ministers, Pierre Joxe and Volker Rühe, is endorsed. The construction of a Eurocorps is agreed. |
| 30 | May | The UN Security Council imposes wide-ranging economic, cultural and other sanctions on the FRY. |
| 2 | June | Denmark votes "no" in a referendum on the Maastricht treaty on European Union. |
| 4 | June | *ESDI/ESDP.* NATO and the WEU offer peacekeeping forces to the CSCE in order to allow time to settle disputes. |
| 5 | June | UNPROFOR negotiates an agreement with the parties to the BiH conflict on handing over Sarajevo airport to the UN force. |
| 8 | June | The UN Security Council enlarges UNPROFOR's mandate and increases the force's strength to include the supervision of the withdrawal of anti-aircraft weapons and the concentration of heavy weapons at agreed locations in Sarajevo. |

| | | |
|---|---|---|
| 19 | June | *ESDP.* WEU Petersberg Summit: WEU countries adopt the Petersberg Declaration, whereby "forces answerable to WEU" (FAWEU) can henceforth undertake humanitarian missions, rescue tasks, peacekeeping tasks and tasks of combat forces in crisis management (including peacemaking). WEU ministers also call for a more coherent relationship between NATO's IEPG and the emerging Western European Armaments Group (WEAG). |
| 20 | June | *ESDP.* The WEU admits Greece as a full member; Iceland, Norway and Turkey as associate members; and Denmark and Ireland as observers. |
| 20 | June | *ESDP.* The WEU establishes a Forum for Consultation, in which WEU members and Eastern and Central European states will participate. |
| 29 | June | UNPROFOR's mandate is further expanded to ensure the security and functioning of Sarajevo airport and the delivery of humanitarian assistance to Sarajevo and environs. |
| | June | Georgia and Albania join the NACC. |
| | June | *ESDP.* The WEU Farfadet Exercise combines forces from France, Greece, Italy, the Netherlands, Portugal, Spain and the UK, as well as Eurocorps. |
| 1 | July | *ESDP.* A provisional staff for Eurocorps is created at Strasbourg. |
| 3 | July | United Nations observers and troops are deployed to Sarajevo, and the airport is reopened for a humanitarian airlift. |
| 3-6 | July | The CSCE Parliamentary Assembly meets and agrees to hold a review conference every two years. |
| 9-10 | July | CSCE heads of state and government meet in Helsinki and agree to appoint a high commissioner on national minorities. They also confirm the suspension of the FRY as a participating state. |
| 10 | July | *ESDP.* The WEU decides to dispatch naval forces to the Adriatic to support an operation to prevent the flow of arms to former Yugoslavia. |
| 13 | July | The UN Security Council calls on states to "take nationally or through regional agencies or arrangements all necessary measures to facilitate, in coordination with the UN, the delivery ... of humanitarian assistance to Sarajevo and wherever needed in other parts of Bosnia and Herzegovina." |
| throughout | July | The Yugoslav War escalates as the siege of Sarajevo and the discovery of death camps hit headlines in the West. |
| 28 | August | *ESDP.* WEU ministers agree to send a 5,000-strong force on a humanitarian mission to former Yugoslavia. |

| | | |
|---|---|---|
| 28-16 | August-September | Europe faces a monetary crisis following the Danish "no" vote on the Maastricht treaty and increasingly negative public-opinion polls in France. These events make financial markets pessimistic concerning the future of the European Exchange Rate Mechanism (ERM) and the broader Monetary Union project. Speculative attacks begin on the overvalued pound and lira, and, by mid-September, the German *Bundesbank* stops supporting these currencies. As a result, the pound and lira fail to remain within the exchange-rate range permitted by the ERM; they are forced to leave the mechanism. The EC monetary authorities establish a new ERM that has much larger fluctuation bands. Governments realise that a system as tight as the first ERM is impossible without a central currency, which implies, however, giving up independent monetary policy. |
| 14 | September | The UN Security Council expands the strength and mandate of UNPROFOR to include the provision of support and protection for humanitarian relief efforts conducted by the Office of the United Nations High Commissioner for Refugees, as well as for convoys of released civilian detainees. The enlarged UNPROFOR is to be deployed into new zones in Bosnia and Herzegovina, and a separate Bosnia and Herzegovina Command is established within UNPROFOR. |
| 20 | September | A referendum in France only narrowly supports the Maastricht treaty. |
| 1 | October | *ESDP.* A WEU Military Planning Cell is established in Brussels. |
| 1-2 | October | *ESDI.* Headquarters Allied Rapid Reaction Corps (HQ ARRC) are officially activated in Bielefeld, Germany. UK Lieutenant-General Jeremy McKenzie takes command. |
| 2 | October | In the US, the Hatfield-Exon-Mitchell amendment enters into force. It imposes a nine-month moratorium on US nuclear testing and places strict conditions on any further US testing. It also requires the president to complete negotiations for a Comprehensive Test Ban Treaty (CTBT) by September 1996. |
| 9 | October | The UN Security Council bans all military flights over BiH except for UNPROFOR flights and other flights in support of UN operations. |
| 14 | October | The first meeting of the WEU Forum for Consultation takes place. It is composed of WEU members and most Central and Eastern European states. |
| | October | The US Senate approves START I. |
| | October | *ESDP.* The UK and France establish the Franco-British Joint Commission on Nuclear Policy and Doctrine. |
| 3 | November | William Jefferson (Bill) Clinton is elected US president. |
| 9 | November | The CFE treaty enters into force. |

| | | |
|---|---|---|
| 11 | November | The president of Macedonia requests that the UN secretary-general deploy UN observers to prevent the fighting that is going on in other parts of former Yugoslavia from spreading to Macedonia. UN envoy Cyrus Vance and EC mediator Lord Owen support this request. |
| 20 | November | *ESDP.* WEU ministers meeting in Rome cement relations with Iceland, Norway and Turkey (associate members) as well as with Denmark and Ireland (observers). Greece becomes a full member. NATO Secretary General Manfred Wörner is invited to attend the meeting. A proposal for the creation of a trilateral, temporary air-maritime force for the Mediterranean is also made at the meeting. EUROFOR (European Operational Rapid Force) and EUROMARFOR are born. On IEPG, ministers agree that, "a transfer of IEPG functions to WEU would represent an important step towards enhanced cooperation in the field of armaments with the aim of creating a WEU European Armaments Agency. The WEU Permanent Council has been mandated to take all necessary steps in the light of the results of the next meeting of IEPG Ministers." |
| 28 | November | UN Secretary-General Boutros Boutros-Ghali sends an assessment mission to Macedonia that is to report on the possibility and desirability of a deployment of UNPROFOR to that country. |
| 3 | December | *ESDI/ESDP.* France and Germany agree that, in case of attack, the Eurocorps can be assigned to NATO for crisis management and humanitarian missions. |
| 4 | December | *ESDI/ESDP.* At a WEU meeting in Bonn, the 13 IEPG defence ministers decide "to dissolve IEPG and to transfer its functions forthwith to the WEU." |
| 6 | December | Swiss voters very narrowly reject Swiss membership of the EEA. This leaves the EEA with Norway, Iceland and Liechtenstein. |
| 11 | December | The UN Security Council approves a report by the secretary-general and establishes an UNPROFOR presence in Macedonia. |
| 11-12 | December | *ESDP.* The Edinburgh European Council adopts a "Report on Joint Action and the Development of the CFSP in the Field of Security", which describes in more detail the potential areas or issues in the security field suitable for early joint action by the EU envisaged in the declaration of 12 December 1991. |
| 15 | December | Kyrgyzstan signs the Open Skies treaty. |
| 15-16 | December | Chancellor Kohl visits Moscow and offers extra aid if Russia will accelerate the withdrawal of troops from Germany. |

| | | |
|---|---|---|
| 17 | December | NATO ministers announce their readiness to back further UN action in former Yugoslavia and agree to strengthen Alliance co-ordination in peacekeeping and to develop practical measures to enhance the Alliance's contribution in the area. |
| 29 | December | An Austrian tourist and a hotel worker are killed in a bomb explosion in Yemen. Al-Qaeda is blamed for the attack. The new terrorism starts. |
| | December | France approves the design of a new strategic missile, the M5-S5. |

| At a Glance – Major Events and Themes | |
|---|---|
| | **Czechoslovakia breaks up** |
| | **START II signed** |
| | **Three new NATO multinational corps agreed** |
| | **The Treaty on European Union (Maastricht treaty) comes into effect** |
| | **Eurocorps inaugurated** |
| | **Balladur Plan proposing a European Stability Pact for Central and Eastern European states endorsed** |
| | **Russia and the EU sign an agreement on political relations** |

# 1993

| Day | Month | Event |
|---|---|---|
| 1 | January | Czechoslovakia peacefully breaks up into the Czech Republic and the Slovak Republic. |
| 3 | January | START II is signed. |
| | January | Shortly before having to leave office, US Defense Secretary Dick Cheney identifies four critical areas of US regional defence strategy for the 1990s:<br>a) Strategic defence and deterrence;<br>b) Forward presence;<br>c) Crisis response; and<br>d) Reconstitution. |
| 20 | January | Bill Clinton is inaugurated as US president. Warren Christopher becomes US secretary of state. |
| 21 | January | Les Aspin is appointed US secretary of defense. |
| 21 | January | *ESDI/ESDP.* German General Klaus Naumann, SACEUR John M. Shalikashvili and French Admiral Jacques Lanxade sign an agreement placing Eurocorps under NATO command in the event of war. |
| | January | Chancellor Kohl announces troop cuts below the level agreed by the Two-Plus-Four Treaty of 1990. |
| | January | The WEU Secretariat moves from London to Brussels. |
| | January | Secret negotiations take place between Israeli and Palestinian delegations in Oslo. |
| 18 | February | The US signs an agreement with Russia to purchase highly enriched uranium for 20 years. |
| 24 | February | The US Joint Chiefs of Staff present the House of Representatives with a report entitled "Roles, Missions & Functions of the Armed Forces of the United States". |

| | | |
|---|---|---|
| 25 | February | *ESDI.* US Secretary of Defense Les Aspin and German Minister of Defence Volker Rühe agree on the creation of two German-American corps. The purpose is to create a multinational force that is a central element of NATO's new main defence force. Initially, however, co-operation is limited to an exchange of headquarters officers. |
| 26 | February | A car-bomb attack on the World Trade Center in New York kills six people and injures more than 1,000. Al-Qaeda is believed to be behind the attack. |
| 30 | March | *ESDI/ESDP.* The ministers of defence of the Netherlands and Germany, Relus ter Beek and Volker Rühe, respectively, acting upon the London Declaration of July 1990 and the Rome Declaration of November 1991, sign a common declaration on the creation of a multinational corps. This new multinational corps is designed to involve more than the two initial member states and is wholly in line with NATO's New Strategic Concept. |
| 5 | April | *ESDP.* WEU member states agree to provide assistance to Bulgaria, Hungary and Romania in their efforts to enforce UN sanctions on the Danube. |
| 8 | April | *ESDI/ESDP.* In a landmark legal decision, the German Constitutional Court agrees that German air crews can remain on NATO AWACS over BiH, even though operations are technically out of NATO area. However, the operation is allowed under a UN Security Council resolution. |
| 17 | April | The UN Security Council extends the sanctions against the FRY and strengthens their implementation. Certain requirements regulating the shipment to and through areas in Croatia and BiH controlled by local Serbian authorities are also put in place. |
| 21 | April | Germany agrees to send 1,600 troops to Somalia. |
| 23 | April | The two German-US corps are constituted in Giebelstadt, Germany. |
| 28 | April | *ESDP.* The WEU Satellite Information Interpretation Centre is inaugurated at Torrejon, Spain. |
| | April | The WEU Military Planning Cell in Brussels becomes operational. |
| | April | French Prime Minister Edouard Balladur proposes a European Stability Pact to solve disputes concerning ethnic minorities and other CSCE-related topics. It becomes known as the Balladur Plan. |

| | | |
|---|---|---|
| 6 | May | The UN Security Council passes a resolution declaring several cities and towns in BiH, in particular Sarajevo, Tuzla, Zepa, Gorazde, Bihac and Srebrenica, so-called safe areas. Armed attacks or any hostile act against these safe areas must cease immediately, all Bosnian Serb military or paramilitary units must withdraw from them, and UNPROFOR and international humanitarian agencies in these areas must be fully respected and have unimpeded access to them. The setting for the 1995 Srebrenica massacre unfolds. |
| 18 | May | In a second referendum, the Danes say "yes" to the EU Maastricht treaty after obtaining certain exemptions and clarifications. |
| 19 | May | *ESDP.* At the Rome meeting of the WEU Council, it is agreed that Eurocorps and a part of the UK-Netherlands Amphibious Force will be "forces answerable to WEU" (FAWEU). In order to ensure the practical transfer of the IEPG to the WEU, IEPG defence ministers decide at the same meeting to "meet at least once a year, before a WEU Council Meeting, to oversee the activities of the armaments cooperation forum, which will henceforth be known as the Western European Armaments Group (WEAG)." WEAG work will be organised in three panels: Joint Programmes and Equipment, Research and Technology, and Procedures and Economic Matters. It is agreed that Denmark, Norway and Turkey can continue to participate fully in the group's activities. |
| 24 | May | Eurogroup's training and medical activities are transferred to NATO and its publicity and communications activities to the WEU. |
| 25 | May | The UN Security Council passes a resolution establishing the International Criminal Tribunal for the former Yugoslavia (ICTY). |
| 25-26 | May | NATO defence ministers agree to stabilise shrinking defence budgets. |
| 8 | June | *ESDI/ESDP.* A Joint WEU/NAC session agrees to combine the NATO and WEU naval forces deployed for the enforcement of the UN embargo against Serbia and Montenegro in the Adriatic under a single command. |
| 10 | June | NATO foreign ministers agree to offer protective air power should UNPROFOR be attacked and should the UN request it. |
| 11 | June | The NACC publishes a report on co-operation in peacekeeping and launches a programme on co-operation in preparation of joint peacekeeping activities in support of the UN and the CSCE. |
| 15 | June | *ESDI/ESDP.* The Joint NATO/WEU Operation Sharp Guard begins. Its task is to monitor the embargo in the Adriatic against former Yugoslavia. |

| | | |
|---|---|---|
| 21-22 | June | *ESDP.* At the Copenhagen European Council, the EU draws up a report on the future of European security interests and common principles for the future CFSP. |
| 21-22 | June | EU leaders at the same European Council agree that Central and Eastern European states can join the EU when they have fulfilled the so-called Copenhagen Criteria. These criteria comprise the following: stability of institutions guaranteeing democracy; achievement of rule of law and respect for human rights, including respect for, and protection of, minorities; a functioning market economy, including the ability to cope with competitive pressure and market forces within the EU; and the ability to assume duties of membership, including adherence to aims of political, economic and monetary union. Moreover, admitting a member must not undermine the dynamic of European integration. |
| 21-22 | June | Also at the Copenhagen European Council, proposals by France for more-detailed criteria for admission, the so-called Balladur Plan, are endorsed. The Pact on Stability in Europe, as it is officially called, encourages applicant states to solve minority and border questions by mutual agreement in a common framework and to stimulate regional co-operation among states. |
| 22 | June | *ESDP.* The Belgian Government decides to seek participation in Eurocorps. |
| 24 | June | The EU and Russia sign a Partnership and Co-operation Agreement at Corfu. It establishes a framework for bilateral relations, defines their principal common objectives and calls for activities and dialogue in a number of policy areas. |
| 25 | June | *ESDP.* Belgium officially accedes to Eurocorps. |
| 30 | June | The Czech Republic joins the CoE. |
| 3 | July | President Clinton extends the US moratorium on nuclear testing and establishes a no-first-test policy, which allows for no US nuclear testing as long as other nations do not test. |
| 8 | July | The Rwandan radio station Radio Télévision Libre de Mille Collines begins broadcasting. It disseminates hate messages and incites the Hutu majority to slaughter the Tutsi minority and opponents of the regime. |
| 13 | July | The first French Le Triomphant-class SSBN is rolled out. |
| | July | NATO commences reorganisation. |
| | July | It is agreed at the Franco-British Summit to make the Franco-British Joint Commission on Nuclear Policy and Doctrine a permanent entity. |
| 2 | August | A second US proposal for air strikes against Bosnian Serbs is accepted by NATO Allies. |

| | | |
|---|---|---|
| 14 | August | The first UK Vanguard-class SSBN is commissioned. |
| 1 | September | The Convention Implementing the Schengen Agreement enters into force. However, since the necessary technical and legal prerequisites are not yet in place, the Common Area of Security and Justice does not exist in practice. |
| 6 | September | A meeting in Cairo sees the first handshake between Israeli Prime Minister Yitzhak Rabin and Palestinian leader Yasser Arafat. |
| 13 | September | Rabin and Arafat agree in Washington to an historic peace agreement negotiated in Oslo. Israel recognises the PLO, whilst the PLO renounces the goal of reconquering the whole of Israel. Israeli troops are to withdraw from the West Bank and Gaza by April 1994, a Palestinian Council with legislative and executive powers is to be elected and civil responsibilities for Gaza and the West Bank are to be handed over to the Palestinians over a period of five years. February 1999 is set as the deadline for a final settlement. |
| 20 | September | *ESDP.* The Joint Declaration Stating the Conditions for the Use of the European Corps Within the Framework of Western European Union is agreed. |
| | September | *ESDI/ESDP.* The EFA makes its first flight. |
| | September | At a congress of Bosnian Muslim intellectuals, the term "Bosniaks" (Bosnians) is adopted to designate the community of Bosnian Muslims. |
| 3-4 | October | The US Army Task Force Ranger is ambushed in the Somali capital Mogadishu as they attempt to capture local militia leader Mohammed Farah Aideed. During hours of heavy fighting, 18 US soldiers and hundreds of Somalis are killed. Pictures of a dead US soldier being dragged through the streets of Mogadishu spark an international outcry. |
| 5 | October | The UN Assistance Mission for Rwanda (UNAMIR) is established by the UN Security Council to help parties implement the Arusha peace agreement. |
| 7 | October | US President Clinton announces a short-term reinforcement of US troops in Somalia, as well as a complete withdrawal by 31 March. |
| 12 | October | *ESDP.* The German Constitutional Court gives the go-ahead to German ratification of the Maastricht treaty. |
| 12 | October | *ESDI/ESDP.* Belgium signs the so-called SACEUR agreements on the use of Eurocorps by NATO. |
| 21-29 | October | *ESDP.* Under the code name Ardente 93, 10,000 troops hold joint exercises simulating the evacuation of civilians in Italy's Tuscany province. Sponsored by Italy and conducted with the participation of France, Greece, the Netherlands, Spain, Turkey and the UK, exercise Ardente is the first true WEU exercise. |

| | | |
|---|---|---|
| 1 | November | *ESDP.* The TEU enters into force, creating the so-called pillar structure. The first pillar is the Community Pillar, which includes the three European Communities (Economic, Coal and Steel and Atomic Energy) and deals with the Common Market and a common currency. In the second pillar, which concerns the CFSP, and the third pillar, dealing with Justice and Home Affairs, decisions are mostly intergovernmental, i.e., by unanimity. EU members agree to develop a CFSP "including the eventual framing of a Common defence policy which might in time lead to a common defence." A Declaration on Western European Union by the 10 WEU members that are also members of the EU is annexed to the treaty and states that the "WEU will be developed as the defence component of the European Union and as a means to strengthen the European Pillar of the Atlantic Alliance. To this end, it will formulate a common European defence policy and carry forward its concrete implementation through the further development of its own operational role." |
| 5 | November | *ESDP.* At the Eurocorps inauguration ceremony, German Defence Minister Volker Rühe states that: "Eurocorps is the central building stone for European defence. We are creating an instrument for a joint foreign and security policy of the Europeans. At the end of the road Europe's unification will be waiting." |
| 11 | November | Wider UN sanctions are imposed on Libya, including a travel ban and financial sanctions. |
| 22 | November | *ESDI/ESDP.* The WEU Council of Ministers in Luxembourg votes for a strong transatlantic partnership and suggests that the WEU should have the possibility of using "not only European Allies' forces and resources but also the collective assets of the Atlantic Alliance such as communication systems, command facilities and headquarters." |
| 22 | November | *ESDP.* At the same meeting, the WEU also decides to draw up an enhanced status for those consultation partners that have concluded or will conclude a Europe Agreement (framework for bilateral co-operation with associated countries, normally leading to membership) with the EU. |
| | November | *ESDP.* The Italian initiative for a EUROFOR and EUROMARFOR covering the Mediterranean is welcomed by the assembled WEU ministers. In a statement, they say that they have "welcomed and agreed to study the Italian initiative envisaging a multinational ground force aimed at enhancing the operational significance of the air-maritime initiative." |
| 7 | December | *ESDI/ESDP.* It is announced that several Eurogroup subgroups will either be incorporated into NATO or transferred to the WEU and that Eurogroup itself will cease to exist as of 1 January 1994. |

| | | |
|---|---|---|
| 8-9 | December | At a NATO defence ministers meeting, the concept of Combined Joint Task Forces (CJTF) is discussed. Ministers stress that they "are committed to improving [their] ability to participate in a range of peacekeeping operations and to facilitate closer co-operation between NATO and the WEU in this field, including the possibility of making Alliance assets available for use in European-led operations following consultations within the Alliance. An aim of the concept of Combined Joint Task Forces is to give further impetus towards achieving this." |
| 9 | December | Russia and the EU sign a bilateral political declaration on future relations. |
| 10-11 | December | On the basis of the Balladur Plan, the Brussels European Council decides to launch a diplomatic process that should result in the conclusion of a Pact on Stability in Europe and calls upon the Council of Ministers to implement this initiative as a joint action. The inaugural conference is set to take place in Paris in April 1994. |
| 14 | December | *ESDI.* NATO and the WEU fail to agree on a practical way to implement proposals for CJTF. |
| 19 | December | *ESDP.* A high-level group presents an adjusted version of the Pact on Stability in Europe to the EU as part of a CFSP plan that involves a three-phase process, including an inaugural Paris conference in May 1994. |
| 20 | December | The EU Council of Ministers adopts the Pact on Stability in Europe as a joint action. |
| | December | *ESDP.* The UK and Italy make a joint proposal to develop more-concrete links between the six Eastern European associates and the CFSP. |
| | December | UN sanctions against Libya are tightened. |
| | December | Georgia joins the Commonwealth of Independent States (CIS). |

| At a Glance – Major Events and Themes | |
|---|---|
| | **The debate over European defence intensifies** |
| | **Formal decision to create a European Security and Defence Identity within NATO** |
| | **NATO creates the Partnership for Peace programme** |
| | **Combined Joint Task Forces formally agreed by NATO** |
| | **Rwanda genocide** |
| | **Eurocorps Headquarters fully operational** |
| | **Troops of the Four Powers withdraw from Berlin** |

# 1994

| Day | Month | Event |
|---|---|---|
| 1 | January | The EEA comes into being, thus creating a zone of free movement of people, goods, services and capital between EU member states and Norway, Iceland and Liechtenstein. |
| 1 | January | Eurogroup ceases to exist, as most of its subgroups have been incorporated into NATO or transferred to the WEU. |
| 10-11 | January | *ESDI/ESDP.* At a NATO Summit in Brussels, heads of state and government give their "full support to the development of a European Security and Defence Identity ... The emergence of a European Security and Defence Identity will strengthen the European pillar of the Alliance while reinforcing the transatlantic link and will enable European Allies to take greater responsibility for their common security and defence. The Alliance and the European Union share common strategic interests." They also "support strengthening the European pillar of the Alliance through the Western European Union, which is being developed as the defence component of the European Union." |
| 10-11 | January | The Partnership for Peace (PfP) programme is also initiated at this NATO Summit. PfP is a defence co-operation programme aimed at increasing the participants' ability to act in concert, thereby reinforcing stability and reducing conflict. |
| 10-11 | January | *ESDI/ESDP.* Also at the Brussels Summit, the Combined Joint Task Forces (CJTF) concept is endorsed. Ministers agree that WEU states can utilise the "collective assets of the Alliance" and that the CJTF initiative be developed "as a means to facilitate contingency operations, including operations with participating nations outside the Alliance". CJTF is designed to provide a flexible and efficient multinational, tri-service HQ capability for non-Article 5 contingency operations, facilitating the use of NATO collective assets by the WEU |

| | | |
|---|---|---|
| | | should NATO choose not to act, thus preventing duplication. It concerns short-term, quick-reaction multinational (combined) and multi-service (joint) self-contained contingency elements within NATO, which on the basis of an *ad hoc* NAC decision could be detached for certain missions and put under the command of the WEU should NATO choose not to participate in an operation but in support of the so-called Petersberg tasks. |
| 19-20 | January | *ESDI.* Exercise Mapex takes place to study the capacity of the HQ ARRC to operate in BiH. |
| | January | *ESDI/ESDP.* France agrees that the strengthening of ESDI is complementary with the development of NATO and that it must be designed to strengthen the European pillar. |
| 3 | February | William J. Perry replaces Les Aspin as US secretary of defense. |
| 5 | February | A mortar shell explodes in the main market square of Sarajevo, the capital of Bosnia and Herzegovina, killing 68 and wounding more than 200. |
| 9 | February | NATO issues the Sarajevo Ultimatum to Serbs in the wake of the Sarajevo market massacre. Serbs must either pull back all heavy weapons within a 20-kilometre radius from Sarajevo or turn them over to UN control by 20 February. In the event of non-compliance, they will face attack. |
| 28 | February | NATO shoots down four Serbian aircraft violating the no-fly zone established by the UN Security Council on 9 October 1992. |
| 9 | March | The Council of Ministers of the EU agrees to an annual summit involving the president of the European Council, the president of the Commission and the heads of state of the six EU associate states. |
| 9 | March | *ESDP.* The Council of Ministers also proposes holding one Special Council on CFSP matters during each six-month presidency; meetings for the six Central and Eastern European associate states with the Troika (i.e., the current, previous and next holders of the EU presidency aided by the Commission; the Troika represents the EU in external relations under the CFSP); and the opportunity for the Six to take part in Troika *démarches* and Joint Actions under the CFSP. |
| 18 | March | Bosniaks and Bosnian Croats sign a peace agreement creating the Federation of Bosnia and Herzegovina. This reduces the warring parties to two: namely, the Federation and the Republika Srpska. |
| 31 | March | The remaining division of the BAOR is replaced by the 25,000-strong British Forces in Germany. |

| | | |
|---|---|---|
| 1 | April | The German *Heeresführungskommando*, the country's first national military command since 1945, is established in Koblenz. |
| 6 | April | Rwandan President Juvénal Habyarimana and Burundian President Cyprien Ntaryamira are killed as their plane is shot down. This fuels the ongoing violence between Hutu government troops and civilians on the one side and Tutsi rebels on the other. Extremist Hutus slaughter thousands of Tutsis and Hutu moderates that night. UN forces stand by since their mandate does not allow them to intervene. |
| 7 | April | Rwandan Prime Minister Agathe Uwilingiyimana, 10 Belgian paratroopers guarding her and other government officials are killed by soldiers. Thousands of Tutsis accused of collaborating with the rebels are killed by Hutu-dominated government troops and militia. |
| 21 | April | The UN peacekeeping force in Rwanda is cut from more than 4,000 to 270. |
| 21-28 | April | *ESDP.* Exercise Arcade Guard takes place with 2,000 troops in order to validate procedures for deployment to a foreign country under a UN-mandated peace-support mission. |
| 27 | April | In the first South African election in which all parts of the population can participate on an equal basis, the African National Congress under Nelson Mandela wins 62% of the vote. |
| 30 | April | In one day, a quarter million Rwandans flee from the advance of the Tutsi rebel movement Rwandan Patriotic Front (RPF) and cross borders to neighbouring countries. |
| 4 | May | Under the terms of the Cairo agreement, Israel agrees to withdraw its troops from Jericho by 13 March and from 60% of the Gaza Strip by 17 March. Further withdrawals and an agreement on the status of Jerusalem is foreseen within the next five years. Self-administration by Palestinians in Gaza and Jericho enters into force. |
| 9 | May | *ESDP.* WEU Kirchberg Summit: the Kirchberg Declaration is issued, whereby the Council of Ministers authorises the WEU to commence work upon a Common European Defence Policy (CEDP). |
| 9 | May | *ESDP.* At the same summit, the WEU gives associate-partner status to Bulgaria, the Czech Republic, Estonia, Hungary, Latvia, Lithuania, Poland, Romania and Slovakia, but refuses to give security guarantees. |
| 17 | May | The UN Security Council agrees to send a 6,800-strong peacekeeping force to Rwanda to protect civilians. |
| 27 | May | Nelson Mandela becomes president of South Africa. |
| | May | *ESDI.* HQ ARRC are permanently established at Rheindahlen, Germany. |

| | | |
|---|---|---|
| | May | The two German-American corps created in 1993 are given a truly multilateral structure, going beyond the exchange of headquarters. |
| | May | The Pact on Stability in Europe is inaugurated at a conference in Paris. |
| 10 | June | A memorandum of understanding is signed between the EU and the city of Mostar, BiH. The EU is to administer the city. |
| 22 | June | The UN Security Council backs the deployment of 2,500 French troops to Rwanda and refugee camps in Zaire. |
| 24 | June | The EU and Russia sign an Agreement on Partnership and Co-operation. |
| 28 | June | *ESDI/ESDP.* The defence ministers of the Netherlands and Belgium, Relus ter Beek and Leo Delcroix, respectively, sign a Declaration of Common Intent on the Reinforcement of Dutch-Belgian Naval Co-operation in Times of Peace and War and in Times of Crisis and Tension. The agreement calls on both navies to co-operate in operations, logistics, instruction and training. They also stress the importance of closer co-operation between their air forces. |
| 29 | June | *ESDI/ESDP. The* WEU presents a report to NATO on the criteria and modalities for effective use of CJTF. Once the NAC has decided to provide the WEU with a CJTF, NATO will select CJTF HQ elements (including support assets) from one of its major subordinate commands and prepare it for deployment, the control of which will "at a certain moment" be given to the WEU. |
| | June | *ESDP.* Luxembourg requests that the WEU send an interim intervention force to Rwanda: logistical and technical support is offered by various member states, but the WEU itself demurs. |
| | June | *ESDP.* Luxembourg announces its intention to join Eurocorps. |
| 1 | July | *ESDP.* Spain accedes to Eurocorps. Eurocorps headquarters are now fully operational. |
| 1 | July | *ESDI/ESDP.* Denmark reorganises its forces and creates a new force, the Danish Reaction Brigade, with the view to integrating it into the ARRC by the end of 1995. During the summer of 1994, the Danish parliament also agrees that if the WEU seeks to use Danish forces that are part of LANDJUT (NATO's Headquarters Allied Land Forces, Schleswig-Holstein and Jutland), it will permit it to do so. |
| 1 | July | *ESDP.* Eurocorps headquarters become fully operational. Lieutenant-General Helmut Willmann of Germany is the corps commander. |

| | | |
|---|---|---|
| 4 | July | After the death of some 1 million people in the genocide in Rwanda, the Tutsi rebel movement RPF takes the capital Kigali. The Hutu Government flees to Zaire. Ethiopian UN troops take over from the French. |
| 12 | July | *ESDI/ESDP.* Speaking at celebrations attended by US President Clinton to mark the deactivation of allied forces in Berlin, German Chancellor Kohl says that, "Europe needs an America that plays a central role in matters of European security, and at the same time, America needs a Europe that assumes greater responsibility for itself and international security." |
| 12 | July | *ESDI.* The German Constitutional Court confirms that, if approved by a simple parliamentary majority, the German Government may deploy the *Bundeswehr* for UN and NATO operations ranging from peacekeeping missions to combat operations. |
| 14 | July | *ESDP.* Upon an invitation from French President Mitterrand, German soldiers from Eurocorps take part for the first time in the Champs Elysées parade celebrating Bastille Day. |
| 18 | July | The genocide in Rwanda comes to an end. The killing, often for revenge, continues, however, in refugee camps, where epidemics also kill many more. |
| 19 | July | A moderate Hutu-dominated government takes office in Rwanda. |
| | July | *ESDI.* The second round of NATO reorganisation under the New Strategic Concept begins. |
| | July | *ESDP.* The EU administration of Mostar, BiH, is established. The WEU supports the mission with a police contingent. |
| 4 | August | The Rwandan Government and the rebel movement RPF sign a peace agreement that provides for a coalition government. |
| 31 | August | Russian troops withdraw from Berlin. |
| 8 | September | Western allied troops withdraw from Berlin. |
| 23 | September | The UN Security Council reinforces and extends its measures regarding the areas in BiH under control of Bosnian Serb forces. Meanwhile, it suspends, for an initial period of 100 days, certain sanctions against the FRY, citing the FRY authorities' decision to support a proposed territorial settlement and to close the international border between the FRY and BiH for all goods except certain humanitarian items. |
| 29-30 | September | *ESDI/ESDP.* French Defence Minister François Léotard attends the Seville NATO ministerial meeting, indicating a rapprochement between France and the NATO command. |

| | | |
|---|---|---|
| 1 | October | German Army divisions are from now on under the control of the new German *Heeresführungskommando*. |
| 28 | October | BAOR is officially disbanded. |
| | October | *ESDP.* UK Foreign Secretary Douglas Hurd says of EU security and defence that security "goes to the heart of the functions of the nation-state" and that, "public opinion would not understand or accept it if these responsibilities appeared to have been surrendered to a supranational body, however worthy." Commenting upon increased bilateral Anglo-French defence links, he adds that, "although both countries differ occasionally ... neither for Britain nor for France is there attraction in a vision of Europe which erodes national identity." |
| | October | *ESDP.* At a Franco-Spanish summit, President Mitterrand notes that, "contradictions are beginning to emerge [between northern and southern member states of the EU] and we must prevent them from becoming lethal." |
| | October | *ESDI/ESDP.* The French permanent representative to the WEU states that, "the more the Europeans decide to depend upon the Alliance's assets, the more they need to have assets of their own for certain key functions so that recourse to NATO's collective assets does not lead to WEU and the European Union playing a purely superficial role." |
| | October | A peace deal is signed between Israel and Jordan. |
| 7-17 | November | *ESDP.* The first Eurocorps exercise takes place. Code-named Pegasus, it is intended to test the interoperability of the corps staff and the 5,000 troops involved. |
| 8 | November | The UN Security Council establishes the International Criminal Tribunal for Rwanda. It is seated in Arusha, Tanzania. |
| 14 | November | *ESDP.* The WEU Noordwijk summit endorses a document on a CEDP and aims for it "to evolve into a comprehensive Common European Defence Policy Statement in the perspective of the Intergovernmental Conference of 1996." |
| 14 | November | *ESDP.* At the same summit, ministers discuss the progress made by Spain, France and Italy on EUROFOR and EUROMARFOR. |
| 14-25 | November | *ESDP.* In an exercise code-named Tramontana 94, 8,000 troops, mainly French, Italian and Spanish, but supported by other contingents from Greece, the Netherlands, France and a battalion of Eurocorps, conduct exercises in southern Spain. |
| 18 | November | *ESDP.* An Anglo-French summit at Chartres agrees upon the creation of the Franco-British European Air Group, which will designate aircraft in joint missions on a case-by-case basis. |

| | | |
|---|---|---|
| 5-6 | December | The CSCE is renamed the Organization for Security and Co-operation in Europe (OSCE) at the Budapest summit, which also launces a discussion on a common and comprehensive security model for Europe and formally adopts the Code of Conduct on Politico-Military Aspects of Security. |
| 9-10 | December | *ESDP.* The Essen European Council discusses a Mediterranean dimension for the CFSP. At the meeting, a comprehensive pre-accession strategy is also presented, which includes structured dialogue, concrete plans for adopting conditions in areas such as the single market and in-depth analysis of agricultural policy. |
| 13 | December | *ESDI.* The Danish chief of staff of the Armed Forces and his UK counterpart sign a letter of intent on an affiliation between the Danish Reaction Brigade and the 1st UK armoured division. The force is intended to be constituted within the ARRC framework. |

| At a Glance – Major Events and Themes | |
|---|---|
| | **Sweden, Austria and Finland join the EU** |
| | **Review conference decides that the Treaty on the Non-Proliferation of Nuclear Weapons is to continue indefinitely** |
| | **The Srebrenica massacre** |
| | **Eurocorps becomes fully operational** |
| | **General Framework Agreement on Peace in Bosnia and Herzegovina signed** |

# 1995

| Day | Month | Event |
|---|---|---|
| 1 | January | Sweden, Austria and Finland join the European Union, bringing its membership to 15. |
| 10 | January | French President Mitterrand publicly wonders whether a European nuclear-deterrence doctrine would be possible. |
| 30 | January | French Foreign Minister Alain Juppé speaks of *dissuasion concertée*, i.e., a concerted European deterrence. The concept is not meant to signify a unilateral enlargement of the nuclear umbrella, shared decision-making or a replacement of the US nuclear guarantee; rather, it signifies a dialogue between partners on equal footing. France wants to integrate nuclear debate in European construction and give it more than an exclusively Atlantic dimension. |
| | January | *ESDP.* José Cutileiro of Portugal becomes secretary-general of the WEU. |
| 20+21 | March | The Pact on Stability in Europe is signed in Paris. |
| 26 | March | The Convention Implementing the Schengen Agreement takes practical effect. Belgium, France, Luxembourg, the Netherlands, Portugal and Spain create a border-check-free zone between their countries. |
| 28 | March | *ESDI/ESDP.* During the annual meeting of the defence ministers of Benelux, in Alden-Biezen (Belgium), the Belgians and Dutch agree to an intense programme of co-operation between their navies. The two countries also sign an agreement on the creation of a deployable air task force. |
| | March | *ESDI/ESDP.* The HQ of the Dutch-German army corps are established at Münster. |
| 6 | April | *ESDI/ESDP.* The UK and the Netherlands sign an exchange of letters regarding common interests in the area of maritime defence and a reaffirmation and strengthening of the co-operation between their navies in such areas as logistics, personnel, training, research and development, information, hydrography, oceanography, etc. At the same time, UK Defence Secretary Malcolm Rifkind and Dutch Defence Minister Joris Voorhoeve extend co-operation between air and land forces. |

| | | |
|---|---|---|
| 11 | May | The Review and Extension Conference of the Parties to the Treaty on the Non-Proliferation of Nuclear Weapons decides that the treaty should remain in force indefinitely. |
| 15 | May | *ESDP.* France, Italy and Spain sign the EUROFOR and EUROMARFOR founding documents for the creation of an army joint rapid reaction force and a European maritime force to provide extra security for the Mediterranean. |
| 10 | June | *ESDP.* France, Italy and Spain plan to launch Helios 1A, the first European military observation satellite system. A recent WEU study suggests a reasonably comprehensive satellite surveillance system would cost in the region of $19 billion over 25 years. |
| 27 | June | France and the UK officially establish the European Air Group (EAG). |
| 7 | July | *ESDP.* France, Italy and Spain launch the Helios 1A satellite system. |
| 6-16 | July | Srebrenica massacre: Bosnian Serbian forces lay siege to the UN save haven of Srebrenica and start shelling the city. A few days later, Serbian forces enter the city. Under the command of General Radko Mladic, more than 7,000 Bosnian men are massacred. Many attempt to reach safety by taking to the hills but are captured and slaughtered. An estimated 23,000 women and children are deported to Muslim territory. Dutch peacekeepers, ill-prepared, without a clear mandate and without air support, stand by and, in exchange for 14 Dutch hostages, hand over about 5,000 Bosniaks, mostly women, children and the infirm, who sought refuge at a Dutch base. On 16 July, the peacekeepers withdraw. The UN fails in its responsibilities to the Bosnian people. |
| 31 | August | *ESDI/ESDP.* The Dutch-German army corps becomes operational. |
| 1 | September | *ESDP.* The Franco-British European Air Group becomes operational. Based at RAF High Wycombe, UK, it is under the command of a French two-star general. |
| 28 | September | In Washington, Arafat and Rabin sign the Taba Agreement, also named Oslo II. It provides for an extension of self-administration by Palestinians in the West Bank and the Gaza Strip. |
| | September | *ESDP.* France, Spain and Italy, plus several other contingents, conduct Exercise Mistral 95 in southern France. |
| 4 | November | At an Israeli peace rally, Prime Minister Yitzhak Rabin is assassinated by an orthodox Israeli extremist opposed to Rabin's policy towards the Palestinians. Foreign Minister Simon Peres is named acting prime minister. |

| | | |
|---|---|---|
| 13 | November | Car bombs outside a building belonging to a US security/ military firm in Riyadh, Saudi Arabia, kill nine people. Al-Qaeda is thought to be responsible. |
| 15 | November | *ESDP.* The WEU Council of Ministers adopts a document called "European Security: a Common Concept of the 27 WEU States". The document outlines security challenges and risks facing Europe in the politico-military field. It asserts that the WEU can respond to many of these challenges. The concept also identifies ways in which WEU members can contribute to security and stability in Europe, in neighbouring areas and the wider world, with special emphasis on how the WEU can enhance capabilities in the field of crisis prevention and management. |
| 21 | November | The General Framework Agreement on Peace in Bosnia and Herzegovina (Dayton peace accords) is initialled to end hostilities in BiH and to allow the return of refugees and internally displaced persons. |
| 22 | November | The UN Security Council suspends indefinitely most of its sanctions against the FRY. However, the suspension does not apply to the Bosnian Serbian party until certain obligations are met by the latter. Also, all hitherto frozen or impounded funds and assets are released under certain conditions. The sanctions against the FRY and the Bosnian Serbian party are to be terminated on the 10th day following the free and fair elections provided for in the Dayton peace accords. |
| 31 | November | *ESDP.* Eurocorps is declared available for operations. |
| | November | The Barcelona Declaration is signed by 11 Mediterranean states, the Palestinian Authority and the EU. It contains three chapters, or pillars: politico-security, economic and cultural issues. The first pillar contains a mandate to provide the Mediterranean region with a regional security arrangement. |
| 3 | December | *ESDI/ESDP.* The US and the EU issue a New Transatlantic Agenda: "We are committed to the construction of a new European security architecture in which the North Atlantic Treaty Organisation, the European Union, the Western European Union, the Organization for Security and Cooperation in Europe and the Council of Europe have complementary and mutually reinforcing roles to play." An EU-US Action Plan is also adopted as the framework for EU-US partnership in several areas. |
| 5 | December | *ESDI/ESDP.* French Foreign Minister Hervé de Charette announces that France will be more closely involved in NATO's work and will actively participate in the reformation of the Alliance. France will henceforth participate in meetings of the Council of Defence Ministers and be fully involved in NATO's Military Committee, while intensifying its working relations with the military structure. |

| | | |
|---|---|---|
| 8 | December | Carl Bildt of Sweden is designated as the high representative (HR) in BiH. This post is created by the Dayton peace accords, in which the parties request the HR to facilitate and monitor their and others' efforts in implementing the civilian aspects of the agreement. The HR "is the final authority in theatre regarding interpretation of [the Dayton peace accords] on the civilian implementation of the peace settlement." |
| 14 | December | The General Framework Agreement on Peace in BiH is signed in Paris and the post of high representative is created. Carl Bildt is appointed the first HR. |
| 15 | December | The UN Security Council authorises the deployment of an Implementation Force (IFOR) under NATO as provided for in the Dayton peace accords for BiH. |
| 20-21 | December | The NATO-led IFOR begins its work in BiH. The civilian component of the international presence, the United Nations Mission in Bosnia and Herzegovina (UNMIBH), is also deployed, and with it the International Police Task Force (IPTF). |
| | December | Under the US Basic Force Plan, all forces are reduced by 25% compared with 1990 force levels. |

| At a Glance – Major Events and Themes | |
|---|---|
| | **Discussions about a European pillar in NATO and relations with the EU continue throughout the year** |
| | **France conducts and then ceases nuclear testing** |
| | **Intergovernmental Conference on European Union opens in Turin** |
| | **ESDI reinforced within NATO at Berlin summit** |
| | **Boris Yeltsin is re-elected president of the Russian Federation** |
| | **Comprehensive Test Ban treaty signed** |
| | **Bill Clinton re-elected president of the United States** |
| | ***Organisation Conjointe de Coopération en Matière d'Armement* created** |
| | **SFOR replaces IFOR in BiH** |

## 1996

| Day | Month | Event |
|---|---|---|
| | January | *ESDI/ESDP.* The new Dutch-Belgian Naval Force becomes operational. |
| 13 | January | US President Bill Clinton visits US troops stationed in Tuzla, BiH. |
| 17 | January | *ESDI.* The French ambassador to NATO announces more details of France's new approach to NATO. France will fully participate in NATO's Military Committee, but it will not take part in the meetings of the DPC or the NPG. |
| 20 | January | Yasser Arafat is elected president of the Palestinian Authority. |
| 26 | January | START II Treaty is approved by the US Senate. |
| 27 | January | France conducts a nuclear test in the Pacific. |
| 29 | January | President Jacques Chirac announces the cessation of French nuclear tests. |
| 31-2 | January-February | *ESDI/ESDP.* Chirac visits the United States, where he stresses the need to reform NATO to make it a "more equal partnership" between Europeans and Americans. |
| 26 | February | The Government of BiH declares that the siege of Sarajevo is over and that the city is now open. |
| 27 | February | After being informed by IFOR that Bosnian Serbian forces have withdrawn behind the zones of separation established by the Dayton peace accords, the UN Security Council indefinitely suspends its measures against the Bosnian Serbian party. |
| 28 | February | Russia joins the CoE. |

| | | |
|---|---|---|
| | February | *ESDI.* The US and France agree that CJTF can also be under non-NATO command if a prior decision on deployment is made by the NAC and all NATO members. |
| 5 | March | *ESDI.* "The Guardian" reports that European Allies will take over the military control of some NATO operations from the US. |
| 20-21 | March | *ESDI.* NATO Secretary General Javier Solana visits Moscow to discuss NATO-Russia relations. A Memorandum of Understanding on Civil Emergency Cooperation between NATO and Russia is signed. |
| 29 | March | *ESDP.* The IGC reviewing the TEU opens in Turin, Italy. |
| | March | *ESDP.* Pressure increases for the role of the WEU to be defined more clearly, with the WEU founding treaty due for renewal in 1998. |
| 6 | May | *ESDI/ESDP.* NATO Secretary General Javier Solana and WEU Secretary-General José Cutileiro sign a security agreement setting out the procedures for protecting and safeguarding classified information and material provided by either organisation. |
| 7 | May | *ESDP.* The foreign and defence ministers of the WEU member states (as well as five neutral observer countries and 12 associate and partner countries) meet in Birmingham and agree to mount peacekeeping operations out of NATO area. |
| 7 | May | Luxembourg decides to join Eurocorps. |
| 10 | May | *ESDP.* At a working dinner in Bonn, President Jacques Chirac of France and Chancellor Helmut Kohl of Germany emphasise co-operation on European defence. |
| 26 | May | A major political crisis starts in Albania. All major opposition parties pull out of parliamentary elections only hours before polls close, accusing the ruling Democratic Party of widespread irregularities. |
| | May | According to the "Neue Zürcher Zeitung", French Foreign Minister Hervé de Charette states that French reintegration into NATO's integrated military structure may be slowed down if Europe's role in the Alliance does not obtain a more permanent and autonomous basis. |
| 2 | June | A second round of elections is held in Albania, boycotted by most opposition parties. The ruling Democratic Party wins 87% of the vote. The Socialists refuse to recognize the results and do not take their seats. |
| 2 | June | *ESDI.* US Secretary of State Christopher asserts that the US will remain the most significant power in NATO even if space is created for a more visible role for Europe. |

| | | |
|---|---|---|
| 3-4 | June | *ESDI/ESDP.* At a meeting of the NAC in Berlin, it is agreed to build up the European Security and Defence Identity (ESDI) within NATO as part of the internal adaptation of the Alliance (including a new military command structure). These changes are made in response to the removal of the East-West conflict, and they permit European members of NATO to undertake humanitarian and peacekeeping operations without the US through the creation of CJTF in co-operation with the WEU. The so-called Berlin-Plus process commences. |
| 13-14 | June | *ESDI.* The NAC in Brussels agrees that any follow-up force in former Yugoslavia would be assembled by NATO as a whole. The ministers also agree to hold an urgent review of future military options in former Yugoslavia after the elections in BiH. |
| 18 | June | Following the implementation of the Agreement on Regional Stabilisation contained in the Dayton peace accords, sanctions are lifted against former Yugoslavia by the United Nations Security Council. |
| 19 | June | *ESDI/ESDP.* The joint NATO-WEU naval blockade of former Yugoslavia, Operation Sharp Guard, is suspended but not formally terminated. |
| 21-22 | June | *ESDP.* At the Florence European Council, the first three months of the IGC to review the Maastricht treaty are reviewed. |
| 26 | June | Nineteen US airmen are killed in a car-bomb explosion at a US compound in Dhahran, Saudi Arabia. Al-Qaeda claims responsibility for the attack. |
| | June | *ESDI.* The Russian response to the NATO meeting in Berlin is supportive of the development of ESDI. However, Russian officials are still opposed to military structures being built in peacetime in the Czech Republic, Hungary and Poland if they become members and in the Baltic states should they become full NATO members. |
| 2-3 | July | *ESDI.* At a meeting of the Council of Baltic Sea States, Russia reiterates its opposition to NATO's enlargement eastwards. |
| 3 | July | Boris Yeltsin is re-elected president of the Russian Federation. |
| 24 | September | The five declared nuclear powers (China, France, Russia, the UK and the US) sign the CTBT. |
| 25-26 | September | *ESDI/ESDP.* NATO defence ministers meet informally in Bergen, Norway. Discord between France and the US over the threat by France not to reintegrate into the NATO military structure unless two top command posts are given to Europeans dominates the meeting. Russia-NATO relations are also on the agenda; Russia welcomes co-operation with NATO but does not endorse NATO's expansion to the East. |

| | | |
|---|---|---|
| 1 | October | The UN Security Council formally ends the sanctions against the FRY and the Bosnian Serbs that have been suspended since the Dayton peace accords of 1995. |
| 19-25 | October | President Chirac of France visits the Middle East. He confirms European and French commitment to the Middle East and the Middle East peace process and calls for a larger European role in the latter. |
| 5 | November | Bill Clinton is re-elected president of the United States. |
| 12 | November | *L'Organisation Conjointe de Coopération en Matière d'Armement* (OCCAR) is created through an administrative agreement among France, Germany, Italy and the UK. |
| 14 | November | An international conference to assess the implementation of the 1995 Dayton peace accords is held in Paris. |
| 2-3 | December | An OSCE summit in Lisbon on European security issues adopts a Declaration on a Common and Comprehensive Security Model for Europe for the 21st Century. The declaration outlines security challenges facing the participating states and possibilities for co-operative approaches in meeting them, approves the Framework for Arms Control and the Development of the Agenda of the Forum for Security Co-operation, and calls on the Permanent Council to elaborate a mandate for the appointment of an OSCE representative on freedom of the media. |
| 4-5 | December | A Peace Implementation Conference for BiH is held in London. |
| 9 | December | *ESDP.* German Chancellor Kohl and French President Chirac sign an agreement on mutual security and defence, in which they state their readiness to undertake a dialogue on the function of nuclear deterrence in the context of European defence policy. |
| 10 | December | *ESDI.* A ministerial meeting of the NAC in Brussels confirms NATO readiness to organise and lead a Stabilisation Force (SFOR) in BiH, subject to a UN Security Council mandate. Ministers also announce further steps to be taken in the internal and external transformation of the Alliance in preparation for the July 1997 Madrid Summit. NATO issues a statement on the stationing of nuclear forces. |
| 12 | December | The UN Security Council unanimously authorises deployment of SFOR and a UN civilian operation in BiH for 1997. The IPTF can thus continue to operate, as the mandate of UNMIBH is extended until 21 December 1997. |
| 20 | December | The mandate of the NATO-led IFOR in BiH expires. IFOR is replaced by SFOR, which is also led by NATO. |

| | |
|---|---|
| **At a Glance – Major Events and Themes** | **Kofi Annan becomes UN secretary-general** |
| | **Bill Clinton begins his second term as US president** |
| | **NATO enlargement agreed** |
| | **Clinton and Yeltsin meet in Helsinki** |
| | **Operation Alba in Albania** |
| | **Chemical Weapons Convention enters into force** |
| | **New Labour wins UK elections; Tony Blair becomes prime minister** |
| | **Meetings between NATO Secretary General Solana and Russian officials throughout the year result in the Founding Act establishing the NATO-Russia Permanent Joint Council** |
| | **Czech Republic, Hungary and Poland invited to join NATO** |
| | **EU Amsterdam treaty signed** |

## 1997

| Day | Month | Event |
|---|---|---|
| 1 | January | Kofi Annan is appointed secretary-general of the United Nations. |
| 15 | January | The collapse of a pyramid savings system triggers riots in the Albanian capital Tirana. |
| 15 | January | Israeli Prime Minister Benjamin Netanyahu and Palestinian Authority President Arafat sign an agreement under which Israel is to hand over 80% of Hebron to the Palestinian Authority. |
| 20 | January | Bill Clinton is sworn in for his second term as US president. |
| 21 | January | Talks to revise the 1990 CFE treaty begin in Vienna, Austria. |
| 23 | January | Madeleine Albright becomes US secretary of state. |
| 24 | January | William S. Cohen becomes US secretary of defense. |
| 24-late | January-March | Riots in Albania spread over the whole southern half of the country after the collapse of a pyramid savings scheme. More than 10,000 people flee to Italy. The country approaches a state of anarchy. More than 360 people are killed and 3,500 injured. |
| 4 | February | *ESDI.* Bill Clinton says in his State of the Union address that NATO enlargement should be pursued by 1999 and a stable relationship with Russia achieved. |
| 11 | March | *ESDI/ESDP.* A WEU Assembly Colloquium is held in Athens, Greece, to discuss security implications of NATO and EU enlargement. |
| 13 | March | In a letter to the EU Presidency, the Albanian Government requests the deployment of an international force to its country. |

| | | |
|---|---|---|
| 20-21 | March | President Clinton and President Yeltsin meet in Helsinki, Finland, to discuss NATO-Russia relations and European security. |
| 24 | March | The EU Council of Ministers agrees to send an advisory mission to Albania but rules out any major military or police commitment. |
| 27 | March | The OSCE's Permanent Council "appreciates that certain participating States are willing to meet the official request ... made by the Albanian authorities ... for assistance in resolving the security situation in Albania". |
| 28 | March | The UN Security Council welcomes the deployment of an Italian-led Multinational Protection Force (MPF) to Albania (Operation Alba) to monitor the delivery of humanitarian aid and to maintain order, and gives the MPF a three-month mandate. |
| 9 | April | Socialist parliamentarians in Albania end their boycott and take up their seats in parliament. |
| 15 | April | Operation Alba begins as the 6,000-strong MPF arrives in Albania. |
| 15 | April | Non-WEU members Turkey and Norway are permitted to take part in a WEU-led operation mounted with NATO equipment. |
| 15 | April | Leka I, the Albanian pretender to the throne, returns to his country and calls for a referendum on reintroducing the monarchy. |
| 24 | April | The Chemical Weapons Convention (CWC) is approved by the US Senate. |
| 29 | April | Having been ratified by at least 65 states for 180 days, as required in the treaty, the CWC enters into force. |
| 1 | May | New Labour and Tony Blair win UK elections. |
| 2 | May | Tony Blair takes office as the youngest UK prime minister in a century. |
| 27 | May | *ESDI.* The Founding Act on Mutual Relations, Cooperation and Security between NATO and the Russian Federation is signed in Paris, establishing the NATO-Russia Permanent Joint Council. The Founding Act "defines the goals and mechanism of consultation, cooperation, joint decision-making and joint action that will constitute the core of the mutual relations between NATO and Russia" and states that, "NATO and Russia do not consider each other as adversaries. They share the goal of overcoming the vestiges of earlier confrontation and competition and of strengthening mutual trust and cooperation" and that, "NATO and Russia will work together to contribute to the establishment in Europe of common and comprehensive security based on the allegiance of shared values, |

| | | |
|---|---|---|
| | | commitments and norms of behaviour in the interests of all states". The Permanent Joint Council will hold two annual meetings of foreign ministers and two of defence ministers, as well as monthly meetings of ambassadors or special representatives. The Joint Council may also meet, as appropriate, at the level of heads of state or government. Areas for consultation and co-operation include issues such as conflict prevention, crisis management and conflict resolution; peacekeeping operations; strategy; defence policy and military doctrines; arms control; nuclear safety; non-proliferation of weapons of mass destruction (WMD); air traffic; size and role of conventional forces; armaments; civil-emergency preparedness and disaster relief; terrorism and drug trafficking; and public understanding of NATO-Russia relations. |
| 29 | May | Ukraine and Russia sign a co-operation agreement. |
| 30 | May | The concluding meeting of the NACC and the inaugural meeting of its successor, the Euro-Atlantic Partnership Council (EAPC), take place. The EAPC brings together the 19 NATO Allies and 27 partner countries from Central and Eastern Europe, Central Asia and the Caucasus, as well as Switzerland, Ireland, Finland, Sweden and Austria. |
| | May | *ESDP.* The WEU Council formally decides to send a Multinational Advisory Police Element (MAPE) to Albania in the framework of the MPF. The mission is to provide advice and train instructors. |
| 16-17 | June | *ESDP.* The Amsterdam European Council agrees upon a new EU treaty, the Treaty of Amsterdam. It incorporates the Petersberg tasks into the CFSP, opens the possibility of the WEU's full integration into the EU and for a common defence, and creates the post of the secretary-general of the Council / high representative for the CFSP. The Amsterdam treaty also provides for CFSP operations to be financed from the Community's budget. However, this does not apply to operations with military or defence implications. In a declaration annexed to the treaty, it is agreed to set up a policy-planning and early-warning unit under the authority of the high representative for the CFSP. |
| 19 | June | The UN Security Council prolonges the MPF's mandate until 13 August. |
| 20-22 | June | Russia officially joins the G7, making the partnership of industrialised countries the G8. |
| 29+6 | June+July | Albanian parliamentary elections. The Socialist Party wins 100 out of 155 seats. The Socialists say that Albania will be a parliamentary democracy. A referendum on restoring the monarchy is also held; only a third of voters are in favour. |
| 8-9 | July | *ESDI.* At the NATO Madrid summit, the Czech Republic, Hungary and Poland are invited to join the Alliance. |

| | | |
|---|---|---|
| 23 | July | Slobodan Milosevic becomes president of the FRY. |
| | July | *ESDP.* EU foreign ministers agree on the details of EU co-operation with the WEU in developing a common defence. |
| 13 | August | Operation Alba's mandate ends; all MPF troops have left Albania. |
| 1 | September | The Dublin Convention enters into force. It determines which state is responsible for examining applications for asylum lodged in one of the EU member states. |
| 26 | September | The foreign ministers of Russia and NATO countries meet for the first time at the NATO-Russia Permanent Joint Council. |
| 2 | October | *ESDP.* The Amsterdam treaty is signed. |
| 16 | November | *ESDI.* Hungarian citizens vote 85% in favour of joining NATO. |
| 17 | November | Fifty-eight people are killed in a bomb attack at the Egyptian holiday resort Luxor. |
| 18 | November | *ESDP.* WEU foreign and defence ministers meet in Erfurt, Germany, and agree to harmonise the EU and WEU presidencies. |
| 1 | December | Signed already in June 1994, the Agreement on Partnership and Cooperation between the EU and Russia enters into force. |
| 1-11 | December | More than 160 states gather in Kyoto, Japan, to conclude an amendment to the UN Framework Convention on Climate Change, the Kyoto Protocol. Under the protocol, industrialised countries will reduce their collective emissions of certain greenhouse gases by 5.2% compared to 1990. |
| 3 | December | The NATO-Russia Permanent Joint Council holds its first meeting of defence ministers. |
| 18-19 | December | The OSCE Ministerial Council agrees to draft a European Security Charter. |
| | December | *ESDI.* NATO signs Accession Protocols with the Czech Republic, Hungary and Poland. |

| At a Glance – Major Events and Themes |
|---|
| **Kosovo crisis** |
| **Al-Qaeda attacks US embassies in Nairobi and Dar es Salaam** |
| **Gerhard Schröder elected chancellor of Germany** |
| **Iraq temporarily ends co-operation with UNSCOM and then obstructs its work** |
| **St Malo Declaration** |
| **US and UK launch air strikes against Iraq** |

## 1998

| Day | Month | Event |
|---|---|---|
| 15 | January | A CIA report estimates that an ICBM threat is "unlikely" but still worthy of attention. |
| 2 | March | The EU Presidency (United Kingdom) calls for mutual restraint by Serbs and Albanians in Kosovo. |
| 9 | March | The Contact Group, comprising the foreign ministers of France, Germany, Italy, the Russian Federation, the United Kingdom and the United States, "call[s] upon President Milosevic to take rapid and effective steps to stop the violence and engage in a commitment to find a political solution to the issue of Kosovo through dialogue." Specifically, the Contact Group requests that he "withdraw the special police units and cease action by the security forces affecting the civilian population" within 10 days. The Contact Group asserts that, "the principles for a solution of the Kosovo problem should be based upon the territorial integrity of the Federal Republic of Yugoslavia, and be in accordance with OSCE standards, Helsinki principles and the UN Charter. Such a solution also must take into account the rights of the Kosovo Albanians and all those who live in Kosovo." It "support[s] an enhanced status for Kosovo within the Federal Republic of Yugoslavia which a substantially greater degree of autonomy would bring and recognize[s] that this must include meaningful self-administration." |
| 31 | March | The UN Security Council adopts Resolution 1160 (14-0, with China abstaining), imposing an arms embargo on the FRY. |
| 10 | April | The Northern Ireland Good Friday Agreement is signed by the Irish and UK Governments after multiparty negotiations. It provides for devolution of powers to a Northern Ireland Assembly and Executive and establishes North-South as well as UK-Ireland bodies. It also provides for decommissioning of weapons and a reduction of British security forces. Moreover, bodies on human rights and equality are set up, and major police and criminal-justice reforms are agreed. |

| | | |
|---|---|---|
| 20 | April | Libyan leader Muammar Al-Gaddafi agrees to hand over two Libyan Pan Am suspects for trial by a Scottish court in a neutral country. |
| 20 | April | *ESDI/ESDP.* French, German, Italian, Spanish, Swedish and UK defence ministers issue a joint statement to the effect that they intend to make the harmonisation of requirements of their armed forces a priority in order to avoid a duplication of acquisition, research and technological development policies. |
| 27 | April | EU foreign ministers confirm their adherence to the UN arms embargo against the FRY and also agree to ban the export of police equipment and armoured vehicles to Serbia and to deny visas to Serbian officials. However, the ministers reject a proposal to freeze export credits already approved for Serbia. |
| 29 | April | The Contact Group, with the exception of Russia, agrees to freeze the financial assets held abroad of the Governments of the FRY and Serbia. |
| throughout | May-July | More than 13,000 refugees from Kosovo pour into Albania. |
| 22 | May | The Good Friday Agreement is endorsed in a parallel referendum by the populations of both Northern Ireland and the Republic of Ireland. |
| 5-8 | June | FRY President Milosevic is given further warnings by the international community to curb the escalating violence in Kosovo. |
| 11 | June | NATO defence ministers meet in Brussels. They agree to continue SFOR beyond the end of its current mandate on 20 June, subject to a resolution from the UN Security Council. |
| 12 | June | The Contact Group calls for an immediate ceasefire in Yugoslavia, the withdrawal from Kosovo of all Yugoslav and Serbian security forces, the admission of international monitors to the province and fresh talks between Yugoslav and ethnic Albanian leaders in Kosovo. |
| 15 | June | The Cardiff European Council endorses the demand that Serbia halt military operations against civilians in Kosovo. |
| 15 | June | *ESDI.* Operation Determined Falcon, an exercise designed to demonstrate NATO force, takes place over Albania and Macedonia, involving 85 aircraft from 13 member countries. |
| 24 | June | UK Prime Minister Tony Blair warns that use of NATO air strikes and ground forces remains an option unless Serbian and FRY security forces are withdrawn from Kosovo. |

| | | |
|---|---|---|
| 24 | June | NATO begins planning for military action against Milosevic. |
| 6 | July | *ESDI/ESDP.* France, Germany, Italy, Spain, Sweden and the UK sign a letter of intent to facilitate cross-border restructuring of defence industries. Six working groups are established to study specific aspects. |
| 15 | July | The US Commission to Assess the Ballistic Missile Threat to the United States (headed by Donald Rumsfeld) releases its report. It estimates that these "newer threats in North Korea, Iran and Iraq ... would be able to inflict major destruction on the US within about five years of a decision to acquire such a capability (10 years in the case of Iraq)." It also suggests that such attacks would come with "little or no warning". Furthermore, "Concerted efforts by a number of overtly or potentially hostile nations to acquire ballistic missiles with biological or nuclear payloads pose a growing threat to the United States, its deployed forces and its friends and allies." The report explicitly criticises the CIA assessment of January: "The threat to the U.S. posed by these emerging capabilities is broader, more mature and evolving more rapidly than has been reported in estimates or reports by the intelligence community." |
| 15-17 | July | The Statute of the International Criminal Court (ICC) is adopted in Rome. |
| | July | The US and UK agree to hold the trial of the Libyan Pan Am suspects in a third country under Scottish law. |
| 7 | August | Two hundred fifty-seven people are killed and more than 5,000 injured in two car-bomb explosions near the US embassies in Nairobi, Kenya, and Dar es Salaam, Tanzania. Al-Qaeda is believed to have conducted the attacks. |
| 20 | August | In retaliation for the Nairobi and Dar es Salaam attacks and after rejecting a Sudanese proposal for UN on-site inspections, US President Clinton orders cruise-missile strikes on a compound housing supporters of Osama bin Laden in Afghanistan and a pharmaceutical factory in Sudan. The US believes that the factory produces chemical weapons, but doubts soon emerge whether this is really the case. |
| 24 | August | The UK and the US agree to have the Lockerbie trial conducted by a Scottish court in the Netherlands. The Dutch Government agrees. |
| 26 | August | The Libyan Government accepts the terms of the Lockerbie trial. |

| | | |
|---|---|---|
| 9 | September | *ESDP.* After failing to set up OCCAR as a subsidiary body of the WEU, France, Germany, Italy and the UK sign a treaty giving legal personality to OCCAR at Farnborough, UK. |
| 24 | September | NATO defence ministers meet in Vilamoura, Portugal, and approve an activation warning authorising SACEUR General Wesley Clark to ask member nations for the forces necessary to carry out military intervention. |
| 11-12 | October | The health of Russian President Boris Yeltsin deteriorates. |
| 15-23 | October | Palestinian leader Arafat, Israeli Prime Minister Netanyahu and US President Clinton negotiate the Wye Agreement. They agree on the principle of "land for peace": Israel is to withdraw from a further 13% of the West Bank and to free 750 Palestinian prisoners. The Palestinian Authority pledges to prevent attacks on Israel and Israeli citizens. |
| 24-25 | October | *ESDP.* After an informal European Council at Pörtschach, Tony Blair declares at a press conference: "There was a willingness, which the UK obviously shares, for Europe to take a stronger foreign policy and security role ... A Common Foreign and Security Policy for the European Union is necessary, it is overdue, it is needed and it is high time we got on with trying to engage with formulating it ...." He adds: "we need to make sure that the institutional mechanism in no way undermines NATO but rather is complementary to it ...." |
| 26 | October | The Dutch military is cleared of trying to cover up its troops' failings during the 1995 fall of the Bosniak enclave of Srebrenica. |
| 27 | October | *ESDP.* Gerhard Schröder of the Social Democratic Party is elected German chancellor and Joschka Fischer of the Green Party appointed deputy chancellor and federal foreign minister. |
| 31 | October | *The Iraq War.* Iraq ends co-operation with UNSCOM and orders inspectors out. |
| 4 | November | *ESDP.* "The Guardian" reports that EU defence ministers agreed at an informal meeting in Vienna that, in the words of Austrian defence minister Werner Fasslabend, the EU "simply [has] to be willing and able to get to grips with European crises and conflicts, if necessary also by [its] own efforts ... ." |
| 6 | November | Unarmed observers under OSCE control arrive in Kosovo as part of an advanced force. |
| 13-14 | November | *The Iraq War.* US President Clinton orders air strikes against Iraq but holds off at the last minute as Iraq promises renewed unconditional co-operation. |
| 18 | November | *The Iraq War.* UNSCOM inspectors return to Iraq. |

| | | |
|---|---|---|
| | November | *ESDP.* Upon a request by the EU, the WEU Satellite Centre embarks upon "general security surveillance" of the Kosovo region. |
| 3-4 | December | *ESDI/ESDP.* The UK and France issue the St Malo Declaration, which states: "the Union [EU] must be given appropriate structures and a capacity for analysis of situations, sources of intelligence, and a capability for relevant strategic planning, without unnecessary duplication, taking account of the existing assets of the WEU and the evolution of its relations with the EU. In this regard, the European Union will also need to have recourse to suitable military means (European capabilities pre-designated within NATO's European pillar or national or multinational European means outside the NATO framework)." This marks a major shift in UK attitudes towards the European defence project. The UK effectively lifts its decades-long objections to the EU's acquiring an "autonomous" military capacity so long as European defence remains NATO-compatible. The Declaration is soon followed by many further-reaching declarations and proposals. |
| 7 | December | *ESDI.* US Secretary of State Madeleine Alrbright endorses ESDI and the Franco-British St Malo initiative but says that it is important that this happen under the "three Ds", i.e., no diminution of NATO, no discrimination of non-EU NATO members and no duplication of efforts or capabilities. The term "three Ds" later comes to mean "no duplication, no discrimination and no de-coupling". |
| 9-16 | December | *The Iraq War.* UN weapons inspectors from UNSCOM leave Iraq after reporting that their work has been obstructed. |
| 11-12 | December | *ESDP.* European Council in Vienna. The first European Council after St Malo "welcomes the new impetus given to the debate on a common European policy on security and defence." The need to establish the necessary capabilities to conduct a CFSP is for the first time specifically mentioned as "[t]he European Council considers that in order for the European Union to be in a position to play its full role on the international stage, the CFSP must be backed by credible operational capabilities." |
| 16 | December | Under pressure by Orthodox extremists, Israeli Prime Minister Netanyahu announces that he will stop implementing the Wye Agreement. |
| 16 | December | *The Iraq War.* The US and the UK launch air strikes against Iraq to force it to fully comply with UN weapons inspections and to degrade the country's military capability. |

| **At a Glance – Major Events and Themes** | |
|---|---|
| | **Rambouillet talks on Kosovo** |
| | **Kosovo War: NATO Operation Allied Force** |
| | **Poland, Czech Republic and Hungary join NATO** |
| | **EU Amsterdam treaty enters into force** |
| | **NATO 50th anniversary summit in Washington** |
| | **Milosevic indicted** |
| | **Serbs defeated, peace plan for Kosovo signed, Serbs withdraw** |
| | **Stability Pact for South Eastern Europe created** |
| | **Croatian President Franjo Tudjman dies** |
| | **The EU's Helsinki Declaration and Headline Goal agree to create a European Rapid Reaction Force** |

## 1999

| Day | Month | Event |
|---|---|---|
| 14 | January | The US imposes sanctions on three Russian scientific institutions that are suspected of helping the Iranian nuclear-weapons programme. |
| 25-26 | January | Serious disagreements persist throughout US Secretary of State Albright's visit to Moscow over the crisis in Kosovo and a possible US missile defence system. |
| 6 | February | Peace negotiations on Kosovo open at Rambouillet, France. |
| 15 | February | Abdullah Öcalan, leader of the Kurdistan Workers' Party, is taken back to Turkey after being captured by Turkish special forces in Kenya. |
| 23 | February | Rambouillet talks are adjourned. The proposed deal, which foresees substantial autonomy for Kosovo within Serbia, has not been endorsed by the parties to the talks. |
| 12 | March | *ESDI.* Poland, the Czech Republic and Hungary join NATO. They are the first former Warsaw Pact members to do so. |
| 13-14 | March | *ESDP.* At an informal EU foreign ministers meeting, the German Presidency submits a proposal entitled "Strengthening the Common Policy on Security and Defence". |
| 15-19 | March | Rambouillet peace talks resume. The Kosovar Albanians accept the Western proposal, but the Serbs do not. International observers are told to leave Kosovo. |
| 19 | March | In a letter to the UN secretary-general, Libya indicates that suspects in the 1988 bombing of Pan Am Flight 103 over Scotland will be made available to the UN secretary-general. |

| | | |
|---|---|---|
| 22 | March | US special envoy Richard Holbrooke travels to Belgrade to convince Milosevic to accept the peace deal proposed at Rambouillet, but the FRY president refuses. |
| 24 | March | NATO begins Operation Allied Force, which is aimed at destroying Yugoslav air defences. The FRY responds by declaring a state of war. Air bases in Italy are used by eight countries. The campaign is led by the US, with support from Canada, France, Germany, Italy, the Netherlands, Spain and the UK. |
| 25 | March | Yugoslavia responds to the attacks against its territory by severing relations with France, Germany, the UK and the US. Government authorities also state that 40 military installations have been targeted, none destroyed but 10 soldiers killed. |
| 27 | March | Large numbers of ethnic Albanian refugees start leaving Kosovo for Albania and Macedonia, forced out of their homes by Serbian forces and paramilitaries in the North and West of Kosovo. A NATO spokesman declares that "dark things are happening" in the province of Kosovo. |
| throughout | April | NATO aircraft continue to carry out attacks on targets in Yugoslavia on a daily basis. The aim of reducing civilian casualties hampers attempts to eliminate air-defence systems in Yugoslavia. |
| 5 | April | The two Libyan Pan Am bombing suspects are handed over to UN representatives and arrive in the Netherlands for trial before a Scottish court. On the same day, the UN Security Council suspends sanctions against Libya. |
| 6 | April | The Libyan Pan Am bombing suspects make their first appearance before the Scottish court set up in the Netherlands. |
| 13 | April | Calls for more aircraft are made by SACEUR General Wesley Clark. |
| 23-25 | April | *ESDI/ESDP.* The 50th-anniversary summit of NATO leaders is held in Washington. Surprisingly, the final *communiqué* of the summit, inspired by events in Kosovo, shows a much greater acceptance of the EU's efforts to build up its own security and defence than the new Strategic Concept, adopted at the same summit. While the Strategic Concept reflects a view that sees the European capability as developing within ESDI, under WEU command and with NATO's providing headquarters, logistics, intelligence etc., the summit *communiqué* "acknowledge[s] the resolve of the European Union to have the capacity for autonomous action so that it can take decisions and approve military action where the Alliance as a whole is not engaged; ... applaud[s] the determination of both EU members and other European Allies to take the necessary |

| | | |
|---|---|---|
| | | steps to strengthen their defence capabilities, especially for new missions, avoiding unnecessary duplication; ... [and] note[s] Canada's interest in participating in such operations ...." The summit also launches the Defence Capabilities Initiative (DCI), designed to ensure that NATO can deal with every kind of security challenge, from crises such as the one in Kosovo to the defence needs of member states. Five overlapping areas for improvements are identified: mobility and deployability, sustainability, effective engagement, survivability, and interoperable communications. The summit also gives tentative support for EU-led Berlin-Plus missions and formulates the principle of "separable but not separate forces". |
| 28 | April | Montenegro continues to oppose the Milosevic regime, but NATO continues to attack targets in Montenegro, leaving the situation in the Yugoslav province in a state of flux. |
| 1 | May | *ESDP.* Ratified by all EU member states, the EU's Amsterdam treaty enters into force. The Troika ceases to exist. It is replaced by the Presidency, assisted by the secretary-general of the Council in his capacity as the high representative for the CFSP and by the member state next in line for the Presidency. These three parties will from now on represent the EU in external relations. |
| 2 | May | Three US soldiers are released by Yugoslav authorities, their release having been negotiated by US civil-rights leader Reverend Jesse Jackson. |
| 6 | May | General Principles on a Settlement to the Conflict in Kosovo are adopted by the G8 foreign ministers in Bonn. |
| 7 | May | The Chinese Embassy in Belgrade is attacked in error by NATO cruise missiles, killing three Chinese nationals and injuring 20. |
| 10 | May | *ESDP.* The WEU De-mining Assistance Mission to Croatia (WEUDAM) starts operations. |
| 10-11 | May | *ESDP.* WEU ministers meet in Bremen, Germany. They agree to take the necessary steps to allow the EU to have direct and indirect access to WEU resources. |
| 24 | May | FRY President Milosevic is indicted with four other senior Serbian leaders on charges of crimes against humanity and war crimes at the UN's ICTY. This marks the first time that a sitting head of state is indicted for war crimes. |
| 28 | May | *ESDP.* At an informal meeting in Bonn, EU defence ministers establish a working group charged to elaborate defence convergence criteria. |

| | | |
|---|---|---|
| 29 | May | *ESDP.* The Franco-German Defence and Security Council meets in Toulouse. The two countries agree to co-operate more closely in operational and armament matters in order to harmonise these areas. They also state the need for an adaptation of Eurocorps so that it can be transformed into a European rapid reaction corps. |
| 2-3 | June | The president of Finland, Martti Ahtisaari (EU envoy), and Viktor Chernomyrdin (special envoy of the president of the Russian Federation for the Balkans) hold talks in Belgrade with FRY President Milosevic, who accepts the terms of the peace agreement they table based on the 6 May General Principles. |
| 3 | June | The Serbian parliament accepts the peace plan proposed by the G8. |
| 3-4 | June | *ESDP.* At the Cologne European Council, it is decided to develop decision-making procedures for a Common European Security and Defence Policy (CESDP) within the context of the CFSP and to develop capacities to undertake operations. The heads of state and government confirm the St Malo Declaration and recognise that to pursue the CFSP, "the Union must have the capacity for autonomous action, backed up by credible military forces, the means to decide to use them, and a readiness to do so, in order to respond to international crises without prejudice to actions by NATO." They commit themselves "to further develop more effective European military capabilities. The maintenance of a sustained defence effort, the implementation of the necessary adaptations and notably the reinforcement of our capabilities in the field of intelligence, strategic transport, command and control." EU leaders agree to limit the EU defence capacity to the Petersberg tasks, comprising "the full range of conflict prevention and crisis management tasks." Furthermore, they "recognise the need to undertake sustained efforts to strengthen the industrial and technological defence base ...." The Summit also confirms the need to convene an IGC to consider the "left-over" institutional issues that need to be settled before enlargement. |
| 8 | June | G8 foreign ministers meet in Cologne and agree to the text of a draft UN Security Council resolution incorporating the main points of the peace deal worked out by the EU envoy (Ahtisaari) and the Russian envoy (Chernomyrdin). |

| | | |
|---|---|---|
| 9 | June | A Military Technical Agreement, based essentially on the G8 peace plan, is signed by NATO's International Security Force KFOR (Kosovo Force), the FRY Government and the Serbian Government. It foresees a cessation of hostilities, the gradual withdrawal of all Serbian forces from Kosovo within 11 days and the arrival of an international security force in the province. |
| 10 | June | The Stability Pact for South Eastern Europe is adopted in Cologne. More than 40 partner countries and organisations undertake to strengthen South-Eastern European countries "in their efforts to foster peace, democracy, respect for human rights and economic prosperity in order to achieve stability in the whole region." Euro-Atlantic integration is promised to all the countries in the region. The Stability Pact is a political declaration of commitment and a framework agreement on international co-operation to develop a shared strategy for stability and growth for these countries. A special co-ordinator is tasked to bring the political strategies of the partners in line to co-ordinate existing and new initiatives. He chairs the most important instrument of the Pact, the so-called Regional Table. Under the Regional Table, three Working Tables operate: one on democratisation and human rights; a second on economic reconstruction, co-operation and development; and a third on security issues, which is split between security and defence and justice and home affairs. Structures and working methods are modelled on the former CSCE process. The states of South-Eastern Europe are on an equal footing with international organisations and financial institutions under the Pact. |
| 10 | June | The NATO air campaign in Kosovo is suspended. |
| 10-11 | June | Serbian troops withdraw from Kosovo. |
| 10 | June | Resolution 1244 is adopted by the UN Security Council. It authorises the secretary-general "to establish an international civil presence in Kosovo in order to provide an interim administration for Kosovo under which the people of Kosovo can enjoy substantial autonomy within the Federal Republic of Yugoslavia …." It also provides for an international security presence to be established in Kosovo. |
| 11 | June | Russian armoured vehicles unexpectedly cross from BiH into Yugoslavia towards the border with Kosovo, creating a flurry of diplomatic activity between the US and Russia. |
| 11-14 | June | Russian troops move first to occupy Pristina airport, as British, French, German, US and Italian KFOR troops deploy across the province to their respective zones. The troops are welcomed by ethnic Albanians. Yugoslav military withdrawals from Kosovo continue. |

| | | |
|---|---|---|
| 18 | June | The Americans and Russians announce that they have reached an agreement on a role for Russian troops in KFOR. |
| 20 | June | NATO declares that the withdrawal of regular Yugoslav forces from Kosovo has been completed and that the air campaign is over. |
| 21 | June | *ESDI/ESDP.* The EU and NATO issue the Bonn Declaration, which speaks of a "full and equal partnership between Europe and the United States in solving regional and global issues" in economic, political and security affairs. The EU and NATO agree on principles and mechanisms for early recognition of potential transatlantic differences of opinion, particularly in the field of trade. |
| 20 | July | *ESDP.* An Anglo-Italian joint declaration launches the European Defence Capability Initiative. It includes a peer review to measure progress; a road map for more effective defence procurement, including the harmonisation of military requirements and collaborative arms procurement; and the promotion of defence, including restructuring. |
| 29-30 | July | The Stability Pact for South Eastern Europe holds its first summit meeting of heads of state or government from 39 countries and the representatives of 17 international organisations in Sarajevo to discuss Balkan reconstruction. Bodo Hombach is appointed special co-ordinator of the Stability Pact. |
| | July | *ESDP.* The WEU Satellite Centre concentrates its work in Kosovo on finalising a geographic information system, creating a digital map of the entire Kosovo region that can be used to assist in several aspects of reconstruction work (including de-mining). This system is made available to the Geneva International Centre for Humanitarian Demining. |
| | July | *ESDP.* The six working groups established by the letter of intent of 1998 on the transnational restructuring of defence industries present their report. An executive committee is set up to draft a framework agreement. |
| 2 | August | *ESDI.* Lord Robertson (UK) is appointed NATO secretary general. |
| 1 | September | President of the European Commission Romano Prodi invites a high-level group comprising former Belgian Prime Minister Jean-Luc Dehaene, former FRG Federal President Richard von Weizäcker and former UK Minister of State for Trade and Competitiveness in Europe Lord Simon of Highbury to give its views on the institutional implications of EU enlargement. |

| | | |
|---|---|---|
| 5 | September | Palestinians and Israelis sign an agreement on the implementation of the Wye Agreement in Sharm el Sheikh. A further 11% of the West Bank is to be under Palestinian control as of 20 January 2000. Negotiations on the definite status of the autonomous areas are to resume no later than 13 September 1999, and are to lead to the conclusion of a comprehensive agreement on all permanent-status issues within one year from the resumption of status negotiations. |
| 18 | September | *ESDP.* Javier Solana of Spain (former NATO secretary general) is appointed EU high representative for the CFSP, and the transfer of WEU assets to the EU is announced, as the WEU as an organisation is considered to "have completed its mandatory function". |
| 8 | October | General Klaus Reinhardt (Germany) becomes the commander of KFOR, replacing Lieutenant General Sir Michael Jackson (UK). |
| 14 | October | *ESDP.* The merger of German Daimler Chrysler Aerospace and French Aerospatiale Matra SA is announced. The two companies are to form the European Aeronautic, Defence and Space Company (EADS), which will be the world number three behind Boeing and Lockheed Martin. |
| 18 | October | *ESDP.* Javier Solana takes office as EU high representative for the CFSP. |
| 18 | October | *ESDP.* The group of high-level experts appointed by European Commission President Romano Prodi presents its report on the institutional implications of EU enlargement in view of the upcoming IGC. They propose a treaty in two separate parts: a basic treaty with aims, principles, general policy, citizens' rights and the institutional framework and another treaty with all other clauses from the existing treaties. The high-level group calls for an extention of QMV and proposes that the EP should have the power of co-decision where QMV applies in the first pillar. The legal capacity of the EU to act as a unit in all external relations must be established. On flexibility, the experts judge that the treaty clauses are too complex and that there are so many conditions that they are unworkable. Closer co-operation should be possible without the right to veto but with due respect for the interests of non-participating states. It should be open to all members that fulfil the conditions and it should not be used in a way that loosens ties between member states. The CFSP should be included in the scope of closer co-operation. They also assert that the IGC must consider defence. New institutional arrangements on defence will be needed, and they should fit into the single institutional framework and not be set up as a fourth pillar. |

| | | |
|---|---|---|
| 8 | November | Negotiations on the status of the West Bank start between Israelis and Palestinians. |
| 10 | November | Information is reported on mass graves in Kosovo and the exhumation of 2,018 bodies for identification. |
| 10 | November | The European Commission presents a report entitled "Adapting the Institutions to Make a Success of Enlargement". |
| 15 | November | *ESDP.* For the first time ever, EU defence ministers meet with EU foreign ministers at the General Affairs Council in Brussels. |
| 15 | November | *ESDP.* The General Affairs Council allows EU High Representative for the CFSP Javier Solana to accept an expected parallel appointment as WEU secretary-general. |
| 18-19 | November | The Charter for European Security is adopted at the OSCE Istanbul summit. It adopts the Platform for Co-operative Security to enhance co-operation between the OSCE and other international organisations and institutions. It develops the OSCE's role in peacekeeping operations, creates a Rapid Expert Assistance Co-operation Team and expands the OSCE's ability to carry out police-related activities. Moreover, it establishes an Operations Centre at the Secretariat to facilitate effective preparation and planning of rapid deployment of OSCE field operations. A Preparatory Committee to improve the consultation process within the OSCE is also set up. Thirty OSCE participating states also agree to adapt the CFE treaty to the changes brought about by the end of the Cold War. |
| 22 | November | Eurocorps' Common Committee decides to transform the Eurocorps into a rapid reaction corps. |
| 22-23 | November | *ESDP.* The WEU Luxembourg Declaration: "Ministers reaffirm their readiness, ... if the Union so wishes, to continue to provide the Union with access to an operational capability and to elaborate and implement decisions and actions of the Union which have defence implications." Ministers also express "their willingness to allow bodies of the Council of the European Union direct access, as required, to the expertise of the Organisation's operational structures, including the WEU Secretariat, the Military Staff, the Satellite Centre and the Institute for Security Studies." They agree "to authorise the transmission of all WEU's work and analyses, particularly those of the Military Staff, to the High Representative for the CSFP and the other appropriate bodies of the Council of the European Union taking into account the relevant security arrangements." |
| 23 | November | US President Clinton visits Kosovo. |
| 25 | November | *ESDP.* Javier Solana, the EU high representative for the CFSP, is appointed WEU secretary-general. |

| | | |
|---|---|---|
| 25 | November | *ESDP.* In view of the upcoming Helsinki European Council, the UK and France issue a Joint Declaration on European Defence, stressing that Helsinki must "take a decisive step forward for the development of [European] military capabilities and for the setting up of the political and military instruments necessary to use them." They declare their intention "to develop standing arrangements for setting up multinationalised cells within [UK's Permanent Joint Headquarters and France's *Centre Operationnel Interarmées* (proposed as options to command EU-led operations)] including officers from other EU countries." |
| 30 | November | *ESDP.* In light of the upcoming Helsinki European Council, France and Germany declare at a summit in Paris that they have decided to compare their respective plans concerning the reinforcement of their capacities in the fields of intelligence, strategic mobility, command and control, and communications, and to continue to develop their military capacities in this domain. In the intelligence field, they state their determiniation to pool "existing or future means, including in the space area, in order to constitute common European capacities." France and Germany also establish a European Air Transport Command. |
| | November | The Serbian minority in Kosovo continues to be targeted by ethnic Albanians. |
| 2 | December | *ESDP.* The Spanish aerospace and defence company CASA signs an agreement to join EADS. |
| 3 | December | France, Italy and Spain launch Helios 1B, the second European military reconnaissance satellite. |
| 10 | December | President Franjo Tudjman dies in Croatia. |
| 10-11 | December | *ESDP.* The European Council in Helsinki sets an objective of having a capacity, by 2003, to deploy within 60 days and to sustain for at least one year 50,000 to 60,000 military personnel capable of undertaking the full range of Petersberg tasks. This objective becomes known as the Helsinki Headline Goal. A decision is also taken to establish new political and military bodies and structures within the Council to enable the EU to guarantee the necessary political guidance and strategic direction of such operations. Specifically, a standing Political and Security Committee (PSC), a Military Comittee and a Military Staff will be established within the Council. As an interim measure, EU leaders establish an interim Political and Security Committee, an interim body of military representatives of member states' chiefs of defence to give advice to the interim PSC as required, and |

| | | |
|---|---|---|
| | | a detachment of military experts from member states to assist in the work on the CESDP and to form the nucleus of the future Military Staff. EU leaders also call on the Commission to create a civilian rapid reaction facility and pledge to devote particular attention to developing the capabilities necessary to ensure effective performance in crisis management: deployability, sustainability, interoperability, flexibility, mobility, survivability, and command and control. The European Council also expresses its will to develop "appropriate arrangements" for consultation and co-operation with NATO and affirms the principle of full consultation, co-operation and transparency between the EU and NATO, as well as necessary dialogue, consultation and co-operation with non-EU European members of NATO. On institutional implications of enlargement, the European Council decides that the upcoming IGC should look at the following issues: the size and composition of the Commission, the weighing of votes in the Council, the extention of QMV and other institutional adjustments necessary in relation to the above. |
| 17 | December | *The Iraq War.* The UN Security Council replaces the United Nations Special Commission (UNSCOM) with the United Nations Monitoring, Verification and Inspection Commision (UNMOVIC). UNMOVIC's mandate is the verification of Iraq's compliance with Resolution 687 (1991), i.e., its disarmament, and in the longer run ongoing monitoring, verification and inspections. Like UNSCOM, UNMOVIC is a subsidiary body of the Security Council, but unlike UNSCOM it reports directly to the Security Council and not to the secretary-general. The Security Council also provides for a renewable 120-day suspension of sanctions against Iraq to be put in place if and when the latter co-operates in all respects and if the ongoing verification and monitoring scheme is operational. |
| 31 | December | Vladimir Putin becomes acting president of the Russian Federation. |

Part 7

# THE END OF STRATEGIC VACATION

# 2000 - 2005

2000 2003 2005

| At a Glance – Major Events and Themes | |
|---|---|
| | **EU Toolbox Meeting on European Security and Defence Policy** |
| | **Peacekeeping force in Kosovo continues its work amidst ongoing Serb-Albanian conflict** |
| | **Vladimir Putin becomes new president of the Russian Federation** |
| | **Feira European Council** |
| | **Yugoslav President Slobodan Milosevic is replaced by Vojislav Kostunica** |
| | **ESDP Capabilities Commitment Conference in Brussels** |
| | **Nice European Council** |

## 2000

| Day | Month | Event |
|---|---|---|
| 26 | January | The European Commission presents a follow-up on its report "Adapting the Institutions to Make a Success of Enlargement". |
| 31 | January | Sanctions are imposed on Austria by the EU due to the presence of the far-right Freedom Party in a national coalition government. The sanctions have more of a psychological than a practical impact. They involve a freezing of bilateral relations; there are to be no contacts or ambassadorial meetings at the intergovernmental level, and Austrian candidates will not be supported when EU international offices are assigned. |
| 4 | February | The sanctions against Austria come into force. |
| 6 | February | Russian federal forces take control of Grozny, the capital of the separatist Russian republic of Chechnya. |
| 7 | February | NATO is accused of breaching international law during the Kosovo conflict in a report published by Human Rights Watch, owing to the US and UK's use of cluster bombs. It is also suggested that NATO might have contravened international humanitarian law by attacking targets of questionable military legitimacy and by not taking adequate measures to warn civilians of impending attacks. |
| 14 | February | The EU IGC opens in order to "carry out a comprehensive review of the provisions of the Treaties on the composition and functioning of the institutions" before enlargement, as demanded in the Amsterdam treaty. Belgium, France and Italy want the conference to agree on a "significant extension of recourse to qualified majority voting." |
| 24 | February | Acting Russian President Putin dismisses his prime minister and cabinet "for administrative and political reasons." |

| | | |
|---|---|---|
| 28 | February | *ESDP.* At an informal meeting of EU defence ministers, two papers are presented. The Toolbox Paper, initiated by Richard Hatfield of the British Defence Ministry, lays the groundwork for the Capabilities Commitment Conference of November 2000. The UK Food for Thought Paper elaborates the Headline and Capabilities Goals. |
| | February | Allegations emerge of widespread torture of Chechen civilians in Russian military camps. |
| 23-24 | March | *ESDP.* The Lisbon European Council agrees that sanctions against the Serbian regime will remain in force as long as President Slobodan Milosevic is in power. Javier Solana and EU External Relations Commissioner Chris Patten are both given the mandate to oversee the Balkan policy of the EU. EU leaders also decide to establish a committee for civilian crisis management by or at the Feira European Council of June 2000. |
| 26 | March | Vladimir Putin is elected president of the Russian Federation. |
| | March | Violence continues in the ethnically divided town of Mitrovica in Kosovo between Serbs, ethnic Albanians and the NATO-led KFOR peacekeeping force, which struggles to keep the two sides apart. |
| 4 | April | KFOR peacekeepers clash with Serbs, as tension in the disputed Serbian province of Kosovo continue to rise. |
| 17 | April | Israel informs the UN Security Council that it will withdraw from Lebanon by July 2000. |
| 18 | April | *ESDP.* Lieutenant-General Juan Ortuño of Eurocorps takes command of KFOR. He acts under the direct command of SACEUR General Clark. |
| 7 | May | Vladimir Putin is inaugurated as the new president of Russia. |
| 7 | May | *ESDI/ESDP.* EU foreign ministers meeting informally in the Azores decide to back plans for joint EU-NATO working groups on security issues, military capabilities, arrangements for EU use of NATO assets and permanent EU-NATO arrangements. |
| 16 | May | Israel withdraws its troops from southern Lebanon. |
| 22 | May | *ESDP.* The EU Council of Ministers establishes the Committee for Civilian Aspects of Crisis Management. It is to provide information, make recommendations and give its opinion to the Political and Security Committee (PSC). |
| 6 | June | Alija Izetbegovic announces that he will step down as president of BiH for health reasons. |

| | | |
|---|---|---|
| 19-20 | June | *ESDI/ESDP*. Feira European Council: "Principles and modalities for arrangements have been identified to allow non-EU European NATO members and other EU accession candidates to contribute to EU military crisis management. Principles for consultation with NATO on military issues and modalities for developing EU-NATO relations have also been identified in four areas covering security issues, capability goals, the modalities for EU access to NATO assets, and the definition of permanent consultation arrangements." The European Council also endorses the Presidency Report on Strengthening the CESDP and identifies four spheres in which to develop priority areas for intervention: police, rule of law, civilian administration and civilian protection. Concerning police, European leaders undertake to be able to provide by 2003 up to 5,000 police officers for international missions across the range of conflict-prevention and crisis-management operations. The European Council also adds the issue of enhanced co-operation to the agenda of the next IGC. |
| 11-25 | July | Palestinian leader Yasser Arafat, Israeli Prime Minister Ehud Barak and US President Bill Clinton participate in a summit at Camp David, US. It fails over the status of Jerusalem. |
| 27 | July | *ESDP*. France, Germany, Italy, Spain, Sweden and the UK sign a Framework Agreement Concerning Measures to Facilitate the Restructuring and Operation of the European Defence Industry. |
| 12 | August | A torpedo aboard the Russian nuclear-powered submarine "Kursk" explodes, causing the vessel to sink in the Barents Sea. All 118 crew die. |
| 21 | August | The UN Brahimi Report on peacekeeping ("Report of the Panel on United Nations Peacekeeping Operations") is published. It calls for "clear, credible and achievable mandates" and insists that "peacekeepers, once developed, must be able to carry out their mandates professionally and successfully and must be capable of defending themselves, other mission components and the mission mandate, with robust rules of engagement, against those who renege on their commitments to a peace accord or otherwise seek to undermine it by violence." The report also recommends "a substantive increase in resources for Headquarters support of peacekeeping operations" and makes several proposals for structural adjustments to the UN Department of Peacekeeping Operations. |
| 12 | September | The EU lifts the diplomatic sanctions against Austria but says the participation of the far-right Freedom Party in Austria's government is still a "grave concern". |
| 19 | September | *ESDI/ESDP*. The first meeting is held between the NAC and the interim PSC. |
| 24 | September | Presidential, parliamentary and local elections take place in Yugoslavia. |

| | | |
|---|---|---|
| 28 | September | Israeli opposition leader Ariel Sharon visits the Haram Al-Sheif compound in Jerusalem, where the Al-Aqsa Mosque is located. Palestinians feel provoked. Violent riots in Jerusalem, the West Bank and Gaza mark the beginning of the second *intifada*. |
| 28 | September | The Yugoslav Election Commission says Slobodan Milosevic's party has won parliamentary elections. The opposition claims irregularities and victory. It calls for five days of non-violent protest. Milosevic announces he wants to stand for a second round of presidential elections on 8 October. |
| 5 | October | The Yugoslav High Court annuls the 24 September election results. Mass protests continue, and opposition forces take over the parliament building and state-run media. |
| 6 | October | The Yugoslav High Court declares opposition candidate Vojislav Kostunica winner of the presidential elections. |
| 6 | October | Yugoslav President Milosevic surrenders power. |
| 7 | October | Kostunica is inaugurated as the new president of Yugoslavia. |
| 9 | October | EU foreign ministers meet in Luxembourg and agree to lift the oil embargo, flight ban and other financial and travel restrictions against Serbs, except for Milosevic and his family. |
| 14 | October | Alija Izetbegovic, the last of the three war-time leaders in the Balkans, steps down as president of BiH. The other two were Slobodan Milosevic in Serbia/Yugoslavia and Franjo Tudjman in Croatia. |
| 14 | October | An attack on the American guided-missile destroyer "USS Cole" in Yemen kills 17 and injures 39. Al-Qaeda is responsible for the attack. |
| 16-17 | October | Israeli Prime Minister Ehud Barak and Palestinian leader Arafat meet in Sharm el Sheikh, but the summit breaks down almost immediately. Violence in the occupied territories and against Israel continues. |
| 25 | October | Representatives of South Eastern European countries, EU External Relations Commissioner Chris Patten and Stability Pact Special Co-ordinator Bodo Hombach meet in Skopje, Macedonia. Kostunica attends as the new president of Yugoslavia. |
| 7 | November | In the US presidential election, no winner can be declared, as the result in Florida is not yet clear. Neither candidate has enough electoral votes. The Al Gore campaign requests a recount because of irregularities. |
| 11 | November | The George W. Bush campaign takes legal action to stop the recount. A legal battle ensues about the questions of whether recounts should take place; if so, then in which counties; by which means; and by what date. |

| | | |
|---|---|---|
| 13 | November | *ESDP.* The WEU Council of Ministers in Marseille decides that the WEU will cease most activities. The Petersberg tasks are assigned to the EU, together with WEU agencies. WEAG defence ministers also agree to the accession of Austria, the Czech Republic, Finland, Hungary, Poland and Sweden as full members of the WEAG. |
| 14-15 | November | *ESDI/ESDP.* NATO defence ministers agree on EU proposals concerning EU-NATO permanent arrangements for consultation and co-operation. |
| 20-21 | November | *ESDP.* Capabilities Commitment Conference in Brussels: EU defence ministers pledge their initial commitments to the European Rapid Reaction Force (ERRF). The member states commit themselves, on a voluntary basis, to making national contributions corresponding to rapid reaction capabilities identified for attaining the Headline Goal. These commitments are set out in the Force Catalogue. One hundred thousand troops, 400 aircraft and 100 ships are pledged on this day. Also, a number of areas are identified at the conference in which efforts will be made to upgrade existing assets, investment, development and co-ordination, so as gradually to acquire or enhance the capabilities required for autonomous EU action. This conference constitutes the first stage of the process of reinforcing military capabilities for crisis management by the Union with the purpose of achieving the Headline Goal. |
| 7-11 | December | *ESDP.* European Council in Nice, France: Three new permanent bodies are set up: the Political and Security Committee (PSC), the EU Military Committee (EUMC) and the EU Military Staff (EUMS). The Presidency Report on ESDP makes a proposal to NATO for permanent arrangements for EU-NATO consultation and co-operation. The report also includes paragraphs on incorporation of certain WEU functions into the EU (Satellite Centre and Institute for Security Studies, direct management by the EU of a police technical co-operation mission in Albania, to take over from the WEU's MAPE), the achievement of the Headline Goal and of civilian crisis-management objectives. The Treaty of Nice adopted at this European Council states that: "The common foreign and security policy shall include all questions relating to the security of the Union, including the progressive framing of a common defence policy, which might lead to a common defence, should the European Council so decide. ... The policy of the Union in accordance with this Article shall not prejudice the specific character of the security and defence policy of certain Member States and shall respect the obligations of certain Member States, which see their common defence realised in the North Atlantic Treaty Organisation (NATO), |

| | | |
|---|---|---|
| | | under the North Atlantic Treaty and be compatible with the common security and defence policy established within that framework. The progressive framing of a common defence policy will be supported, as Member States consider appropriate, by cooperation between them in the field of armaments." |
| 12 | December | The US Supreme Court makes a final decision in the legal battle regarding the US election and finds that manual recounts are unlawful. Florida is thus called for Bush, who now has enough votes to win the Presidency. |
| 13 | December | Al Gore accepts the US Supreme Court decision and makes his concession speech. |
| 14-15 | December | *ESDI/ESDP.* At the NAC meeting in Brussels, no agreement is reached on permanent arrangements between the EU and NATO. This is due to Turkish dissatisfaction with its participation in EU-led operations. Turkey, concerned about a possible EU intervention in Cyprus or the Aegean Sea area, seeks a say in decision-making and shaping of EU operations with NATO assets or ERRF operations, to which it has pledged over 20,000 troops. |
| 16 | December | George W. Bush nominates Colin Powell as US secretary of state. |
| 31 | December | The US signs the Rome Statute of the ICC on the last day on which it is open for signature. |

| At a Glance – Major Events and Themes | |
|---|---|
| | **NATO-EU joint meetings begin in earnest** |
| | **Conflict in Macedonia** |
| | **Plans for US missile defence system unveiled** |
| | **Tony Blair re-elected UK prime minister** |
| | **First Putin-Bush meeting** |
| | **NATO disarmament operation Essential Harvest in Macedonia** |
| | **Al-Qaeda attacks the United States** |
| | **NATO operation Amber Fox to protect civilian observers in Macedonia** |
| | **Operations commence in Afghanistan against Al-Qaeda and Taleban** |
| | **Operation Eagle Assist deploys NATO radar planes to patrol the skies over the United States** |
| | **Laeken European Council declares ERRF operational but sees deficiencies in achieving the Headline Goal and launches a European Capability Action Plan** |

# 2001

| Day | Month | Event |
|---|---|---|
| 1 | January | The Treaty on Open Skies enters into force. |
| 9-10 | January | *ESDI.* The NAC meets. The US and the UK reject demands by Italy, Germany, Greece and Norway to abandon the use of depleted uranium. This follows widespread debate and media coverage of the possible environmental health risks associated with the use of depleted uranium munitions by NATO in the Balkans. |
| 10 | January | Biljana Plavsic (former president of Republika Srpska) voluntarily surrenders to the ICTY to face charges that include genocide and crimes against humanity. |
| 11 | January | The Commission to Assess United States National Security Space Management and Organization headed by Donald Rumsfeld presents its report. It states that the US has "an urgent interest in promoting and protecting the peaceful use of space and in developing the technologies and operational capabilities that its objectives in space require." The US president should "have the option to deploy weapons in space to deter threats to, and if necessary, defend against attacks on U.S. interests." |
| 20 | January | George W. Bush is inaugurated as US president. He appoints Donald H. Rumsfeld as secretary of defense. |
| 22 | January | US President Bush appoints Condoleezza Rice as national security advisor. |

| | | |
|---|---|---|
| 22 | January | *ESDI/ESDP.* The EU Council of Ministers confirms the setting up of three essential components of the ESDP: the PSC, the Military Committee and the Military Staff. |
| 26 | January | Donald Rumsfeld and Colin Powell are sworn in as US secretary of defense and secretary of state, respectively. |
| 28 | January | *ESDP.* The Organisation for Joint Armaments Cooperation Convention enters into force. The organisation, which is often named after its French acronym OCCAR (*Organisation Conjointe de Coopération en Matière d'Armement*), aims at greater efficiency in the management of collaborative defence-equipment programmes. France, Germany, Italy and the UK are members. |
| 5 | February | *ESDI/ESDP.* The first meeting at the ambassadorial level of the NAC and the EU PSC under the new permanent NATO-EU consultation arrangements takes place at the EU in Brussels. Discussions focus on the way ahead for EU-NATO relations and the management of the crisis in the Western Balkans. |
| 5-6 | February | Ehud Barak loses elections in Israel; Ariel Sharon becomes the new prime minister. |
| 17 | February | The first clashes take place in Macedonia between government forces and fighters of the rebel movement National Liberation Army (NLA) near the village of Tanusevac. The rebels demand a new Macedonian constitution with better rights for Albanians and international mediation of the conflict. Former fighters of the Kosovo Liberation Army are also among the ranks of the NLA. |
| 24 | February | A mass grave is discovered in Chechnya near a major Russian military base. The number of bodies is unknown and disputed (20-200). |
| 26 | February | *ESDP.* EU foreign ministers sign the Treaty of Nice, agreed upon at the European Council in December 2000. The treaty introduces the possibility of closer co-operation in the field of the CFSP, with the exception of military matters and defence policy. The ministers also create the Civilian Rapid Reaction Mechanism (CRRM) to enhance the EU's civilian capacity to intervene fast, easily and effectively in crisis situations in third countries. According to External Relations Commissioner Chris Patten, the CRRM "will act as a catalyser allowing [the EU] to mobilise resources within hours or days rather than weeks or months." |
| 26 | February | Macedonian security forces try to take control of Tanusevac. The situation escalates into a lengthy exchange of fire. |
| 1 | March | Lieutenant-General Rainer Schuwirth (Germany) is appointed the first director-general of the EU Military Staff. UK Major-General Graham Messervy-Whiting is appointed his deputy and chief of staff. |

| | | |
|---|---|---|
| 14 | March | *ESDI/ESDP.* The EU PSC and the NATO NAC meet; the situation in Kosovo dominates discussions. |
| 19 | March | *ESDI/ESDP.* EU foreign ministers meet to discuss the crisis in Macedonia and the possible role of the EU in helping to solve it. In an unprecedented move, NATO Secretary General Lord Robertson is also invited to the meeting in order to synchronise actions by the two organisations. |
| 22 | March | A high-level EU delegation headed by Swedish Foreign Minister Anna Lindt and including Belgian Foreign Minister Louis Michel, Javier Solana, and EU External Relations Commissioner Chris Patten arrive in Macedonia for talks with the two parties to the conflict. |
| 28 | March | President Bush announces that the US will not ratify the Kyoto Protocol. The parties to the protocol need to account for at least 55% of total 1990 carbon dioxide emissions before the treaty can enter into force. Thus, US refusal to ratify constitutes a fatal blow to the protocol unless Russia ratifies. |
| 9 | April | *ESDP.* General Gustav Hägglund from Finland is appointed the first chair of the EU Military Committee. |
| 9-10 | April | German Chancellor Schröder and Russian President Putin meet in St. Petersburg. |
| 11 | April | *ESDP.* "The Guardian" reports that a "House of Commons report describes plans for a European rapid reaction force as confused and lacking democratic accountability." |
| 18 | April | *ESDP.* The Framework Agreement Concerning Measures to Facilitate the Restructuring and Operation of the European Defence Industry enters into force between France, Germany, Italy, Spain, Sweden and the UK. |
| 21-28 | April | The first of a series of events takes place to celebrate the 10th anniversary of North Atlantic East-West co-operation in the framework of the NACC and the EAPC (as of 1997). |
| 1 | May | US President Bush makes a speech in which he advocates deep unilateral cuts in the US nuclear arsenal and at the same time announces his determination to construct a system of national missile defence. This casts doubt on the future of the 1972 Anti-Ballistic Missile (ABM) treaty with Russia. According to Bush, it is safe to leave the ABM behind. Bush asserts that, "Unlike the Cold War, today's most urgent threat stems not from thousands of ballistic missiles in the Soviet hands, but from a small number of missiles in the hands of these states, states for whom terror and blackmail are a way of life." |
| 8 | May | The first financing decision under the new CRRM is taken. It concerns housing reconstruction in the former Yugoslav Republic of Macedonia (FYROM). |

| | | |
|---|---|---|
| 14 | May | *ESDP.* The German and Dutch defence ministers, Rudolf Scharping and Frank de Grave, respectively, sign a Memorandum of Understanding on Mutual Co-operation to Reinforce European Air Transport Capacities, which "enables the Netherlands to call upon Germany to facilitate the deployment of Netherlands forces in future crisis response or humanitarian assistance operations." The Netherlands will provide funds to Germany to strengthen the latter's strategic air-transport capabilities in support of international operations in areas of air-to-air refuelling, medical evacuation, and handling and reception capabilities. |
| 15 | May | *ESDP.* The 13 WEAG members sign a memorandum of understanding entitled European Undertakings for Research Organisations, Programmes and Activities. It is an umbrella arrangement for collaboration in research and technology. |
| 29-30 | May | *ESDI/ESDP.* NATO defence ministers meet in Hungary. Their discussions focus on the situation in FYROM, NATO-EU co-operation and relations with Russia, as well as missile defence and the proliferation of weapons of mass destruction. |
| 30 | May | *ESDI/ESDP.* The first formal NATO-EU ministerial meeting is held in Hungary and is dominated by discussions on stability in the Balkans and EU access to NATO planning capabilities and military assets. |
| 5 | June | Headquarters Eurocorps start adopting a rapid reaction corps structure. |
| 7 | June | New Labour wins UK general elections. Tony Blair starts his second term as prime minister. |
| 7-8 | June | *ESDI.* NATO defence ministers meet in Brussels. US Secretary of Defense Rumsfeld argues for the utility of missile defence against rogue states and that the US considers the 1972 ABM treaty obsolete. ESDI is also discussed. Ministers also review the progress in implementing the DCI and identify a number of deficiencies. These are "effective engagement and survivability of Alliance forces such as in the areas of suppression of enemy air defence and support jamming; combat identification; intelligence, surveillance and target acquisition (including the Alliance Ground Surveillance system); air weapons systems for day/night and all weather operations; air defence in all its aspects, including against theatre ballistic missiles and cruise missiles; capabilities against nuclear, biological, and chemical (NBC) weapons and their means of delivery, and NBC detection and protection." |
| 10 | June | Swiss voters narrowly vote in favour of legislation to allow Swiss troops on international peacekeeping missions to be armed and to allow more automatic and balanced procedures for training of the Swiss military with NATO forces. |
| 11 | June | *ESDP.* The EU Military Staff is declared operational. |

| | | |
|---|---|---|
| 12 | June | *ESDI/ESDP.* The NATO Military Committee and the EUMC meet for the first time at NATO headquarters. They exchange information on issues such as NATO assets and capabilities, the NATO command structure, the future force structure and NATO's DCI, ESDP, its exercise programme and command and control of EU operations. |
| 12 | June | US President Bush arrives on a European tour. He first meets Spanish Prime Minister José María Aznar and then attends a NATO summit. He advocates missile defence and receives support only from the Italian and the UK prime ministers, Silvio Berlusconi and Tony Blair, respectively. |
| 13 | June | *ESDI.* A NATO summit meeting takes place in Brussels. The question of NATO's role in the Macedonian situation dominates discussions. |
| 14 | June | US President Bush meets EU leaders in Gothenburg, where disagreements between the Europeans and the Americans over the Kyoto Protocol on global warming dominate. |
| 15 | June | *ESDI/ESDP.* President Bush delivers a speech in Warsaw in which he argues for the integration of Central and Eastern European countries in European and Atlantic institutions and for a greater role and responsibility of Europe in European security: "I believe in NATO membership for all of Europe's democracies that seek it and are ready to share the responsibilities that NATO brings. ... All nations should understand that there is no conflict between membership in NATO and membership in the European Union. My nation welcomes the consolidation of European unity, and the stability it brings. We welcome a greater role for the EU in European security, properly integrated with NATO. ... the basis for our mutual security must move beyond Cold War doctrines .... We must confront the shared security threats of regimes that thrive by creating instability, that are ambitious for weapons of mass destruction, and are dangerously unpredictable. In Europe, you're closer to these challenges than the United States. You see the lightning well before we hear the thunder. Only together, however, can we confront the emerging threats of a changing world." |
| 15-16 | June | *ESDP.* The European Council in Gothenburg, Sweden, is also attended by the leaders of 12 applicant states. The EU is "committed to developing and refining its capabilties, structures and procedures in order to improve its ability to undertake the full range of crisis prevention and management tasks." To this end, EU leaders agree among other things to improve early-warning procedures. The European Council also sets up specific targets for the Committee for Civilian Aspects of Crisis Management and adopts the EU Programme for the Prevention of Violent Conflicts. |
| 15-20 | June | Negotiations between Macedonian and Albanian government parties on the crisis in Macedonia fail. |

| | | |
|---|---|---|
| 16 | June | Russian President Vladimir Putin and US President George W. Bush meet for the first time in Ljubljana, Slovenia. |
| 19 | June | *ESDP.* At the Le Bourget Air Show, a memorandum of understanding on a joint A400M programme is signed by the defence ministers of Belgium, France, Germany, Luxembourg, France, Spain, Turkey and the UK. Portugal is also interested but has not yet finished its internal approval process. Germany's participation is subject to parliamentary approval. |
| 20 | June | Macedonian President Boris Trajkovski requests NATO assistance. |
| 23 | June | NATO Secretary General Lord Robertson urges the Macedonian Government to stop its offensive against ethnic Albanian rebels. He describes the offensive as "complete folly" and speaks of "unacceptable resort to violent action". "New outbreaks of violence, from whichever side", Robertson says, "are madness at this sensitive time." |
| 24 | June | EU High Representative Javier Solana wins a ceasefire in Macedonia. |
| 28 | June | Former Yugoslav President Milosevic is handed over to the ICTY at The Hague. |
| 28 | June | *ESDP.* The WEU Council holds its last meeting. The WEU now takes up a residual status in Brussels. |
| 29 | June | NATO approves operation Essential Harvest for Macedonia. |
| | June | The Russian and Belarusian ratification procedures for the Open Skies treaty are completed. |
| | June | *ESDP.* The Helsinki Process Catalogue is issued. It lists 40 shortfalls in attaining the Helsinki Headline Goal, i.e., only 104 of 144 capability targets in the Helsinki Headline Goal have been met. |
| 2 | July | Talks aimed at producing a political settlement to the crisis in Macedonia are opened by EU Special Representative in FYROM François Léotard and Special Envoy of the President of the United States James Pardew. |
| 3 | July | Milosevic makes his first appearance before the ICTY. |
| 16 | July | *ESDP.* The EU Council of Ministers adopts two joint actions relating to the transfer of the WEU Satellite Centre (Torrejon) and the Institute for Security Studies (Paris) to the EU, to become effective on 1 January 2002. |
| 19 | July | Peace negotiations in Macedonia are suspended by the Albanian parties. |
| 26 | July | NATO Secretary General Lord Robertson and EU High Representative for the CFSP Javier Solana travel to Macedonia to stop deepening hostilities in that country. |
| 28 | July | Peace talks on Macedonia resume in Ohrid. |

| | | |
|---|---|---|
| 13 | August | The Ohrid Framework Agreement is signed between the Macedonian Government and the National Liberation Army. It includes raising the percentage of ethnic Albanians in the Macedonian police force, increasing the status of the Albanian language so it can be used in official institutions and improving the constitutional status of ethnic Albanians and other minority groups. |
| 15 | August | NATO authorises partial deployment of a Task Force to Macedonia. |
| 22 | August | *ESDI/ESDP.* NATO's NAC and the EU's PSC meet as part of regular consultations. The crisis in Macedonia dominates discussions. |
| 22 | August | NATO launches Operation Essential Harvest in Macedonia, and the full deployment of a 3,500-troop force to collect and destroy rebel arms is thus authorised. |
| 27 | August | NATO's Operation Essential Harvest in Macedonia starts effectively. |
| 11 | September | *9/11.* Al-Qaeda attacks against the United States in New York and Washington. Some 2,800 people die as two hijacked planes are flown into the World Trade Center, another hits the Pentagon and a fourth crashes in a field in Pennsylvania. This is the first time since 1812 that the US has faced a lethal attack by a foreign force on its own territory. As an immediate result, air travel across the United States is – for the first time ever – suspended totally for several days for fear of follow-up attacks. Soon afterwards, Bush declares a Global War on Terror. |
| 12 | September | *9/11.* The UN Security Council unanimously adopts a resolution recognising terrorism as a "threat to international peace and security". |
| 12 | September | *9/11.* NATO invokes Article 5, under which an attack on one member state is considered an attack on all 19 members. |
| 12 | September | *9/11.* President of the European Commission Romano Prodi convenes an emergency meeting to discuss implications of 9/11. |
| 13 | September | *9/11.* The NATO-Russia Permanent Joint Council issues a joint statement condemning the attacks of 11 September. |
| 19 | September | *9/11.* The European Commission proposes a European arrest warrant and a common definition of terrorism, as well as related penalties to tackle cross-border crime, including terrorism. |
| 21 | September | *9/11.* An extraordinary European Council declares that, "The fight against terrorism will, more than ever, be a priority objective of the European Union." An action plan is adopted to this end. It identifies a series of measures: joint investigation teams of police and magistrates from |

| | | |
|---|---|---|
| | | throughout the EU; a common list of terrorist organisations; co-operation agreements on terrorism between Europol and the relevant US authorities; a specialist anti-terrorism team within Europol; Eurojust, a co-ordination body composed of magistrates, prosecutors and police officers; and routine exchange of information between member states of Europol. |
| 21 | September | FYROM authorities request continued NATO assistance. |
| 23 | September | Operation Essential Harvest completes its work of disarming the ethnic Albanian NLA in Macedonia, and Operation Amber Fox is to take over. The mission changes from the collection of weapons to the protection of civilian observers. |
| 26 | September | The UN Security Council gives Operation Amber Fox an initial three-month mandate. |
| 27 | September | NATO Operation Amber Fox is deployed in FYROM. |
| 28 | September | *9/11.* The UN Security Council decides on a range of measures that nations must take against terrorism. |
| 29 | September | *9/11.* The EU warns that retaliation for the attacks against the US must be "targeted" and "proportional" to remain legitimate under the authority of UN Security Council Resolution 1368. |
| | September | *ESDP.* The European Air Transport Co-ordination Cell in Eindhoven, set up by the seven members of the European Air Group, becomes operational. |
| 3 | October | *ESDI/ESDP.* Russian President Putin meets with senior EU officials and NATO Secretary General Lord Robertson. It is agreed that the EU will inform Russia of discussions within the PSC. Putin hints that Russia will not oppose NATO expansion to the Baltic region due to his country's growing co-operation with the organisation. |
| 3 | October | French General Marcel Valentin becomes head of NATO-led KFOR operations in Kosovo. |
| 4 | October | A Russian airliner *en route* from Tel Aviv to Novosibirsk is accidentally hit by a Ukrainian missile fired during military exercises, killing all 78 people on board. |
| 4 | October | *9/11.* NATO responds positively to a US request for help in the fight against terrorism by introducing a number of measures to support the United States. |
| 7 | October | *9/11.* Owing to the continuing refusal of the Taleban Government in Afghanistan to surrender Osama bin Laden and other Al-Qaeda members, the US, UK, Australia, Canada, France and Germany begin military operations against the country. Operation Enduring Freedom is underway. |
| 8 | October | The Russian nuclear submarine "Kursk" is raised. |

| | | |
|---|---|---|
| 8 | October | *9/11.* UK Prime Minister Blair establishes a war cabinet to supervise Great Britain's participation in the US-led military action in Afghanistan. |
| 9 | October | *9/11.* NATO launches Operation Eagle Assist by deploying STANAVFORMED to the eastern part of the Mediterranean and announces the sending of five AWACS to the US. The latter is the first time NATO assets are deployed to defend the continental United States. |
| 18 | October | NATO Secretary General Lord Robertson, EU High Representative Javier Solana and OSCE Chairman-in-Office Mircea Dan Geoana (as well as SACEUR General Joseph Ralston) travel to Macedonia to urge government officials to resume the country's political process. |
| 19 | October | *9/11.* EU leaders meet at an informal European Council in Ghent, Belgium, to discuss EU enlargement, the introduction of the Euro and a proposed European Constitution. They also make a declaration on follow-up to the 11 September attacks and the fight against terrorism and endorse a "road map" of all measures and initiatives to be taken in the fight against terrorism. Following up on the action plan endorsed on 21 September, EU leaders approve practical details of the common arrest warrant and the common definition of terrorist offences, as well as anti-money-laundering measures. They also agree on increased co-operation between Europol, Eurojust, intelligence services, police forces and judicial authorities, which should enable them to draw up the requested list of terrorist organisations by the end of the year. During the meetings, disagreement among EU leaders concerning US military action in Afghanistan becomes apparent. |
| 26 | October | *9/11.* NATO launches Operation Active Endeavour, deploying parts of its STANVFORMED to patrol the eastern Mediterranean and monitor shipping. |
| 9-10 | November | *9/11.* Police in Strasbourg arrest six suspected members of an Islamic fundamentalist cell believed to be linked to Osama bin Laden. |
| 13-15 | November | Russian President Putin meets US President Bush in Washington and at Bush's Texas ranch. They fail to reach an agreement on the missile defence shield sought by the US. |
| 19-20 | November | *ESDP.* EU foreign and defence ministers meet in Brussels to discuss capability improvements. They agree a European Capability Action Plan (ECAP). It is intended to remedy the 55 identified shortcomings in the development of European crisis-management capabilities. The conference makes several proposals, including making forces and capabilities that have not yet been declared already available; making existing capabilities more effective and efficient; seeking |

| | | |
|---|---|---|
| | | creative responses outside traditional military procurement programmes; and co-producing, financing and acquiring capabilities particularly for large-scale or very specific projects. The ECAP is based on four principles: enhanced effectiveness and efficiency of European military capability efforts, a bottom-up approach to European defence co-operation, co-ordination between EU member states and co-operation with NATO, and the importance of broad public support. The conference decides to set up panels of experts to analyse remaining deficiencies and identify specific solutions. |
| 25 | November | *9/11.* US troops move into southern Afghanistan. Troops in the US-led coalition include forces from Australia, Canada, Japan, Turkey, the Czech Republic, France, Italy, the Netherlands, Poland, Spain, the United Kingdom, and Germany, which is undertaking its first military action outside of Europe since World War II. |
| 2 | December | *ESDP.* Turkey endorses the so-called Ankara compromise, elaborated by the UK, the US and Turkey, on the participation of European non-EU states in EU crisis-management operations. Under the compromise, Turkey would be given a consultative role in the ERRF decision-making process. |
| 5 | December | The participants in the UN talks on Afghanistan sign the Bonn Agreement. It provides for an Interim Authority to be established on 22 December. The Interim Authority is to be composed of an Interim Administration, a Special Independent Commission for the Convening of the Emergency *Loya Jirga* (great assembly), and a Supreme Court of Aghanistan. The *Loya Jirga* is to be convened within six months of the establishment of the Interim Authority, and is to decide on a Transitional Authority, including a broad-based Transitional Administration, to lead Afghanistan until a fully representative government can be elected through free and fair elections, which are to be held no later than two years after the *Loya Jirga* convenes. Within 18 months of the establishment of the Transitional Authority, a Constitutional *Loya Jirga* is to be convened to adopt a new constitution for the country. The participants also "request the United Nations Security Council to consider authorizing the early deployment to Afghanistan of a United Nations mandated force. This force will assist in the maintenance of security in Kabul and its surrounding areas. Such a force could, as appropriate, be progressively expanded to other urban centres and other areas." |
| 7 | December | NATO foreign ministers announce the creation of a NATO-Russia Council. Russia seeks, but fails to get, a veto over NATO activities. |

| | | |
|---|---|---|
| 13 | December | Bush announces US withdrawal from the 1972 ABM treaty. Russian President Putin says this step by the US does not pose any threat to the security of the Russian Federation. However, he calls Bush's move a mistake and calls for the rapid creation of "a new framework of our strategic relationship". |
| 14-15 | December | *ESDP.* European Council in Laeken, Belgium. The main topic under discussion is a plan to draft an EU constitution. Former French President Valéry Giscard d'Estaing is appointed chairman of the Convention on the Future of Europe, which is drafting the constitution. On ESDP, the Presidency Conclusions state that, "the EU is now capable of conducting some crisis-management operations". The European Rapid Reaction Mechanism (ERRM) is thus declared operational. However, the draft Presidency Report on ESDP also asserts that, "To enable the European Union to carry out crisis-management operations over the whole range of Petersberg Tasks, ... substantial progress is to be made." This includes reaching an agreement on EU-NATO relations, which fails, however, due to Greece's objecting to the Ankara compromise of 2 December. Greece thinks that the long consultation process that is foreseen with non-EU countries would compromise the decision-making authority of the EU. EU leaders assert that the ERRF "does not imply the creation of a European Army." The Laeken summit also sees the launching of the ECAP. |
| 18 | December | *9/11.* NATO defence ministers meet to discuss how the Alliance will adapt to the war on terror, notably addressing how to increase the organisation's ability to dispatch forces out of NATO area. |
| 18 | December | US Secretary of Defense Rumsfeld announces that US troops in Bosnia will be reduced from 3,100 to 2,000 in 2002. |
| 18 | December | *ESDP.* The A400M contract is signed, as are more-detailed arrangements for the management of programmes within OCCAR. |
| 20 | December | The UN Security Council authorises the establishment of an International Security Assistance Force (ISAF) for Afghanistan. |
| 21 | December | The first British troops arrive in Afghanistan to set up ISAF, of which it will be the first lead nation. |

| At a Glance – Major Events and Themes | |
|---|---|
| | **Co-operation between Russia, the EU and NATO increases** |
| | **Conflict in Macedonia continues** |
| | **EU Police Mission established in BiH** |
| | **Decision taken to form Serbia and Montenegro** |
| | **Barcelona European Council** |
| | **French President Jacques Chirac re-elected** |
| | **Russian President Putin and US President Bush meet in Moscow** |
| | **NATO-Russia Council formed** |
| | **Row over International Criminal Court** |
| | **Seville European Council** |
| | **NATO-Russia Council established** |
| | **First NAC-PSC meeting** |
| | **Gerhard Schröder re-elected chancellor of Germany** |
| | **Brussels European Council** |
| | **Franco-German proposal on Common Security and Defence in EU constitutional treaty** |
| | **NATO Prague summit: Bulgaria, Estonia, Latvia, Lithuania, Romania, Slovakia and Slovenia invited to join** |
| | **EU-NATO Berlin-Plus agreement** |
| | **EU-NATO Declaration on the ESDP** |
| | **Final report of the European Convention working group on defence** |

## 2002

| Day | Month | Event |
|---|---|---|
| 1 | January | *ESDP.* Eurojust, a co-ordination body composed of magistrates, prosecutors and police officers, is launched by the EU. |
| 1 | January | *ESDP.* The two WEU subsidiary bodies – the Torrejon Satellite Centre and the Institute for Security Studies – become EU agencies. |
| 10 | January | The UK officially assumes command of ISAF in Kabul, Afghanistan. |
| 29 | January | *9/11.* In his State of the Union address, US President Bush, speaking of North Korea, Iraq and Iran, states that, "states like these, and their terrorist allies, constitute an axis of evil, aiming to threaten the peace of the world." |

| | | |
|---|---|---|
| 1-3 | February | *9/11/The Iraq War.* Munich Conference on Security Policy: US Deputy Secretary of Defense Paul Wolfowitz, citing Donald Rumsfeld, says that, "the mission must determine the coalition", not vice versa, and that otherwise, "the coalition is reduced to the lowest common denominator". He advocates "flexible coalitions", i.e., "different coalitions for different missions". |
| 3-4 | February | *9/11.* A NATO-Russia conference on combating terrorism is held. |
| 11-12 | February | An opening gathering is held in Brussels for the ECAP. Nineteen panels are set up, each headed by one or two member states. The panels are to submit a report in March 2003. |
| 12 | February | The trial of former Yugoslav President Slobodan Milosevic opens at the ICTY in The Hague. |
| 18 | February | NATO's NAC extends Operation Amber Fox for a further three months at the request of the Government of Macedonia. |
| 18-19 | February | *ESDP.* EU foreign ministers, meeting as the General Affairs Council (GAC), announce the EU's readiness by 1 January 2003 to follow up on the UN IPTF in BiH. The Spanish Presidency seeks "to enable Defence Ministers to discuss certain agenda items, limited to issues covering military capabilities", at the GAC. |
| 26 | February | Saudi Crown Prince Abdullah launches an initiative calling for normalisation of all Arab relations with Israel in return for Israeli recognition of an independent Palestinian state based on the 1967 borders, with East Jerusalem as its capital. |
| 28 | February | The European Airlift Co-ordination Cell set up by the EAG (currently comprising Belgium, France, Germany, Italy, Spain, the UK and the Netherlands) is officially inaugurated at Eindhoven Air Base. |
| 28 | February | The Steering Board of the Peace Implementation Conference (PIC) accepts an EU offer for a European Police Mission (EUPM) in BiH. At the same meeting of the PIC, Lord Ashdown is designated as the new high representative, succeeding Wolfgang Petrisch. |
| 1-15 | March | *ESDI.* NATO tests its ability to handle two simultaneous operations (a collective defence operation and a crisis response) in Norway and Poland. |
| 3 | March | Some 54.6% of Swiss people vote in favour of UN membership. |
| 5 | March | The UN Security Council welcomes the acceptance by the Steering Board of the PIC of the offer made by the EU to set up a European Union Police Mission (EUPM) in BiH from 1 January 2003, to follow the end of UNMIBH's mandate. |

| | | |
|---|---|---|
| 11 | March | *ESDP.* The Council of the EU establishes the EUPM, which is to take over the mission of the UN's IPTF in BiH. Lord Ashdown is appointed EU special representative in BiH. |
| 11 | March | *9/11.* At a Council of Ministers meeting, EU foreign ministers issue a declaration on the terrorist attacks of 11 September, stating that: "Actions taken against those responsible for these barbaric acts and their accomplices are not targeted against any people or religion. They aim at the reinforcement of international security and the rule of law as well as the security of the countries affected by the scourge of terrorism. The global fight against terrorism represents, more than ever, a priority goal for the European Union ...." |
| 12 | March | The UN Security Council speaks for the first time of an independent Palestinian state, "affirming a vision of a region where two states, Israel and Palestine, live side by side within secure and recognised borders." |
| 14 | March | The leaders of Serbia, Montenegro and the FRY sign an Agreement in Principle in Belgrade to maintain a joint state under the name of Serbia and Montenegro. |
| 15-16 | March | *ESDI/ESDP.* The Barcelona European Council declares the EU's "availability" to take over NATO's operation in the former Yugoslav Republic of Macedonia, "on the understanding that the permanent arrangements on EU-NATO cooperation ('Berlin plus') would be in place by then." It is decided that the EU Presidency, the secretary-general/high representative and Greece will hold meetings in an effort to promote a settlement of the participation issue. |
| 27-28 | March | The Arab League endorses Saudi Crown Prince Abdullah's peace initiative. Jordan and Egypt do not attend the meeting. |
| | March | *ESDP.* The 19 ECAP panels start their work of addressing the 21 Helsinki shortfalls that are regarded as significant (out of 40 total shortfalls identified by the Helsinki Process Catalogue). |
| 10 | April | The Netherlands Institute for War Documentation publishes an official report on the Srebrenica massacre. It finds that, "humanitarian motivation and political ambitions drove the Netherlands to undertake an ill-conceived and virtually impossible peace mission", and it blames the Dutch peacekeepers for handing over Muslim civilians to Serbian forces and says that the UN failed to give the troops enough support to defend the city's inhabitants. Although the report blames former Serbian President Milosevic for the disintegration of Yugoslavia, it also states that, "no evidence had been found that suggests the involvement of the Serbian authorities in Belgrade [in the killings in Srebrenica]." |
| 15 | April | Israel announces that it will build a "security fence" to prevent Palestinian terrorists from reaching Israeli territory. |

| | | |
|---|---|---|
| 16 | April | Dutch Prime Minister Wim Kok endorses the findings of the Srebrenica Report, which he commissioned in 1997, and resigns with his entire cabinet. Queen Beatrix, however, immediately asks him to form a caretaker administration until the elections scheduled for 15 May. |
| 17 | April | The Dutch Army chief of staff resigns over the Srebrenica massacre. |
| 30 | April | *ESDI/ESDP.* Javier Solana; Lord Robertson; and the chairman of the PSC, Ambassador Carles Maria Casajuana, meet at NATO headquarters in Brussels for NATO-EU talks on security issues. |
| 5 | May | President Jacques Chirac decisively defeats far-right candidate Jean-Marie Le Pen to take the French presidency for a second term. |
| 6 | May | The US declares that it "does not intend to become a party to the [Rome Statute of the ICC]", and that accordingly, it "has no legal obligation arising from its signature on December 31, 2000." |
| 8 | May | Lord Robertson meets in Brussels with the new high representative and EU special representative in BiH, Lord Ashdown. |
| 13 | May | *ESDP.* EU defence ministers participate for the first time in the GAC. |
| 14-15 | May | *ESDI/ESDP.* NATO and EU foreign ministers meet in Iceland and discuss use of Alliance capabilities and infrastructure by the EU. Turkey rejects the proposal. Little progress on the issue is made. |
| 16 | May | *9/11.* NATO's operation Eagle Assist ends in the United States. |
| 17 | May | *ESDI/ESDP.* A co-operation forum to discuss NATO and EU defence and security policies called the the New Defence Agenda holds its first session. |
| 21 | May | NATO member countries agree to extend operation Amber Fox in Macedonia. |
| 22-28 | May | *ESDP.* The first EU crisis-management exercise (CME02) involves all EU capitals, the Council, the Commission and High Representative Javier Solana. It also makes use of the Torrejon Satellite Centre. |
| 23-24 | May | US President George W. Bush and Russian President Vladimir Putin meet in Moscow. They sign the Treaty of Moscow, reducing stockpiles of nuclear weapons by two-thirds over 10 years, and agree to co-operate on energy policy and anti-terrorism measures. Differences between the two countries remain, primarily over trade and nuclear non-proliferation. |

| | | |
|---|---|---|
| 28 | May | At a NATO summit in Rome, a new NATO-Russia Council is formed: "NATO member states and Russia will work as equal partners in areas of common interest." Other issues discussed include nuclear non-proliferation, missile defence, and combating terrorism. |
| 29 | May | The EU formally recognises Russia as a market economy at a Russia-EU summit in Moscow. Serious disagreements over the future status of Russia's Kaliningrad Region are also discussed. |
| 17 | June | *ESDP.* The GAC agrees on the financing of EU operations that have military or defence implications, i.e., the breakdown of EU and national budgets. |
| 18 | June | Objecting to the possible subjection of American military personnel in the Balkans to the jurisdiction of the ICC, the US presents two draft resolutions to the UN Security Council to exempt peacekeepers from the ICC. The opposition of some Security Council members to these proposals leads to the US's threatening to withdraw from peacekeeping operations in the Balkans. |
| 20 | June | As ISAF command passes from the UK to Turkey, Major-General John McColl hands over command to Major-General Hilmi Akin Zorlu. |
| 21-22 | June | *ESDP.* European Council in Seville:<br>a) On the EUPM, member states make commitments to contribute police forces, judges, prosecutors and legal administrators to build up the EU's capacity in the area of developing rule of law in crisis-management operations;<br>b) The scope of the ESDP is broadened to include the fight against terrorism, as the EU endeavours to increase its involvement in this area through a co-ordinated, interdisciplinary apporach; the ESDP is thus given a vital strategic mission for the coming years, beyond peacekeeping in the Balkans;<br>c) The EU indicates its willingness to take over from NATO in FYROM;<br>d) A Presidency Report on the EU programme for the prevention of violent conflict is also presented. |
| 25 | June | *ESDI/ESDP.* The NAC and the PSC meet at EU headquarters in Brussels. Discussions focus on NATO and EU contributions to the international fight against terrorism, the situation in the Balkans and progress made in initiatives for NATO-EU co-operation. |
| 1 | July | Having been ratified by 60 states, the Rome Statue of the ICC enters into force. |

| | | |
|---|---|---|
| 12 | July | A compromise is eventually reached on the question of ICC jurisdiction over peacekeepers (UNSC Res. 1422). This compromise agreement allows the US to drop its demand that the UN Security Council grant US citizens serving in UN peacekeeping missions permanent immunity from investigation or prosecution by the new court. The UN Security Council meets the same day to extend the mandates of SFOR and UNMIBH until 31 December with the unanimous passing of Resolution 1423. |
| 15 | July | The presidents of BiH, Croatia, and Yugoslavia hold a landmark summit meeting in Sarajevo. |
| 16 | July | *ESDP.* The European Advisory Group on Aerospace presents a report entitled "Strategic Aerospace Review of the 21st Century" to the president of the European Commission, Romano Prodi. The report makes recommendations at the European level for Europe to attain a competitive aerospace industry, which the group regards as essential for a successful European economy. |
| 18 | July | *ESDP.* Judging that, "the development of the European Security and Defence Policy is not making sufficient progress", and that, "there is, however, no doubt that public opinion in our countries is convinced of the need for a European defence", Belgian Prime Minister Guy Verhofstadt proposes in a letter to Tony Blair and Jacques Chirac the creation of a limited EU planning and command capability, the setting up of a European Armaments Agency, the introduction of a collective defence guarantee among the 15 member states and an EU operation in Macedonia, despite the unresolved problem of EU use of NATO assets and capabilities. Verhofstadt adds that, "over the last few months, I have perceived a risk of re-nationalisation of defence policies. ... the danger persists, in my opinion, in seeing both the European Union and NATO turn into 'toolboxes' for supporting ad hoc coalitions." Consequently, "we must relaunch the idea of a European defence and rekindle the Saint-Malo spirit." |
| 30 | July | *ESDP.* At a Franco-German summit on defence and security in Schwerin, Germany, the two countries, "intending to give a new impulse to ESDP", state that they favour harmonisation, among the 15 member states, of the planning of military requirements and the "bundling", wherever possible, of capacities and resources. They also confirm their commitment to the A400M heavy-lift aircraft and sign an agreement to create a satellite-assisted Franco-German reconnaissance system. |
| | July | The UK Defence Ministry publishes "UK Strategic Defence Review - A New Chapter". Among the key elements described are: an integrated approach across government to dealing with asymmetric threats before they reach the UK; network-centric capability; developing further the ability to |

| | | |
|---|---|---|
| | | act rapidly, at a distance and in areas with little infrastructure in counterterrorist operations; and, on home defence, an improved ability to deal with rogue aircraft and to provide improved security on the ground. |
| 10 | September | *ESDP.* The mandate of the working group on defence of the European Convention, chaired by Michel Barnier of France, is published. |
| 10 | September | Switzerland is admitted to the United Nations. |
| 17 | September | *The Iraq War.* Iraq says it will allow weapons inspections to take place. |
| 17 | September | The US publishes its National Security Strategy, which focuses on spreading freedom and democracy, the fight against terrorism and the spread of WMD, global economic growth and the transformation of national-security institutions in the US. |
| 22 | September | Gerhard Schröder is elected to a second term as chancellor of Germany. |
| 24 | September | *The Iraq War.* Tony Blair launches a report that concludes that Iraq could deploy WMD within 45 minutes. |
| 30 | September | The EU Council of Ministers adopts guidelines for member states regarding how to deal with possible agreements with the US regarding conditions for a surrender of individuals to the ICC. |
| 4 | October | The EU and BiH sign an agreement on the actvities of the EUPM. According to the agreement, the EUPM will have a mandate until the end of 2005. |
| 4-5 | October | *ESDP.* In a speech at an informal meeting of EU defence ministers in Rethymnon, Greece, Javier Solana makes an assessment of progress and shortfalls in the Helsinki process. The Union's military deficiencies, which have been studied by several groups of experts within the ECAP since April 2002, are acute in force projection, precision weapons and intelligence and will only be overcome gradually. |
| 12 | October | *9/11.* Bomb attacks in a club on Bali kill more than 180 people, mostly Australian, British and Indonesian citizens. Al-Qaeda's complicity is assumed. |
| 24-25 | October | *ESDI/ESDP.* At the European Council in Brussels, the EU says that it is determined to reach an agreement with Turkey regarding forthcoming enlargement (especially with respect to Cyprus's membership) and on the question of the EU's access to NATO's infrastructure. The presidency conclusions refer to the principles and provisions of the CFSP that non-EU European Allies have to respect and abide by. The Brussels Document, also called the Nice Implementation Document, is also issued. It contains modalities for implementing the Nice |

| | | |
|---|---|---|
| | | provisions on the involvement of non-EU Allies in the ESDP. In contrast with the earlier Ankara compromise, it contains a mutual pledge that NATO military crisis management will not be used against the EU or an EU member state and that no action will be taken that violates principles of the UN Charter. |
| 3 | November | The moderate Islamist Justice and Development Party (AKP) wins general elections in Turkey. AKP leader Tayyip Erdogan cannot take office as prime minister, however, as he was banned from holding any elected office when he was convicted of Islamist sedition in 1998. |
| 8 | November | *The Iraq War.* UN Security Council Resolution 1441 gives Iraq one final opportunity to fully comply with its international obligations. The Security Council imposes an enhanced inspection regime because of Iraq's material breach of its obligations under Resolution 187 (1999) and because of its failure to co-operate with UN inspectors and the IAEA. The resolution also recalls that the UN Security Council "has repeatedly warned Iraq that it will face serious consequences as a result of its continued violation of its obligations." |
| 11 | November | The main issues discussed at a Russia-EU summit include the fight against terrorism, Russia's conduct in the conflict in Chechnya, and the type of travel documents that should be issued to Russian citizens travelling between the Kaliningrad Region and the rest of the Russian Federation once Poland and Lithuania, which surround Kaliningrad, become EU members in 2004. |
| 14 | November | *ESDP.* Javier Solana makes a one-day visit to Turkey to discuss the participation issue. |
| 19 | November | *ESDP.* EU foreign ministers meet at a Civilian Crisis Management Capability Conference on the sidelines of the General Affairs and External Relations Council "to [review] progress achieved and challenges ahead in developing the EU's civilian crisis management capacity." |
| 21 | November | *ESDP.* The French and German foreign ministers, Dominique de Villepin and Joschka Fischer, respectively, issue a joint proposal to the European Convention in which they call for a section on "common security and solidarity" in the treaty. They also argue for "enhanced co-operation" in the ESDP, i.e., flexibility within the EU that would allow groups of member states to co-operate more closely with other members. Their proposal further includes sections on military capacities and a European armament policy. |

| | | |
|---|---|---|
| 21-22 | November | *ESDI/ESDP.* NATO Prague summit. Bulgaria, Estonia, Latvia, Lithuania, Romania, Slovakia and Slovenia are invited to join. NATO heads of state and government also approve new, more-specific commitments on operational capabilities, replacing the DCI, considered too ambitious and overtaken by 9/11. The DCI thus becomes the Prague Capabilities Commitment (PCC). Furthermore, it is agreed to set up a 21,000-strong NATO Response Force (NRF), deployable within a few days, as the spearhead of a larger force. The Turkish president makes a declaration at the summit, expressing Turkey's readiness to start preparing for a joint NATO-EU crisis-management exercise in 2003. In a statement on Iraq, ministers pledge their "full support for the implementation of Security Council resolution 1441 [of 2002] ... [and] recall that the Security Council in this resolution has warned Iraq that it will face serious consequences as a result of its continued violation of its obligations." |
| 25 | November | *9/11.* The new US Department of Homeland Security is established. It is intended to consolidate the work of agencies engaged in homeland security. |
| 27 | November | *The Iraq War.* UN inspections in Iraq resume with the United Nations Monitoring, Verification and Inspection Commision (UNMOVIC) under Executive Chairman Hans Blix (Sweden). |
| 29 | November | Following a request by Macedonian President Boris Trajkovski, NATO agees to continue supporting the country with a new mission after 15 December, which is to "assist the government of the FYROM in taking ownership of security throughout the country." |
| 1 | December | A group of left-wing, moderate Israeli and Palestinian leaders launch the Geneva Initiative. They propose a detailed peace plan that includes the renouncement by Palestinians of the right of return, shared sovereignty of Jerusalem, withdrawal of Israeli troops from most of the Palestinian territory occupied in 1967 and the evacuation of around 30% of settlers. |
| 7 | December | *The Iraq War.* Iraq provides UNMOVIC with a 122,000-page declaration supposedly of all its weapons and missile programmes. |
| 12-13 | December | *ESDI/ESDP.* European Council in Copenhagen. Accession negotiations are concluded with Cyprus, the Czech Republic, Estonia, Hungary, Latvia, Lithuania, Malta, Poland, the Slovak Republic and Slovenia. The Council endorses a Presidency Proposal entitled "European Defence: NATO/EU Consultation, Planning and Operations". Javier Solana formally transmits the text of the Nice Implementation Document to NATO. EU leaders also indicate the "Union's willingness to lead a military operation in Bosnia following SFOR" and "confirm the Union's readiness to take over the military operation in FYROM as soon as possible in consultation with NATO ...." |

| | | |
|---|---|---|
| 13 | December | *ESDI/ESDP.* The NAC gives the go-ahead for the advancement of all outstanding issues regarding EU-NATO relations. NATO Secretary General Lord Robertson transmits the final text of the NAC decision to the EU. |
| 16 | December | A UN Security Council presidency statement reiterates support for the EUPM. |
| 16 | December | NATO Operation Allied Harmony takes over from Amber Fox in Macedonia. |
| 16 | December | *ESDI/ESDP.* The secretary general of NATO, Lord Robertson, and the secretary-general of the EU Council and high representative for the CFSP, Javier Solana, sign a formal framework for co-operation: the EU-NATO Declaration on ESDP. It provides for the "fullest possible involvement" of non-EU members of NATO with the ESDP. Thus, the Berlin-Plus permanent arrangements on EU access to NATO's planning, logistics and intelligence for operations in which NATO as a whole is not involved are finally agreed after three years of difficult negotiations. Solana declares that the EU aims to be ready by the end of February 2003 to take over the military operation in Macedonia and that, together with NATO, the EU is going to analyse the possibilities for an EU military role in Bosnia and Herzegovina (EUFOR) after the SFOR mission. A joint exercise with NATO, scheduled for November 2003, is also going to be prepared. |
| 16 | December | *ESDI/ESDP.* The final report of the European Convention working group on defence is issued, reviewing the legal context and the developments in European security and defence policy since the Cologne European Council in June 1999, the progress made and the gaps remaining. It proposes the creation of a European Armament and Strategic Research Agency, as well as a solidarity clause among EU member states. |
| 27 | December | Chechen suicide bombers kill 80 people at the Russian Government headquarters in Grozny. |
| | December | An amendment of the Turkish Constitution is passed that allows AKP leader Erdogan to stand for elections. |

| | |
|---|---|
| **At a Glance – Major Events and Themes** | **The EU undertakes three missions: an EU Police Mission in Bosnia and Herzegovina (EUPM), Concordia (Macedonia) and Artemis (Democratic Republic of the Congo)** |
| | **Federal Republic of Yugoslavia dissolved and Serbia and Montenegro established** |
| | **The US and UK invade Iraq** |
| | **European Security Strategy** |
| | **Libya renounces WMD** |

# 2003

| Day | Month | Event |
|---|---|---|
| 1 | January | *ESDP.* An EU Police Mission (EUPM) is launched in BiH, taking over from the IPTF. The EUPM is given a mandate for three years to monitor, mentor and inspect the police in BiH to ensure that they are a legitimate, professional and executive force. The mission has no executive power and focuses on fighting organised crime and corruption and ensuring the security of returning refugees. |
| 14 | January | *The Iraq War.* Tony Blair says that Iraq's WMD programme is "active, detailed and growing", that "[t]he policy of containment is not working" and that "[t]he case for ensuring Iraqi disarmament ... is overwhelming." |
| 15 | January | The French *Assemblée Nationale* adopts the *Loi de Programmation* 2003-2008, which contains significant increases in defence. These increases will be used to modernise forces in the fields of reconnaissance, command and force protection; to increase the "*moyens d'action dans la profondeur*"; to amplify research efforts to respond to new threats; and to restore the operational availability of forces. These efforts should allow "France to contribute significantly to the constitution of a multinational force." |
| 18-19 | January | Macedonian President Boris Trajkovski formally requests that the EU take over the military mission from NATO. |
| 20 | January | *The Iraq War*. France announces its opposition to a UN Security Council resolution that would allow military action against Iraq, saying that at this moment nothing would justify the use of military force. Foreign Minister Dominique de Villepin states that he believes that the inspections have frozen Iraq's weapons programmes. |

| | | |
|---|---|---|
| 22 | January | *ESDP.* The 40th anniversary of the Elysée Treaty: celebrations provide Germany and France with the background for announcing a number of common projects. On ESDP, the two countries "propose to further develop the ESDP into a European Security and Defence Union (ESDU), which should also contribute to strengthening the European Pillar of the Alliance" and pledge their commitment to advance the EU's rapid reaction capacity; common utilisation of funds, resources and personnel; a common threat analysis; prevention of, and fight against, terrorism; a common armaments co-operation policy; and the common training of personnel. Germany and France also repeat their willingness to further the areas highlighted in their proposal on 21 November 2002. They also present joint proposals for EU reform, including for a dual Presidency (of the Commission and the European Council) and qualified majority voting in CFSP but not in ESDP. On a number of other issues, they intend to "intensify in exemplary fashion their bilateral co-operation within the Union." Projects cover issues such as cultural exchanges; harmonisation of legislation and policies, e.g., in international bodies such as the UN Security Council; the opening of joint Franco-German embassies; and, in the area of defence, the harmonisation of military requirement planning and the pooling of capabilities and resources. Franco-Geman summits will in future take the form of a German-French Council of Ministers. The German-French Defence and Security Council, whose 15th anniversary the two countries are celebrating the same day, and its committee will take place on the occasion of meetings of this Council of Ministers. France and Germany aim for their projects "to create a basis for European policies". |
| 22 | January | *The Iraq War.* At the Elysée Treaty anniversary, France and Germany also adopt a common position on the use of force in Iraq, saying that they will do everything they can to avert a war in Iraq. Russia asserts on the same day that, "there is no evidence that would justify a war in Iraq." |
| 24 | January | *9/11.* The US Department of Homeland Security begins operations. |
| 27 | January | The EU Council of Ministers adopts a joint action to deploy a military mission in FYROM with recourse to NATO assets and capabilities. |
| 27 | January | *The Iraq War.* UNMOVIC presents its first report. Even though several questions remain unanswered and full Iraqi co-operation on substance is still lacking, UNMOVIC so far has no proof that Iraq possesses illegal weapons. |
| 28 | January | *The Iraq War.* After the weapons inspectors report that Iraq has not yet shown a genuine acceptance of the need to disarm, Russian President Putin slightly modifies Russia's position on Iraq. Russia will now support a war if Iraq's reluctance to co-operate fully with the inspections continues. But he insists on a UN mandate for such military action and on giving the inspections more time. |

| | | |
|---|---|---|
| 30 | January | *The Iraq War*. Eight European leaders (the Czech Republic, Denmark, Hungary, Italy, Poland, Portugal, Spain, and the UK) send an open letter to the US (entitled "United We Stand") that backs the US position on Iraq. The letter states that, "The Iraqi regime and its weapons of mass destruction represent a clear threat to world security", and it insists that the international community "must remain united in insisting that his regime be disarmed" and that, "the Security Council must maintain its credibility by ensuring full compliance with its resolutions." |
| 1 | February | The EU Treaty of Nice enters into force. |
| 4 | February | The FRY is renamed Serbia and Montenegro, as the state's new constitution comes into force. The constitution foresees a loose union between the two parts of the country, with the option for each member to break away from the union after three years. |
| 4 | February | *ESDP.* At a meeting in the French town of Le Touquet, France and the UK sign a joint Declaration on Strengthening European Co-operation in Security and Defence. Agreeing that, "the potential scope of ESDP should match the world-wide ambition of the European Union's Common Foreign and Security Policy and should be able to support effectively the EU's wider external policy objectives to promote democracy, human rights, good governance and reform", they "propose that the European Union should set new capability objectives", and that to "support this, an inter-governmental defence capabilities development and acquisition agency could be established in the EU." The two countries also emphasise that they "regard developing the capacity for rapid reaction as a European priority" and that "air-naval capabilities are a key element in power projection." |
| 5 | February | *The Iraq War.* US Secretary of State Colin Powell convenes a meeting of the UN Security Council to present an "accumulation of facts and disturbing pattern of behavior" that allegedly "demonstrate that Saddam Hussein has made no effort ... to disarm as required by the international community" and that, "Saddam Hussein and his regime are concealing their efforts to produce more weapons of mass destruction." Powell presents various intelligence sources, including recorded conversations between Iraqi officials, satellite pictures and human sources, to convince his audience that Iraq still possesses and is further developing biological and chemical weapons, that it is seeking to develop nuclear weapons, that it is developing delivery systems for all these weapons and that it is collaborating with Al-Qaeda, providing them with a base and help with the acquisition of WMD. |

| | | |
|---|---|---|
| 5 | February | *The Iraq War.* Ten Central and Eastern European states and future members of NATO issue a statement expressing support of the US position on Iraq. Asserting that the US has "presented compelling evidence to the United Nations Security Council detailing Iraq's weapons of mass destruction programs, its active efforts to deceive UN inspectors, and its links to international terrorism" and that "it has now become clear that Iraq is in material breach of U.N. Security Council Resolution 1441", the 10 countries are "prepared to contribute to an international coalition to enforce its provisions and the disarmament of Iraq." |
| 6 | February | *The Iraq War.* While UK Foreign Secretary Jack Straw states that "time is now very short" to avoid war in Iraq, French Foreign Minister Dominique de Villepin asserts that the weapons inspections have shown "significant results" and have not yet been "explored to the end". He advocates a strengthening of the inspection regime. According to de Villepin, France does not rule out recourse to force, but the risks and uncertainties of such an option would need to be addressed clearly beforehand. |
| 6 | February | *The Iraq War.* NATO's North Atlantic Council meets to consider a US proposal to task NATO military authorities to begin planning deterrent and defence measures in relation to a possible threat to Turkey. |
| 10 | February | *The Iraq War.* In a joint declaration on Iraq, Russia, Germany and France state that they "favour the continuation of the inspections and a substantial reinforcement of their human and technical capacities through all possible means and in liaison with the inspectors. ... Russia, Germany and France are determined to ensure that everything possible is done to disarm Iraq peacefully." |
| 10 | February | *9/11.* A Dutch and German command under Lieutenant-General Norbert van Heyst (Germany) takes over ISAF in Afghanistan from Turkey. Van Heyst's deputy is Brigadier-General Robert Bertholee (the Netherlands). The new command is resorting to NATO planning and logistical structures. |
| 10 | February | *The Iraq War.* Turkey invokes Article 4 of NATO's founding treaty, by which the Alliance will consult whenever any member feels that the territorial integrity, political independence or security of any NATO country is threatened. |
| 12 | February | *The Iraq War.* France details its proposal of a strengthened inspection regime in Iraq in a so-called non-paper. |
| 14 | February | *The Iraq War.* The chief UN weapons inspector in Iraq, Hans Blix, presents a report on UNMOVIC activities and findings to the UN Security Council. Blix judges the Iraqis to be more proactive in their co-operation. He questions some of Powell's arguments, such as his interpretation of satellite images and the assertion that Iraq has a nuclear-weapons programme. Blix also says that the Iraqis have not received early warning of inspections. |

| | | |
|---|---|---|
| 14 | February | *The Iraq War.* According to UK Foreign Secretary Jack Straw, the UNMOVIC report proves that Iraq is still in material breach of its obligation and that a peaceful solution of the crisis would "require a dramatic and immediate change by Saddam". He states that the 12 years since Resolution 687, which obliged Iraq to disarm, have been "a period of humiliation" for the Security Council and that the behaviour of the Security Council vis-à-vis Iraq sends a signal to proliferators elsewhere. |
| 14 | February | *The Iraq War.* French Foreign Minister Dominique de Villepin's reaction to the weapons inspectors' report is quite different: he asserts that ,"real progress is beginning to be apparent", that France is convinced "that the option of inspections has not been taken to the end" and "that the use of force would be so fraught with risks for people, for the region and for international stability that it should only be envisioned as a last resort." He also asserts that,"given the present state of [France's and its Allies'] research and intelligence, nothing allows [them] to establish the alleged links between Al-Qaeda and the Iraqi regime." |
| 15-16 | February | *The Iraq War.* More than 10 million people demonstrate worldwide against a possible war in Iraq. Most of the demonstrations take place in Europe, with the largest in Rome, where some estimate up to 3 million protesters. Demonstrations in Madrid, Barcelona and London each attract about 1 million people. |
| 16 | February | *The Iraq War.* Belgium, France and Germany issue a statement on Iraq stressing that, "the use of force can only be the last resort and that not all options offered by UNSCR 1441 have, as yet, been fully exploited." They also state that Belgium and Germany have agreed "to invite the military authorities to provide military advice on prudent defensive contingency planning in support of Turkey" but that the implementation of the measures to be proposed would need a new decision. |
| 17 | February | *The Iraq War.* Extraordinary European Council on the crisis in Iraq: "We are committed to the United Nations remaining at the centre of the international order. We recognise the primary responsibility for dealing with Iraqi disarmament lies with the Security Council. … War is not inevitable. Force should be used only as a last resort. It is for the Iraqi regime to end this crisis by complying with the demands of the Security Council. We reiterate our full support for the ongoing work of the UN inspectors. They must be given the time and resources that the UN Security Council believes they need. However, the inspections cannot continue indefinitely in the absence of full Iraqi cooperation. … The Iraqi regime alone will be responsible for the consequences if it continues to flout the will of the international community and does not take this last chance. … We recognize that the unity |

| | | |
|---|---|---|
| | | and firmness of the international community ... and the military build-up have been essential in obtaining the return of the inspectors. In [the] regional context, ... the European Union reiterates its firm belief in the need to invigorate the peace process in the Middle East and to resolve the Israeli-Palestinian conflict." |
| 19 | February | *The Iraq War.* NATO's DPC authorises the Alliance's military authorities to deploy NATO AWACS, missile, chemical and biological defences to Turkey. |
| 24 | February | *The Iraq War.* France states that a new UN Security Council resolution on Iraq, sought above all by the US and UK, is "neither useful nor necessary" and that France opposes such a resolution as long as the weapons inspectors are making progress. However, France also says that the possible use of its veto is "not an issue". |
| 1 | March | *ESDP.* ECAP panels present their final reports. |
| 2 | March | *The Iraq War.* The UK and the US say that they might use force against Iraq even without a second UN Security Council resolution if it is to be vetoed as a matter of principle by France. They also describe Iraq's promise to destroy al-Samoud 2 missiles as "propaganda" and "a cynical attempt to divide the Security Council". |
| 5 | March | *The Iraq War.* Russia, Germany and France issue a declaration stating that the objective of full and effective Iraqi disarmament can be achieved by inspections but that the latter need to be speeded up. They insist that they "will not let a proposed resolution pass that would authorise the use of force." |
| 7 | March | *The Iraq War.* The head of UNMOVIC, Hans Blix, and the head of the IAEA, Mohamed ElBaradei, present another report to the UN Security Council. France reacts to the report by proposing that inspectors should prioritise their disarmament tasks and present progress reports every three weeks and |
| | | that a schedule for assessing the implementation of the inspectors' work programme should be established. France again states that it "will not allow a resolution authorising the automatic use of force to go through." De Villepin also asserts that France does "not subscribe to what may be the other objectives of a war" and insists that, "there is nothing today that indicates a link between the Iraqi regime and al-Qaida" and that it is convinced that a military intervention in Iraq would not make the world a safer place. |
| 9 | March | The AKP wins Turkish by-elections. AKP leader Erdogan wins a seat. |
| 10 | March | *9/11.* NATO's Operation Active Endeavour is expanded to include escorting civilian ships through the Strait of Gibraltar. |

| | | |
|---|---|---|
| 10 | March | *The Iraq War.* France and Russia declare that they are ready to use their veto in the UN Security Council if the US and the UK demand a vote on a resolution that would authorise the use of force against Iraq. |
| 11 | March | Erdogan is appointed Turkish prime minister. |
| 11 | March | The ICC is inaugurated in The Hague. |
| 13 | March | *The Iraq War.* UK leaders say that a diplomatic solution for the Iraq crisis is "probably less likely than at any time" and the prospects of the use of force "more likely", blaming France's intransigent stance on a possible second UN Security Council resolution. |
| 14 | March | *ESDI/ESDP.* The EU formally adopts the Berlin-Plus agenda: NATO may support EU-led operations without committing itself militarily as an alliance. |
| 14 | March | *ESDI/ESDP.* A NATO-EU Agreement on Security of Information is signed. It provides for full and effective consultation and co-operation between NATO and the EU on the basis of classified information exchanged between the two parties. This is an important step in the implementation of Berlin-Plus. |
| 17 | March | NATO decides to terminate Operation Allied Harmony as of 31 March in view of the upcoming EU takeover. |
| 17 | March | *ESDI/ESDP.* A Comprehensive Framework for EU-NATO Permanent Arrangements is finalised and adopted. They provide details on EU access to NATO resources for EU operations (Berlin-Plus). |
| 17 | March | *The Iraq War. The* US and UK fail to obtain UN Security Council backing for a military operation in Iraq. The US advises UN inspectors to leave Iraq. |
| 18 | March | *The Iraq War.* UN weapons inspectors are withdrawn from Iraq. |
| 19 | March | *The Iraq War*. In a meeting shortly before the announced military action against Iraq is to begin, French Foreign Minister Dominique de Villepin insists that the choice between the peaceful disarmament of Iraq through continued inspections and the use of military force is one "between two visions of the world". |
| 20 | March | *The Iraq War.* The US and the UK launch air strikes against Iraq. |
| 21 | March | *The Iraq War.* US and UK ground troops invade Iraq. |

| | | |
|---|---|---|
| 21-22 | March | *ESDP.* The Brussels European Council "recognises the role that defence and security related R&D could play in promoting leading-edge technologies and thereby stimulate innovation and competitiveness; welcomes the Commission's Communication 'Towards an EU Defence Equipment Policy'; invites the Council to analyse the role of defence R&D procurement in the context of the overall R&D activities in the Union, including the possible creation by the Council of an inter-governmental defence capabilities development and acquisition agency." This paragraph is the starting point for work on the idea of an EU agency in the field of armaments and defence capabilities. |
| 27 | March | *ESDP.* The EP Committee on Foreign Affairs, Human Rights, and Common Security and Defence Policy issues a Report on the New European Security and Defence Architecture, listing priorities and deficiencies. |
| 27 | March | *The Iraq War.* US Ambassador to the UN John D. Negroponte says that the use of military force against Iraq is legitimate since it is authorised under UN Security Council Resolution 678 (1990). He also insists that the coalition aspires to liberate, not occupy, Iraq; that Iraq must be disarmed and its terrorist infrastructure destroyed; that its territorial integrity and structure as a unified state must be preserved; and that a process of economic and political reconstruction leading towards prosperity and freedom must begin. |
| 31 | March | *ESDI/ESDP.* The EU's mission Operation Concordia is launched in Macedonia with NATO support. Thirteen EU member states contribute personnel and 14 non-EU countries participate in the mission, which consists of 350 personnel and is scheduled to end on 30 September 2003. The purpose is to support the Ohrid peace agreement and to more generally support the emergence of a stable and secure environment. The mission, which was established on the basis of a host-state request and Security Council Resolution 1371, constitutes the EU's first use of NATO assets and capabilities. |
| | March | *ESDP.* The ECAP Report is finalised. |
| 9 | April | *The Iraq War.* Baghdad falls. |
| 14-15 | April | *The Iraq War.* The coalition in Iraq declares that the military phase of the conflict is over. |
| 15 | April | *9/11.* The EU Council of Ministers adopts a so-called targeted initiative to respond effectively to the international threat of terrorism. |
| 16 | April | *9/11.* NATO decides that it will take over the ISAF mission in Afghanistan. |

| | | |
|---|---|---|
| 16 | April | An informal EU summit is held in Athens for the signing of accession treaties with Cyprus, the Czech Republic, Estonia, Hungary, Latvia, Lithuania, Malta, Poland, Slovakia and Denmark. |
| 23 | April | Turkish Cypriot leader Rauf Denktasch allows Turkish Cypriots to cross the "green line" and visit the South and Greek Cypriots to visit the North. |
| 29 | April | *ESDP.* The leaders of Belgium, France, Germany and Luxembourg meet in the Brussels suburb of Tervuren to discuss increasing EU defence co-operation. They call for the creation of a European Security and Defence Union and a new rapid reaction force. The latter would be built around the Franco-German brigade and supplemented by Belgian commandos and units from Luxembourg, and it can also be reinforced by troops from other interested countries. They also pledge to set up autonomous EU military headquarters by 2004, which draws negative reactions from the UK and the US. |
| 30 | April | The EU, the UN, Russia and the US publish the so-called Performance-based Road Map to a Permanent Two-State Solution to the Israeli-Palestinian Conflict, which foresees a final and comprehensive settlement by 2005. |
| 1 | May | *The Iraq War.* President Bush announces the end of major combat operations in Iraq but stops short of saying the war is over. |
| 6 | May | US President Bush announces the appointment of Paul Bremer as presidential envoy to Iraq. Bremer is to "oversee Coalition reconstruction efforts and the process by which the Iraqi people build the institutions and governing structures that will guide their future...." |
| 11 | May | *The Iraq War.* "The Washington Post" reports that a Coalition Provisional Authority (CPA) has been set up by the US in Iraq. It is to restore security and stability in Iraq and to oversee the country's reconstruction and return to civilian rule. |
| 13 | May | US Secretary of Defense Rumsfeld designates Paul Bremer as CPA administrator. |
| 13 | May | *9/11.* Three simultaneous bomb explosions occur in a residential area largely inhabited by Westerners in Riyadh, Saudi Arabia, killing 34 people and injuring some 200 more. Al-Qaeda is involved in the attacks. |
| 19 | May | *ESDP.* The EU General Affairs and External Relations Council holds an ECAP Conference. On the ERRF, EU defence ministers declare that the EU "now has operational capability across the full range of Petersberg tasks" but that this capability remains "limited and constrained by recognised shortfalls". The Council establishes 15 project groups that are |

| | | |
|---|---|---|
| | | to focus on "implementation of concrete projects, including solutions through acquisition or other solutions such as leasing, multinationalisation and considering possibilities for role specialisation." |
| 22 | May | *ESDI/ESDP.* German Defence Minister Peter Struck issues new guidelines on defence policy. The main tasks of the *Bundeswehr* are identified as prevention and management of international conflicts and the internal fight against terrorism. Future deployment cannot be limited territorially or in terms of intensity. Conscription is maintained. International armed deployment will only take place with NATO Allies and partners from the UN, NATO and the EU. The ESDP does not replace NATO; it is merely a necessary complement thereto. The commitment to rapid military reaction within the framework of NATO and the EU makes rapid political decision-making at the national level indispensable. |
| 22 | May | *The Iraq War.* A UN Security Council resolution gives the occupying powers in Iraq a mandate to administer the territory of Iraq and at the same time reminds them of their responsibilities and obligations towards the population and the country. |
| 5 | June | *ESDP.* The EU agrees to send 1,400 troops to Bunia, Democratic Republic of the Congo (DRC), as an Interim Emergency Multinational Force (Operation Artemis). This mission, which is backed by a UN Security Council resolution, constitutes the first EU military deployment outside of Europe and independent from NATO. France acts as the lead nation. The EUMC is responsible for the military direction of the mission, whilst strategic direction is undertaken by the PSC. The Security Council mandate for Artemis runs until 1 September to allow the UN secretary-general to strengthen the UN mission in the country (MONUC) in the meantime. |
| 10 | June | *ESDP/9/11.* The PSC adopts Basic Principles for an EU Strategy Against Proliferation of Weapons of Mass Destruction, which include an action plan for the implementation of the basic principles. |
| 12 | June | *ESDP.* Operation Artemis troops are deployed. |
| 13 | June | *ESDP.* The European Commission issues a report on the Convention on the Future of Europe: "the new provisions on the common foreign and security policy, together with the creation of an EU Foreign Affairs Minister, will help to enhance the Union's role on the international stage; ... the provisions on defence will make it possible to improve military capabilities and will enable these member states which are willing and able to do so to engage in structured cooperation that will strengthen the credibility of the EU's foreign policy." However, "The Commission has to conclude |

| | | |
|---|---|---|
| | | that the result is not always as ambitious as it would have liked ... [and that] there are still shortcomings on some important matters", such as QMV, institutional balance and clarification of the role of institutions, economic governance and external representation, and possibility to revise the Constitution by a reinforced majority procedure without recourse to national ratification procedures. |
| 16 | June | *ESDP/9/11*. The PSC presents its Basic Principles for an EU Strategy Against Proliferation of Weapons of Mass Destruction to the EU Council of Ministers. |
| 19-20 | June | *ESDP.* Thessaloniki European Council. Javier Solana presents a draft for a European Security Strategy. A Declaration on Non-Proliferation of Weapons of Mass Destruction including the Basic Principles and the action plan is adopted. The Italian Presidency is tasked to draw up plans for establishing an EU agency in the field of armaments. Giscard d'Estaing presents the draft Treaty Establishing a Constitution for Europe. The draft is accepted as a working basis for the IGC that is to be convened to agree on a definite treaty. |
| 25 | June | *9/11*. A transatlantic summit between the EU and NATO is held in Washington. It leads to the signing of Mutual Legal Assistance and Extradition Agreements and to the launch of a Transatlantic Aviation Act. A Joint Initiative Against the Proliferation of WMD is also undertaken. Discussions focus on the implementation of the Middle East road map. |
| 10 | July | The European Convention concludes its work by adopting by consensus a draft treaty establishing a Constitution for Europe, which includes a Charter of Fundamental Rights. |
| 13 | July | *The Iraq War.* Iraq's Governing Council is established by the CPA and meets for the first time. |
| 18 | July | Valéry Giscard d'Estaing hands over the draft European Constitution to the Italian Presidency. |
| 21 | July | The EU Council of Ministers extends Operation Concordia to 15 December in accordance with a request by the FYROM Government. |
| 11 | August | *9/11*. NATO takes over control of ISAF in Afghanistan from Germany and the Netherlands. The force is now led by Lieutenant-General Götz Glimeroth. Canadian Major-General Andrew Leslie is his deputy. |
| 14 | August | *The Iraq War.* UN Security Council Resolution 1500 is passed, thereby establishing a United Nations Assistance Mission in Iraq. |
| 19 | August | *The Iraq War.* The UN headquarters in Baghdad are attacked. The special representative of the UN secretary-general in Iraq, Sergio Vieira De Mello, is killed, along with 22 colleagues. |

| | | |
|---|---|---|
| 1 | September | *ESDP.* Operation Artemis in Bunia, DRC, ends, and responsibility is transferred back to the UN mission in DRC (MONUC). |
| 12 | September | Sanctions against Libya are lifted. |
| 16 | September | FYROM authorities invite the "EU to assume responsibility for an enhanced role in policing and the deployment of an EU Police Mission." |
| 20 | September | *ESDP.* French, UK and German leaders meet at an informal summit in Berlin. They do not reach agreement on Iraq, but their differences on the issue of independent EU military headquarters diminish. Tony Blair accepts the principle that the EU should have autonomous military planning and operational capacities. A joint paper states: "We are together convinced that the EU must be able to plan and conduct operations without the backing of NATO assets and NATO capability. ... Our goal remains to achieve such a planning and implementation capacity in consensus with the 25 [member states] but also in a circle of interested partners." |
| 24 | September | The EU and the UN issue a joint declaration on crisis management. The two organisations "agree to establish a joint consultative mechanism at the working level to examine ways and means to enhance mutual co-ordination and compatibility" in the areas of planning, training, communication and best practices. |
| 29 | September | *ESDP.* The EU decides to conform with the request made by FYROM to establish a police mission in FYROM in December 2003. |
| 3-4 | October | *ESDP.* At an informal EU defence ministers meeting in Rome, France proposes the formation of a European police force. Javier Solana speaks of the development of a new capabilities objective, including ensuring that forces declared are usable in real operations as a mid-term objective for 2010. He sees 2010 as a reasonable target date for significant progress in filling the gaps identified in the ECAP exercise. EU defence ministers also discuss the plan to establish independent EU military headquarters. The UK comes forward with the idea to establish the EU HQ at the same location as the NATO HQ, in Mons, Belgium. At the same meeting, it is agreed that the EU will take over peacekeeping in BiH from NATO in 2004. |
| 4 | October | An IGC starts to finalise the proposed EU Constitution. |
| 10 | October | *ESDP.* Javier Solana appoints Annalisa Giannella (Italy) as his personal representative on non-proliferation of WMD. |
| 15-16 | October | *ESDI/ESDP.* The US ambassador to NATO, Nicholas Burns, describes the recent EU plans to step up autonomous EU defence and to set up independent military headquarters as the "most significant threat to NATO's future" and demands an emergency meeting of all NATO members on the issue. |

| | | |
|---|---|---|
| 16 | October | *The Iraq War.* The UN Security Council recognises the Governing Council and its ministers as the principal bodies of the Iraqi interim administration and calls upon the CPA "to return governing responsibilities and authorities to the people of Iraq as soon as practicable." The resolution also mandates the UN to "strengthen its vital role in Iraq". |
| 20 | October | *ESDI/ESDP.* A NATO meeting on the proposed EU strategic military headquarters ends inconclusively, but US fears are somewhat calmed. |
| 20 | October | *ESDP.* The DRC Government addresses a request to the EU for assistance in setting up an integrated police unit. |
| 24 | October | Ther German *Bundestag* votes to send German troops to Kunduz. It is the first time ISAF is going to operate outside Afghanistan's capital, Kabul. |
| 3-23 | November | Following parliamentary elections in Georgia, opposition parties and tens of thousands of demonstrators demand that President Eduard Shevardnadze (Soviet foreign minister from 1985 to 1990 and in 1991) resign and that the election results be annulled because of falsifications. |
| 15 | November | *9/11.* Bomb attacks in Istanbul kill 30 and injure at least 400. Al-Qaeda is suspected. |
| 17-18 | November | *ESDP.* The EU Council of Ministers sets up an Agency Establishment Team to create an agency in the field of developing defence capabilities, including in the areas of research, acquisition and armaments, in the course of 2004. The European Defence Agency (EDA) is born. On ECAP, the Council, stressing the need for an approach identifying objectives, timelines and reporting procedures, asks for the development of an ECAP road map to monitor progress and to allow redirection of work if necessary. |
| 19-25 | November | *ESDI/ESDP.* The first joint EU-NATO crisis-management exercise, CME/CMX 03, takes place. It focuses on the strategic management of civilian and military instruments for an envisaged EU-led operation with recourse to NATO assets and capabilities. |
| 20 | November | Bomb attacks in Istanbul, the second series within a week, kill 27 people. Al-Qaeda is suspected. |
| 22 | November | Protesters in Georgia storm the parliament building in Tbilisi. |
| 23 | November | Georgian President Shevardnadze steps down, and a group of three reformers, consisting of Mikheil Saakashvili, Nino Burjanadze and Zurab Zhvania, takes power *ad interim*. |
| 25 | November | The Georgian Supreme Court annuls the results of a part of the parliamentary elections of 2 November, namely those mandates allocated through proportional representation (the mandates allocated through majoritarian constituencies were not challenged). |

| | | |
|---|---|---|
| 25 | November | *ESDP.* The Italian Presidency of the EU issues a proposal on defence for the proposed constitution. It speaks of "structured cooperation" for defence issues, i.e., that decisions in the CFSP can be taken by QMV, thereby enabling pioneer groups to lead the ESDP forward. The Italian Presidency also proposes to add a reference to the provisions on mutual defence to the effect that co-operation in this area has to conform to NATO commitments. |
| 26 | November | *ESDP.* France, Germany and the UK reach a deal on autonomous EU headquarters at a defence ministers meeting in Naples. They also agree a new force concept that becomes known as battle groups, i.e., rapid-deployment joint tactical groups of around 1,500 soldiers each that would be deployed in support of UN operations. |
| 28-29 | November | *ESDP.* At an EU foreign ministers meeting in Naples, a proposal by the Italian Presidency allows a breakthrough in the definition of the ESDP in the Constitution. The proposal foresees structured co-operation that needs a minimum number of participants and provides for the whole Council to decide on setting up and expanding membership of structured co-operation. Ministers also agree to set up independent European military headquarters at NATO headquarters in Belgium. The headquarters will only be called upon when NATO is not involved in an operation and national headquarters need assistance. The presidency proposal also eliminates the term "mutual defence", which has worried neutral countries (and the UK), from the draft Constitution. However, the conference reaches no compromise on the issue of the allocation of votes in the Council. |
| 29 | November | *ESDP.* France, Germany and the UK present a joint paper to other EU defence ministers that "sets out how the collective capability of the EU can be strengthened, including the ability to plan and run certain operations, and describes how consideration of the options involved would take place between UN Partners and NATO Allies." The three countries, "in order to improve the preparation of EU operations having recourse to NATO assets and capabilities under the Berlin plus arrangements, ... propose that a small EU cell should be established at SHAPE and to invite NATO to establish liaison arrangements at the EUMS. This will also ensure full transparency between EU and NATO embodying their strategic partnership in crisis management." The paper also proposes that the EUMS enhance its early-warning, situation-assessment and strategic-planning capacity. Regarding autonomous EU operations, the countries propose to use national headquarters, which can be multi-nationalised, or, when it is necessary, to draw on the collective capacity of the EUMS. A civilian-military cell within the EUMS is to act as an operations centre. France, Germany and the UK also make proposals on structured co-operation. |

| | | |
|---|---|---|
| 30 | November | Following the resignation of Shevardnadze, the Georgian parliament sets 4 January 2004 as the date for extraordinary presidential elections. |
| 1 | December | *ESDP.* The Italian Presidency issues several revised documents on European defence in the wake of the 28-29 November Naples meeting. In contrast to the proposals made at the meeting, the new texts reintroduce the words "mutual defence" and speak of a minimum number of participants required for structured co-operation in defence. |
| 12-13 | December | *ESDP.* The Brussels European Council approves the EU defence planning document on an autonomous EU civilian-military planning cell that was introduced as a joint paper by the UK, France and Germany on 29 November. EU leaders also adopt the new Headline Goal 2010 and agree on an EU Strategy Against Proliferation of Weapons of Mass Destruction. |
| 12-13 | December | *ESDP.* The Brussels European Council approves a report drafted by the office of the EU high representative for the CFSP, Javier Solana, entitled "A Secure Europe In A Better World – European Security Strategy". It states that: "Europe should be ready to share in the responsibility for global security and in building a better world. ... An active and capable European Union would make an impact on a global scale. In doing so, it would contribute to an effective multilateral system leading to a fairer, safer and more united world." |
| 12-13 | December | The Brussels European Council fails to finalise the European Constitution because of serious disagreements over the allocation of votes to each member state. While Germany and France want to change the distribution of votes agreed at the 2000 Nice Summit to better take into account population size, Poland and Spain prefer to stick to the Nice structure. |
| 13 | December | *The Iraq War.* Saddam Hussein is captured outside of Tikrit, Iraq, by US military forces. |
| 15 | December | *ESDP.* The EU Police Mission in FYROM, code-named EUPOL PROXIMA, is launched. |
| 15 | December | *ESDP.* The PSC agrees to support the setting up of an integrated police unit in DRC with a three-strand approach comprising rehabilitation and refurbishing of a training centre and the provision of basic equipment; training of the unit; and follow-up, monitoring and mentoring of the concrete implementation of the unit's mandate after the initial training phase. |
| 19 | December | US President Bush and UK Prime Minister Blair announce that, after nine months of negotiations between Libyan leader Al-Gaddafi and US and UK diplomats, Libya has agreed to renounce its nuclear- and chemical-weapons programmes and the production of relevant delivery means. Libya will also "immediately and unconditionally" welcome international inspectors. |

| | |
|---|---|
| **At a Glance – Major Events and Themes** | **Iraqi armed resistance against the US-led occupation intensifies** |
| | **Battle-group concept presented** |
| | **Madrid attacked** |
| | **New reformist government in Georgia** |
| | **Seven new member states join NATO** |
| | **10 new member states join the EU** |
| | **Headline Goal 2010 formally adopted** |
| | **Iraqi civilian Interim Government replaces Coalition Authority** |
| | **Javier Solana to become EU minister for foreign affairs upon entry into force of EU Constitution** |
| | **European Gendarmerie Force created** |
| | **EU Constitution signed** |
| | **George W. Bush re-elected US president** |
| | **Yasser Arafat dies** |
| | **Orange Revolution in Ukraine** |
| | **EUFOR/Althea launched** |
| | **The EU to start accession negotiations with Turkey in October 2005** |

## 2004

| Day | Month | Event |
|---|---|---|
| 4 | January | An Afghan *Loya Jirga* adopts a new constitution that endows Afghanistan with a strong president. |
| 4 | Janaury | Opposition leader Mikheil Saakashvili is elected president of Georgia with more than 96% of the vote in an extraordinary presidential election called in the wake of the resignation of former President Shevardnadze. |
| 9 | January | Georgia's acting president, Nino Burjanadze, announces that repeat parliamentary elections will take place on 28 March. |
| 25 | January | Mikheil Saakashvili takes office as Georgian president. |
| 28 | January | *ESDP.* Javier Solana appoints Briton Nick Witney as leader of the Agency Establishment Team for the EDA. |
| 2 | February | Israeli Prime Minister Sharon announces a unilateral withdrawal from all settlements in Gaza, independent of a possible peace agreement with the Palestinians. |
| 9 | February | *9/11*. Lieutenant-General Rick Hillier of Canada takes over command of ISAF in Afghanistan. The operation is still under NATO command. Hillier's deputy is Major-General Werner Korte of Germany. |

| | | |
|---|---|---|
| 10 | February | *ESDP.* France and the UK submit their proposal for battle groups, or technical groups (as France calls them), to the PSC. |
| 11 | February | *ESDP.* The German defence minister decides that Germany will participate in the proposed battle groups. |
| 16-18 | February | India and Pakistan hold low-level bilateral talks. Higher-level talks over the issue of Kashmir are scheduled for later in the year. |
| 18 | February | *ESDP.* The PSC asks the Military Committee for an opinion on the technical aspects of the battle-group concept. |
| 19 | February | Israeli Prime Minister Sharon's plan for withdrawing all settlements from the Gaza Strip and four from the northern West Bank wins a clear majority in a cabinet vote. However, each evacuation of a settlement is subject to a prior assessment of the situation. Implementing a decision by the Israeli Supreme Court, the cabinet also approves a modified line for the so-called security fence between Israel and the West Bank, which will now be closer to the "green line". |
| 23 | February | *ESDP.* The EU Council of Ministers approves a decision to create a new mechanism for administering the common costs of EU-led missions with military or defence implications. This new mechanism should reduce the time needed to launch a mission, as it eliminates the need for a separate Council decision on the financing of common costs for every operation. |
| 1 | March | *The Iraq War.* Iraq's Governing Council announces that it has agreed on an interim constitution. |
| 2 | March | *The Iraq War.* Suicide attacks on Shi'a Muslims in Karbala and Baghdad during the religious festival of Ashoura kill at least 169 people. |
| 8 | March | *The Iraq War.* Iraq's Governing Council signs an interim constitution. |
| 11 | March | Greek and Turkish Cypriots fail to agree a peace deal. |
| 11 | March | *3/11.* A series of bomb attacks on commuter trains in Madrid kills 191 people. The Spanish Government instantly blames the radical Basque separatist movement ETA. |
| 14 | March | *3/11/The Iraq War.* Elections in Spain are won by the Social-Democratic opposition. Voter turnout is unusually high, and the ruling Conservatives pay a price for blaming ETA for the bomb attacks despite indications that Al-Qaeda was involved. Many US commentators see the election result as giving in to terrorist blackmail since the Conservatives have supported US policy on Iraq while the Social-Democrats have not. |
| 14 | March | Vladimir Putin is elected to serve a second term as Russian president. |

| | | |
|---|---|---|
| 15 | March | *ESDP.* The so-called Group of Personalities, consisting of high-level industry executives and policy-makers, presents a report called "Research for a Secure Europe" to the president of the European Commission, Romano Prodi. The report calls for an increase in European funding for, and co-ordination of, security-related research. Specifically, the report recommends the creation of a European Security Research Programme with a minimum funding of 1 billion euros for the development of security-related technology. |
| 15 | March | *The Iraq War/3/11.* The newly elected prime minister of Spain, José Luis Rodríguez Zapatero, promises to pull Spanish troops out of Iraq as soon as it becomes feasible. |
| 16 | March | Riots break out in Kosovo after ethnic Serbs are blamed for the drowning of two ethnic Albanian children. |
| 22 | March | Macedonia applies for EU membership. |
| 22 | March | Israel kills Hamas leader Sheikh Ahmed Yassin. |
| 22 | March | Former US cyber-terrorism advisor Richard Clarke accuses US President Bush of not having taken the Al-Qaeda threat seriously before 9/11. He also asserts that there was no reason for the US to have gone to war in Iraq in 2003. |
| 25-26 | March | *3/11.* The European Council in Brussels adopts a Declaration on Combating Terrorism. It focuses on making better use of existing agencies and policies rather than setting up new bodies in the wake of the Madrid attacks. It does, however, appoint a counter-terrorism co-ordinator, Gijs de Vries from the Netherlands, and calls for the integration of an intelligence structure on terrorism within the Council Secretariat and the strengthening of border controls. The declaration also puts forward the idea of keeping records of telephone and Internet operators, and it urges progress on a database of persons suspected of terrorist involvement and other serious crimes. Moreover, the document contains a Declaration on Solidarity Against Terrorism, which, however, is but a "political commitment" and leaves it to each state "to choose the most appropriate means to comply with this solidarity commitment towards the affected State." |
| 28 | March | The united National Movement-Democrats bloc of Saakashvili, Burjanadze and Zhvania wins a majority of 67.75% in a rerun of the parliamentary elections in Georgia that were initially held in November 2003 but annulled because of widespread falsifications. |
| 1 | April | Talks fail between Greek and Turkish Cypriot leaders on a UN peace plan that would foresee a loose union between the two parts of the island. |
| 1 | April | The conflict in southern Sudan makes the headlines in the West. |

| | | |
|---|---|---|
| 2 | April | Bulgaria, Estonia, Latvia, Lithuania, Romania, Slovakia and Slovenia join NATO. |
| 3 | April | *3/11*. Islamist suspects in the Madrid bombings die, as they blow up the building where they are hiding after it is surrounded by police. One police officer also dies. |
| 5-6 | April | *ESDP.* At an informal meeting, EU defence ministers and chiefs of defence staff give a very positive response to the battle-group proposal. They set a target date of 2007 for achieving the first operational groups, which should be deployable worldwide within 15 days and for up to four months until larger units can be deployed. The number of groups is expected to be between six and ten. |
| 15 | April | *The Iraq War/3/11*. Spain begins withdrawing its troops from Iraq. |
| 17 | April | Israel kills Abdel Aziz Al-Rantissi, who replaced Yassin as Hamas leader. |
| 23 | April | US lifts sanctions on Libya, rewarding the country for its decision to abandon its WMD programmes. |
| 24 | April | Greek Cypriots vote "no" in a referendum on a peace agreement submitted by UN Secretary-General Kofi Annan. |
| 26 | April | Macedonian President Boris Trajkovski dies in a plane crash. |
| 29 | April | *The Iraq War.* Pictures and videos emerge of mistreatment of Iraqi prisoners by US troops at Abu Ghraib prison. Subsequent investigations reveal that these practices are widespread and have been going on since October 2003. One of the several military investigations launched by the US, the so-called Schlesinger Report, states: "There is no evidence of a policy of abuse promulgated by senior officials or military authorities. Still, the abuses were not just the failure of some individuals to follow known standards, and they are more than the failure of a few leaders to enforce proper discipline. There is both institutional and personal responsibility at higher levels." In contrast, investigations by Amnesty International find a "systematic pattern of torture and ill-treatment". |
| 1 | May | Estonia, Latvia, Lithuania, the Czech Republic, Slovakia, Slovenia, Poland, Hungary, Malta and Cyprus join the EU. |
| 11 | May | *The Iraq War.* Islamist extremists behead a US civilian and distribute a video of the act. |
| 17-18 | May | *ESDP.* Whilst noting that "further progress will be required on the recognised shortfalls and deficits from the 2003 Headline Goal", the Council of Ministers approves Headline Goal 2010. The battle-group concept is included in the new Headline Goal. The ECAP road map and a capability improvement chart 2004 are also endorsed. |

| | | |
|---|---|---|
| 28 | May | Ayad Allawi, a former member of Iraq's interim Governing Council, is elected by the latter to become interim prime minister after the handover to civilian rule scheduled for 30 June. |
| 1 | June | *The Iraq War.* Iraq's Governing Council chooses one of its members, Ghazi Mashal Ajil Al-Yawer, as the new president of the Iraqi Interim Government. The Governing Council is then dissolved by its members. |
| 9 | June | The G8 present the so-called Greater Middle East Initiative, a programme initiated by the US to promote democracy in the region. The initiative is criticised by some of the regions's countries for not having been discussed and elaborated with them. |
| 17-18 | June | *ESDP.* The Brussels European Council agrees on a text for a European Constitution and endorses the new Headline Goal 2010. EU leaders also agree to take over SFOR from NATO. Regarding the fight against terrorism, the EU leaders decide that they will review their anti-terrorism action plan and road map (endorsed in September and October 2001, repectively) twice a year, starting in December 2004. The European Council also agrees "to take forward work on the establishment of a civilian/military cell within the EU Military Staff", "of a small EU cell at SHAPE and NATO liaison arrangements with the EUMS" and of "an operations centre". EU leaders insist "that this [operations centre] will not be a standing HQ, that the main option for autonomous military operations remains national HQ and that a decision to draw on the collective capacity of the EUMS would be taken, upon the advice of the Military Committee, in particular where a joint civil/military response is required and where no national HQ is identified." EU leaders also review progress of the follow-up to the European Security Strategy, particularly welcoming the focus on effective multilateralism. |
| 28 | June | *The Iraq War.* Iraq returns to civilian rule, as the CPA is dissolved and power transferred to the Iraqi Interim Government. |
| 28 | June | The EU and the UN Development Programme establish a strategic partnership to strengthen their "ability to deliver efficient, high-quality aid to developing countries, particularly in the areas of governance, conflict prevention and post-conflict reconstruction." |
| 28 | June | *ESDP.* The EU Council of Ministers, following an invitation by the Georgian prime minister on 3 June, decides to launch a rule-of-law mission to Georgia, EUJUST THEMIS, "to support the Georgian authorities in addressing urgent challenges in the criminal justice system." |

| | | |
|---|---|---|
| 29 | June | *ESDI.* NATO Istanbul summit. NATO heads of state and government decide to expand ISAF in Afghanistan, including several additional provincial reconstruction teams; to conclude operations in Bosnia and Herzegovina; to offer assistance to the Government of Iraq with the training of its security forces; to enhance the contribution of Operation Active Endeavour in the Mediterranean to the fight against terrorism; and to further transform the Alliance's military capabilities. NATO leaders also agree "an enhanced set of measures to strengthen [their] individual and collective contribution to the international community's fight against terrorism". Moreover, they decide to enhance the Mediterranean Dialogue and to offer to co-operate with the countries of the broader Middle East region through the Istanbul Cooperation Initiative. Concerning the transformation of the Alliance's military capabilities, NATO leaders state that the NATO Multinational CBRN Defence Battalion has become operational, that the NRF will reach initial operational capability later in 2004, that the implementation of NATO's streamlined command arrangements is on track, that the implementation of the PCC is progressing and that they are "examining options for addressing missile threat to Alliance territory, forces and population centres through an appropriate mix of political and defence efforts." An Istanbul Declaration entitled Our Security In a New Era is also issued. It states that: "Collective defence remains the core purpose of the Alliance. But the threats that NATO faces have changed substantially. ... NATO is transforming its military capabilities in order to adapt to the changing strategic environment. ... But transformation is a process, not an event." |
| 29 | June | *ESDP.* Meeting at the level of heads of state or government, the EU Council of Ministers decides that Javier Solana will be EU minister for foreign affairs when the EU Constitution enters into force. |
| 9 | July | The International Court of Justice (ICJ) renders an advisory opinion, requested by the UN General Assembly, on the Legal Consequences of the Construction of a Wall in the Occupied Palestinian Territory. The ICJ says the construction of the wall is contrary to international law. |
| 12 | July | *ESDP.* The EU Council of Ministers decides to replace NATO's SFOR in BiH in 2004 with an EU force (EUFOR) dubbed Operation Althea. After meeting with Iraqi Foreign Minister Hosyar Zebari, the Council also agrees to establish, conditions permitting, an EU exploratory mission to Iraq that will concentrate, in particular, on the fields of rule of law and civilian administration. |
| 16 | July | EUJUST THEMIS, the EU's first rule-of-law mission, is launched in Georgia. |

| | | |
|---|---|---|
| 22 | July | The US Senate passes a resolution describing events in Darfur, Sudan, as constituting genocide. |
| 23 | July | The restored bridge over the Neretva is inaugurated in Mostar, BiH. The destroyed bridge was a symbol of the ethnic division in Mostar and the country as a whole. |
| 9 | August | After conducting a fact-finding mission in Sudan, an EU delegation says that the situation does not amount to genocide. |
| 9 | August | Eurocorps, headed by Lieutenant-General Jean-Louis Py, takes over command of ISAF. Dutch Major-General Leonardus van der Born is his deputy. The operation remains under NATO control. |
| 26 | August | After three weeks of fighting between US troops and militia under Shi'a leader Moqtada Al-Sadr in Najaf, Grand Ayatollah Ali Sistani negotiates a ceasefire. |
| 29-31 | August | *The Iraq War/ESDP.* The EU conducts an exploratory mission in Baghdad. The purpose of the mission is to consider options for specific forms of EU engagement in the areas of police, rule of law, civilian administration, and elections. |
| 1 | September | Chechen rebels take over a school in Beslan, North Ossetia, taking some 1,200 people hostage. The hostages are packed into a small gymnasium with no food or water. After two days, Russian special forces storm the building following the shooting of fleeing hostages by the attackers. Three hundred thirty-nine hostages and all but one of the hostage-takers die in the ensuing firefight. |
| 4 | September | EU foreign ministers offer to send police officers to Darfur should the African Union wish them to do so. EU ministers also agree to put more pressure on the Sudanese Government to protect the civilian population but do not impose sanctions. |
| 9 | September | At talks with Iran in the Netherlands, the foreign ministers of France, Germany and the UK, Michèle Alliot-Marie, Peter Struck and Geoff Hoon, respectively, issue a two-month ultimatum for Iran to stop its uranium-enrichment activities. |
| 13 | September | *ESDP.* The EU Council of Ministers adopts staff provisions and a budget for the EDA. On the basis of the report on the first EU exploratory mission to Iraq, ministers also agree "that the suggested activities that the EU could engage in, in the civilian crisis management areas of police, rule of law and civilian administration, should be further examined and elaborated." Planning for an EU civilian crisis-management fact-finding mission to Iraq is therefore to be started. This mission should prepare a package of concrete assistance proposals. |

| | | |
|---|---|---|
| 20 | September | *ESDP.* France, Italy, the Netherlands, Spain and Portugal sign an agreement creating a European Gendarmerie Force to be based in Vicenza, Italy. |
| 28 | September | Speaking at the UN General Assembly, North Korea's Vice Foreign Minister Choe Su Hon says that his country has turned plutonium from 8,000 wasted fuel rods into arms. This is the first time that North Korea has publicly declared that it has nuclear weapons. |
| 30 | September | The Russian Government endorses the Kyoto Protocol and sends it to the Russian parliament, the Duma, for approval. |
| 9 | October | Afghani voters elect Hamid Karzai, the leader of the Transitional Authority, as president. |
| 21 | October | France, Germany and the UK offer Iran "valuable nuclear technology" if it ceases all its uranium-enrichment activities. |
| 22 | October | The Russian Duma approves the Kyoto Protocol. Russian ratification allows it to enter into force. |
| 24 | October | EU High Representative for the CFSP Javier Solana visits Sudan and declares that the EU will support the planned African Union peace operation with approximately $100 million. |
| 26 | October | The Israeli parliament, the Knesset, approves Prime Minister Sharon's plan to unilaterally abolish all settlements in the Gaza Strip and four more in the West Bank. |
| 29 | October | EU leaders sign the Treaty Establishing a Constitution for Europe in Rome. Some key institutional changes with regard to the CFSP have found their way into the Constitution, including the creation of the post of European minister for foreign affairs, who will be responsible for carrying out the Union's external policy as a whole, and the creation of a European Armaments, Research and Military Capabilities Agency. Furthermore, a solidarity clause in the event of a terrorist attack or natural disaster is included. The Petersberg tasks are expanded to include disarmament, military advice, post-conflict stabilisation and the fight against terrorism, including actions carried out on the territory of third countries. New forms of flexibility and co-operation are made possible in defence matters: the Council can entrust a group of member states with a mission to uphold the Union's values; a permanent structure of co-operation can be created beween countries that meet criteria and subscribe to commitments regarding military capability; closer co-operation in the field of reciprocal defence is introduced; and a start-up fund for military defence independent of the Union budget is set up. Also, a procedure to allow rapid access to appropriations in the Union budget is defined. CFSP procedures are largely left untouched, however. |

| | | |
|---|---|---|
| 29 | October | Al-Jazeera broadcasts a new video of Al-Qaeda leader Osama bin Laden, in which the latter asserts that "the motivations are still there for what happened to be repeated" and that American citizens hold their security "in their own hands". He also says that, "Any nation that does not attack us will not be attacked." |
| | October | *ESDP.* The Helios 1B satellite that was launched in 1999 is allowed to disintegrate because of power problems. |
| 2 | November | George W. Bush wins a second term in US presidential elections. |
| 2 | November | France, Germany and the UK issue a statement calling on Iran to cease its uranium-enrichment activities in exchange for nuclear technology, access to nuclear fuel, increased trade and assistance with regional security concerns. Iranian President Mohammad Khatami states Iran's willingness to reach an agreement as long as the country's right to peaceful nuclear technology is recognised. |
| 2 | November | Controversial Dutch film director Theo van Gogh is killed by a Dutch Islamist terrorist of Moroccan origin. This spurs a debate on the integration of Muslim immigrants in Western societies. |
| 6 | November | *The Iraq War.* US and Iraqi troops storm the city of Falluja, where several thousand insurgents have been entrenched for months. |
| 11 | November | President of the Palestinian Authority Yasser Arafat dies in a hospital in Paris. Rawdi Fattuh becomes new caretaker president of the Palestinian Authority and Mahmud Abbas new chairman of the PLO. |
| 11 | November | The Lithuanian parliament approves the European Constitution. |
| 14 | November | Elections for a new president of the Palestinian Authority are scheduled for 9 January 2005. |
| 14 | November | The IAEA publishes an agreement between Iran, France, Germany and the UK. Iran reaffirms its commitment not to acquire nuclear weapons and agrees "on a voluntary basis, [to] continue and extend its suspension to include all enrichment-related activities." Meanwhile, Iran's right to develop nuclear technology for peaceful purposes is recognised. |
| 15 | November | US Secretary of State Colin Powell announces that he will step down from his post. |
| 16 | November | US President Bush nominates his national security advisor, Condoleezza Rice, as the new secretary of state in his second term. |

| | | |
|---|---|---|
| 22 | November | *ESDP.* At a military capability commitment conference in Brussels, EU defence ministers review progress of, and the way ahead for, battle groups and ECAP. Initial commitments for the battle groups are outlined. Ministers agree that during the initial operational capability period, set for 2005-2006, the EU should at any time be able to undertake at least one battle-group-sized operation. Full operational capability is set to be reached in 2007. EU defence ministers also adopt guidelines on the EDA's work programme for 2005. |
| 22 | November | Iran officially suspends all its nuclear activities including uranium enrichment. |
| 23 | November | *ESDP.* EU defence ministers back the formation of battle groups. |
| 23 | November | Ukrainians take to the streets in great numbers after the government-supported candidate, Prime Minister Viktor Yanukovych, is declared the winner of the presidential election, although exit polls show a clear lead for the opposition candidate, Viktor Yushchenko. The protests are soon called the Orange Revolution, after the colour of the opposition parties, which dominates the rallies. The EU calls for a repeat election, whilst Russian President Putin sees no reason to do so. |
| 24 | November | Iran demands that it be allowed to continue research and development with centrifuges during the suspension of its nuclear activities. The EU rejects this demand. |
| 27 | November | Iran declares that, "suspension of enrichment is an illogical demand." |
| 30 | November | Iranian top negotiatior Hassan Rowhani says that Iran has not given up its right to enrich uranium, as the suspension of all its nuclear activities is only a temporary measure during the IAEA inspections of Iranian nuclear sites. |
| 1 | December | The Ukrainian parliament passes a vote of no confidence in Prime Minister Yanukovych. The vote requires the signature of President Leonid Kuchma to become effective, however. |
| 2 | December | *ESDP.* Operation Althea is launched in BiH, replacing the NATO-led SFOR. |
| 2 | December | The United Nations Secretary-General's High-Level Panel on Threats, Challenges and Change issues a report entitled "A More Secure World: Our Shared Responsibility". The report addresses such issues as the use of force, peace-building, conflict prevention and reform of the UN, and it also emphasises the need for collective security. |

| | | |
|---|---|---|
| 3 | December | The Ukrainian Supreme Court rules on a claim filed by opposition candidate Yushchenko that the second round of the election was indeed fraudulent and the results cannot stand. The ruling goes into great detail about the types of violations that occurred. |
| 7 | December | Hamid Karzai is sworn in as Afghanistan's president. |
| 8 | December | The Ukrainian parliament adopts a reform package introducing changes to the electoral law, paving the way for a re-run of the presidential election, and constitutional changes transferring some powers from the president to parliament. This constitutes a compromise between government and opposition demands. President Kuchma immediately signs the reform package into law and mass demonstrations in Kyiv end. |
| 8-9 | December | The NATO-Russia Council agrees on an action plan against terrorism. Ministers also sign a memorandum of understanding on Russia's participation in NATO's anti-terrorism operation in the Mediterranean, known as Operation Active Endeavour. |
| 9 | December | UK police announce the prevention of an attack in London on the scale of the Madrid bombings. |
| 9 | December | *ESDP.* The EU Council of Ministers decides to launch a Police Mission in Kinshasa, DRC, EUPOL KINSHASA. The mission will monitor, mentor and advise on the setting up, and the initial running of, an integrated police unit in Kinshasa. |
| 15 | December | The election campaign for the Iraqi National Assembly gets under way. |
| 16-17 | December | The Brussels European Council agrees to start accession negotiations with Turkey on 3 October 2005. EU leaders also endorse the Civilian Headline Goal 2008. Civilian missions under the ESDP should be deployable within 30 days and can be deployed autonomously, jointly or in close collaboration with military operations. |
| 18 | December | *ESDP.* The Helios A2 satellite is launched into Outer Space as a successor to the Helios 1B. It will serve the security and surveillance needs of France and other involved European nations. |
| 20 | December | Hungary's parliament approves the European Constitution. |
| 26 | December | An underwater earthquake some 160 kilometres west of the Indonesian island of Sumatra causes a huge *tsunami* that spreads across the Indian Ocean and as far as Africa's eastern coast. The countries directly affected include Indonesia, Sri Lanka, India, Thailand, the Maldives, Malaysia, Myanmar, Bangladesh, Somalia, Kenya, Tanzania, the Seychelles, South Africa and Yemen. Around 300,000 people die or go missing (including several thousand foreign tourists), some 1.5 million are displaced, homeless and/or left with no livelihood. Around 125,000 are injured. An enormous international relief effort gets under way in the following days. |

| | | |
|---|---|---|
| 26 | December | Ukrainians are again asked to elect a new president. |
| 31 | December | In the wake of the *tsunami* disaster, France's President Chirac calls for a humanitarian rapid reaction force for natural disasters to be set up by Europe and the United Nations. |
| | December | *ESDP.* The EU sends a fact-finding mission to the DRC to examine different options for an EU response, including through the ESDP, in the field of security-sector reform, including army integration and training. |

| At a Glance – Major Events and Themes | |
|---|---|
| | **Mahmud Abbas wins presidential elections in the Palestinian Authority** |
| | **Popular elections in Iraq for a Transitional National Assembly conducted** |
| | **Israeli-Palestinian ceasefire agreed in Egypt** |
| | **NATO to expand ISAF into western Afghanistan but there are disagreements over training of Iraqi soldiers** |

## 2005

| Day | Month | Event |
|---|---|---|
| 9 | January | PLO Chairman Mahmud Abbas wins popular elections and becomes president of the Palestinian Authority, succeeding Yasser Arafat. |
| 10 | January | Ukraine's Central Election Commission declares opposition candidate Victor Yushchenko the winner of the repeat presidential election, but his opponent Victor Yanukovych appeals the decision. |
| 12 | January | The United States announces that it has abandoned its search for WMD in Iraq. |
| 16 | January | Zhao Ziyan, a reformist former Chinese prime minister and general secretary of the Chinese Communist Party, dies. He was ousted from the party for opposing the use of military force against the Tiananmen demonstrators in 1989. |
| 17 | January | The EU high representative for the CFSP, Javier Solana, appoints Michael Machiessen (Denmark) as his personal representative on human rights. |
| 18 | Janaury | The Ukrainian Supreme Court allows the publication of the repeat presidential election results, making them legal. |
| 20 | January | The Ukrainian Supreme Court rejects Yanukovych's final of a series of appeals against the result of the repeat presidential election. |
| 20 | January | George W. Bush is inaugurated for a second term as US President. |
| 23 | January | Victor Yushchenko is sworn in as Ukrainian president. |
| 25 | January | The Italian Chamber of Deputies approves the European Constitution. |
| 26 | January | Condoleezza Rice is sworn in as US secretary of state. |
| 28-29 | January | At an informal meeting in Luxembourg, European justice and home affairs ministers discuss a plan for a central register of criminal convictions but express concern over costs and data protection. At the same meeting, ministers do agree that the new Permanent Internal Security Committee, to be created under the Constitution, should promote and strengthen operational co-operation between police and other internal-security authorities. |

| | | |
|---|---|---|
| 30 | January | The Iraqi people elect a Transitional National Assembly. Voter turnout is between 60% and 75% on average, according to the Independent Election Commission of Iraq, but very low in Sunni areas. The United Iraqi Alliance, a Shi'a-led list backed by Grand Ayatollah Ali Sistani, wins over 47% of the vote. Second comes a united list of Kurdish parties, with around 25%. Interim Prime Minister's Allawi's list of secular Shi'a wins just under 14% of the vote. On the same day, 260 insurgent attacks take place in the country, killing at least 44 people. |
| 1 | February | The Slovenian parliament approves the European Constitution. |
| 1 | February | The European Commission agrees to start membership negotiations with Croatia on 17 March 2005 under the condition that the latter co-operates with the ICTY. |
| 1-3 | February | NATO holds Exercise Allied Reach 05 at NATO's Joint Warfare Centre in Stavanger. The exercise features a simulated scenario that examines planning, operational and capability issues related to the deployment of the NRF. |
| 3 | February | Georgia's Prime Minister Zurab Zhvania dies from apparently accidental gas poisoning. Georgia's President Mikheil Saakashvili takes over his post *ad interim*. |
| 4 | February | Yuliya Tymoshenko, one of the leaders of the Ukrainian Orange Revolution, is confirmed as prime minister by the Ukrainian parliament. |
| 8 | February | Israeli and Palestinian leaders agree a ceasefire at a summit in Egypt. |
| 9-10 | February | At an informal meeting in France, NATO defence ministers agree to gradually take over full command of ISAF in Afghanistan and to expand the Alliance's presence into the west of the country. However, they fail to agree to expand training of the Iraqi military in Iraq itself. Ministers also review and discuss the Alliance's ability to field complex military operations when and where necessary, including the planning and financing of operations, the decision-making processes and the "usability" of member countries' forces. |
| 12 | February | At the Munich Conference on Security Policy, German Chancellor Schröder asserts that, "As part of the European Union, Germany today feels that it shares responsibility for international stability and order. ... We Germans are living up to this responsibility. ... However, this responsibility also brings with it a right to be involved in decision-making. Our wish to see Germany become a permanent member of the UN Security Council derives from the need to base responsibility on legitimacy." On the transatlantic partnership, Schröder says that it "must take such changes into consideration. And, to be honest, it does so insufficiently at present. ... [NATO] is no longer the primary venue where transatlantic partners dis- |

| | | |
|---|---|---|
| | | cuss and co-ordinate strategies. The same applies to the dialogue between the European Union and the United States, which in its current form does justice neither to the Union's growing importance nor to the new demands on transatlantic co-operation." He proposes "a high-ranking panel of independent figures from both sides of the Atlantic to help us find a solution." Also, he stresses that, "A strong European pillar gurantees Europe's loyal partnership in the transatlantic alliance and its willingness to share the burden of the task. This is also in the vested strategic interest of the US." |
| 13 | February | Turkey takes over command of ISAF from Eurocorps. Lieutenant-General Ethem Erdagi takes over from Lieutenant-General Jean-Louis Py of France. Turkey already led ISAF from June 2002 to February 2003. NATO remains in charge of the mission. |
| 16 | February | The Kyoto Protocol enters into force. One hundred forty states are party to the agreement. |
| 20 | February | Some 76.73% of Spanish voters endorse the European Constitution in a referendum. |
| 1 | March | Greece's Foreign Policy and Defence Council adopts a new defence doctrine. The document cites terrorism, illegal arms trade, regional destabilisation and organised crime in general as the biggest security and defence challenges. This means that for the first time since 1974, Turkey does not figure as the biggest threat to Greece. The new doctrine also replaces the so-called unified defence area Greece-Cyprus, which stipulated that any attack on Cyprus would be considered a *casus belli* for Greece, with a promise to support Cyprus on all levels in the event of an emergency. |

# SOURCES


- Keesing's Contemporary Archives 1945-2002 (http://www.keesings.org).
- Edward Fursdon, "The European Defence Community: A History" (London: Macmillan, 1980)
- Kevin Ruane, "The rise and fall of the European defence community: Anglo-American relations and the crisis of European defence, 1950-1955" (Basingstoke [etc.]: Macmillan [etc.], 2000)
- Andrew J. Priest, "The Failure of Alliance Politics: The United States, Europe and the Multilateral Force" (in "49th Parallel. An Interdisciplinary Journal of North American Studies")
- Michael Boas Pedersen, "Historien om et aflag – MLF og US's kamp for sit nukleare hegemoni"
- Robert S. Norris, William M. Arkin and William Burr, "Where they were", in Bulletin of the Atomic Scientist, 55(06), November-December 1999, pp. 26-35 (http://www.thebulletin.org/article.php?art_ofn=nd99norris_024)
- Ansgar Baums, "Deutsche Anerkennungspolitik 1991 / 1992 - Die Anerkennung Sloweniens und Kroatiens: Bewertung eines 'diplomatischen Traumas', seminar paper, Freie Universität Berlin, Otto-Suhr-Institut für Politikwissenschaft, July 1999 (http://www.hausarbeiten.de/faecher/hausarbeit/poj/918.html)
- Ralph Piotrowski, "Sprache und Aussenpolitik - Der deutsche und US-amerikanische Diskurs zur Anerkennung Kroatiens", PhD dissertation, Freie Universität Berlin, Fachbereich Politik und Sozialwissenschaften, December 2003, chapter 3 (www.diss.fu-berlin.de/2004/23/piotrow.pdf)
- http://europa.eu.int
- http://www.nato.int
- http://www.weu.int
- http://www.osce.org
- http://www.un.org
- The websites of the governments whose activities and positions are covered in this chronology
- http://www.isn.ethz.ch/php/collections/coll_gladio.htm
- International Institute for Security Studies, "The Military Balance"
- EU Institute for Security Studies, Chaillot Papers
- http://www.bbc.co.uk
- http://www.cnn.com
- The Economist
- Neue Zürcher Zeitung
- http://en.wikipedia.org/wiki/Main_Page
- Lebendiges virtuelles Museum Online (http://www.dhm.de/lemo/home.html)
- http://www.wordiq.com
- http://www.infoplease.com
- RFE/RL Newsline (http://www.rferl.org/newsline/)
- Hellenic Resources Network (http://www.hri.org)
- www.bits.de/CESD-PA/NEWCESDMAIN.html

# INDEX

## Symbols



## A



## B

## C

# D

# E

# F

# G

# H



# I



INDEX

## J



## K



## L

# M



# N

# O



# P

# Q



# R



# S

# T



# U



# V

## W



## X



## Y



## Z

UK PRICE
£3·99

# THE OFFICIAL LIVERPOOL

## 1990 ANNUAL

STAN LIVERSEDGE

HAMLYN

FOREWORD BY BOB PAISLEY

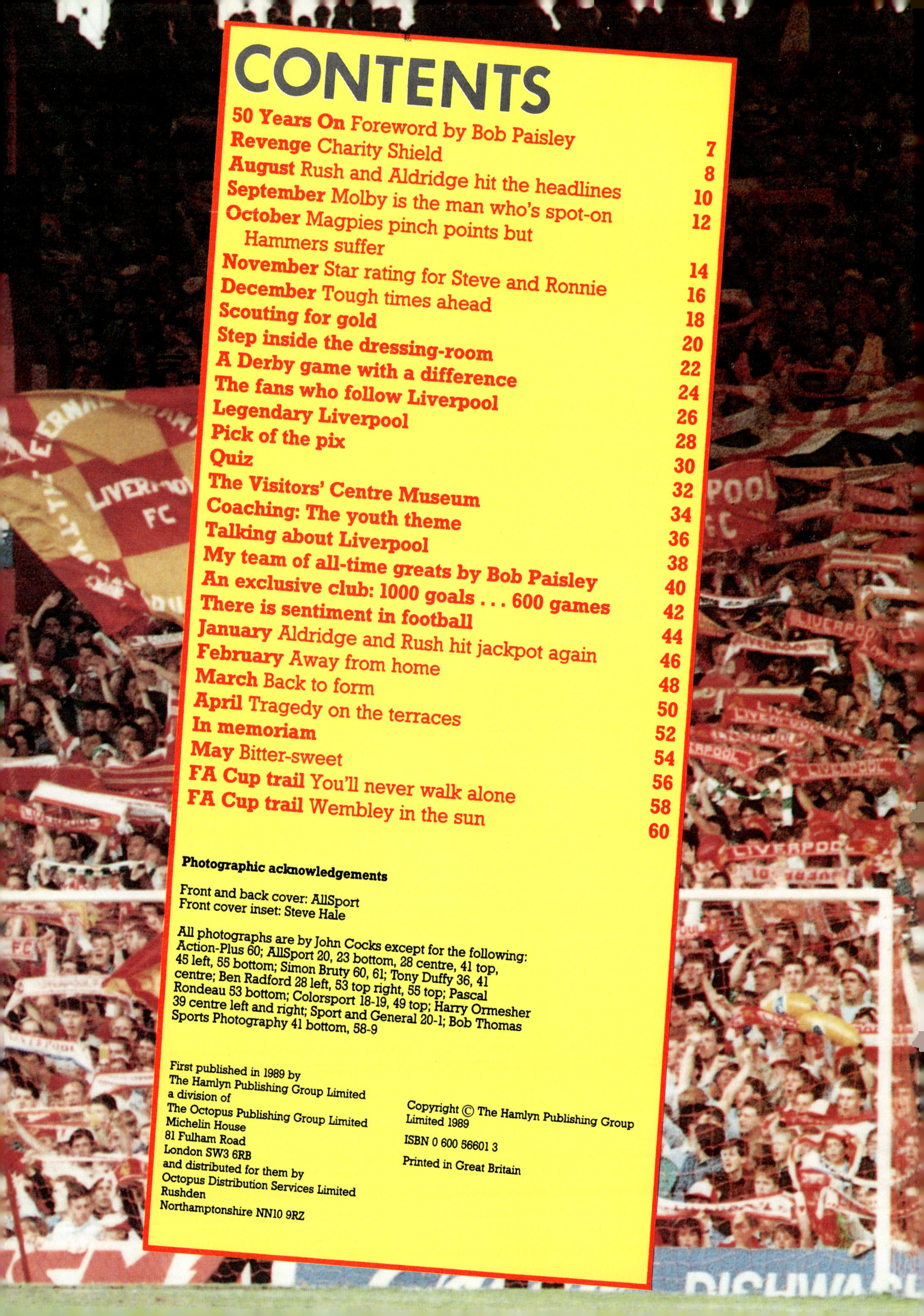


# CONTENTS




**Photographic acknowledgements**

Front and back cover: AllSport
Front cover inset: Steve Hale

All photographs are by John Cocks except for the following: Action-Plus 60; AllSport 20, 23 bottom, 28 centre, 41 top, 45 left, 55 bottom; Simon Bruty 60, 61; Tony Duffy 36, 41 centre; Ben Radford 28 left, 53 top right, 55 top; Pascal Rondeau 53 bottom; Colorsport 18-19, 49 top; Harry Ormesher 39 centre left and right; Sport and General 20-1; Bob Thomas Sports Photography 41 bottom, 58-9

First published in 1989 by
The Hamlyn Publishing Group Limited
a division of
The Octopus Publishing Group Limited
Michelin House
81 Fulham Road
London SW3 6RB
and distributed for them by
Octopus Distribution Services Limited
Rushden
Northamptonshire NN10 9RZ




ISBN 0 600 56601 3

Printed in Great Britain

# 50 YEARS ON

**It's been said often enough that you should look forwards, rather than backwards, and while no-one can tell what the future holds, it seems certain that during the next two years or so Anfield will be undergoing a massive facelift, with the terraces of the famous Kop being replaced by seating, so that the whole stadium will be able to accommodate everyone in comfort and – more important – safety.**

Liverpool Football Club has an enviable reputation around the world for the standards it sets, both on and off the playing field, and we are now entering an era where Anfield seems destined to become an all-seater stadium with a reduced capacity of around 40,000. So, once again, Liverpool will have given a lead . . . although, sadly, the changes will have been brought about because of a major football disaster.

Successive generations of families have stood on the Kop, which for many years has been the most famous landmark in our game of football. Bill Shankly once made a symbolic gesture by taking his place there among the thousands of regulars. But times change, and we all hope that change itself, so far as this club is concerned, will be for the better.

Having been what I call 'part of the furniture' at Liverpool for 50 years, I have seen a great many changes as people have come and gone. I'm referring, of course, mainly to players – and we've had some great teams through the years. I started out as a player with Liverpool when I arrived at Anfield on 8 May 1939 – Billy Liddell had signed professional forms a few weeks earlier – and when I hung up my boots I graduated to the backroom side, serving as trainer, physiotherapist, assistant manager and manager, before I was invited to join the board.

Elsewhere I have written about my Liverpool team of all-time greats, and I think you'll find my choice interesting, to say the least. Everyone has his own ideas, of course, and we all enjoy being armchair managers. As for the Liverpool Annual as a whole, it really is something which I feel the fans will treasure . . . and for obvious reasons.

What happened at Hillsborough on a sunny afternoon in April 1989 will never be forgotten by anyone associated with this club, and these pages contain pictures and words which will be a lasting tribute to those who lost their lives. Lighter moments are also reflected, as the Liverpool players come under the spotlight, and the events of what turned out to be a traumatic season are recorded.

I hope and believe that you will feel the Liverpool Annual truly does justice to a great club and its supporters. I am sure you will agree that every effort has been made to achieve this.

*Bob Paisley*

LIVERPOOL FOOTBALL CLUB
Carlsberg
ROYAL
Candy
THE FOOTBALL ASSOCIATION
CHARITY SHIELD

# REVENGE

*Far left: Steve McMahon in action against Wimbledon in the Charity Shield match*

*Left: John Fashanu (left) in the middle of the action against Liverpool*

*Below left: Skipper Ronnie Whelan and John Barnes parade the Charity Shield*

*Right: Barry Venison beats John Fashanu to the ball during the Charity Shield game*

Charity, they say, begins at home . . . and Liverpool look upon Wembley as their second home. In fact they've been there so often through the years that they now call it Anfield South. When they went to Wembley in August 1988 for the Charity Shield match against Wimbledon, they were also men with a mission – they wanted to make up for their FA Cup final defeat by Wimbledon the previous May.

There's an old song in which the refrain runs: 'But it's a long, long time from May to September . . .' In Liverpool's case, after their experience of May, they couldn't wait for August to come round, never mind September.

In May, Wimbledon had gone to Wembley for the final of the FA Cup. They were rated very much the under-dogs. Liverpool had been installed as the red-hot favourites to add the Cup to their League championship crown and so achieve an historic second double.

Wimbledon upset all the pundits' calculations, however, and spoiled the party for Liverpool, because they actually managed not just to score, but to win. While their Cup-winning hero, Lawrie Sanchez, could look back with pride, one Liverpool marksman in particular would much rather forget that final.

For once John Aldridge – normally a cucumber-cool and expert spot-kick marksman – failed to take advantage of the chance, when Liverpool were awarded a penalty which could bring them an equaliser. Although 'Aldo' struck the ball firmly enough, he saw Wimbledon 'keeper Dave Beasant dive to his left and make the save. From then on Liverpool simply could not draw level, let alone get their noses in front.

## 'Aldo' makes it two

Come August, and Liverpool – as champions of the Barclays League – were on their way back to Wembley to take on the team which had beaten them in the FA Cup final . . .

It was the pipe-opener to season 1988-89. John Aldridge was reckoned to be the man under most pressure to keep his place, especially with Ian Rush about to don the red jersey once again, after his return from Juventus. Back at Wembley 'Aldo' provided the perfect answer by showing that he hadn't lost the knack of finding the net.

This time, it wasn't Dave Beasant who barred the way, because the Dons' Cup final 'keeper had departed for Newcastle United. In his place Wimbledon had the relatively inexperienced Simon Tracey. Yet he played well, although he was still beaten twice by John Aldridge. So Liverpool scored a 2-1 victory and returned home with the trophy, having avenged that FA Cup final defeat and put Wimbledon in their place.

# August

## Rush and Aldridge hit the headlines...

Ian Rush and John Aldridge made headline news, as the English soccer season got under way in August 1988. 'Rushy' returned to Liverpool from Italy; 'Aldo' – who had succeeded him as leading marksman – got away to a flier in the goal-den-boot stakes. In fact he followed Ian Rush by winning the prestigious adidas Golden Shoe award. The presentation was made before the Barclays League game against Manchester United at Anfield.

### Stepping up for the Golden Shoe

The award had been made annually in the United Kingdom since 1978 to the top scorer in each Football League division. In 1984 Rush had won the UK and European awards, after hitting 32 goals, while Aldridge's 26 goals in season 1987-88 brought him the adidas accolade. By the time Liverpool met United, 'Rushy' had already been reintroduced to the Anfield faithful, while Aldridge had scored the two goals which beat Wimbledon in the Charity Shield and a hat-trick against Charlton Athletic at Selhurst Park on kick-off day.

### The numbers game

'Rushy' got his first taste of English League action again against Charlton, though he started out on the bench at number 12. In the second match – the Centenary tournament quarter-final against Nottingham Forest at Anfield – Aldridge was on the bench at number 12 and Rush wore the number 9 shirt, with Ray Houghton switching to number 8. The match was memorable for Barry Venison too ... he drilled in his first-ever goal for Liverpool.

Like Ian Rush before him, John Aldridge collects the prestigious adidas Golden Shoe award

Liverpool's first home game and Ian Rush (9) is back in action

Barry Venison (3) is congratulated after scoring his first-ever goal for Liverpool

# QUOTE

*Ian Rush's reaction, as he donned a Liverpool jersey for the second time around: 'I didn't need much persuading to come back . . . I spent seven years here, and I missed it a bit because of the fans and the people around the club. Juventus are a great club and I don't regret going there – I think I'm a lot better off for the experience, though I don't know if it will make me a better player. We'll have to wait and see. If I go anywhere again from Liverpool, it will be a step downwards . . . so, hopefully, I'm here to stay.'*

## ...RESULTS...

**FA Charity Shield, 20 August**

| | |
|---|---|
| Liverpool 2<br>*John Aldridge (2)* | Wimbledon 1<br>*John Fashanu* |

**Football League, 27 August**

| | |
|---|---|
| Charlton Athletic 0 | Liverpool 3<br>*John Aldridge 3* |

**Centenary tournament quarter-final, 29 August**

| | |
|---|---|
| Liverpool 4<br>*Barry Venison*<br>*Jan Molby (penalty)*<br>*Ray Houghton*<br>*John Barnes* | Nottingham Forest 1<br>*Neil Webb* |

# September

## MOLBY IS THE MAN WHO'S SPOT-ON

The first match of the month was an Anfield crowd-puller – despite the high-noon kick-off, more than 42,000 fans packed the ground to see which, if any, of four ace marksmen (Ian Rush, John Aldridge, Brian McClair, Mark Hughes) would be able to cast their spell on the game. United were brimming with confidence, since they hadn't lost at Anfield for almost 10 years . . . on Boxing Day 1979.

Jan Molby's penalty was a match-winner

In the event Rush, wearing number 12, went on for Aldridge; but the hero of the day as far as Liverpool were concerned, was Danish-international Jan Molby who, for the second game in succession, was given the job of scoring from the penalty spot. When he slotted the ball past 'keeper Jim Leighton, it meant Liverpool wound up as winners.

## Steve's delight

Ray Houghton hit his second goal of the season to earn Liverpool a point at Villa Park, and Peter Beardsley beat Tottenham 'keeper Bobby Mimms for the second season on the trot at Anfield – the previous term, his goal had clinched the League title but this time it earned Liverpool just one point.

The Centenary semi-final at Highbury brought Liverpool's first defeat of the season. However the match was memorable for young Steve Staunton. He was in the starting line-up *and* he scored Liverpool's only goal. Then Liverpool cruised to a 3–1 win at Southampton, with a Molby penalty and goals from Aldridge and Beardsley.

## Dalglish in; Grobbelaar . . . out

The first leg of the Littlewoods Cup tie against Walsall was notable not just because defender Gary Gillespie gave Liverpool a slender lead for the return game. The 18,000 fans were treated also to the spectacle of team-boss Kenny Dalglish emerging from the dug-out and making a rare appearance as a player, when he went on for John Aldridge.

By the end of the month Liverpool were becoming accustomed to the absence of another man who, season after season, had been a key player: 'keeper Bruce Grobbelaar, who had gone down with meningitis. So, as in the previous season, Mike Hooper stepped up from the reserves. He was to stay in the side for 25 matches.

## . . . RESULTS . . .

**Football League, 3 September**

Liverpool 1 — Manchester United 0
*Jan Molby (penalty)*

**Football League, 10 September**

Aston Villa 1 — Liverpool 1
*Alan McInally* — *Ray Houghton*

**Football League, 17 September**

Liverpool 1 — Tottenham Hotspur 1
*Peter Beardsley* — *Terry Fenwick*

**Centenary tournament semi-final, 20 September**

Arsenal 2 — Liverpool 1
*Perry Groves* — *Steve Staunton*
*Brian Marwood*

**Football League, 24 September**

Southampton 1 — Liverpool 3
*Derek Statham (penalty)* — *John Aldridge*
*Peter Beardsley*
*Jan Molby (penalty)*

**Littlewoods Cup second round – first leg, 28 September**

Liverpool 1 — Walsall 0
*Gary Gillespie*

LEAGUE POSITION

| | P | W | D | L | F | A | Pt | Position |
|---|---|---|---|---|---|---|---|---|
| Liverpool | 5 | 3 | 2 | 0 | 9 | 3 | 11 | 2nd |

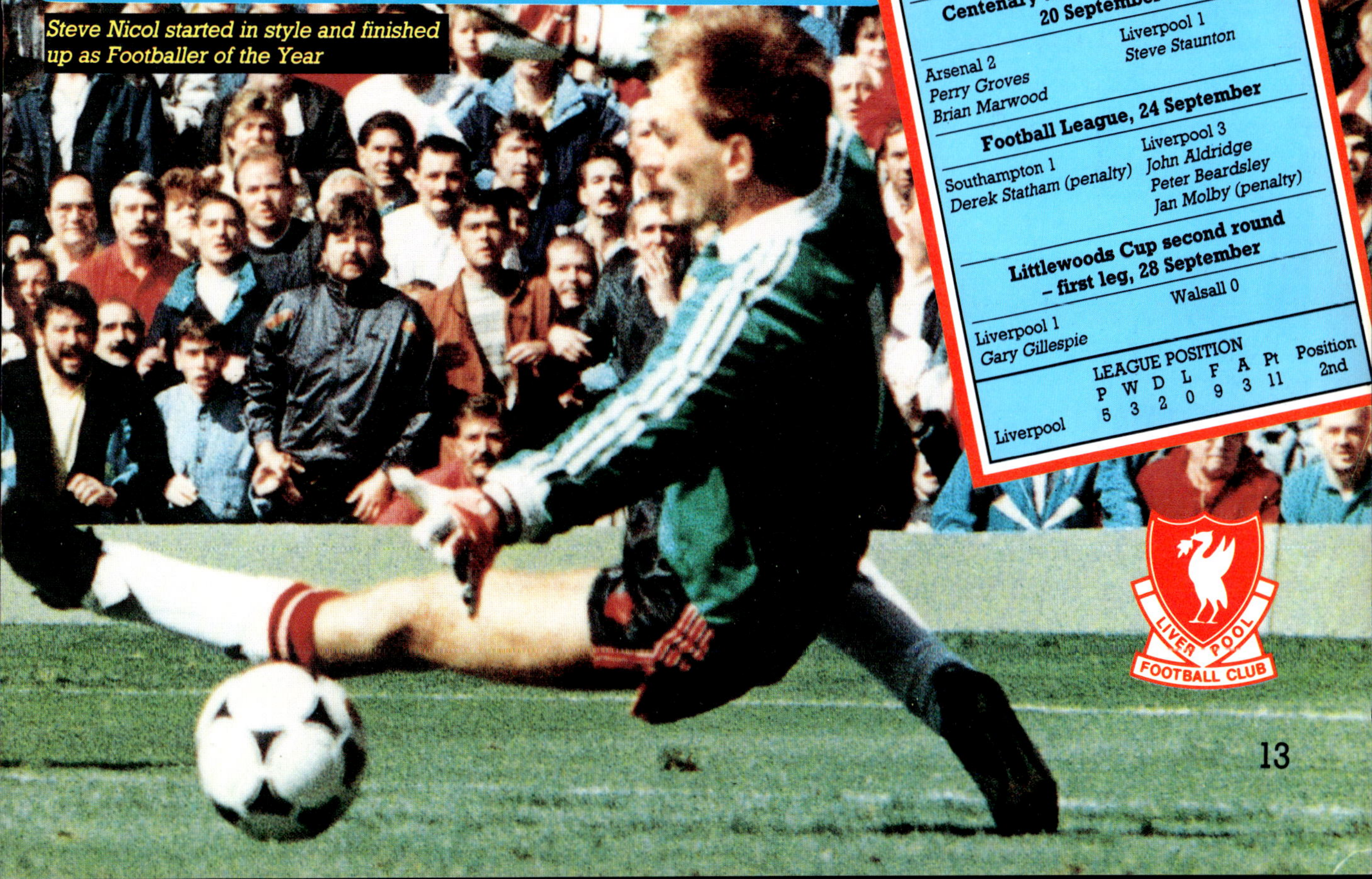

Steve Nicol started in style and finished up as Footballer of the Year

# October

# MAGPIES PINCH POINTS BUT HAMMERS SUFFER

The first day in October saw Gary Gillespie scoring at Anfield for the second successive game . . . unfortunately for Liverpool, it wasn't enough as Newcastle United, anchored near the foot of the table, sprang a shock 2–1 win. Worse befell Liverpool as they lost at Luton; in the first couple of minutes, Mick Harford scored what turned out to be the match-winner.

## Rush stops the rot

So the trip to Walsall for the Littlewoods Cup return was viewed by some as a tricky one, since Liverpool had only a one-goal lead. Ian Rush got off the mark for the first time since his return from Italy, Jan Molby chipped in with another penalty goal, and John Barnes helped Liverpool record a 3–1 win on the night.

There were no goals when Coventry City came to Anfield, and despite a Rush goal at Nottingham Forest's City Ground, Liverpool went down 2–1 to make it three defeats, a draw and only one victory as they came to the end of the month, with Upton Park the last stop. But West Ham were made to suffer as Ian Rush made it two goals on the trot and Peter Beardsley also scored, for Liverpool to clock up a 2–0 win.

## Hooper and Ablett make the grade

And if 'Rushy' was back on the goal trail, 'keeper Mike Hooper at the other end deserved credit, as well, for his displays during the absence of Bruce Grobbelaar. The game at Upton Park was Mike's ninth outing, and if results hadn't gone Liverpool's way, Mike certainly hadn't let the side down. It was becoming clear, in fact, that when Bruce was fit again, he faced a fight to regain his place.

There was also praise for defender Gary Ablett, who stepped up from reserve-team duty to take the place of the injured Gillespie. Ablett was to show that he could perform equally well at left-back or in the centre of the defence, as Liverpool's injury problems bit deeply into their squad's strength

*Liverpool defender Gary Gillespie shows he also knows how to attack, although his goal against Newcastle United wasn't enough to prevent an Anfield defeat*

## ...RESULTS...

**Football League, 1 October**

| | |
|---|---|
| Liverpool 1 | Newcastle United 2 |
| *Gary Gillespie* | *John Hendrie* |
| | *Mirandinha (penalty)* |

**Football League, 8 October**

| | |
|---|---|
| Luton Town 1 | Liverpool 0 |
| *Mick Harford* | |

**Littlewoods Cup second round – second leg, 12 October**

| | |
|---|---|
| Walsall 1 | Liverpool 3 |
| *Craig Shakespeare* | *Jan Molby (penalty)* |
| | *Ian Rush* |
| | *John Barnes* |

**Football League, 22 October**

| | |
|---|---|
| Liverpool 0 | Coventry City 0 |

**Football League, 26 October**

| | |
|---|---|
| Nottingham Forest 2 | Liverpool 1 |
| *Brian Rice* | *Ian Rush* |
| *Neil Webb* | |

**Football League, 29 October**

| | |
|---|---|
| West Ham United 0 | Liverpool 2 |
| | *Ian Rush* |
| | *Peter Beardsley* |

LEAGUE POSITION

| | P | W | D | L | F | A | Pt | Position |
|---|---|---|---|---|---|---|---|---|
| Liverpool | 10 | 4 | 3 | 3 | 13 | 8 | 15 | 4th |

*Ian Rush was among the scorers in Liverpool's Cup tie against Walsall.*

# November

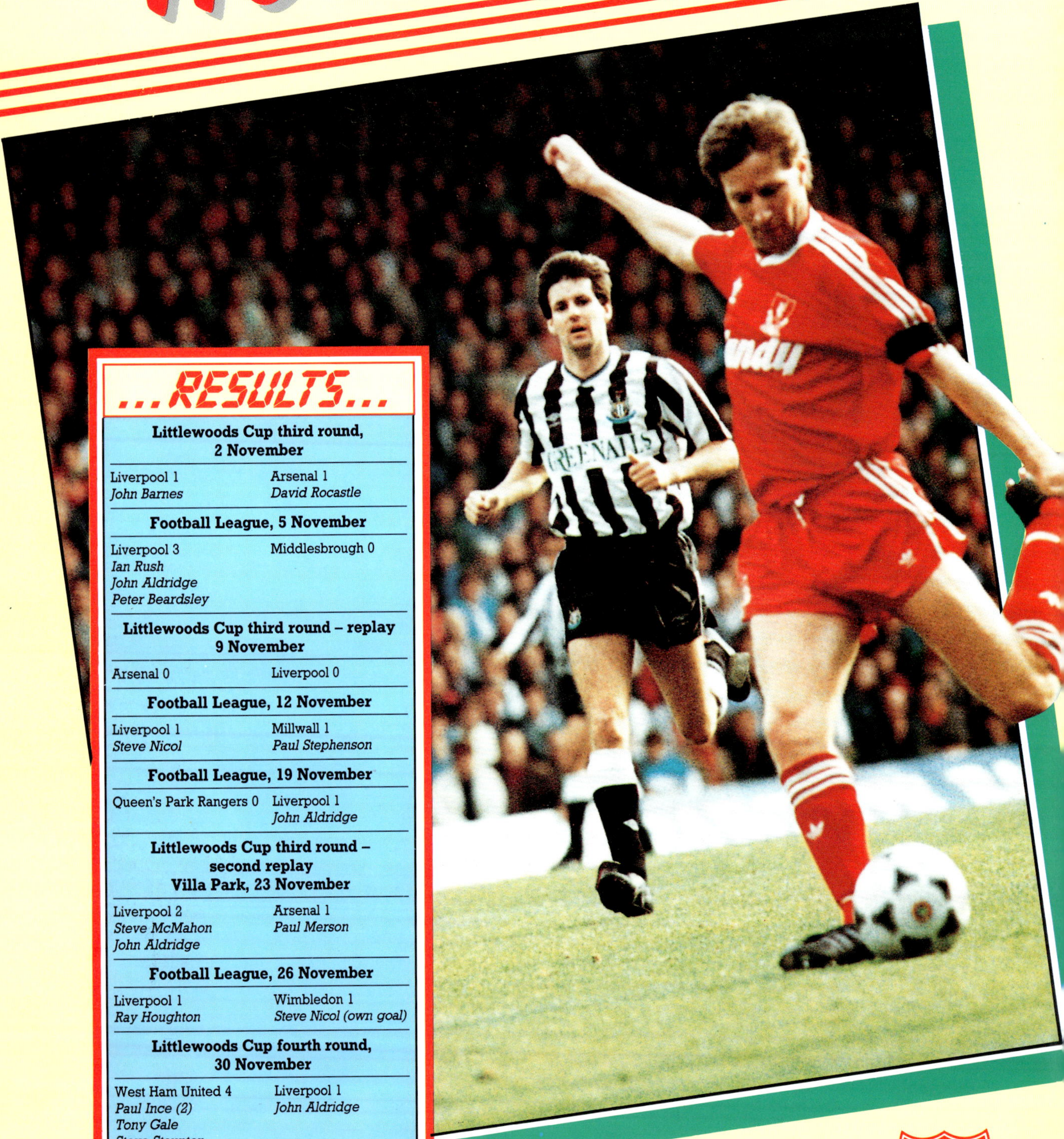


## ...RESULTS...

**Littlewoods Cup third round, 2 November**

| | |
|---|---|
| Liverpool 1 | Arsenal 1 |
| *John Barnes* | *David Rocastle* |

**Football League, 5 November**

| | |
|---|---|
| Liverpool 3 | Middlesbrough 0 |
| *Ian Rush* | |
| *John Aldridge* | |
| *Peter Beardsley* | |

**Littlewoods Cup third round – replay 9 November**

| | |
|---|---|
| Arsenal 0 | Liverpool 0 |

**Football League, 12 November**

| | |
|---|---|
| Liverpool 1 | Millwall 1 |
| *Steve Nicol* | *Paul Stephenson* |

**Football League, 19 November**

| | |
|---|---|
| Queen's Park Rangers 0 | Liverpool 1 |
| | *John Aldridge* |

**Littlewoods Cup third round – second replay Villa Park, 23 November**

| | |
|---|---|
| Liverpool 2 | Arsenal 1 |
| *Steve McMahon* | *Paul Merson* |
| *John Aldridge* | |

**Football League, 26 November**

| | |
|---|---|
| Liverpool 1 | Wimbledon 1 |
| *Ray Houghton* | *Steve Nicol (own goal)* |

**Littlewoods Cup fourth round, 30 November**

| | |
|---|---|
| West Ham United 4 | Liverpool 1 |
| *Paul Ince (2)* | *John Aldridge* |
| *Tony Gale* | |
| *Steve Staunton (own goal)* | |

LEAGUE POSITION

| | P | W | D | L | F | A | Pt | Position |
|---|---|---|---|---|---|---|---|---|
| Liverpool | 14 | 6 | 5 | 3 | 19 | 10 | 23 | 4th |

LIVERPOOL FOOTBALL CLUB

# Star Rating for Steve and Ronnie

No question about it, the Littlewoods Cup dominated the month; though after the Lord Mayor's show came the big let-down! Having despatched Walsall, Liverpool met the toughest possible opposition in Arsenal, though the third-round tie was at Anfield, where John Barnes gave Liverpool the lead, only for the Gunners to make it all square at 1–1.

## Arsenal at bay

So, after a 3–0 home League win over Middlesbrough, it was a 200-mile trek to Highbury for the Cup replay. Interest was so intense that with 54,000 fans jammed into the ground and an estimated 6000 still outside, the game was delayed 15 minutes to overcome the crowd problems. At the end of the night Liverpool – outplayed by Arsenal at Anfield – had turned the tables on the Gunners and gone close to winning.

Two players especially received praise for their displays: Steve Nicol, switched to centre-back and skipper Ronnie Whelan, doing a stint at right-back, inspired Liverpool to a peak performance. In fact former West Ham and England star Trevor Brooking went out of his way to pay a tribute to both men.

By then Nicol and Whelan were Liverpool's only ever-presents. Steve struck his first goal of the season to equalise against Millwall at Anfield, then John Aldridge was the match-winner against Queen's Park Rangers at Loftus Road. Buoyed by this victory, Liverpool went to Villa Park for a third confrontation with Arsenal.

## Gunners' fire quelled

They went, they saw – and they conquered. The Gunners beat Mike Hooper once but goals from Steve McMahon and John Aldridge saw them off. Which left Liverpool with games against Wimbledon and West Ham to complete the course for the month. Fortune, however, didn't favour Liverpool, because after Ray Houghton had given them the lead against the Dons, Steve Nicol scored an own goal three minutes from time. Shortly afterwards Liverpool had a collective off-night at Upton Park as the struggling Hammers avenged their earlier League defeat by winning 4–1 and ending Liverpool's interest in the Littlewoods Cup.

One bright note was the form of David Burrows, Liverpool's £500,000 buy from West Brom. Though ineligible for the Littlewoods Cup, he had slotted into the League side and shown he could measure up to the demands of First Division football, even by Anfield standards. In fact he claimed a Barclays Young Eagle award.

*Steve Nicol had a starring role for Liverpool when he switched to centre-back*

*Ronnie Whelan: the skipper who helped to inspire Liverpool to a peak performance*

*David Burrows: the new recruit who settled in quickly at Anfield*

# December

## TOUGH TIMES AHEAD

**There couldn't have been a sterner test for Liverpool than that posed by the games scheduled for the last month of the year: Arsenal at Highbury, Everton at Anfield, First Division leaders Norwich City at Anfield and high-riding Derby County at the Baseball Ground. Two games – against the Gunners and Everton – were televised live on Sunday afternoons, yet between them they attracted more than 74,000 spectators.**

At Highbury Liverpool put on another first-class show, just as they had done in the Littlewoods Cup replay there. When John Barnes gave Liverpool the lead by beating John Lukic for the second time during the season, it looked as if they would collect three points. However Arsenal weren't prepared to concede best again. Once they had equalised it became clear that this game was going to end all square – which it did, to leave both these championship contenders no further forward, although Liverpool, perhaps, were entitled to feel the more satisfied with this result.

Ray Houghton, whose goal had knocked Everton off the Wembley trail in the FA Cup the

*Steve McMahon in derby-game action against his old club Everton*

previous season, became Liverpool's man of the match in the Anfield derby game as he shot them ahead once again; but this time Wayne Clarke scored an equaliser from the penalty spot, so the result was 1–1. When Norwich tried their luck at Anfield, they found it was in . . . because they chalked up only their third victory in 13 encounters there. It was certainly unlucky 13 for Liverpool when Andy Townsend scored the only goal of the game.

## Rush to the rescue

Liverpool knew they needed to get a result when they met Derby County at the Baseball Ground on Boxing Day and when Ian Rush struck his fifth goal of the season it was sufficient to send Derby spinning to defeat. Derby were always looking second-best as Liverpool took a firm grip on the game. The result meant that the gap between the clubs had widened.

### ...RESULTS...

**Football League, 4 December**

| | |
|---|---|
| Arsenal 1<br>*Alan Smith* | Liverpool 1<br>*John Barnes* |

**Football League, 11 December**

| | |
|---|---|
| Liverpool 1<br>*Ray Houghton* | Everton 1<br>*Wayne Clarke (penalty)* |

**Football League, 17 December**

| | |
|---|---|
| Liverpool 0 | Norwich City 1<br>*Andy Townsend* |

**Football League, 26 December**

| | |
|---|---|
| Derby County 0 | Liverpool 1<br>*Ian Rush* |

LEAGUE POSITION

| | P | W | D | L | F | A | Pt | Position |
|---|---|---|---|---|---|---|---|---|
| Liverpool | 18 | 7 | 7 | 4 | 22 | 13 | 28 | 3rd |

*John Barnes scored some vital goals for Liverpool*

# SCOUTING FOR

Ron Yeats was a tower of strength at the heart of Liverpool's defence for many years, as he totalled more than 450 appearances . . . and now in his capacity as chief scout he's constantly scouring the length and breadth of Britain for talent. Ron says: 'I clock up at least 40,000 miles a year, covering three or four matches a week, Saturday to Saturday – and sometimes on a Sunday.

'I suppose you could say I take over where Steve Heighway leaves off, because I and the scouts who work for the club are more concerned with players aged 18 or over. The job embraces all aspects of the game, from non-League to the international scene.

'Altogether there are about 10 of us involved in the scouting network and we cover more than 850 matches a season. There are times when the scouting staff will be augmented by other people from inside the club, and my job literally means I can be travelling around from Land's End to John O'Groats . . . not to mention Ireland and Wales.

## Local talent

'If we get a tip about a player, we try to follow it up as soon as possible. You never know when a tip will turn up someone who is worth signing. For instance, we received tips about a couple of lads who were playing football locally. When we'd taken a look at them, we signed them for Liverpool.

'One was John Durnin, who became a regular in our reserve side and who, last season, broke through to Second Division football when he moved to Oxford United; and the other was Mike Marsh, who also became a regular in our Central League side and, in fact, made his first-team debut when he went on as substitute in the League game against Charlton Athletic.

'We're looking all the time for the best talent in Britain. When your standards are as high as Liverpool's that makes the job just a little bit harder. It's always difficult assessing talent. To appreciate what's involved let me say that, whenever I'm at a game, you can bet there will be scouts from five or six other top clubs there as well. So, as well as backing your own judgment, you are competing with people whom you know to be very keen rivals.'

*Ron Yeats in his days as captain of Liverpool*

*Left: Ron holding the League Championship trophy*

# GOLD

'But when you do spot a player who's a little bit special, and he makes good at your club, then you feel that all the miles you've covered and all the effort you've put into the job are really worthwhile.'

*Top right: Ron is now Liverpool's chief scout and travels thousands of miles a year in the search for talent*

## THE CHIEF SCOUT'S WEEK

**Friday**
Receive a complete list of all match fixtures for the following week. Study the list carefully, and get down to planning which games should be covered.

**Monday, Tuesday, Wednesday**
Out at a match each evening.

**Thursday**
The one day, normally, when there are no games – but as usual the day starts with a visit to Anfield.

**Friday**
Having sorted out the fixtures for the following week, take in a match that same evening.

**Saturday, Sunday**
Scouting missions again.

P.S. If there's a mid-week international involving Liverpool players – for instance, Scotland playing at Hampden Park – I may drive up on the Wednesday, watch the game, then act as chauffeur to players such as Steve Nicol and Gary Gillespie, maybe arriving back on Merseyside around three o'clock in the morning. This attention to detail is well worthwhile, though, because it means the players can report back to the club by Thursday lunch-time.

*Liverpool's coaches Roy Evans*
*Ronnie Moran*

# STEP INSIDE THE DRESSING-ROOM

It's match day at Anfield, with the fans flocking through the turn-stiles to see Liverpool in action. There's a while to go, though, before the players appear – they're still in the dressing-room, where the kit (as you can see on the left) has already been laid out by coaches Ronnie Moran and Roy Evans, who are usually the first to get changed.

Across the corridor, above the steps which lead down and out to the playing area, a sign says 'This is Anfield'. It's been there for years and is calculated to inspire Liverpool's players and make the opposition acutely aware of the testing time they face.

So as the minutes tick by, let's step inside the Liverpool dressing-room and savour the atmosphere.

Bruce Grobbelaar has a special pre-match routine

## Lights out for Brucie

Bruce Grobbelaar's pre-match routine involves kicking a ball against the light switches until one of the lights goes out.

Barry Venison is an early starter: he usually begins to get changed three-quarters of an hour before kick-off, then he'll sit quietly, mentally tuning himself up for the game.

Gary Gillespie is another who doesn't hang about. He's a good singer and has been known to lead the lads in a sing song.

Skipper Ronnie Whelan isn't really superstitious, though number 5 is his favourite shirt. He has two dislikes: being beaten and bad time-keeping.

Steve Nicol really likes his food but he never seems to put on weight. He likes to touch the 'This is Anfield' sign as he goes out third in line.

## Aldo's dream come true

For the man who wears number 8, being in the Liverpool dressing-room is a dream come true. As a nipper John Aldridge used to go with his Dad to watch his favourite team. It was real Roy-of-the-Rovers stuff when he hit the winner on his home debut.

*When John Aldridge started playing for Liverpool it was a dream come true*

The most famous jersey in the dressing-room over the past 20 years must be the number 7. Both Kevin Keegan and Kenny Dalglish wore it. Now it's Peter Beardsley's turn. Remarkably he has been a team-mate of both his predecessors.

Three of the youngest and least-experienced players in the dressing-room are Gary Ablett, Steve Staunton and David Burrows. Not surprising, then, that they're still ready and willing to soak up the atmosphere and listen and learn.

# A DERBY GAME WITH A DIFFERENCE

Liverpool resumed League business after the Hillsborough tragedy by making the short trip down the road to Goodison Park. Having tested the temperature with a game against Glasgow Celtic at Parkhead the previous Sunday, they started out once more on the quest for the championship when they faced up to Everton. The date: Wednesday, 3 May 1989.

As the teams walked out, led by the clubs' chairmen and the managers, the crowd of close on 46,000 gave them an emotional welcome. You could have heard a pin drop during the pre-match minute's silence. Television captured the moment and, with it, a banner which on this occasion had a wealth of meaning.

## Supporters side by side

Draped along the front of a stand, it said: 'The Kop thanks you all. We never walked alone.' Liverpool and Everton supporters stood side by side, proud to be called Merseysiders and joined together by a bond which had been forged by the tragedy that had so deeply affected all. This truly was a derby game with a difference.

As for the action, both sides were totally committed and if there were no goals there was plenty of good football. Everton manager Colin Harvey summed up the feeling of everyone afterwards as he said: 'It was a fair result, on the night. His Liverpool counterpart, Kenny Dalglish, said: 'It was a tremendous occasion and both sets of supporters rose to it. Once

*Above: Steve McMahon in action against his old club*

*Left: my ball! Everton 'keeper Neville Southall makes sure John Aldridge misses out, on this occasion*

*Right: rival supporters stand side by side in the city that's united*

again, they have covered themselves in glory.'

As to the result and how it affected Liverpool's title hopes, Kenny added: 'You can only tell if it's a point lost or a point gained when you count them up at the end of the season. Altogether, we're quite happy with the way we played, taking everything into consideration.'

FIFA referee Neil Midgley reflected: 'It was very touching at the start, but I had told my linesmen that once the minute's silence was over, we had to put that to the back of our minds. They did, and I'm sure the players did, as well. There's only one way to play football. It was a very competitive match and everyone responded brilliantly.'

David Burrows presents Kop fan A C Thomson with a £1000 prize

Tim Langford travels all the way from Newton Abbot to Anfield

Liverpool fan Mariusz Gamza at home in Poland

# CROWD-PULLERS

Liverpool are just about the top crowd-pullers in the country, as clubs like Charlton Athletic, Luton Town, Derby County, Southampton, Queen's Park Rangers and West Ham United would be happy to testify. Because when Liverpool play them on their own grounds they can count on having their highest crowd of the season. When you consider that clubs keep their home-gate receipts, this means a lot of revenue!

Liverpool chairman John W Smith

# THE FANS WHO FOLLOW LIVERPOOL

It goes without saying that chairman John W. Smith is one of Liverpool's most ardent fans. Indeed having supported the team in red for more than half a century, Liverpool has become 'almost a religion' to him. He will readily admit to having played truant from school more than once in his younger days, just to get a glimpse of his idols on the playing field of Anfield.

## Childhood memories

His father was a shareholder of the club and John Smith saw his first Liverpool match as a mere four-year-old. He can look back and recall the days when the gates used to be opened a quarter of an hour from the end of the match, and the youngsters would then descend upon Anfield and get in free. His father used to remark that the 'shareholders' were arriving.

Until recently John Smith was chairman of the Sports Council. He is a member of the Football League's management committee and has been chairman of Liverpool Football Club throughout its greatest years, since the mid-1970s. Most of all, though, he has remained a Liverpool fan, with red blood running through his veins.

## From Devon to Anfield

Liverpool fans come from all around the country, of course – and some live abroad – yet, one way or another, they try to get to Anfield as often as possible. One of the club's most loyal supporters is also an agent for the Liverpool Development Association; his name is Tim Langford and he lives in Newton Abbot, Devon, where he is mine host at the Saracen's Head hotel.

Remarkably Tim travels to just about every match at Anfield and he has sold the club's lottery tickets for a long time, which made it a fair exchange a few seasons ago when he found himself a winner. Yes, the ticket he had bought turned out to be worth £1500!

Another supporter, from Northampton, clicked for a £250 prize at a night match . . . then found he'd won £1000 when he travelled up for another game. Then there is the long-distance lorry driver who's a regular at Anfield. He stands on the Kop with his two daughters. Like Mr Wright from Northampton, Mr Thompson – who lives on Merseyside – won a top prize. No wonder he yelled with delight from his vantage point on the Kop when he heard he'd won £1000.

## Thousands of miles away

Much further afield there is Andrew Eustace, living in Brisbane, Australia – a Liverpool supporter 'for as long as I can remember' – and Tore Hansen, from Farsund in Norway, who paid his own tribute to seven English-based fans: 'Where there's a game involving Liverpool, they'll be there. It doesn't matter if it's the FA Cup final or a pre-season friendly north of the Arctic Circle in Norway. They'll still travel to support the Reds. They're great ambassadors of the Kop.'

Tore mentions one fan in particular: Jim Gardiner, a Kop season-ticket holder who has seen every League game during the past five or six years and who has cheered Liverpool on in Norway, Denmark, Sweden, West Germany and Spain, as well.

*The kind of action which makes Liverpool top crowd-pullers*

# Legendary LIVERPO

Left: *Steve Nicol Footballer of the Year in season 1988-89, followed in the footsteps of his team-mate John Barnes, the previous winner.*

*Right: Ian Rush who, like John Barnes, Kenny Dalglish and Terry McDermott, was a double award winner*

*Below: Emlyn Hughes another award winner with Liverpool*

Of all the clubs in the Football League, Liverpool hold a unique record – and in more than one respect. For instance their 17 successes in the First Division championship stakes make them far and away the top club in the country, and no other club can match their four triumphs in the European Champions Cup competition.

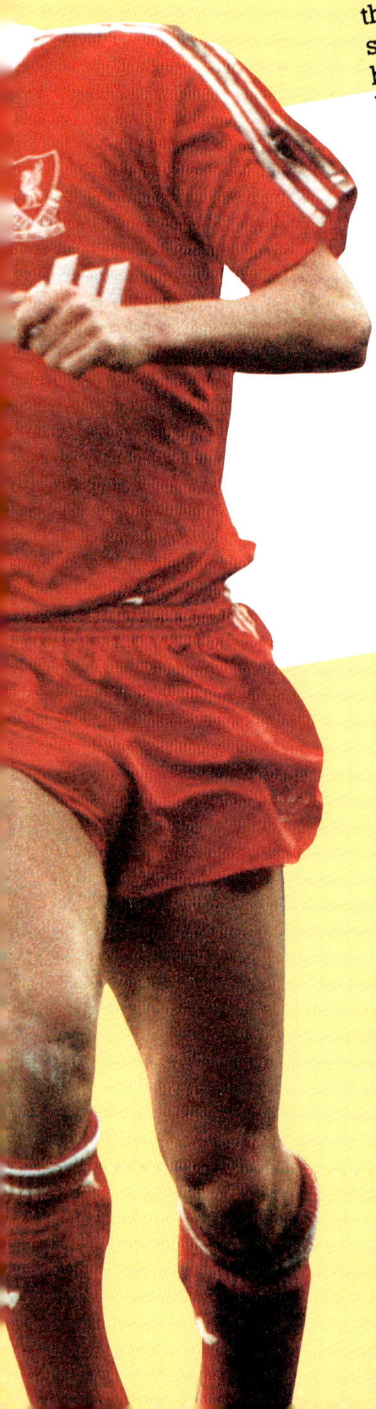

## Footballers of the Year

As for individual awards, few clubs – if any – can compare with Liverpool. Ian Callaghan became their first recipient of the Football Writers' Association award for the Footballer of the Year in season 1973-74. He was followed by Kevin Keegan (1975-76), Emlyn Hughes (1976-77), Kenny Dalglish (1978-79), Terry McDermott (1979-80), Kenny Dalglish again (1982-83), Ian Rush (1983-84), John Barnes (1987-88) and Steve Nicol (1988-89). Terry McDermott, Kenny Dalglish, Ian Rush and John Barnes were double-award winners: they also topped the Professional Footballers' Association polls for the Player of the Year.

## Manager of the Year

On the managerial side, Liverpool have an incomparable record going back nearly 20 years. Bill Shankly became the first Liverpool manager to win the Manager of the Year award (at the end of season 1972-73), then Jack Charlton (Middlesbrough) and Ron Saunders (Aston Villa) followed him. But Shankly's successor, Bob Paisley, held a virtual monopoly on the trophy after that, being named as Manager of the Year in 1976, 1977, 1979, 1980, 1982 and 1983 . . . and he was followed immediately by Joe Fagan, while Kenny Dalglish claimed the trophy in seasons 1985-86 and 1987-88.

All of which meant that four Liverpool managers in succession had won the prestigious award . . . a feat not achieved by any other club in the country.

## The boys in the backroom

Liverpool have long had a reputation for preserving continuity, but it is doubtful if any club can match them when it comes to former players being on the current staff. Including team-manager Kenny Dalglish, no fewer than six men who have worn Liverpool's colours are now working on the backroom side . . . and between them, they totalled close on 2300 appearances.

Now they're still serving the cause of Liverpool Football Club: Ronnie Moran and Roy Evans as the men on the bench when the first team is in action; Phil Thompson, in charge of the reserve side; Ron Yeats as chief scout; and Steve Heighway as Youth development officer.

## Top admin man

The man who rose from office boy to chief executive is widely regarded as one of the top administrators in football – not just in this country, but in Europe. He's been at Liverpool now for close on 25 years. In fact it was June 1965 when Peter Robinson took over as secretary at the club – and he had come up through the divisions.

As a 17-year-old he was the office boy at Stockport County. Five years later, he had become assistant secretary. His travels took him to Crewe Alexandra as secretary, then Scunthorpe United and after that to the south coast, where he worked for Brighton. Finally he arrived at Anfield where he is now Liverpool's chief executive.

# PICK OF THE PIX

Aerial combat and John Aldridge is a high-flier in the game against Coventry City

*Left: man of many parts . . . Steve Nicol claimed the Footballer of the Year award*

This duel for possession features John Barnes and Mickey Phelan, then of Norwich City but now wearing the colours of Manchester United

Peter Beardsley shows his Millwall opponent a clean pair of heels

Action man Ian Rush in the Littlewoods Cup tie against Walsall

## 1

The player in white wearing number 8 and the team-mate looking left could almost be each other's double . . . but can you name them and their club?

5 Kenny Dalglish scored on his debut for Liverpool, against which club?

6 During his career with Liverpool, John Wark hit a hat-trick in a European Cup match. Against which club?

7 Phil Thompson played in Liverpool's European Cup-winning sides of 1978 and 1981, true or false?

8 Name two former England internationals John Toshack signed from Liverpool, when he was manager of Swansea City.

9 Kenny Dalglish scored the only goal in the 1978 European Cup final against FC Bruges. Who supplied the pass?

10 When Alan Hansen played against Nottingham Forest in the 1989 FA Cup semi-final at Old Trafford, how many times had he appeared in semi-finals?

11 Bruce Grobbelaar has one League goal to his credit. For which club did he score it?

12 Two Liverpool players of the 1970s had university degrees: one a BSc, the other a BA. Name the players.

# QUIZ..

## 2

Here's a goalkeeper with a look of some anxiety on his face, as Liverpool attack. Name the 'keeper and his club.

## 4

It's a goal! That's the message from Ian Rush to John Barnes. Can you name the opposition, though, and the referee?

This referee is one of the top officials in the game . . . now can you name him?

## ANSWERS

1 The player wearing number 8 is Neil Webb, the team-mate is Colin Foster and the club, of course, is Nottingham Forest.
2 The goalkeeper is Nigel Spink, who was in action for Aston Villa.
3 The referee's name is Keith Hackett.
4 The opposition came from Middlesbrough, the referee was Brian Stevens.
5 Kenny Dalglish scored on his Liverpool debut, against . . . Middlesbrough.
6 John Wark's hat-trick was against Lech Poznan.
7 Phil Thompson played in both the 1978 and 1981 European Cup finals
8 John Toshack signed Tommy Smith and Ian Callaghan from Liverpool.
9 Graeme Souness supplied the pass for Kenny Dalglish to score the winner, in the 1978 European Cup final.
10 The Old Trafford game was Alan Hansen's 11th semi-final appearance.
11 Bruce Grobbelaar was playing for Crewe Alexandra when he scored the goal.
12 Brian Hall has the BSc and Steve Heighway the BA.

# THE VISITORS' CENTRE MUSEUM

Match day at Anfield is the big attraction for thousands of Liverpool fans – whether they are the rich and the famous or the folk who stand anonymously on the Kop. Yes, Anfield has its fair share of VIPs . . . even when there isn't a game, the trek to Anfield continues week in, week out, because the Visitors' Centre Museum has proved a tremendous drawing card since it was opened in June 1988.

Fans from all over the country – yes, and some from abroad – have taken advantage of the opportunity to tour the Visitors' Centre Museum; so much so that by the end of the first 12 months it had attracted more than 15,000 people. Christine Moss, the club's public relations officer, says: 'Right from the start, it caught on and we were averaging around 300 visitors a week. In the first six months the total rose to 8500, with the number increasing all the time.'

There are daily visits (Monday to Friday) starting at 2pm, 3pm and 4pm, and each one lasts for about three-quarters of an hour. The admission charge is £1.50 per adult (£1 each for children and senior citizens), and £1 a head for parties exceeding 20. Bookings can be made by arrangement, by writing or phoning (051-263 2361) for a booking form.

The Visitors' Centre Museum portrays the history of Liverpool Football Club, with audio-visual effects which set the scene. There is a Bill Shankly corner and a Bob Paisley corner, while memorabilia has also been donated by former Liverpool players and fans.

And, of course, a visit to Anfield would not be complete without seeing the ground.

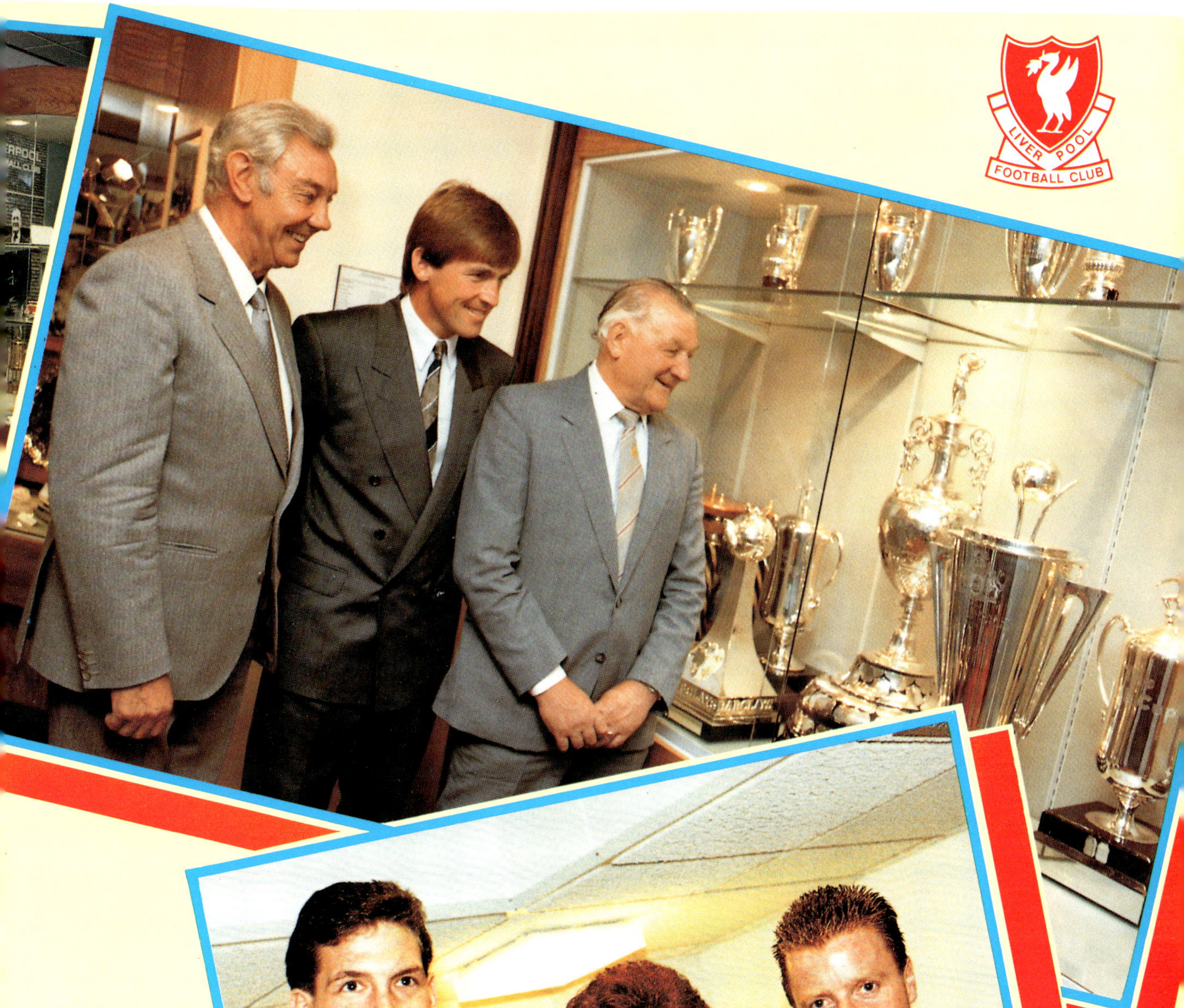

*Top left: Liverpool's public relations officer, Christine Moss, who arranges bookings for the Visitors' Centre Museum*

*Top right: former Liverpool managers Bob Paisley (right) and Joe Fagan, with team-boss Kenny Dalglish, admiring some of the silverware in the Visitors' Centre Museum*

*Right: a VIP visiting Anfield – Cilla Black meets players Gary Gillespie and Steve Nicol*

Steve Heighway in action when he played for Liverpool

# COACHING THE YOUTH THEME

**Soccer is virtually a seven-day-week job for Steve Heighway, Liverpool's youth development officer. Steve himself was once a Liverpool player – he clocked up more than 460 first-team appearances and was capped 29 times by the Republic of Ireland. And, since he was recruited from non-League football, when he was playing for Skelmersdale United, no-one knows better what it takes to make the transition from playing for fun to playing at the highest level.**

Steve says: 'In a nutshell, I'm responsible for the recruitment, coaching and welfare of all the players involved with the club up to the age of 18. There is the school of excellence, for players up to the age of 14; there's the group of schoolboys aged 14 to 16; and there are the lads aged 16 to 18 who come through the youth training scheme.

'We've got almost a score of YTS lads on the books, about 30 schoolboys aged 14 to 16, and around 80 aged under 14 who come to the school of excellence. One school is run at Crosby, the other at Stanley Park. We also do some coaching at Liverpool's Melwood training headquarters.

## Best of the bunch

'It's my responsibility to organise the coaching, and I'm helped by Frank Skelly, who's heavily involved with the administration of the school of excellence, and

*Steve Heighway . . . now he's putting young hopefuls through their paces*

Dave Shannon and Hughie McAuley, who are both full-badge FA coaches. Dave is the son of Les Shannon, a former well-known professional footballer, and Hughie used to be on Liverpool's books.

'Taken all round, the job is to identify the best young players and attract them to this club, then give them top-class coaching and playing experience, while creating an environment which gives a youngster the best possible chance of progressing through to full-time professional football.

'It's a programme of development where we work with the kids and, hopefully, bring them through the A and B teams, with the most talented finding their way on from there.'

## THIS IS STEVE'S WEEK

**Monday**

Arrive Anfield 9.00 am, go through paper work, then down to Melwood training ground. Work with John Bennison until 12.15 coaching YTS boys, then back to Anfield and carry on with paper work until around 6.00 pm. Maybe, take in a youth game.

**Tuesday**

Routine as on Monday, except finish at Anfield about 4.30 pm to go to school of excellence at Crosby and work from 5.00 pm to 7.00 pm. Alternatively go back to Melwood and coach schoolboys from 6.00 pm to 7.30 pm.

**Wednesday**

Routine during day as before, but from 5.00 pm to 8.00 pm attend indoor centre at Stanley Park.

**Thursday**

Usual daily routine but return to Melwood to coach schoolboys from 6.00 pm to 7.30 pm.

**Friday**

Usual routine during day . . . but the evening free . . . unless there's a game to see.

**Saturday**

Games for A and B teams, maybe watch reserve team if they're playing at Anfield, or go to watch a youngster who has been recommended to the club.

**Sunday**

Watching a game somewhere. It may be at Blackpool, or it may be a schoolboy international in Scotland.

# Talking about LIVERPO

'Ronnie Whelan has played in midfield, as an anchor man and going forward, and at left-back . . . now he's slotted in at right-back as if he'd been playing there all his career. As for Steve Nicol – what can you say about him?'

Former West Ham and England midfield star Trevor Brooking

Trevor Brooking

'Typical Rush. He hasn't lost it. Give him half a chance and he's in there. A great strike . . . If we play like that against 90 per cent of the First Division, we'll be all right. But Rushy and Liverpool are a bit different.'

West Ham captain Alvin Martin after Liverpool's 2–0 win at Upton Park, with one of the goals coming from . . . Ian Rush

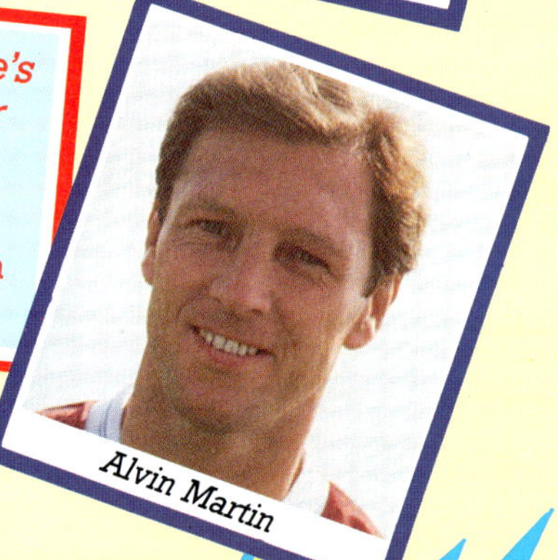

Alvin Martin

'Liverpool are the best in the business, when it comes to dealing with this kind of match. They can take the sting out of it, soak up the pressure and then impose their own authority. They're the best-equipped team in the country to do that and they've been the best for 25 years.'

Former Liverpool skipper Emlyn Hughes, now a Hull City director, on the eve of Hull's FA Cup tie against Liverpool

'Some people say Liverpool have started to crack – that's nonsense. They're still special. They're in the thick of the title race, despite all the injuries they have suffered, and that takes some doing. As for Ian Rush, he's the best in the country and no-one should even suggest he's no longer the force he was.'

Derby County striker Paul Goddard just before Liverpool won at the Baseball Ground with a goal from . . . Ian Rush

'I'm not saying Liverpool will win the championship, but they're still the team Arsenal will have to beat.'

Jim Smith, who moved from Queen's Park Rangers to become manager of Newcastle United

George Graham

'Liverpool deserved to win more convincingly. They were in top gear and we never fired on all cylinders. While we were disappointing, Liverpool played the stuff which is still the yardstick for our football.'

Arsenal manager George Graham, after Liverpool's Littlewoods Cup victory

'We are approaching the standards Liverpool have set for so long.'

George Graham, after the Gunners' 1–1 draw in the first Littlewoods Cup tie at Anfield

'I think he is one of the most under-rated players in the country. But in the game, we know how good he is.'

George Graham, paying tribute to Steve Nicol

'The man's priceless . . . I wouldn't know where to start putting a fee on him. Any club on the Continent would snatch Liverpool's hand off at almost any price – but they'll knock the Kop down before they sell Steve Nicol.'

Former Liverpool star Mark Lawrenson paying tribute to his one-time team-mate

Mark Lawrenson

Nigel Spackman

'Liverpool are the biggest club in the country and it is only with great reluctance that you decide to leave. But I needed first-team football.'

Nigel Spackman, after moving from Anfield to Queen's Park Rangers

'The challenge of Aston Villa in the remaining three years of my contract is to attempt to see the club progress not simply to another fleeting period of the odd Cup or League win, but to start being established along the same permanent lines as Liverpool. It would be wonderful if we could win something worthwhile in the remaining three years of my contract, but I would want this to be the start of a Liverpool-style quarter of a century and more.'

Aston Villa manager Graham Taylor, paying tribute to Liverpool

Graham Taylor

Bob Paisley and his final team selection

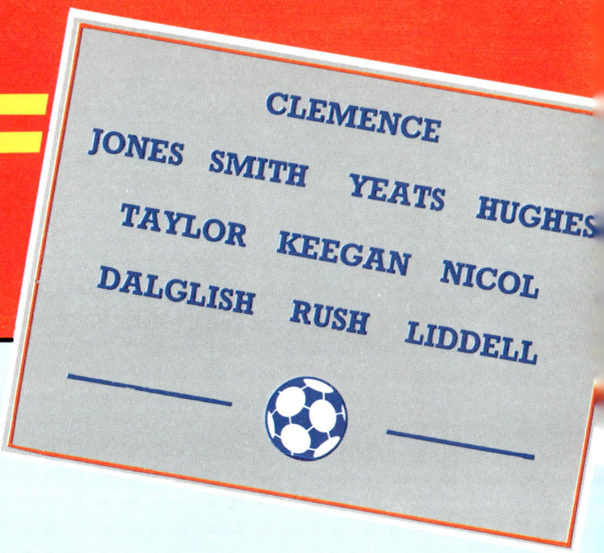


# My Team of ALL-TIME

In more than 50 years at Liverpool, I've seen some very fine teams assembled . . . teams which have won championships and other trophies, at home and abroad. In those teams were some excellent players and you can be sure that when it comes down to naming just 11, plus two substitutes, as my team of all-time greats, I've had to do a great deal of thinking. Not once, not twice, but three or four times. I even changed my mind a couple of times!

## Goalkeeper

I'll start at the back. My short list came down to three: Ray Clemence, Tommy Lawrence and Bruce Grobbelaar. Though Bruce ran Ray close, with Tommy not far behind either, I gave my vote to 'Clem', who won me over during a game against West Brom, when he made three tremendous saves inside the first 15 minutes. He was still learning, but I sensed that he had arrived to stay in the side. Stay he did, as well as becoming an England regular.

## Over 40 to choose from

I've picked a back-four line, a midfield three and a front three; and what a job I had to whittle down the list from something like 40 candidates! Right-back? Try Chris Lawler, Tommy Smith, Bill Jones, Steve Nicol, Phil Neal for starters . . .

Central defenders? Try Bill Jones, Laurie Hughes, Ron Yeats, Chris Lawler, Tommy Smith, Emlyn Hughes, Phil Thompson, Mark Lawrenson, Alan Hansen, Steve Nicol . . . and for left-back try Gerry Byrne, Alec Lindsay, Emlyn Hughes, Steve Nicol . . . then, when you've made your choice, have a go at picking just three players for midfield!

You could start with Phil Taylor, go on to Emlyn Hughes, Phil Thompson, Graeme Souness, Ray Kennedy, Ronnie Whelan, Steve McMahon . . . and a few more who have played in other roles. Such as Steve Nicol, Peter Beardsley, John Barnes, Kenny Dalglish – oh, yes, and Kevin Keegan. And that means treating Ian Callaghan purely as a winger!

Talking of wingers, what about Billy Liddell, 'Cally', Peter Thompson, Steve Heighway and John Barnes? And for men to operate as strikers I can think back to Albert Stubbins, Roger Hunt and Ian St John, come closer to the present by naming Kevin Keegan and John Toshack, get even more up to date with Kenny Dalglish, Ian Rush, Peter Beardsley and John Barnes.

*Emlyn Hughes goes in at left-back*

# GREATS

*Ray Clemence: Bob Paisley's choice for goalkeeper*

## My final 11

I'm sure by now you'll have started to appreciate the problems I've had in limiting my choice to 11 names, plus those two substitutes. The list of players includes Bill Jones and Phil Taylor, who were team-mates of mine; Billy Liddell, another team-mate; Ron Yeats, Emlyn Hughes, Phil Thompson and Tommy Smith who, in the final analysis, got the nod from me as skipper, playing alongside Ron Yeats – a giant of a man from the granite city, Aberdeen – at the heart of the defence. Which left Bill Jones for right-back, Emlyn Hughes for number 3.

Now for the midfield department. I feel Phil Taylor must go in here, along with Kevin Keegan and Steve Nicol, who is so versatile he can operate either at full-back, in the middle of the defence, or on either side of midfield.

Remembering that I've already left out wingers like Ian Callaghan, Peter Thompson, Steve Heighway and John Barnes, I'm now left with Dalglish, Rush and Liddell as my three men up front. Which gives me this team of all the talents: Clemence, Jones, Smith, Yeats, Hughes, Taylor, Keegan, Nicol, Dalglish, Rush, Liddell.

I consider these players would give the side balance, mobility and skill, not to mention a touch of steel when defending and a real cutting edge when it came to the business of scoring goals.

However, since I'm the sole selector, and since I'm a bit greedy, I'm going to go one step further and make up the squad to 15 players, rather than just name two substitutes. That way I'll still be able to call on Roger Hunt, Ian St John, Peter Beardsley and John Barnes, if anyone cries off through injury!

Bob Paisley

*Kenny Dalglish goes into Bob Paisley's team alongside Ian Rush and Billy Liddell up front*

Players who score 100 goals or more become members of an exclusive club and so do players who clock up 600 or more appearances during their careers. Liverpool can boast five men who, between them, have scored more than 1000 goals and half a dozen who have each totalled more than 600 games.

When it comes to long-serving players, Ian Callaghan played more than 600 games in the League alone and 850 in all competitions during his career with Liverpool between 1960 and 1978, while Ray Clemence, who went on to 1000 appearances in his career with Scunthorpe, Liverpool and Spurs, chalked up 656 games for the Anfield club between seasons 1968-69 and 1980-81.

## Skippers' 600-plus

Another member of the 600 Club was Emlyn Hughes, who captained Liverpool to success in almost every competition at home and abroad. Emlyn played 657 games for Liverpool between 1966 and 1979, while another one-time skipper, Phil Neal, totalled 635 games for Liverpool between 1974 and 1986. Then there was a third former captain, Tommy Smith – known affectionately to the fans as 'The Anfield Iron' – and he totalled 633 appearances between 1962 and 1978.

Moving on to the present, Liverpool have two current members of the 600 Club: team-manager Kenny Dalglish and skipper Alan Hansen. Kenny can point to a total of 838 appearances in his career with Glasgow Celtic and Liverpool, and he has played more than 500 of those games since he moved to Anfield. As for Alan Hansen, his tally for Liverpool is 578 and his career total 686 . . . and this in spite of the fact that he missed almost the whole of season 1988-89 through injury.

## Goals galore

Then, of course, there are the goals . . . which prompts another question – and it's this: Is there another club in British football which can boast five players who, between them, have totalled more than 1000 goals? Liverpool can make this claim as they point to Kenny Dalglish, Ian Rush, John Aldridge, Peter Beardsley and John Barnes.

Pride of place, of course, goes to Liverpool's team boss who – as well as having been capped by Scotland more than 100 times – has hit a century of goals for both Liverpool and Glasgow Celtic. Indeed his overall total in 838 games stands at 339. And 172 of those goals have been scored for Liverpool.

Ian Rush added a handful of goals to his Liverpool total while he was spending a season with the Italian giants, Juventus. He has now totalled more than 200 goals during his career at Anfield and around 250 overall.

John Aldridge has scored goals in all four divisions (and, like Ian Rush, hit hat-tricks); his overall tally now exceeds 230. Both Peter Beardsley and John Barnes have totalled more than a century of

# AN EXCLUSIVE CLUB: 10

Left: *Alan Hansen is heading for a career total of 700 games*

*Right: Peter Beardsley is one of five Liverpool players who together have totalled more than 1000 goals*

goals in their respective careers.

Add them all up and the goals come to more than 1000 . . . a staggering tally for five men at the same club.

As a final footnote it's worth remembering that Phil Thompson and Phil Neal each picked up seven League championship medals while they were wearing the colours of Liverpool. That's another one for the record books.

# ...00 GOALS... 600 GAMES

*John Aldridge like Ian Rush has topped the 200 mark for goals*

# THERE *IS* SENTIMENT IN FOOTB

**They say there's no sentiment in football – and it can certainly be a cruel game, at times. Yet one of the most refreshing things about the competition between Bruce Grobbelaar and Mike Hooper has been the way each man has given full and ungrudging credit to the other.**

Two seasons ago Mike Hooper had a brief taste of first-team football, but when Bruce was fit again he got the nod for the FA Cup tie against Aston Villa which was televised live. Mike had just kept four clean sheets, and team-boss Kenny Dalglish had called both players in to explain why he was picking Bruce for the Villa tie, even though there was nothing to choose between the 'keepers.

'The manager said he was picking Bruce on experience, plus the fact that if he did make a mistake in front of the cameras he would get over it immediately. 'The boss feared that if I made an error, with millions watching, it might set me back six months.'

## Another first-team chance

Five matches into season 1988-89 Bruce Grobbelaar went down with meningitis; so Mike stepped up to the first team again, knowing that – all things being equal – Liverpool's recognised number one 'keeper would be out of action for six weeks at least.

Mike also knew, however, that if he didn't produce the goods Liverpool would almost certainly move into the transfer market and that if they did sign a 'keeper it could signal the end for him at Anfield.

There was no animosity between the two 'keepers. Indeed when Liverpool met Arsenal in the Littlewoods Cup – when Bruce was still lying ill in a darkened room – he sent Mike Hooper a good luck telegram and took the trouble to phone him as well.

Mike played to such good effect that he stayed in the side. And when Bruce was fit again, it was the Zimbabwe international who found himself on the outside, looking in. But that didn't mean Mike Hooper could afford to feel complacent! Knowing that Bruce was breathing down his neck, he was also keenly aware that he couldn't afford to relax. And that didn't apply just to first-team matches. Mike conceded that 'I must keep matching him in training . . . I daren't allow him to look better than me! He's a superb 'keeper, and I'm still working towards being as good as Bruce when he's at his best.'

Eventually, Bruce did regain his place in the side, when Liverpool played Southampton at Anfield. By then, though, Mike Hooper had held down the job for 25 consecutive matches. Although Mike went back to the reserves, Bruce Grobbelaar was under no illusions. He knew that he, too, had to keep on his toes, because now it was Mike who was breathing down his neck.

Mike returned to reserve-team duty knowing that he had established himself as a genuine alternative – and not merely a stop-gap.

# ALL

Bruce Grobbelaar . . . the challenge from Mike Hooper keeps him on his toes

Mike Hooper . . . 'I'm still working towards being as good as Bruce when he's at his best'

# January

## ALDRIDGE AND RUSH HIT JACKPOT AGAIN

The New Year started badly for Liverpool. After taking the lead against Manchester United at Old Trafford, they were made to pay for it as United hit back with three goals. However Liverpool recovered to beat Aston Villa 1–0 at Anfield. It was Ronnie Whelan who rated headline treatment next morning: the first goal he had scored for 15 months turned out to be the match-winner.

### Cup delight

The remainder of the month saw Liverpool cruising to victory in three out of four matches, two of them FA Cup ties. Fourth Division strugglers Carlisle United were never good enough to present real problems, even on their own Brunton Park ground. Goals from John Barnes and Steve McMahon (2) despatched the Cumbrians from the Cup.

Sheffield Wednesday hadn't been doing too well in the First Division either, when Liverpool travelled to Hillsborough for the League game. But there were some raised eyebrows when the half-time score was flashed around the country . . . Wednesday were leading 2–0. Liverpool's second-half fight-back was typical, though, and Steve Nicol and John Aldridge (who had substituted for Steve McMahon) scored the goals that earned a point.

### Number 7 comes up for Watson

Back home, against Southampton, there were changes: Bruce Grobbelaar came back to end Mike Hooper's 25-match run; and Steve McMahon was on the bench as John Aldridge teamed up with Ian Rush. The Rush-Aldridge combination worked as each man scored to bring Liverpool maximum points. They stayed together for the difficult assignment at Millwall in the fourth round of the FA Cup.

Team-boss Kenny Dalglish sprang a shock when he named Alex Watson at number 7 and restored Steve McMahon, leaving almost £3 million-worth of talent – Peter Beardsley and Ray Houghton – on the substitutes' bench. The team selection paid off, however, as Liverpool played Alex Watson in the back line alongside Jan Molby and Gary Ablett, with Steve Nicol and David Burrows at full-back. Molby turned in a superb display, while McMahon did well in midfield, and after Liverpool had soaked up early pressure, they started to gain control just before the break.

Early in the second half, John Aldridge rose to plant a John Barnes corner into the net, then Ian Rush wrapped it up as he steered a shot home, after some nifty sleight-of-foot from Barnes. So Liverpool were through to round five.

Men on the mark: John Barnes (left) and John Aldridge helped to see off Carlisle United and Millwall in the FA Cup and Southampton in the League

# RESULTS...

**Football League, 1 January**

| | |
|---|---|
| Manchester United 3 | Liverpool 1 |
| *Brian McClair* | *John Barnes* |
| *Mark Hughes* | |
| *Russell Beardsmore* | |

**Football League, 3 January**

| | |
|---|---|
| Liverpool 1 | Aston Villa 0 |
| *Ronnie Whelan* | |

**FA Cup third round, 7 January**

| | |
|---|---|
| Carlisle United 0 | Liverpool 3 |
| | *John Barnes* |
| | *Steve McMahon (2)* |

**Football League, 14 January**

| | |
|---|---|
| Sheffield Wednesday 2 | Liverpool 2 |
| *Mark Proctor* | *Steve Nicol* |
| *Imre Varadi* | *John Aldridge* |

**Football League, 21 January**

| | |
|---|---|
| Liverpool 2 | Southampton 0 |
| *Ian Rush* | |
| *John Aldridge* | |

**FA Cup fourth round, 29 January**

| | |
|---|---|
| Millwall 0 | Liverpool 2 |
| | *John Aldridge* |
| | *Ian Rush* |

LEAGUE POSITION

| | P | W | D | L | F | A | Pt | Position |
|---|---|---|---|---|---|---|---|---|
| Liverpool | 22 | 9 | 8 | 5 | 28 | 18 | 35 | 4th |

# AWAY FROM HOME

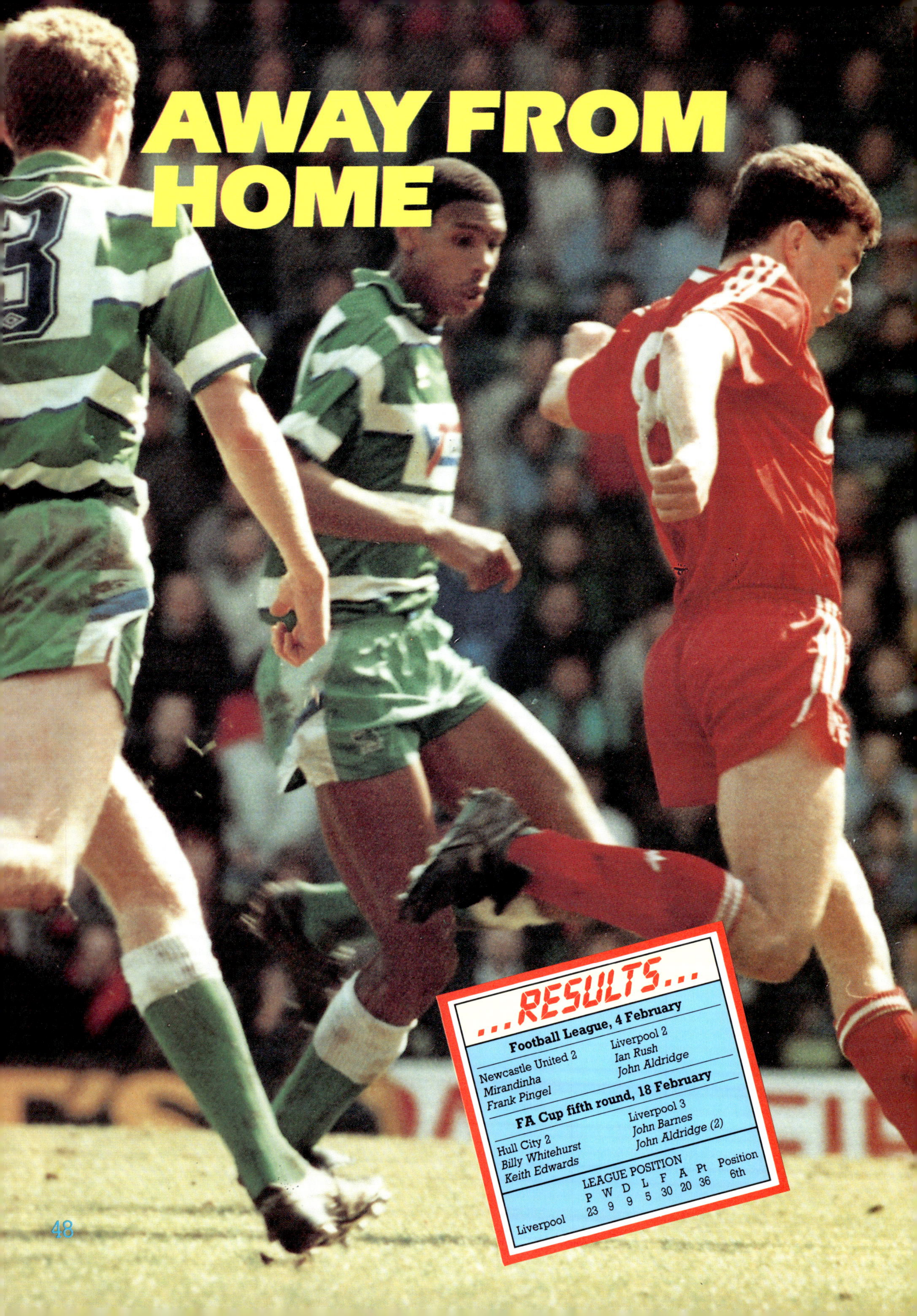

## ...RESULTS...

**Football League, 4 February**

| | |
|---|---|
| Newcastle United 2 | Liverpool 2 |
| *Mirandinha* | *Ian Rush* |
| *Frank Pingel* | *John Aldridge* |

**FA Cup fifth round, 18 February**

| | |
|---|---|
| Hull City 2 | Liverpool 3 |
| *Billy Whitehurst* | *John Barnes* |
| *Keith Edwards* | *John Aldridge (2)* |

LEAGUE POSITION

| | P | W | D | L | F | A | Pt | Position |
|---|---|---|---|---|---|---|---|---|
| Liverpool | 23 | 9 | 9 | 5 | 30 | 20 | 36 | 6th |

# February

February was the month when Liverpool, for various reasons, never managed to get in a game at Anfield. Indeed they were not to play on home ground from 21 January when they beat Southampton, until 1 March when they met Charlton Athletic. If the injury problems were easing up somewhat, the fixture problems were starting to cause headaches!

The original fixture list had Liverpool scheduled to meet Newcastle United, Luton Town, Coventry City and Nottingham Forest during February. In the event, Liverpool went to St James's Park and drew 2-2, then had their home game against Luton postponed because of Luton's televised Littlewoods Cup semi-final.

Liverpool should have played a League game at Coventry on 18 February – but, instead, they travelled to Hull for the fifth round of the FA Cup; and their home game against Nottingham Forest on 25 February went by the board because Forest's Littlewoods Cup semi-final against Bristol City was being televised live on the Sunday.

Action-men John Aldridge (left), John Barnes (right) and Ian Rush (above right). It was the Barnes-Aldridge combination which knocked Hull City out of the FA Cup

## Cup scare

However the month did have its compensations, because Liverpool came through their testing Cup tie at Boothferry Park – though not without a scare – after John Barnes had given them the lead. Hull made it 2-1 at the break, then John Aldridge scored twice in as many minutes to take the sting out of the Tigers' claws.

Aldridge, minus his striking partner, Ian Rush, deserved praise for the clinical way he took his chances. Peter Beardsley produced an outstanding display as he laid on a pinpoint pass for Barnes to head the first goal, produced another teasing cross which Aldridge flicked home, then centred again for Steve McMahon to nod forward and give Aldridge the chance to stab the ball past 'keeper Iain Hesford.

# March

Liverpool's performances during March made them, without question, the Team of the Month. And their fortunes were reflected in various ways as they won their six First Division games and a sixth-round FA Cup tie, because they had Kenny Dalglish named as Manager of the Month and defender Steve Staunton named as the Barclays Young Eagle of the Month. Most of all, they whittled down Arsenal's lead from a massive 19 points on 1 March to a mere couple of points by the first day of the following month.

*Above left: Peter Beardsley . . . six goals in as many matches*

*Above: John Barnes . . . another match-winner for Liverpool*

Individually there were outstanding performances from John Aldridge, Peter Beardsley, Steve McMahon and John Barnes, while all round there wasn't a weak link in the side. First Liverpool beat Charlton Athletic 2-0 at Anfield, then they went to Ayresome Park and inflicted a 4-0 defeat on Middlesbrough. They returned to Anfield to go one better by beating Luton Town 5-0, with an Aldridge hat-trick taking pride of place – in fact, those goals took his haul to 10 in seven successive games.

## Into the semi-final

Brentford were beaten 4-0 in the sixth round of the FA Cup, Coventry went down 3-1 at Highfield Road, Tottenham Hotspur – having taken the lead – lost 2-1 at White Hart Lane, and Derby County were beaten 1-0 at Anfield. Peter Beardsley, the match-winner at Tottenham,

# BACK TO FORM

*Left: John Aldridge . . . hat-trick hero and 10 goals in seven matches*

*Below left: Steve McMahon . . . a marksman in three successive games*

## ...RESULTS...

**Football League, 1 March**

Liverpool 2 — Charlton Athletic 0
*John Aldridge*
*Peter Beardsley*

**Football League, 11 March**

Middlesbrough 0 — Liverpool 4
*John Aldridge*
*Peter Beardsley*
*Ray Houghton*
*Steve McMahon*

**Football League, 14 March**

Liverpool 5 — Luton Town 0
*John Aldridge 3*
*Peter Beardsley*
*Steve McMahon*

**Football League, 22 March**

Coventry City 1 — Liverpool 3
*Gary Bannister*
*John Aldridge*
*Ronnie Whelan*
*John Barnes*

**Football League, 26 March**

Tottenham Hotspur 1 — Liverpool 2
*Terry Fenwick*
*John Aldridge*
*Peter Beardsley*

**Football League, 29 March**

Liverpool 1 — Derby County 0
*John Barnes*

**FA Cup sixth round, 18 March**

Liverpool 4 — Brentford 0
*Peter Beardsley 2*
*John Barnes*
*Steve McMahon*

LEAGUE POSITION

| | P | W | D | L | F | A | Pt | Position |
|---|---|---|---|---|---|---|---|---|
| Liverpool | 30 | 18 | 9 | 3 | 48 | 22 | 57 | 2nd |

struck six goals in as many games; Steve McMahon was a marksman in three successive matches; Aldridge added a couple of goals to that 10-goal haul, and Barnes claimed three goals in four games, including the winner against Derby.

All round, it was an impressive display by Liverpool as they finally managed to keep a settled side and convince the bookmakers that they should be installed as the new favourites to carry off the League title, as well as the FA Cup. But true to form, Liverpool's team boss and his players would make no predictions, other than to admit that while they had enjoyed the month's run of results, the club hadn't won anything yet.

# April

# TRAGEDY ON THE TERRACES

After seven straight wins in March, Liverpool faced a stern test on the first day of April . . . the return game against Norwich City at Carrow Road. The Canaries were still chasing leaders Arsenal and could pull away from Liverpool should they win. But with more than 26,000 fans watching, they failed to take advantage of the occasion.

Liverpool, poised and still full of confidence, scored through Ronnie Whelan after 21 minutes. That goal was the match-winner. So Liverpool returned home to meet struggling Sheffield Wednesday the following Saturday and in front of nearly 40,000 fans, they really turned on the style.

Eight minutes gone and Steve McMahon was tucking away a chance; three minutes to half-time and Peter Beardsley was making it 2-0. Just inside the hour Ray Houghton scored. Within another 10 minutes it was 4-1 as Dean Barrick pulled a goal back with a stunning effort, followed by Peter Beardsley as he hit his second for Liverpool. John Barnes made it five goals with 10 minutes to go

*Ray Houghton scored a goal in Liverpool's 5-1 thrashing of Sheffield Wednesday*

John Barnes was on the mark against Sheffield Wednesday and when Liverpool won at Millwall

Ronnie Whelan . . . the match winner at Norwich

. . . so Liverpool were now only three points adrift of Arsenal, with a game in hand.

## Double talk

Not surprisingly there was talk of the double, with an away game against Millwall the following Wednesday and an FA Cup semi-final against Nottingham Forest on the Saturday. When Liverpool won 2-1 at The Den to go top on goal difference, they appeared to be invincible.

They were certainly the favourites to beat Forest at Hillsborough – though Brian Clough, having steered his team to victory in the final of the Littlewoods Cup, and to the final of the Simod Cup, was looking for a hat-trick of Wembley appearances. But fate decreed otherwise . . .

Hillsborough was the scene of a crowd disaster; the worst tragedy in British sporting history. The semi-final was abandoned after just six minutes and, with 95 Liverpool fans having died, football was relegated to the background as Liverpool players and their wives attended funerals and comforted the bereaved.

One of the many floral tributes which were placed on the Anfield pitch as fans paid homage to the 95 victims of the Hillsborough disaster

When they did play again, Liverpool travelled to Parkhead, the home of Glasgow Celtic, for a fund-raising match on Sunday, 29 April. They scored four goals and showed they had regained their appetite for the game.

### . . . RESULTS . . .

**Football League, 1 April**

| | |
|---|---|
| Norwich City 0 | Liverpool 1<br>*Ronnie Whelan* |

**Football League, 8 April**

| | |
|---|---|
| Liverpool 5<br>*Peter Beardsley 2*<br>*Steve McMahon*<br>*Ray Houghton*<br>*John Barnes* | Sheffield Wednesday 1<br>*Dean Barrick* |

**Football League, 11 April**

| | |
|---|---|
| Millwall 1<br>*Danis Salman* | Liverpool 2<br>*John Aldridge*<br>*John Barnes* |

**FA Cup semi-final Hillsborough, 15 April**

| | |
|---|---|
| Liverpool 0 | Nottingham Forest 0 |

*Abandoned after six minutes*

LEAGUE POSITION

| | P | W | D | L | F | A | Pt | Position |
|---|---|---|---|---|---|---|---|---|
| Liverpool | 32 | 18 | 9 | 5 | 55 | 24 | 63 | 2nd |

# IN MEMORIAM

For a week they flocked to Anfield to pay their respects to those who had lost their lives in the Hillsborough soccer disaster.

In the beginning, just a few hours after it had happened, there were just a few people who, while stunned by the shock of Britain's worst-ever sporting tragedy, were nevertheless drawn to Anfield as if, simply by being there, they could derive some crumbs of comfort.

*Liverpool return to League action with a game against Everton at Goodison Park and the Kop says its thanks as the fans of both clubs help to make it a match to remember*

At the start a few scarves and favours were draped on the famous Shankly Gates and isolated wreaths and bouquets of flowers were left on the terraces of the Kop and in the goalmouth in front of the Kop. But as the days passed, the throng became ever greater, with people standing patiently in line for hours, just so that they could pay their last respects to those who had died.

## Carpet of flowers

By the end of a week the Anfield pitch had become a shrine, a veritable carpet of flowers, the Shankly Gates almost hidden by the scarves and colours left by the fans. Liverpool, Everton, Manchester United . . . these and many other clubs were represented. The queues stretched a mile and more from the ground; and people continued to arrive until, by the final day, it was estimated that more than one million had been, seen and, in many cases, shed their tears.

Everton's footballers arrived to pay homage; Craig Johnston flew back from Australia, and another former Liverpool favourite, John Toshack, paid a return visit to Anfield from Spain. Meantime Liverpool team-manager Kenny Dalglish and the players, having already attended a memorial service, walked with family mourners as the funerals took place. And the wives of players helped social workers and Salvation Army officers by offering comfort to the bereaved in a specially set-up counselling room at Anfield.

From all corners of these islands, and from abroad, the tributes poured in. So did the donations towards the Hillsborough relief fund. It was estimated that the final total could be anything between £3 million and £10 million.

*John Barnes in action as Liverpool meet Glasgow Celtic in the Hillsborough memorial match at Parkhead*

*A poignant tribute to those who died in the Hillsborough disaster*

This, then, was the aftermath of what had started out as an exciting trip to a football match at Hillsborough, Sheffield on a day blessed by April sunshine. It was a day which had ended in April showers . . . showers of tears.

And for those Liverpool fans who so reverently laid their wreaths, bouquets, scarves, teddy-bears and other toys on the pitch, Anfield now is a place which will forever hold the most poignant of memories.

# BITTER-SWEET May

After April's tears of sadness, May blossomed into a month of magical promise for Liverpool, as they swept Everton aside to win the FA Cup in dramatic fashion, then swamped West Ham in the penultimate League game, to leave championship rivals Arsenal with a mountain to climb. But their season ended on a note of near-heartbreak . . . they matched Arsenal on points and goal difference, but lost the title on goals scored.

Liverpool resumed serious action on 3 May, with a derby game against Everton at Goodison Park. It was a scoreless stalemate.

### Forest twice in a week

Sunday 7 May saw Liverpool taking on Nottingham Forest in the restaged FA Cup semi-final, this time at Old Trafford, and Liverpool surged to a 3-1 triumph.

Three nights later it was Liverpool versus Forest again, this time in the League at Anfield. David Burrows was brought down in the penalty area by Carr and John Aldridge despatched the spot-kick past 'keeper Steve Sutton, to make the final scoreline Liverpool 1, Forest 0.

On 13 May Liverpool came from behind to beat Wimbledon 2-1 in the second half at Plough Lane, while the Gunners were going down 2-1 against Derby County at Highbury. That meant the scales had been tilted in favour of the Anfield Reds.

For the third game in succession, John Aldridge was on the mark as Liverpool met and mastered Queen's Park Rangers (2-0) at Anfield, to go top; then, 24 hours later, Wimbledon did Liverpool a good turn by drawing 2-2 at Highbury, though the Gunners regained the top spot by virtue of goals scored.

The FA Cup final saw Aldridge striking after just four minutes, Everton levelling with mere seconds to go, and super-substitute Ian Rush putting Everton on the rack as he scored twice to make the extra-time result 3-2.

### Almost there

Liverpool had a League date with West Ham at Anfield the following Tuesday night . . . and the Hammers, having won five of their previous six matches, were making an 11th-hour bid to save themselves from relegation.

Ray Houghton, given a free transfer from Upton Park some years previously, scored twice to deliver killer blows, and more goals from Ian Rush and John Barnes despatched the Hammers to Division 2, while Liverpool shot back to the top of the First Division, leaving Arsenal to ponder the fact that they needed to win at Anfield by two clear goals, if they were to snatch the title.

*Above: Steve Staunton stepped up to claim a winner's medal at Wembley*

*Top right: Ray Houghton was a two-goal marksman against his old club West Ham*

*Right: Steve McMahon, a Wembley winner against his old club Everton, though he lost out in the title clash with Arsenal*

## ....RESULTS...

**Football League, 3 May**

Everton 0 — Liverpool 0

**FA Cup semi-final, 7 May · Old Trafford**

Liverpool 3 — Nottingham Forest 1
*John Aldridge 2* — *Neil Webb*
*Brian Laws (own goal)*

**Football League, 10 May**

Liverpool 1 — Nottingham Forest 0
*John Aldridge*

**Football League, 13 May**

Wimbledon 1 — Liverpool 2
*Alan Hansen (own goal)* — *John Aldridge*
*John Barnes*

**Football League, 16 May**

Liverpool 2 — Queen's Pk Rangers 0
*John Aldridge*
*Ronnie Whelan*

**FA Cup final, 20 May · Wembley**

Liverpool 3 — Everton 2
(after extra time: 1-1 after 90 minutes)
*John Aldridge* — *Stuart McCall 2*
*Ian Rush 2*

**Football League, 23 May**

Liverpool 5 — West Ham United 1
*Ray Houghton 2* — *Leroy Rosenior*
*Ian Rush John Aldridge*
*John Barnes*

**Football League, 26 May**

Liverpool 0 — Arsenal 2
*Alan Smith*
*Michael Thomas*

FINAL LEAGUE TABLE

| | P | W | D | L | F | A | Pt |
|---|---|---|---|---|---|---|---|
| Arsenal | 38 | 22 | 10 | 6 | 73 | 36 | 76 |
| Liverpool | 38 | 22 | 10 | 6 | 65 | 28 | 76 |
| Nottingham Forest | 38 | 17 | 13 | 8 | 64 | 43 | 64 |
| Norwich City | 38 | 17 | 11 | 10 | 48 | 45 | 62 |
| Derby County | 38 | 17 | 7 | 14 | 40 | 38 | 58 |
| Tottenham Hotspur | 38 | 15 | 12 | 11 | 60 | 46 | 57 |

### The Gunners clinch the title

So the stage was set for a full-house showgame, with millions watching also on television. And still neither Liverpool nor Arsenal conceded that the race had been won or lost . . .

At half-time it was a scoreless stalemate. The odds still favoured Liverpool, though Arsenal were playing positive football. Soon after the restart, the Gunners broke the deadlock, and though Liverpool appealed, Alan Smith's goal stood, after the referee had consulted a linesman.

At times it was desperate stuff at both ends, but with seconds only left on the clock, it seemed Liverpool would cling to the championship. Then Arsenal swept forward in their final assault, and Michael Thomas broke through to beat 'keeper Bruce Grobbelaar and ensure that the Gunners took the title for the first time since 1971. For Liverpool, stunning winners at Wembley less than a week earlier, it was a shattering conclusion to their season – yet they could still be proud of what they achieved after so much heartache.

FA CUP TRAIL

# You'll ne

**Never has there been an FA Cup competition more dramatic and emotional than that of season 1988-89. For Liverpool, it became almost a crusade, after a traumatic experience along what turned out to be a long and tortuous road to Wembley stadium.**

It started sedately enough with a visit to homely Brunton Park, where Liverpool beat Carlisle United 3-0, with two goals from Steve McMahon and one from John Barnes. Peter Beardsley, playing against the club where he first made his mark, turned on the style as well.

## Away at the Den

The fourth round pitched Liverpool in against high-riding Millwall and once again they were drawn away. When they ventured into the Lions' Den, they left almost £3 million-worth of talent (Peter Beardsley and Ray Houghton) on the bench, as they paraded a back-five line of Nicol, Ablett, Molby, Watson and Burrows.

Liverpool's defensive barrier proved too good for strikers Teddy Sheringham and Tony Cascarino to break down, even with the aid of Jimmy Carter's service from the wing; and goals from John Aldridge and Ian Rush enabled Liverpool to go through to round five.

Yet again, they had to travel – to Hull City's Boothferry Park ground. And a former Liverpool skipper, Emlyn Hughes – who had collected the Cup on a previous occasion – was now a director at Hull. So he couldn't lose whichever way the game went.

## A swarm over the Bees

Liverpool scored first, through John Barnes, but 60 seconds before half-time Hull were leading 2-1. However goals from John Aldridge after 52 and 54 minutes enabled Liverpool to finish the match 3-2 ahead; so they could look forward to the visit of Brentford for the sixth round – although the Bees had already despatched Manchester City and Blackburn Rovers from the Cup.

In the end Liverpool won comfortably, by a 4-0 margin, though they had only a single goal lead at half-time. The marksmen: Peter Beardsley (2), John Barnes and Steve McMahon. That victory set up Liverpool for a repeat of the previous season's semi-final against Nottingham Forest at Hillsborough.

## Tragedy at Hillsborough

There, in front of a 53,000 crowd, Liverpool and Forest were expected to produce a classic . . . but with the match a mere six minutes old, crowd problems led to a tragedy which halted play for the day and brought about the deaths of 95 people. The Hillsborough disaster left Liverpool Football Club pondering on whether or not to pull out of the FA Cup but, after much soul-searching, the decision was made to carry on, though the semi-final was not staged until the afternoon of Sunday 7 May.

*John Aldridge scored two goals against Nottingham Forest in the FA Cup semi-final for the second successive season*

Then, as on 15 April, the sun shone; but this time, at the Old Trafford venue, there were no crowd problems, though the kick-off was delayed for 15 minutes because of traffic jams. The only problems were the ones Liverpool presented for

# ver walk alone

*Right: Liverpool beat Everton in extra time. John Barnes salutes two-goal hero Ian Rush*

*Below: Walking out at Wembley*

Nottingham Forest, as John Aldridge scored twice against them for the second season in succession.

While Neil Webb pulled one back for Forest, team-mate Brian Laws scored an own goal, so Liverpool were on their way to meet Everton at Wembley. They deserved their victory, having outplayed Forest virtually right through the game.

# FA CUP TRAIL

The FA Cup final was an emotional occasion, with fans of both clubs standing side by side and joining in the minute's silence before the start. But when the game began there was an explosion of sound as John Aldridge found the Everton net after only four minutes. The ball went from Steve Nicol to Steve McMahon and on for Aldridge to deliver a crisp shot which zipped into the top right-hand corner, leaving 'keeper Neville Southall stranded.

For the remainder of the half Liverpool kept control, while at the same time conserving energy as they played under a sun which took the temperature on the pitch to 90 degrees. Indeed such was Liverpool's grip on the game that they could easily have scored three or four goals. Aldridge himself might well have had a hat-trick.

The second half followed the pattern of the first, until Everton injected new blood by sending on Stuart McCall and Ian Wilson as their substitutes; yet there were mere seconds to go and the Cup was all ready to be tagged with Liverpool's colours, as Everton launched their final assault.

## Into extra-time

As the ball came across the goalmouth, McCall got a foot to it and steered it over the line, to snatch a dramatic, last-gasp equaliser. So it meant extra time . . .

Liverpool had already replaced Aldridge with Ian Rush, and they now sent on Barry Venison for Steve Staunton, which meant a switch to left-back for the indomitable Steve Nicol. And he was to play a part again in helping Liverpool to score, although it was Rush who made the headline news.

First Liverpool's Welsh-international striker collected the ball, turned the defence and drove in a shot which left even the redoubtable Southall helpless; and that, everyone thought, was it. But along came McCall again to hammer in a drive which beat Bruce Grobbelaar and give Everton visions of pulling off a staggering victory.

## Victory at last

However it was Rush again who turned the tide and ensured that Liverpool took the lead for the third time in the match. His first goal had already enabled him to overtake the 19-goal record of Dixie Dean as a derby-game marksman, and when he sent a header spinning out of Southall's reach, to make it Liverpool 3, Everton 2, he was taking his own tally of goals in derby games to 21 . . . and more important winning the FA Cup for Liverpool.

So Ian Rush became the first player also to have scored two goals twice in Wembley FA Cup finals. Ironically, the previous occasion had been in the 1986 final against Everton. For good measure this was the first time two substitutes (Rush and McCall) had scored in an FA Cup final. So at long last Liverpool had reaped their reward; and none disputed that they had thoroughly earned it. They had come back magnificently after the tragedy of Hillsborough. They had won the glittering trophy in style.

*Above: Liverpool fans fly the flag at Wembley*

*Right: John Barnes and Pat Nevin battle for possession*

Above: Ian Rush beats Neville Southall for Liverpool's second goal

# WEMBLEY IN THE SUN

*Right: moment of triumph as Liverpool skipper Ronnie Whelan hoists the FA Cup aloft*

## ROLL OF HONOUR

**Football League champions**

| | |
|---|---|
| 1900-01 | 1976-77 |
| 1905-06 | 1978-79 |
| 1921-22 | 1979-80 |
| 1922-23 | 1981-82 |
| 1946-47 | 1982-83 |
| 1963-64 | 1983-84 |
| 1965-66 | 1985-86 |
| 1972-73 | 1987-88 |
| 1975-76 | |

**FA Cup winners**

1964-65
1973-74
1985-86
1988-89

**European Cup winners**

1976-77
1977-78
1980-81
1983-84

**UEFA Cup winners**

1972-73
1975-76

**League/Milk Cup winners**

1980-81
1981-82
1982-83
1983-84

# CONTENTS

# DIRECTOR'S FOREWORD

The *Taylor Wessing Photographic Portrait Prize* is awarded to an outstanding photograph that successfully transmits the circumstances and character of a sitter or group. Many photographic portraits may seem to do this, but for a winning work, a brilliant combination of location, lighting, style and subject is necessary. Visitors to the exhibition first learn about the subject simply by viewing the image; regardless of the information that becomes available later, it is the great skill of the photographer who produces a portrait that *demands* attention from viewers. Given the speed of communication today, it seems increasingly important to slow down and engage with an image, literally face to face.

Competition was fierce for inclusion in the exhibition this year, and the final choices emerged as a result of intense debate. The enthusiasm of individual judges took us in different directions, and the final selection reflects the best of the work submitted.

My congratulations go to this year's winners: Spencer Murphy, Giles Price, Anoush Abrar and Dorothee Deiss. I am very grateful to the many photographers who submitted 5,410 images to this year's competition. I am also grateful to Simon Crocker, Chairman of the John Kobal Foundation, and to Michael Hoppen, Trustee, for their special support through which a younger photographer is awarded the 2013 John Kobal New Work Award and a commission to make a new portrait in the world of the film industry.

I should like to thank my fellow judges: Kate Bush, Suki Dhanda, Tim Eyles, Terence Pepper and Rebecca Valentine. They were hugely attentive and reached the final choices through excellent discussion and persuasion. My thanks also go to National Portrait Gallery staff, designers NB: Studio and interviewer Richard McClure for all their hard work on the project. I am grateful to The White Wall Company for their excellent contribution to the organisation of the submission and judging process.

I am delighted that Taylor Wessing has renewed its partnership with the Gallery, and my considerable thanks go both to the company and to Tim Eyles, UK Managing Partner. The partnership is an important part of the Gallery's work, and makes it possible to create this very special international exhibition each year.

**SANDY NAIRNE**
**DIRECTOR, NATIONAL PORTRAIT GALLERY**

# SPONSOR'S FOREWORD

Art is an important intellectual stimulant and instrument of change. Artists have the ability to advance society and culture, often challenging commonly held perspectives with innovative thinking, raising awareness about social issues, provoking discussion and breaking down obstacles to cross-cultural understanding. Art educates, entertains and enriches us.

Institutions such as the National Portrait Gallery play a central role in helping us to broaden our knowledge by encouraging analytical thinking and understanding of different ideas and opinions. Yet in times of financial instability, the arts are often first in line for cuts. At Taylor Wessing, we place great value on creativity and art as an important part of our social capital, which is why we are now in our sixth year of supporting the *Photographic Portrait Prize*.

For many people, photography is more accessible than other media. The diversity and popularity of photography make it relatively easy for people to engage with a photograph – particularly these days when millions of photographs are uploaded to the internet every minute. The advent of digital cameras has ushered in a new era in photography, and it is a prolific one. But technology, however advanced, will never turn an ordinary photographer into a great one. A great photographer needs to have a creative gift and the ability to see more deeply, or from an original perspective. A truly distinctive photographic portrait uncovers something innately truthful about the subject, and often about us as viewers too.

This year's exhibition is as diverse, challenging and stimulating as ever; a journey through the whole spectrum of human emotion, communicating across cultures, telling the stories of the past and present, and, hopefully, inspiring minds. One of the mission statements on the National Portrait Gallery's website is "to stimulate debate and to address questions of biography, diversity and fame, which lie at the heart of issues of identity and achievement." This exhibition unquestionably achieves that.

The sixty portraits here were selected from thousands submitted from around the world, so the shortlisted photographers are truly deserving of our congratulations. Our thanks and appreciation also go to the inspiring team at the National Portrait Gallery, with whom our relationship has gone from strength to strength; long may it continue.

**TIM EYLES**
**MANAGING PARTNER, TAYLOR WESSING LLP**

TaylorWessing

# FINDING MRS CAMERON
# **KATE BUSH**

As a child, I used to wait for what seemed like interminable, freezing hours in the dark mornings for the train to take me to school. I don't recall when I first noticed the ranks of photographs on the walls of the waiting room, or the impact that these deep, brooding portraits had on my eleven-year-old mind. I had no idea who the people in the pictures were, but they stayed with me, and when I came across them again in a book, many years later, it was like discovering a lost family album.

Sometime around 1945, a man called Helmut Gernsheim had also been struck by these photographs in the railway station waiting room at Brockenhurst, a village in the heart of the New Forest. Herr Gernsheim set about investigating and it was his research that was to ensure that one of the great photographers, and arguably the greatest photographic portraitist in the history of the medium, did not drift away, forgotten in the mists of time.

Julia Margaret Cameron (1815–79) used to take the train from Brockenhurst to Lymington and from there, the boat to the Isle of Wight and on to her home at Freshwater. In a typically eccentric gesture, she donated in 1871 a set of her pioneering portraits to the little country station, to mark a happy reunion with one of her sons on its platform after they had endured a long separation.

The Irish poet William Allingham recorded in his journal, on Monday 10 June 1867, his encounter with the redoubtable photographer:

> Down train comes in with Mrs Cameron, queenly in a carriage by herself surrounded by photographs. We go to Lymington together, she talking all the time. "I want to do a large photograph of Tennyson, and he objects! Says I make bags under his eyes – and Carlyle refuses to give me a sitting, he says it's a kind of Inferno! The greatest men of the age (with strong emphasis), Sir John Herschel, Henry Taylor, Watts, say I have immortalised them – and these other men object!! What is one to do – Hm?

Alfred, Lord Tennyson, Mrs Cameron's Isle of Wight neighbour, eventually capitulated – as did Carlyle – no match for the woman who had converted her chicken coop into a darkroom and had conquered complex chemistry, hands dripping on the table linen, to achieve her first successful photographs in 1864. She made what was to be Tennyson's favourite portrait. He is pictured in profile, swathed in a cloak with a book in his hand. He called it 'The Dirty Monk'.

Mrs Cameron's photography runs the gamut of possibility in portraiture, and in this sense, she is the grandmother of all subsequent photographic portraitists. Her images are calibrated finely between observation and imagination. Allegorical concoctions, carefully stage-directed, sit alongside life-size, closely observed faces, bold in their minimalism and shorn of all extraneous detail. Gazing at the unforgettable portraits of her niece Julia Stephen, mother-to-be of Virginia Woolf and Vanessa Bell, is to be shocked by the new. It is to meet a woman of the past figured in a newly modern way. Mrs Cameron reached – as all good portraitists do – for the 'inner man'; the psychological as well as the physical essence of her sitters. And at the same time, she was equally adept at co-opting her models to dramatise an idea. People either play themselves in her pictures, or they play a part.

There is still a Julia Margaret Cameron photograph at Brockenhurst station. It is in the ticket office now. No longer an original, the print has faded and fallen out of its *passe partout* to lie crooked in the frame. Forgotten again, sadly. In the meantime, I live with my own walls lined with portraits, photographs and paintings of people from other times and places; people I will never know, but who hold my attention. Portraits hold a particular charge, a charge that is different to the experience of a landscape or a still life. They trigger a moment of mutual recognition between humans, between viewer and subject. Judging the *Taylor Wessing Photographic Portrait Prize* 2013 was a process of seeking out those images that ignited this charge in the minds of the judges, and that sustained our interest over two intense days of looking.

As Mrs Cameron wrote once to a friend, 'the history of the human face is a book we don't tire of, if we can get its grand truths, & learn them by heart.'

# THE PRIZES

**TAYLOR WESSING PHOTOGRAPHIC PORTRAIT PRIZE**

The *Taylor Wessing Photographic Portrait Prize* is open to photographers from around the world aged eighteen or over.

The first prize winner is Spencer Murphy, who receives £12,000.

The second prize winner is Giles Price, who receives £3,000.

The third prize winner is Anoush Abrar, who receives £2,000.

The fourth prize winner is Dorothee Deiss, who receives £1,000.

**THE JOHN KOBAL NEW WORK AWARD**

The John Kobal New Work Award is awarded to a photographer under the age of thirty selected for the exhibition. The winning photographer receives a cash prize of £4,000 to include undertaking a commission from the Gallery to photograph a sitter connected with the UK film industry.

The winner is Hana Knizova.

If you would like to join the mailing list to receive an entry form for next year's *Photographic Portrait Prize*, please register your interest online at: www.npg.org.uk/photoprize or send your full contact details to:

Photographic Portrait Prize 2013
Marketing Department
National Portrait Gallery
St Martin's Place
London WC2H 0HE

PHOTOGRAPH BY SUKI DHANDA, 7 AUGUST 2013

THE JUDGES, LEFT TO RIGHT: TIM EYLES, SUKI DHANDA, TERENCE PEPPER, REBECCA VALENTINE, SANDY NAIRNE, KATE BUSH.

# THE JUDGES

**CHAIR: SANDY NAIRNE**

DIRECTOR, NATIONAL PORTRAIT GALLERY

As in previous years, the extraordinary range of the portraits submitted to the *Taylor Wessing Photographic Portrait Prize* leaves me amazed by the diversity of ways in which humans can be represented – and I am struck again and again by the vitality and ingenuity of the best images. These are fascinating photographs and I am grateful, as always, to the many photographers from around the world who decide to enter this competition.

**KATE BUSH**

HEAD OF BARBICAN ART GALLERIES

This is a prize that celebrates and recognises the diversity of contemporary photographic portraiture. As judges, we came from different professional backgrounds, and each of us brought a distinctive viewpoint to the process. Yet it was interesting that, our differences notwithstanding, the most powerful portraits stood out from a stream of some 5,000 images and that they generally gathered a consensus around them. Whether immediately bold and iconic, or quieter and closely observed, the portraits in this selection have been created in many different registers, each unique, and together amounting to a fascinating compendium of human presence in photographic form.

**SUKI DHANDA**

PHOTOGRAPHER

Judging the selection was not an easy task – we all had our own ideas and criteria for what makes a great portrait. When looking at the work, questions arise. Does it capture an emotion or a sense of stillness? Is it captivating? Does it tell a story and have a distinctive ambience? I saw some great work that did not make the final selection, and I could see the effort that had gone into many of these pictures. For a photographer, it is interesting to be part of the selection process for this major award and to see how the end result is reached. The exhibition will certainly present a diversity of styles, celebrating portraiture on an international level.

**TIM EYLES**

MANAGING PARTNER, TAYLOR WESSING LLP

It was with excitement and a sense of privilege that I approached the judging for this year's awards – and all the anticipation was duly fulfilled. There was a mesmerising array of photographic talent on display, capturing a rich diversity of styles, international settings, technical virtuosity and colour. Our emotions were engaged in myriad ways, with images illustrating many aspects of the human condition: achievement, exuberance, the bizarre – but also defiance, suffering, isolation. The judging process is passionate and intense and the editing is daunting; wistfully, we had to leave some much-admired works behind. The winning photographers fully deserve our congratulations but so do the rest of those shortlisted: the selection of their portraits for exhibition from the thousands submitted is a great testament to their manifest quality.

**TERENCE PEPPER**

HEAD OF PHOTOGRAPHS COLLECTION, NATIONAL PORTRAIT GALLERY

Being a judge of this competition since its inception more than twenty years ago has been a truly revelatory experience and a highlight of my year. The 2013 competition has, yet again, brought to our attention an army of photographers with whom we were unfamiliar. Because the prize is judged anonymously, there are always many pleasant surprises when the sixty finalists are revealed – among them a number of well-established names, who are judged alongside emerging new talent.

**REBECCA VALENTINE**

PHOTOGRAPHIC AGENT/OWNER OF VAARTA.CO.UK

When editing on such a large scale as this, the most powerful images truly sing out from the rest. I thoroughly enjoyed the selection process and, unlike constructing a portfolio or curating a collection for a book or exhibition, there was no requirement for a collective narrative. This was incredibly liberating, allowing us to focus entirely on the impact of each individual image. Recurring themes and parodied styles were evident throughout, and I yearned for images that broke the mould and demanded I look at an old subject through new eyes. Many of those shortlisted carry a narrative beyond the immediate aesthetic, which for me is the essence of an award winner.

# FIRST PRIZE
# SPENCER MURPHY

Awarded third place in last year's *Taylor Wessing Photographic Portrait Prize* for his study of actor Mark Rylance, Spencer Murphy has now capped that achievement by winning first prize for his portrait of Irish jump jockey Katie Walsh. This year's success means that Murphy's work has been selected for exhibition in the competition an unprecedented six years running.

His winning entry was commissioned by Channel 4's creative agency, 4creative, for a poster campaign entitled The Original Extreme Sport, designed to promote the TV channel's coverage of the Grand National. Over the course of a lengthy shoot at Kempton Park on a wet and windy race day, he photographed several jockeys in their mud-spattered silks, keeping the entire series to one location in order to provide a 'cohesive thread' running through the images.

By his own admission, thirty-five-year-old Murphy knew little about his sitter, or indeed horse racing, beyond a modicum of research in the days leading up to the shoot. 'I was asked to show how demanding a job the jockeys have,' he says. 'Until then, I had not realised the kinds of extreme diets they endure and the injuries many have suffered in their careers.'

Each sitting took around thirty minutes, with Murphy using a large-format film camera that, he believes, gives the images a look and feel that could not be achieved using a digital camera or a smaller format. 'There's a depth of field and a grain and texture with large-format film that you can only try to replicate after the event with digital,' he explains. 'What I love is that it's not instant or disposable; there's that exciting period of about twenty-four hours where you don't know exactly what you've got.'

Walsh, who claimed the best Grand National finish for a female jockey when she came in third last year on Seabass, proved to be more comfortable in the saddle than in front of the lens. 'She is quite shy and reserved and not at all fond of having her picture taken. It was hard for her being in a room full of strangers and having to turn on some aggression. Because she was the only woman in the series, I wanted her to be one of the toughest-looking portraits but still retain some of her femininity and empathy.'

Another image from the series, showing a battered and bruised A.P. McCoy, one of the greatest National Hunt jockeys of all time, was acquired by the National Portrait Gallery earlier this year, the ninth portrait by Murphy to be held in the Gallery's permanent collection. His pictures have been exhibited around the world and published in *GQ*, *Time*, *Rolling Stone* and the *Financial Times*.

In order to keep his portraiture fresh and varied, the London-based photographer meticulously plans each assignment, often sketching out the picture before he takes it to help visualise what he is setting out to achieve. 'I'm trying to be more spontaneous but, generally, I don't like to leave anything to chance,' he explains. 'I tend to have a pre-conceived idea of what I want the picture to look like, and it's a matter of coaxing that out of the sitter. But, equally, it's about remaining open to the moment, recognising when something good is happening, and recording that.'

INTERVIEW BY RICHARD MCCLURE

**SPENCER MURPHY**

*KATIE WALSH*

MARCH 2013

**GILES PRICE**
*KUMBH MELA PILGRIM – MAMTA DUBEY AND INFANT*
FEBRUARY 2013

# SECOND PRIZE
# GILES PRICE

Giles Price developed his interest in photography while serving with the Royal Marine Commandos in northern Iraq during the first Gulf War in 1991. Having enlisted straight from school, he travelled to the war zone with a 35mm compact camera in his kit bag, recording his military experiences in a snapshot diary. Those photographs, several of which were taken hanging from the side of a Blackhawk helicopter, are now held in the collection of the Imperial War Museum in London.

At the age of twenty, Price was medically discharged from the forces after suffering severe bowel damage caused by ingesting the residue of phosphates contained in Saddam Hussein's chemical weapons. 'I had always seen myself in the Royal Marines and had signed up for twenty-two years, so this was a major life change,' he recalls. 'I had no qualifications and there was little open to me. Fortunately, photography gave me the purpose and focus that I needed.'

His Iraq images earned him a place at the University of Derby where he gained a BA (Hons) in Photographic Studies before working as a photographer's assistant in London for seven years, setting up on his own in 2005. His first project was a series of twelve portraits of the last surviving First World War veterans, now in the collection of the National Portrait Gallery, while he has continued to carry out aerial photography by documenting the construction of London's Olympic Park from above.

His entry in the *Photographic Portrait Prize* was taken at this year's Kumbh Mela pilgrimage in India where one hundred million Hindus congregate at the confluence of two sacred rivers to pray and cleanse themselves in the holy waters. As a regular traveller to the country, Price had long been aware of the vast gathering, and resolved to chronicle the 'hypnotic and surreal' spectacle after scattering his mother's ashes in the Ganges last year.

Plans to photograph the pilgrimage from a helicopter were abandoned after Indian authorities expressed fears that it could cause the crowds to panic and possibly stampede. Instead, he set up a pop-up studio, using a background of cloth bought in the local market and shooting on a Phase One P65+ medium-format digital camera with flash lighting. Working over eleven days, Price shot 130 portraits, including that of Mamta Dubey, a mother from Uttar Pradesh, and her baby.

'As soon as I had set up, a crowd of people massed, all wanting their picture taken. Apart from placing the sitters where I wanted them, everything was pretty uncontrolled and not posed,' says Price, who intends to publish the portraits as a book, accompanied by an exhibition in India next year.

'I like this particular image for the contrast of colours, and the difference between the baby's western-looking clothing and Mamta's more traditional Indian dress. There's also a likeness in pose to the Madonna and child images we are used to looking at in western religion. But, of course, because Mamta is a Hindu, there is an interesting reverse iconography.'

INTERVIEW BY RICHARD MCCLURE

**ANOUSH ABRAR**
*KOFI ANNAN*
FEBRUARY 2013

# THIRD PRIZE
# **ANOUSH ABRAR**

Anoush Abrar was presented with a number of constraints when commissioned by *Zeitmagazin*, the supplement of German newspaper *Die Zeit*, to take the portrait of Kofi Annan, former Secretary-General of the United Nations. Not only did his subject's busy schedule mean the Iranian-born photographer had just three minutes of his time at the offices of the Kofi Annan Foundation in Geneva, but a tight brief from *Zeitmagazin* editors demanded that the Ghanaian diplomat be pictured in black and white, and with his eyes closed.

Having photographed Annan on a previous occasion, in a session restricted to just five minutes, Abrar was well prepared for the task at hand. 'Annan is not much interested in having his photograph taken, and you know you won't get much time,' he explains. 'When you shoot him you need to know what to do, so I went into the session with the image already in my head.'

Using a black background, flash and reflector, Abrar finally persuaded a reluctant Annan to close his eyes for the portrait. 'He is a natural negotiator, and in the beginning he didn't want to do it,' he reveals. 'He has a powerful face and it is a simple photograph, all about shades of grey and playing with the shadows. I like it because there is something real here; it is not lying.'

Abrar was born in Tehran in 1976 and moved to Switzerland as a child. Disregarding his parents' wish that he become an engineer or doctor, he studied at the Ecole Cantonale d'Art de Lausanne, switching from graphic design to photography in his final year of studies. 'I saw that photography was made for my curiosity. For me, photography is a key: the best and the fastest way to access the intimacy of someone.'

Working with both digital and film cameras, Abrar is best-known for his lavish fashion spreads for a range of European publications, while he also pursues highly diverse personal projects, including a series depicting the Iranian-Jewish community in Los Angeles, and portraits of models and actresses seeking to make it in Hollywood. 'There are always pros and cons when you use film or digital. It is not better or worse, just different. It always depends on the project you are working on. You must keep in your mind that all these cameras and technical aspects are just tools, nothing else. What is important is the finality of your work.'

For the past eighteen months, Abrar has been living in London, and he credits his move from Switzerland to the UK with stimulating his creativity. 'Coming to England has been so refreshing. Here, the visual culture is more pure, more real. Even walking on the street or being on the Underground is an inspiration,' he says. 'In France or Switzerland, the fashion editors only want colour and glamour, which is something I don't like any more. Being in London has allowed me to come back to art photography, my first love. That has been a wonderful rediscovery.'

INTERVIEW BY RICHARD MCCLURE

**DOROTHEE DEISS**
*THE TWINS*
MARCH 2013

# FOURTH PRIZE
# DOROTHEE DEISS

German photographer Dorothee Deiss was attending a bat mitzvah at a Berlin synagogue when she observed identical twins Esther and Ruth in the congregation. Recognising the potential for a striking portrait, she later contacted the Russian-born sisters, who were happy to pose together at Esther's house. Deiss convinced the seventy-five-year-old widows to change from their matching clothes into their bathrobes, and shot the image digitally with a Nikon D800, using both flash and natural light.

'Although Esther and Ruth did not know me, they had prepared a huge Russian meal as a welcome,' she recalls. 'They were dressed identically in fancy black-and-white suits, because they expected to be portrayed in the conventional way, and they paused when I asked them to put on bathrobes and lie down on the bed. It was very out of the ordinary for them, but they tried their best to do as I asked. I wanted to depict their relationship in all its honesty, tenderness and strength.'

Born in Münsingen in 1961, Deiss began taking photographs aged eleven after realising that her father's SLR camera could effect an escape into a 'wonderfully exciting second world'. Her interest deepened in her teens with the discovery of the Magnum photographers, yet after leaving school she decided on a career in medicine. 'I was not brave enough to pursue photography as a job,' she explains. 'Also, I thought it would be too selfish to become an artist.'

Deiss currently works full-time as a pediatric endocrinologist at a Berlin clinic, a role involving the diagnosis and treatment of hormone-related conditions. Although her demanding job largely restricts photography to her spare time, she has built up a substantial body of personal projects, including a series of images taken along the 155km stretch of land where the Berlin Wall once stood. 'It is very hard to combine both medicine and photography in regard of time, but I would love to make at least a part of my living from my camera.'

At times, Deiss's dual passions dovetail. She has previously photographed a Polish GP on house calls to his patients, and young children at an American summer camp for diabetics. This summer, she graduated with a Master of Fine Arts degree in Photography from a limited-residency programme at Hartford Art School in Connecticut. Her thesis project, *VisibleInvisible*, comprised portraits of people who have transformed a mental or physical affliction into an inner strength.

'The pictures are mostly of people who live at the fringes, or do not fit the dominant ideal of beauty. But for me, they are ambassadors of human dignity, so I want to continue working on that,' says Deiss, who contends that there are parallels between medicine and photography.

'As a doctor, I strongly believe in the importance of facial language. Faces are vivid maps of human experience which I have to read in order to understand somebody to some extent,' she says. 'In my relationship with a patient, I depend on what their facial expression tells me about them, beyond their spoken words. This is the same in portraiture.'

INTERVIEW BY RICHARD MCCLURE

**HANA KNIZOVA**
*ELZA AND NELLIE*
FROM THE SERIES *FAMILY MATTERS*
JUNE 2013

# JOHN KOBAL NEW WORK AWARD
# HANA KNIZOVA

Hana Knizova's early aspiration to be a photographer was sparked by the discovery of her high-school darkroom, only for her ambitions to be put on hold when she was scouted by a model agency on the streets of Prague while a student at Charles University. She was a sought-after face in the fashion world over the next five years, until she gradually tired of the business and chose to pursue a career on the other side of the camera.

'At the time, modelling seemed like a wonderful part-time job. It was a great experience, but often all that glitters is not gold,' says Knizova, who is twenty-nine. 'In modelling, success depends mainly on youth and beauty, two factors that are very ephemeral, so your time in the industry tends to be limited.'

Moving to the UK in 2010, Knizova graduated with an MA in Photography from the London College of Communication and continues to live and work in the city. Predominantly, her photographs focus on themes of self-perception, body image and family dynamics. Current personal projects include portraits of young couples in East London, and adolescents from problematic backgrounds in her native Czech Republic.

'Having been a model, I am definitely more patient and sympathetic with my sitters. They are often very glad to know that I have been there myself and that I understand any possible uncertainties they might have in front of the camera.'

Her portrait of identical twin sisters Nellie and Elza Jenkins comes from her series *Family Matters*, which explores physical resemblance and depicts her subjects at home. The twins recently relocated to London hoping to further their media careers after appearing on the television series New Zealand's Next Top Model, and agreed to pose for the portrait at their flat in Camden.

'I met Nellie through a mutual friend and I was immediately captivated by her striking presence, before I realised there were two of them,' says Knizova. 'I come from a very small family, and as an only child, the thought of having a sibling, in particular a twin, always fascinated me. It was great to observe the twins' similarities and differences, and especially their mutual close attachment.'

Using a digital Canon DLSR in order to gain 'more control over the editing process', Knizova only partially styled and directed the shoot, deliberately aiming to capture the 'in-between moment' when the twins were not yet ready to pose. 'I like how the anticipation of the final image can be read in their pose, leading to a slight awkwardness. They know they are being photographed, but they don't know when I am going to press the shutter or what exactly I am seeing through the lens.'

As winner of the John Kobal New Work Award, given to a photographer under the age of thirty selected for the exhibition, Knizova receives a cash prize of £4,000 from the National Portrait Gallery to photograph a sitter connected with the UK film industry. 'I would love to photograph Tilda Swinton,' she reveals. 'She is an amazing actress, and has a striking beauty that has overturned many deep-rooted stereotypes.'

INTERVIEW BY RICHARD MCCLURE

# THE TAYLOR WESSING PHOTOGRAPHIC PORTRAIT PRIZE

# **EXHIBITORS**

**ANDY MASSACCESI**
*FABIO*
OCTOBER 2012

**OLIVER ABRAHAM**
*GERHARD RICHTER, COLOGNE, 2012*
FROM THE SERIES *PORTRAITS OF ARTISTS*
OCTOBER 2012

**CARL COURT**
*THE QUEEN – GREY*
MAY 2012

**CARMEN BALLVÉ**
*GIRLS IN BARRACÓN*
FEBRUARY 2013

**ERIK ALMAS**
*HOLY MOTHER*
FEBRUARY 2012

**TOM STEWART**
*THREE COLOURS RED*
MAY 2013

**PAUL WENHAM-CLARKE**
*CINDY & SHIRLEY AGED TEN HOLDING BABY TERRY ON HIS CHRISTENING DAY*
FROM THE SERIES *THE URBAN GYPSIES*
MAY 2012

**JOHN NASSARI**
*NO. 61, EAST LONDON*
JUNE 2013

**WILLIAM LAKIN**

*MARTYN, SEAN AND JACOB*

FROM THE SERIES *FLORIDA CLUB*

MARCH 2013

**ROSIE HALLAM**
*CHOIR MASTER*
OCTOBER 2012

**RICHARD ALEXANDER PILNICK**
*CAT & PHIL – PAINTING OF LOVE*
FROM THE SERIES *YOGIS*
JULY 2013

**CAROL ALLEN STOREY**
*JAMES, EX-PRISONER*
FROM THE SERIES *FRACTURED LIVES*
MAY 2012

**IAN ATKINSON**
*MEMORIES OF CHILDHOOD 5*
FEBRUARY 2013

**DAN BURN-FORTI**
*MITCH WINEHOUSE*
JUNE 2012

**LINDA BROWNLEE**
*ZADIE SMITH*
JULY 2012

**JASON CLARKE**
*HER STORY – ANIMATA, FREETOWN*
JUNE 2013

**ANGUS FRASER**
*FAMILY OF SANTA MUERTE DEVOTEES, MEXICO*
FROM THE SERIES *SANTA MUERTE (SAINT DEATH)*
NOVEMBER 2012

**DAVID BRUNETTI**

*DREAMING OF SYRIA #1*

FROM THE SERIES *DREAMING OF SYRIA*

MAY 2013

**GAVIN PARRY**
*AHMEDABAD #8*
FROM THE SERIES *SILENT DIALOGUE*
MAY 2013

**DEANA KOLENCIKOVA**
*MAN WITH OWL AND LUCY*
FROM THE SERIES *IS THIS IT?*
OCTOBER 2012

**LUKE WATSON**

*JANET MANDERSON, LUPUS SUFFERER – 1*

FROM THE SERIES *ECLIPSE*

JULY 2013

**VINCENT VOIGNIER, IN COLLABORATION WITH BARBARA BERNARDI**
*OLIVIA*
FROM THE SERIES *NACHTGESTALTEN (CREATURES OF THE NIGHT)*
JUNE 2012

**ANTONIO OLMOS**

*SOL CAMPBELL, EX-FOOTBALLER, AT HIS HOME IN LONDON*

JULY 2012

**DAVID VINTINER**

*LAKSHMAN DONGARI*

FROM THE SERIES *RECALL (WORLD MEMORY CHAMPIONSHIPS)*

DECEMBER 2012

**ANTONIO OLMOS**

*SOL CAMPBELL, EX-FOOTBALLER, AT HIS HOME IN LONDON*

JULY 2012

**DAVID VINTINER**
*LAKSHMAN DONGARI*
FROM THE SERIES *RECALL (WORLD MEMORY CHAMPIONSHIPS)*
DECEMBER 2012

**KIRK CRIPPENS**
*PORTRAITLANDIA: MARY KOZLOV*
APRIL 2013

**ROSIE HALLAM**
*LILY COLE*
MAY 2013

**CHRISTOPHER LANE**
*VANESSA REDGRAVE*
MARCH 2013

**LYDIA PANAS**

*MARIA AND CORINNE*

FROM THE SERIES *AFTER SARGENT*

JULY 2012

**ILONA SZWARC**
*LEXI, LINDENHURST, NEW YORK*
FROM THE SERIES *AMERICAN GIRLS*
JULY 2012

**CLAUDIO RASANO**
*STREET GANGS IN SOUTH AFRICA*
MARCH 2013

**PATRICK FRASER**
*CARLA KÖRBES*
MARCH 2013

**JARI SALO**

*JARI AND TERHI*

FROM THE SERIES *HEROIN FATHERS*

FEBRUARY 2012

**ANTOINE DE RAS**
*OSCAR PISTORIUS – IN THE DOCK*
FEBRUARY 2013

**NÉSTOR DÍAZ**
*SOFÍA*
FROM THE SERIES *VIVÍ. WOMEN WITH A PRESENT LIFE.*
APRIL 2013

**CLARE HEWITT**
*UNTITLED (LATVIA) #3*
AUGUST 2012

**TEREZA ČERVEŇOVÁ**
*SISTERS*
APRIL 2013

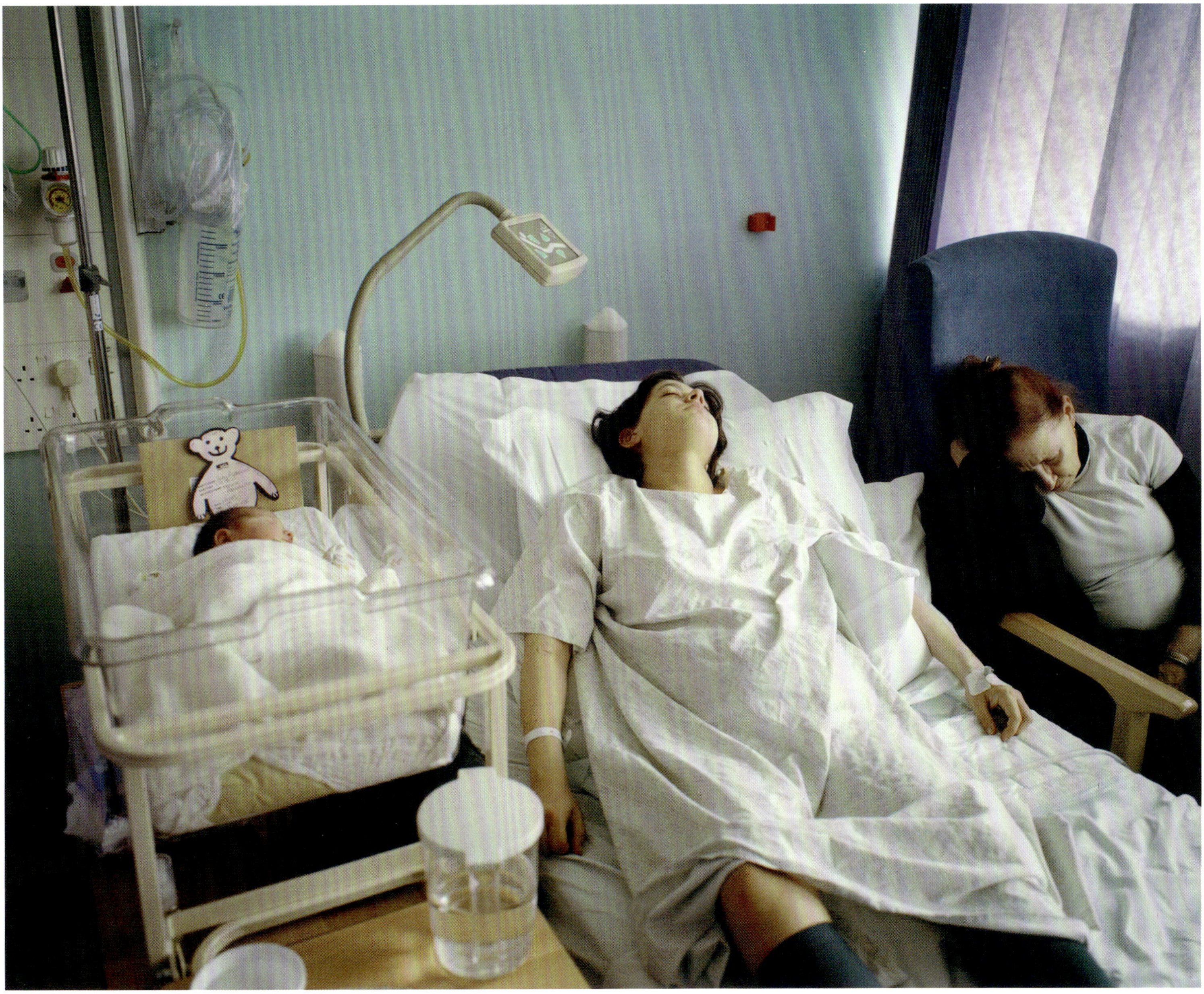

**SIPKE VISSER**

*THREE GENERATIONS*

FROM THE SERIES *FAMILY EXTENSION*

APRIL 2013

**JI YEO**
*BEAUTY RECOVERY ROOM 01*
FROM THE SERIES *BEAUTY RECOVERY ROOM*
JANUARY 2012

**ANDY WILSON**

*EVENING WALK, PRIOZERSK, LAKE BALQASH, KAZAKHSTAN*

JUNE 2012

**LAURA STEVENS**
*PHOEBE AND THE RAT*
OCTOBER 2012

**OLIVER MARK**
*CAMERON CARPENTER AND HIS PERSONAL TRAINER*
JULY 2012

**KATE ESHELBY**

*RETURNING HOME*

OCTOBER 2012

**JONATHAN TORGOVNIK**

*GRANNIE MARY MOKHETHOA WITH HER THREE ORPHAN GRANDCHILDREN*

FROM THE SERIES *A GENERATION LOST – GRANNIES AND AIDS ORPHANS*

OCTOBER 2012

**ADRIAN PEACOCK**
*MARY BEARD*
MAY 2013

**CHRIS FLOYD**
*CHARLIE BROOKER*
JUNE 2012

**JILLIAN EDELSTEIN**
*HORST VON WÄCHTER*
DECEMBER 2012

**JULIA FULLERTON-BATTEN**
*HARAJUKA, TOKYO, 2013*
FEBRUARY 2013

**JAMES STROUD**
*LITTLE HEART*
FROM THE SERIES *SILENCE*
NOVEMBER 2012

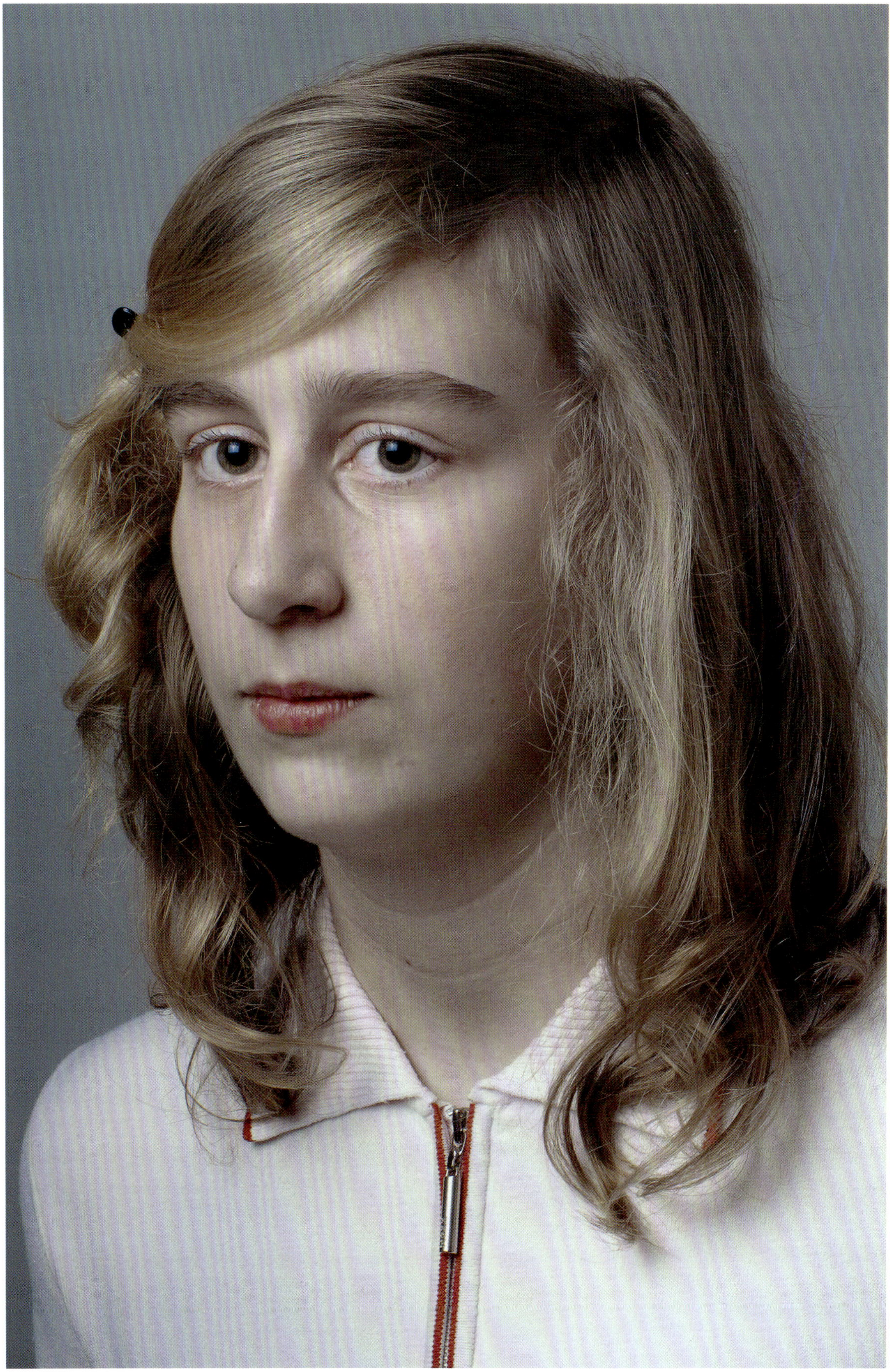

**PAUL DEWITTE**
*ELISE*
FROM THE SERIES *IN DE HUID*
JANUARY 2012

**PROYECTO MÍRAME LIMA**
*HOMBRES DE MAR (FISHERMEN)*
FROM THE SERIES *MÍRAME – LIMA*
MARCH 2012

**SOPHIE BROCKS**
*THE WARD FAMILY*
NOVEMBER 2012

**JILL WOOSTER**
*OF ARIELLE*
NOVEMBER 2012

**LEONCE RAPHAEL AGBODJELOU**

*UNTITLED (CITIZENS OF PORTO-NOVO)*

JULY 2012

**DIRK REES**
*WOMEN OF KHOWARIB*
FROM THE SERIES *HIMBA WOMEN*
NOVEMBER 2012

**MIRI MOR**
*GEORGE*
FROM THE SERIES *BIRDS' ELEGY*
NOVEMBER 2012

# LIST OF EXHIBITORS